FINANCIAL MODELING

Kasturi Mazumdar

Toronto Academic Press

FINANCIAL MODELING

Kasturi Mazumdar

Toronto Academic Press
4164 Lakeshore Road
Burlington ON L7L 1A4
Canada
www.tap-books.com
Email: orders@arclereducation.com

ISBN: 978-1-77956-318-7

ABOUT THE AUTHOR

Kasturi Mazumdar is a dynamic financial analyst with extensive knowledge in investment management and analysis. Her journey into the industry began after completing her bachelor's in engineering from India. Motivated by her love for learning, she pursued a program at UCLA and continues to enhance her skillset through programs at top business schools. She finds inspiration from influential figures like Mr. Ratan Tata, Dr. Devi Shetty and Roger Federer, and passionately dedicates her time and expertise to volunteer work focused on healthcare and public well-being. In her downtime, Kasturi finds joy in reading, painting, and has recently developed a passion for Himalayan hiking. Embracing the value of spirituality, she is committed to living a more harmonious and holistic life.

Table of Contents

8 ASSET PRICING MODELS 241

9 PORTFOLIO MODEL 277

List of Figures

List of Tables

PREFACE

In the past three centuries, human civilization has made remarkable strides in progress and development, evident even in the most impoverished and underdeveloped nations through significant improvements in living standards, healthcare accessibility, and education opportunities. However, this progress has often been pursued with minimal consideration for social equity and environmental preservation. Such a development paradigm, focused solely on economic growth without holistic sustainability, is inherently unsustainable in the long term.

The private sector plays a pivotal role as a major stakeholder in shaping sustainability efforts. Its actions and decisions profoundly impact environmental conservation and social equity. Companies are increasingly recognizing the need to integrate sustainability into their core strategies, not merely as a compliance measure but as a fundamental driver of long-term success and resilience. This entails adopting practices that minimize environmental footprint, promote social responsibility across supply chains, and foster inclusive growth.

Financial modeling stands as a critical tool in navigating the complexities of modern business landscapes. It is a sought-after skill in financial analysis, yet often misunderstood due to its technical nature. At its core, financial modeling involves synthesizing accounting principles, financial metrics, and business forecasts to predict a company's future performance. Typically crafted in software like Microsoft Excel, a comprehensive financial model includes the three primary financial statements—income statement, balance sheet, and cash flow statement—alongside supplementary schedules.

Advanced financial models, such as Discounted Cash Flow (DCF), Leveraged Buyout (LBO), and Mergers and Acquisitions (M&A) models, utilize historical data and projections to assess various financial scenarios. These models are instrumental in decision-making processes, enabling stakeholders to evaluate investment opportunities, assess risk, and optimize financial strategies. Sensitivity analysis further enhances the robustness of these models by testing how changes in key variables impact outcomes, thereby enhancing decision-making under uncertainty.

Content/Structure of the book

This book offers a structured exploration of essential concepts and practical applications in financial analysis across its 10 comprehensive chapters.

Chapter 1 introduces readers to the fundamentals of financial modeling, outlining its significance in decision-making processes within business and investment contexts. It provides a foundational understanding of modeling techniques and their applications in various financial scenarios.

Chapter 2 focuses on Excel for Financial Modeling, emphasizing the software's capabilities in data organization, manipulation, and visualization. Readers learn to leverage Excel's tools and functions to construct robust financial models that facilitate analysis and decision-making.

Financial Statements and Ratio Analysis are covered in Chapter 3, highlighting how these documents serve as crucial indicators of a company's financial health. Ratio analysis techniques are explored to assess profitability, liquidity, and solvency, aiding in informed financial modeling and forecasting.

Chapter 4 examines into Fore casting Financial Statements, guiding readers through methodologies to project future financial performance based on historical data and market trends. This chapter equips analysts with skills to predict revenues, expenses, and cash flows essential for strategic planning.

Discounted Cash Flow (DCF) Analysis is the focus of Chapter 5, demonstrating how to evaluate the present value of future cash flows to determine the intrinsic value of investments. This method aids in investment decision-making by accounting for the time value of money and risk factors.

Financial Valuation Techniques are discussed in Chapter 6, covering approaches such as comparable company analysis and precedent transactions to assess the worth of businesses and assets. These techniques aid in mergers and acquisitions, investment evaluations, and financial reporting.

Chapter 7 shifts to Corporate Finance and Capital Structure Modeling, exploring methods to optimize capital allocation, leverage ratios, and financing decisions within organizations. Readers gain insights into modeling scenarios to optimize corporate finance strategies.

Asset Pricing Models are examined in Chapter 8, detailing frameworks like the Capital Asset Pricing Model (CAPM) to determine expected returns on investments based on risk and market performance.

Chapter 9 introduces Portfolio Modeling, guiding readers on constructing diversified portfolios to manage risk and optimize returns through asset allocation strategies.

Finally, Chapter 10 addresses Risk Analysis and Management, focusing on techniques to identify, measure, and mitigate financial risks within models, enhancing decision-making under uncertainty.

Through these 10 chapters, this book equips finance professionals, analysts, students, and anyone interested in financial analysis with comprehensive knowledge and practical skills to construct, interpret, and apply sophisticated financial models in diverse business and investment contexts.

Audience

This book is designed for professionals and students in finance, accounting, economics, and related fields who are looking to develop practical skills in financial analysis and decision-making. It caters to individuals interested in mastering the art of constructing and using financial models to assess investment opportunities, analyze business performance, and make informed financial decisions.

Professionals working in corporate finance, investment banking, asset management, and financial consulting will find the book invaluable for enhancing their quantitative skills and applying them to real-world financial scenarios. It provides a comprehensive framework for building robust financial models that can handle complex financial data, forecast future outcomes, and support strategic planning and risk management processes within organizations.

Students pursuing degrees in finance, accounting, or economics will benefit from the book's structured approach to learning financial modeling techniques. It serves as a practical guide that bridges theoretical knowledge with hands-on experience, helping students develop proficiency in Excel and other modeling tools commonly used in the industry. The book covers fundamental concepts such as valuation techniques, cash flow forecasting, scenario analysis, and sensitivity testing, equipping students with the necessary skills to excel in their academic studies and future careers.

Entrepreneurs and small business owners seeking to enhance their financial planning and analysis capabilities will also find the book useful. It offers practical insights and methodologies for creating financial models that facilitate budgeting, forecasting revenues and expenses, evaluating investment opportunities, and optimizing business operations.

Therefore, this book is structured to cater to a diverse audience interested in mastering financial modeling techniques and applying them effectively in various professional and academic settings. Whether you are looking to advance your career in finance, deepen your understanding of financial analysis, or enhance your business's financial management capabilities, this book provides the tools and knowledge needed to succeed in the complex world of financial modeling.

Learning Features

- Start-of-chapter learning objectives
- Key terms in each chapter
- Summary Points at the end of each chapter
- Review Questions at the end of each chapter
- Case Studies and Activities in each chapter for solving real problems
- References at the end of each chapter

CHAPTER

1 Financial Modeling

LEARNING OBJECTIVES

After studying this chapter, you will be able to:

- Discuss the financial modeling: objectives and fundamental
- Explain the financial modeling types.

KEY TERMS FROM THIS CHAPTER

Cash flow analysis
Discounted cash flow (DCF)
Financial analysis
Initial public offering (IPO)
Debt service cover ratio
Economic policy
Financial performance

INTRODUCTION

Financial modeling involves analyzing various aspects of an organization's functioning. The process of creating an abstract representation of a real-world financial situation—referred to as a financial model—is known as financial modeling. It is a mathematical model created to represent an abridged representation of the financial asset or portfolio performance of a company, undertaking, or other investment.

The process of creating a model that depicts a real-world financial scenario is known as financial modeling. They are meant to be instruments for making decisions. Executives in the company may utilize financial models to project the expenses and earnings of a suggested new project. Financial analysts predict how an event, such as a change in economic policy, will affect a company's stock price using financial models.

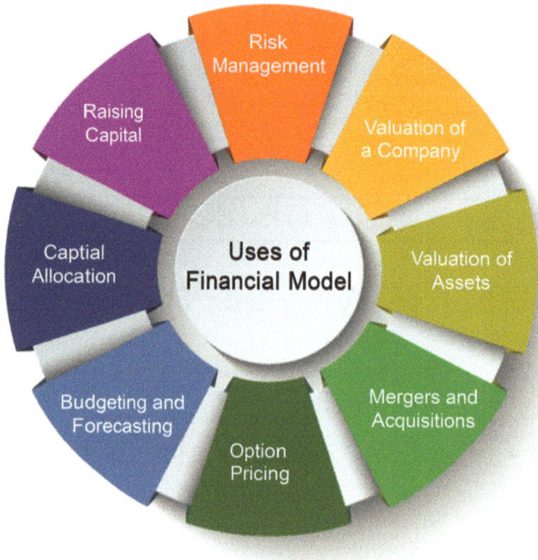

Figure 1.1. *Financial model.*

Source: https://s3-us-west-2.amazonaws.com/content.edupristine.com/images/web/fm.png.

The process used to create a company's financial representation is called financial modeling. Using these financial models, financial analysts project the company's earnings and performance in the future. The analysts replicate business operations using various forecast theories and valuations supplied by financial modeling through these financial models. When finished, financial models show a mathematical representation of the business events (Figure 1.1).

The excel spreadsheet is the main tool used to create the financial model. The method by which a business creates a financial depiction of some or all of its features or a particular security. Typically, the model performs computations and generates recommendations based on the results. In addition to summarizing specific events for the user, the model may also offer guidance on potential courses of action or other options.

1.1. FINANCIAL MODELING: OBJECTIVES AND FUNDAMENTAL

Financial models are used in many different fields to project a company's financial performance and guide historical analysis of the company. These financial models are designed for various uses and are primarily utilized by financial analysts. By building financial models, financial modeling aids management in decision-making and the preparation of financial analyzes (Figure 1.2).

The following are the objectives of creating financial models:

- Valuing a business
- Raising capital
- Growing the business
- Making acquisitions
- Seling or divesting assets and business units
- Capital allocation
- Budgeting and forecasting

Figure 1.2. *Financial models help in steering historical analysis of a company.*

Source: https://financerewind.com/wp-content/uploads/2020/08/871358_599e.jpg.

Top financial models provide a set of fundamental presumptions. For instance, sales growth is one line item that is frequently forecasted. Gross margin growth (or decline) from the previous quarter to the current one is used to measure sales growth. These are the only two inputs that financial models require in order to compute sales growth.

Two cells will be created by financial modeling: cell A will represent sales from the previous year, and cell B will represent sales from the current year. The formula that divides the difference between cells A and B by cell A would be applied to the third cell, or cell C. This will be the recipe for growth. The formula, found in Cell C, would be integrated into the model. The input cells A and B are modifiable by the user.

1.1.1. The Basics of Financial Modeling

Financial modeling is the process of using numbers to depict the operations of a business in the past, present, and anticipated future. These models are meant to be instruments for making decisions.

They could be used by business executives to project the expenses and earnings of a new project that is being proposed. They are used by financial analysts to explain or predict how events, whether internal or external (such as a shift in economic policy or regulation) will affect a company's stock price. Examples of internal factors include strategy or business model changes.

Financial models are used to compare a company's performance to that of its industry peers or to estimate the valuation of a business. Additionally, they are employed in strategic planning to evaluate potential outcomes, estimate project costs, establish budgets, and distribute company resources. Financial models can take many forms, such as sensitivity analysis, discounted cash flow analysis, or comprehensive appraisal.

1.1.1.1. Applications

A fundamental ability that is practically required for anyone hoping to pursue a career in finance is financial modeling. It is helpful for sales and marketing professionals as well as for anyone wishing to launch their own company, as it is essential for project bidding, campaign utility calculations, and other related tasks.

Every time we have to make a financial decision, we project the expected revenue and expenses and then determine whether or not that was the right choice based on those estimates. In a stock market analysis, we consider a company's historical performance to estimate its future revenue, expenses, and profit, and consequently determine whether to purchase, sell, or hold that particular share.

- **Investment Banking/Equity Research:** Financial Modeling is the basic tool for fundamental analysis and valuations. Investment banker use it to arrive at a valuation in M&A or fund-raising transactions. Equity Analysts use it to value stocks and come up with buy/sell/hold recommendations.
- **Project Finance/Credit Rating:** Financial model help bankers, credit analysts to project future revenues and costs and to make an informed judgment about a projects viability. They are then able to decide if they should extend loans or what the credit rating of a project or company should be.
- **Corporate Finance:** Financial Modeling is used by companies to assess their own finances and projects. It is hence an input in creating funding plans for corporate projects.
- **Entrepreneurs/Private Equity:** Entrepreneurs use Financial Models to present their plans to potential investors as much as to plan their strategies. Running different simulations can often be an important tool in avoiding potential risks.

1.1.2. Financial Modeling: Points to Follow

The process of financial modeling is iterative. When building financial models, analysts have to work on individual components until they can finally bring everything together (Figure 1.3).

Below is a step-by-step breakdown of where they should start and how to finally connect all the dots.

1. Historical results and assumptions
2. Start the income statement
3. Start the balance sheet

4. Build the supporting schedules
5. Complete the income statement and balance sheet
6. Build the cash flow statement
7. Perform the Discounted Cash Flow (DCF) analysis
8. Add sensitivity analysis and scenarios
9. Build charts and graphs
10. Stress test and audit the model

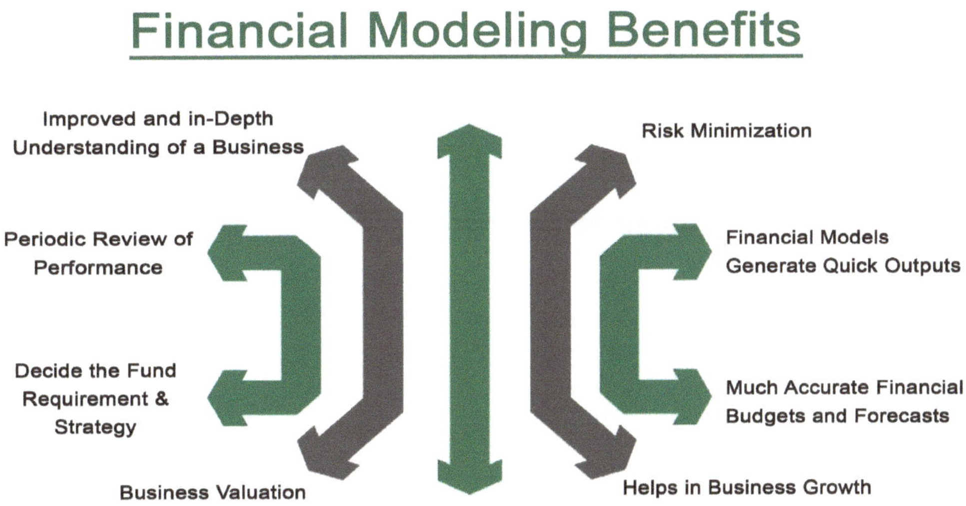

Figure 1.3. *Financial modeling benefits.*

Source: https://cdn.wallstreetmojo.com/wp-content/uploads/2020/12/Financial-Modeling-Benefits.jpg.

1.1.3. Financial Modeling: Categories

Different types of financial modeling tools are used depending on why and how it needs to be done. Financial models are divided into different categories to address various business issues. Although most financial models focus on valuation, some are designed to estimate and forecast risk, portfolio performance, or regional or industry-specific economic trends. A thorough understanding of corporate finance and the use of high-quality templates are essential for successful finance modeling.

Examples of financial models available include:

1.1.3.1. Project Finance Models

The project finance model is a useful tool for determining the capital and project structure of large infrastructure projects that are being assessed for feasibility. Only when the project can generate enough revenue to pay for all operating and debt-servicing costs for the duration of the debt is project financing feasible.

Since these projects are typically long-term, loans and the related debt repayments are an essential component of project finance models, as lenders must determine whether the project can generate enough revenue to cover the debt. Stated differently, the project finance model is employed by the organization as a financial tool for evaluating the project's economic viability.

This category of financial modeling includes metrics like debt service cover ratio (DSCR), which can be a useful gauge of project risk and potentially impact the lender's interest rate. The lender and borrower agree on the DSCR and other metrics at the outset of the project, with the requirement that the ratio not fall below a specific value. Accounting rules dictate the calculation algorithm and the uniform output of a project finance model through financial modeling, but the input is highly project specific (Figure 1.4).

Generally, it can be subdivided into the following categories:

- Variables needed for forecasting revenues
- Variables needed for forecasting expenses
- Capital expenditures
- • Financing

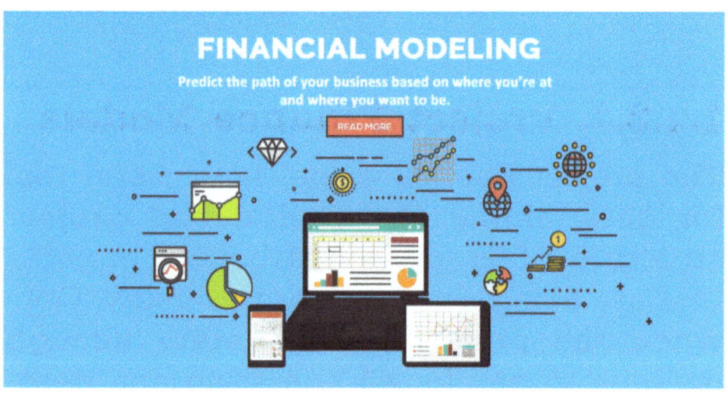

Figure 1.4. *Project finance models.*

Source: https://i1.wp.com/external-cfo.com/wp-content/uploads/2017/05/financial-modeling-my-guwen.png?fit=1042%2C521&ssl=1.

1.1.3.2. Pricing Models

This category of financial models is built for the idea of establishing the price that can or should be charged for a product. One of the most important elements of the marketing mix is price. Companies use cost-based pricing, value-based pricing, value pricing, and competition-based pricing as their four main pricing strategies to determine the right price for their goods and services. The lower limit is determined by production costs, and the upper limit is determined by how customers view the good or service. Price is the input and profitability is the output of a pricing model. An income statement, or profit-and-loss statement, of the company or product should be prepared first, based on the current price or a price that has been entered as a placeholder, before creating a pricing model through financial modeling.

At a very high level:

Units × Price = Revenue

Revenue – Expenses = Profit

On the other hand, these financial models can be fairly simple, residing on a single page, or extremely complex, involving numerous tabs and calculations. The financial modeler can use a goal seek or a data table to perform sensitivity analysis on the price entered once this structure model is in place.

1.1.3.3. Integrated Financial Statement Models

This category of financial models is also known as a three-way financial model. The three kinds of financial statements included in the financial modeling of an integrated financial statement model are the following (Figure 1.5):

1. Income statement, also known as a profit-and-loss (P&L) statement
2. Cash flow statement
3. Balance sheet

Figure 1.5. *Integrated financial statement models.*

Source: https://wsp-blog-images.s3.amazonaws.com/uploads/2018/01/24145803/comboskillsFSM.gif.

While not all financial model categories must include all three forms of financial statements, many do, and these are referred to as integrated financial statement models. From the perspective of financial modeling, it's critical that the financial statements be correctly linked together during the financial modeling process for an integrated financial statement. This way, if one statement changes, the others will follow suit.

1.1.3.4. Valuation Models

For the purpose of joint ventures, refinancing, contract bids, acquisitions, or other types of transactions or deals, this category of financial models values assets or businesses. Deals modelers are the term used to describe those who create these models. It takes specific knowledge of valuation theory, experience with various asset valuation methods, and financial modeling expertise to create these kinds of financial models.

When valuing a company as a going concern there are three main valuation methods used by industry practitioners:

1. DCF analysis
2. Comparable company analysis
3. Precedent transactions

In the majority of financial fields, including corporate development, investment banking, equities research, private equity, mergers and acquisitions (M&A), and private equity, these are the most widely used methods of valuation. Leveraged buyout (LBO) and initial public offering (IPO) models are two popular examples of these types of financial models.

1.1.3.5. Reporting Models

The income statement, cash flow statement, balance sheet, and other financial statements are just a few examples of the financial statements that are condensed in these models. There is a school of thought that claims these financial models are not true financial models because they examine historical events.

Financial modeling uses the same foundations as other financial models, including principles, layout, and design. Actual versus budget reports, which include forecasts and rolling forecasts that are influenced by assumptions and other factors, are frequently produced using reporting models.

1.1.4. Financial Modeling Using Excel & VBA

Utilizing financial models is facilitated by a solid foundation in Excel, VBA, fundamental math, and background finance knowledge. Models are useful for financial projections of all kinds because they use mathematical expressions and "what-if" scenarios to show the relationships between two or more variables. This results in a wealth of information that can be used to make wise financial decisions. To ask, respond to, and resolve your financial questions and problems, start with Excel functions and formulas and then use Visual Basic for Applications macros to extend the functionality of models.

- **Facts:** The most popular framework for financial models, both personal and business, is the deterministic model. Deterministic models aim to establish a relationship between historical data and important dependent variables by basing projections mostly on historical data. A deterministic financial model and a standard Excel spreadsheet may appear to be similar at first glance, but there are often more intricate formulas and functions at work behind the scenes, many of which are accessible through the Data Analysis Toolpak add-in. The inclusion of VBA macros, which help with intricate computations and financial model automation, sets these models apart from standard spreadsheets even more.
- **Organization:** An effective financial model must be well-organized and structured. Your model will be easier to read and comprehend if it has a straightforward, well-organized interface, even though the underlying calculations may be complicated. Commence by providing a thorough explanation of the model's goal or goals and a plan outlining how you intend to reach them. For brief, straightforward models, use a single worksheet; however, think about dividing models with a lot of data into several worksheets. To make data easier to read, group input and output, and designate model components with color-coding, descriptive titles, and column and row names.
- **Coding Components:** Dynamic independent variables, along with static intermediate and immediate dependent variables, are used in calculations by Excel functions and VBA code to generate complex "what-if" scenarios. Independent variables give a model the data it needs to do calculations, such as user input and optional parameters. While their immediate counterpart is the visible, final

result of modeling calculations, intermediate dependent variables are an interim result in a multi-step calculation. In a basic financial model that determines your after-tax income, your gross income is the dynamic independent variable, your income tax due is the intermediate dependent variable, your tax bracket and rate information are static dependent variable parameters, and your after-tax income is the immediate dependent variable.

- **Considerations:** Gaining proficiency in financial modeling requires education, experience, and practice. Let your skill level, the intricacy of a calculation, and the frequency of use dictate whether an Excel function or a VBA macro is the better option as you proceed up the learning curve. Built-in functions are generally suitable for "one-time" or brief computations, but VBA macros can be helpful for more involved or frequently needed calculations. If you're new to financial modeling, using built-in functions from the Data Analysis Toolpak add-in or Excel itself is a good option. You can accelerate your progress by taking advantage of free training offered by Microsoft and independent websites like the Financial Modeling Guide, Chandoo, and the Family Computer Club on both general Excel topics and the intricacies of financial modeling.

1.2. FINANCIAL MODELING TYPES

Creating an abstract representation, or model, of a real-world financial scenario is the task of financial modeling. This is a mathematical model created to show, in a simplified form, how a financial asset or portfolio of a company, project, or other investment performed. Therefore, financial modeling is generally understood to refer to a quantitative exercise in corporate finance or asset pricing. It involves converting a set of theories regarding how markets or agents behave into numerical forecasts. However, the term "financial modeling" is ambiguous and can have different meanings for different people. It is typically used in relation to quantitative finance applications or accounting and corporate finance applications. Financial models come in a wide variety of forms in real life. The top 10 financial models that financial modeling experts use on a regular basis are listed here.

1.2.1. Three-Statement Model

The income statement, balance sheet, and cash flow statement are combined into a single dynamically connected financial model through the use of a three-statement model. These financial models provide the foundation for more complex financial models, including leveraged buyout (LBO), merger, and discounted cash flow (DCF) models, among others. It fits into both reporting models and integrated financial statement models, which are types of financial models.

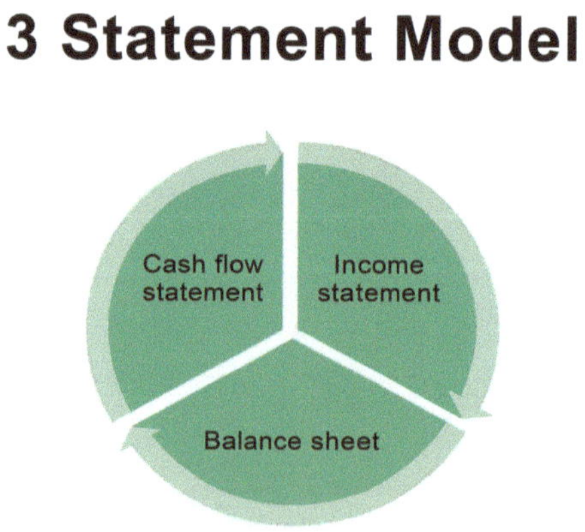

Figure 1.6. *Three-statement model.*

Source: https://cdn.wallstreetmojo.com/wp-content/uploads/2020/08/3-Statement-Model.jpg.webp.

A three statement model is a type of financial modeling that creates a dynamically connected single financial model from the connection of three important financial statements, such as the cash flow statement, balance sheet, and income statement. This type of model is then used as the foundation for more complex financial models, such as leverage buyout, discounted cash flow, merger, and other financial models (Figure 1.6).

1.2.1.1. Explanation

A 3-statement model is a sophisticated financial model that integrates the three essential financial statements—the cash flow statement, the balance sheet, and the income statement—into one cohesive model. This model serves as the foundation for additional crucial models, such as merger and acquisition models and DCF valuation models. Additionally, scenario and sensitivity analysis make use of it. The main benefit of these models is that we can simultaneously capture the principles of three statements in a single Excel file. There's less chance of incorrect formula correlations. When everything is contained in a single Excel file instead of three separate models, it appears more organized. Additionally, it offers a wider range for multi-business organizations to consolidate.

1.2.1.2. Create a 3 Statement Model

A 3 statement model requires several steps to finally integrate all the three financial statements into a single model. The steps required are as follows:

- **Step 1: Gathering or Collating Historical Information from Financial Statement in Single Excel File.** In this step, financial information is obtained from the company website or their press release, and these are considered historical information. These data are either downloaded to a single excel file or copy-pasted into it. After doing this, the excel file needs to be formatted a bit to make the data readable and understandable.
- **Step 2: Chalking Out Assumptions which will Determine Forecasting.** Now once we have the historical data in our excel file, we can implement some formulas to calculate or evaluate the historical performance of the company. Metrics such as margins, growth of revenues, capital expenditures, and working capital calculation can be considered as the following.
- **Step 3: Income Statement Forecasting.** After all the assumptions taken into consideration, it is now the stage to forecast the income statement. It all begins from the revenue and drills now further to the calculation of the EBITDA. In this stage, we also require support scheduling methods for financing activity processes and capital assets.
- **Step 4: Capital Asset Forecasting.** Here forecast is made on aspects like plant and machinery, property, and only after this, one can end the income statement part of the model. Here the closing balance of the last period is considered, and then the capital expenditure is added, or depreciation deducted to arrive at the final closing balance.
- **Step 5: Financing Activity Forecasting.** Here we need to set up a schedule of debt plan to arrive at the interest expense on the income statement. Here too, we

consider the last period's closing balance and then add to this any increase or decrease in the value of the principal to conclude the closing balance.

- **Step 6: Balance Sheet Forecasting.** Here we consider the balance sheet information and working capital elements are forecasted here, taking into consideration assumptions like average payable days, average receivables, inventory turns, etc. Capital assets come here from the schedule. Here the cash balance is not forecasted or completed, which is the last step of the 3-statement model.
- **Step 7: Cash Flow Statement Completion.** The last stage of three-statement modeling is the completion of the cash flow statement. This statement requires a simple linking of the earlier items, calculated to arrive at the cash balance. There are three main sections: cash from operations, cash from investing activity, and cash from financing activity. Thus, by linking these three to the other statements, we arrive at the final cash in hand/bank balance.
- **Example**

You have attached a template for the 3-statement model based on Excel. In this case, we have projected until 2025 based on historical data up to 2020.

The profit and loss statement, balance sheet, and cash flow statement are the three main financial statements that have been utilized.

Finally, a schedule plan is attached, and the template starts with the assumptions that have been taken into account.

1.2.1.3. Approaches

There are five steps to build a 3-statement model, and we rely on our base on historical.

Assumptions are essential because we need to assume many factors like growth rate, interest rate, etc.

1. Thus the first and foremost important approach is our assumptions, which means how the business will drive itself in the forecasted period.
2. Next comes the income statement, which is a summary of profit and loss, and thus, based on the historical data, the future is predicted.
3. After this, we have the balance sheet, which explains the position of the company at a particular point in time. Same as profit and loss statement here too based on historical data, we forecast the future period.
4. After this, from data points in the above two statements, we build our cash flow statement, which is the ultimate goal of our 3-statement modeling. Here few data gets populated from profit and loss statement and balance sheet. Thus, we find all three statements are linked to one another. It shows the different levels of cash from operations, investing activity, and financing activity and finally arrives as closing cash balance or net cash balance.
5. The last part of the three-statement model is the supporting schedules, which help calculate the depreciation or interest and other such factors.

1.2.2. Discounted Cash Flow (DCF) Model

These financial models are classified as valuation models and are commonly, though not exclusively, employed in capital markets and equities research. One particular kind of financial model used to determine a company's value is the DCF model. The DCF model projects an organization's unlevered free cash flow, which is then discounted back to its current value and known as the Net Present Value (NPV).

The three-statement financial model, which connects the financials, is the fundamental component of a DCF model. The DCF model uses the XNPV function in Excel to discount the cash flows back to the current day at the company's Weighted Average Cost of Capital (WACC) after making any necessary adjustments to the three-statement financial model (Figure 1.7).

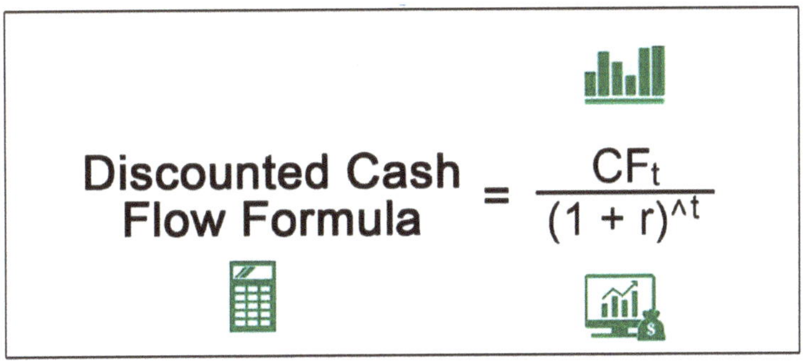

Figure 1.7. *Discounted cash flow (DCF) model.*

Source: https://cdn.wallstreetmojo.com/wp-content/uploads/2021/05/Discounted-Cash-Flow-Formula.jpg.

A valuation technique called discounted cash flow (DCF) is used to calculate an investment's value based on anticipated future cash flows. By estimating how much money an investment will make in the future, DCF analysis aims to determine the investment's current value. This pertains to choices made by investors in businesses or securities, such as purchasing stock or a company, as well as choices made by managers and owners of businesses regarding capital budgets and operating expenses.

Estimating the amount of money an investor would receive from an investment after time value of money is taken into account is the goal of DCF analysis. Because a dollar can be invested, the time value of money assumes that a dollar today is worth more than a dollar tomorrow. Therefore, in any scenario where an individual is making a payment now with the expectation of receiving a larger payment later, a DCF analysis is appropriate.

For instance, $1 in a savings account will be worth $1.05 over the course of a year, assuming a 5% annual interest rate. In a similar vein, if a $1 payment is postponed for a year, you cannot transfer it to your savings account to accrue interest, so its present value is only 95 cents. Using a discount rate, DCF analysis determines the present value of anticipated future cash flows. The notion of present value of money can be utilized by investors to ascertain if the projected future cash flows of a project or investment match or surpass the initial investment's value. The opportunity should be taken into consideration if the value determined using the DCF is greater than the investment's current cost. An investor must estimate future cash flows and the asset's ending value, such as equipment or other assets, in order to perform a DCF analysis.

A suitable discount rate for the DCF model must also be chosen by the investor; this will vary based on the project or investment in question, the investor's or company's risk tolerance, and the state of the capital markets. When an investor lacks access to future cash flows or the project is highly intricate, DCF becomes less valuable and other models ought to be utilized.

1.2.2.1. Example of DCF

A company typically uses its weighted average cost of capital (WACC) as the discount rate when evaluating the DCF when determining whether to invest in a particular project or buy new equipment. The average rate of return that firm shareholders anticipate for a given year is factored into the Weighted Average Cost of Capital (WACC).

Let's take an example where you want to invest in a project and your company's WACC is 5%. In this case, your discount rate will be 5%. The initial investment is $11 million, and the project will last for five years, with the following estimated cash flows per year:

Cash Flow	
Year	Cash Flow
1	$1 million
2	$1 million
3	$4 million
4	$4 million
5	$6 million

Therefore, the discounted cash flows for the project are:

Discounted Cash Flow		
Year	Cash Flow	Discounted Cash Flow (Nearest $)
1	$1 million	$952,381
2	$1 million	$907,029
3	$4 million	$3,455,350
4	$4 million	$3,290,810
5	$6 million	$4,701,157

If we add up all of the discounted cash flows, we get a value of $13,306,727. Subtracting the initial investment of $11 million, we get a net present value (NPV) of $2,306,727. Because this is a positive number, the cost of the investment today is worth it because the project will generate positive discounted cash flows above the initial cost. If the project had cost $14 million, the NPV would have been -$693,272, indicating that the cost of the investment would not be worth it.

1.2.3. Merger Model (M&A)

Financial models that fall under the valuation category include the M&A model as well. This kind of financial modeling, as the name implies, is geared toward a more sophisticated model used to evaluate the pro forma accretion/dilution of a merger or acquisition. For every company, a single tab model is frequently used, with the consolidation shown as Company A + Company B = Merged Co. The most common uses for this level of complexity are in investment banking and/or corporate development, though it can vary greatly.

The purpose of merger models is to replicate the effects of a merger or acquisition of two companies. The analysis depicts the possible union of two businesses that join through a M&A procedure. The model evaluates the effect on the acquirer's finances and clarifies how an acquisition would be made possible. Building a merger model involves several key steps or components, starting with M&A model inputs (assumptions about financial statements and valuation inputs needed to drive the rest of the analysis), which are followed by a variety of M&A model assumptions, model analysis, and model outputs.

Mergers and Acquisitions (M&A) are, to put it simply, transactions that result in the buying and/or joining of one business with another. Due diligence is necessary to determine whether or not these deals can be advantageous. It is important to consider whether acquirers pay a premium over the share price of the target company for acquisitions or control, evaluate the factors that could drive value creation, and look for possible synergies (Figure 1.8).

The mains steps for building a merger model are:

1. Making Acquisition Assumptions
2. Making Projections
3. Valuation of Each Business
4. Business Combination and Pro Forma Adjustments
5. Deal Accretion/ Dilution

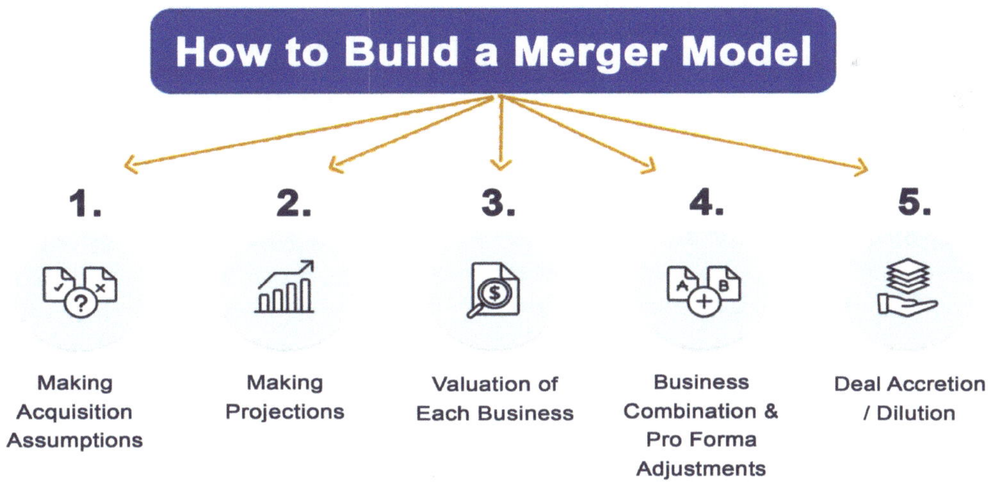

Figure 1.8. *The mains steps for building a merger model.*

Source: https://corporatefinanceinstitute.com/resources/knowledge/modeling/build-merger-model/.

Each of these steps will be explored in more detail below:

1. **Making Acquisition Assumptions.** Since they would have to give up a sizable number of shares to the target company, a buyer whose stock is undervalued might choose to use cash rather than equity consideration. On the other

hand, because equity may be worth more than cash, the target company might prefer to receive it. A key component of reaching an agreement is identifying a factor that both sides can agree upon.

The target company, on the other hand, might prefer to get equity because it might be thought to be worth more than cash. A key component of reaching an agreement is identifying a factor that both sides can agree upon.

Key assumptions include:

i. Purchase price of the target
ii. Number of new shares to be issued to the target (as consideration)
iii. Value of cash to be paid to the target (as consideration)
iv. M&A synergies can occur from cost savings or revenue upside. There are various types of synergies in mergers and acquisition. This guide provides examples. A synergy is any effect that increases the value of a merged firm above the combined value of the two separate firms. Synergies may arise in M&A transactions from the combination of the two businesses (cost savings)
v. Timing for those synergies to be realized
vi Integration costs
vii Adjustments to the financials (mostly accounting-related)
viii. Forecast/financial projections for target and acquirer

2. **Making Projections.** Forecasting in a merger model is analogous to forecasting in a standard DCF model. One particular kind of financial model used to determine a company's value is the DCF model. All that the model is, is a projection of the unlevered free cash flow (or any other kind of financial model) of the company. The DCF model, MandA model, LBO model, budget model, and three statement model are the most popular forms of financial models.

Find out which are the top 10. An analyst will make assumptions regarding capital structure, capital expenditures, fixed and variable costs, revenue growth, margins, and all other accounts on the company's financial statements in order to forecast. We refer to this procedure as "building a 3 Statement Model."

The income statement, balance sheet, and cash flow statement are combined into a single dynamically connected financial model by means of a three statement model. Linking the cash flow statement, balance sheet, and income statement is necessary and is facilitated by examples.

3. **Valuation of Each Business.** The third step in creating a merger model is to analyze each company's DCF. Following the completion of the forecast, each business needs to be valued. The discounted cash flow (DCF) model will be used for valuation. This is the most subjective step, and there will be a lot of assumptions involved. Because of this, having a highly qualified financial analyst can really help to produce extremely accurate and trustworthy numbers in this area.

The steps in performing the valuation include:

i. Performing comparable company analysis. This guide shows you step-by-step how to build comparable company analysis ("Comps") and includes a free template and many examples.

ii. Building the DCF model. A DCF model is a specific type of financial model used to value a business. The model is simply a forecast of a company's unlevered free cash flow

iii. Determining the weighted average cost of capital (WACC is a firm's Weighted Average Cost of Capital and represents its blended cost of capital including equity and debt.)

iv. Calculating the terminal value are a great way to improve technical knowledge of finance, accounting, financial modeling, valuation, trading, economics, and more of the business

4. **Business Combination and Pro Forma Adjustments.** The balance sheet items of company B are added to company A's balance sheet upon acquisition of company B. There will be a number of accounting adjustments needed when the two companies' financials are combined, including figuring out the worth of goodwill, stock shares, options, and cash equivalents. Any effect that raises the value of a combined company above the sum of the values of the two independent firms is referred to as a synergy. Synergies could occur when M&A transactions are made (Figure 1.9).

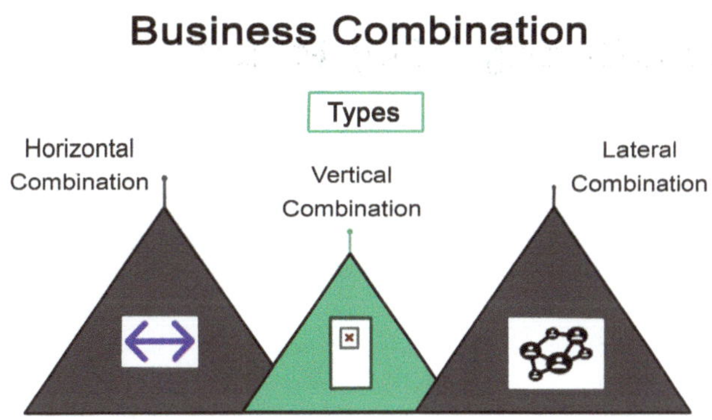

Figure 1.9. *Business combination and pro forma adjustments.*

Source: https://cdn.wallstreetmojo.com/wp-content/uploads/2020/11/Business-Combination-1.jpg.

Key assumptions include:

- The form of consideration (cash or shares)
- Purchase Price Allocation (PPA)
- Goodwill calculation
- Any changes in accounting practices between the companies
- Synergies M&A. Synergies occur when the value of a merged company is higher than the sum of the two individual companies. 10 ways to estimate operational synergies in M&A deals are: 1) analyze headcount, 2) look at ways to consolidate vendors, 3) evaluate any head office or rent savings 4) estimate the value saved by sharing calculation

Determining the goodwill resulting from the acquisition of the target company's assets is a crucial step in developing the merger model. When a buyer purchases a target for more money than the seller's balance sheet's Fair Market Value of Net Tangible Assets, goodwill is created. An impairment charge will be incurred if the acquired entity's book value is less than what the acquirer paid. Consequently, the value of the acquired net assets will be written down to reflect the consideration that was paid.

5. **Deal Accretion/ Dilution.** A straightforward test called dilution analysis is used to assess whether a proposed merger or acquisition will result in a rise or fall in post-transaction EPS. It also assesses how the acquisition will affect the buyer's pro forma. If, following the acquisition of the target company, the buyer's EPS rises, the transaction is considered accretive. On the other hand, if the merger results in a decrease in the buyer's EPS, the transaction is seen as dilutive. Before finalizing a deal, the buyer should calculate the impact of the target's financial performance on the company's EPS.

Key assumptions include:

- Number of new shares issued
- Earnings acquired from the target
- Impact of synergies

1.2.4. Initial Public Offering (IPO) Model

A valuation model is also the IPO model. Investment bankers and other financial experts create Excel IPO financial models to assess a company's worth prior to going public. These financial models compare the analysis of a company to a presumption regarding the price that potential investors would be willing to pay for the company that is being considered.

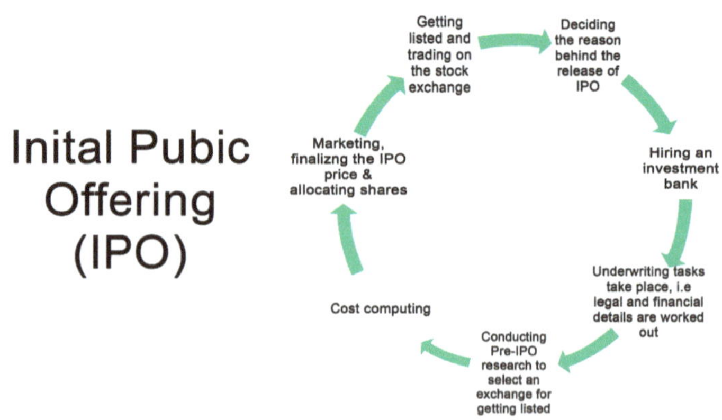

Figure 1.10. *Initial public offering (IPO).*

Source: https://cdn.wallstreetmojo.com/wp-content/uploads/2021/07/IPO.jpg.

To guarantee that the stock trades favorably in the secondary financial market, an IPO discount is included in the valuation in an IPO model. A privately held company becomes a public company whose shares are traded on a stock exchange through an initial public offering (IPO). Going public is another term used to describe this process. A privately held business is owned by the investors who buy its stock when it goes public (Figure 1.10).

A lot of investors in initial public offerings (IPOs) are unaware of how a company's value is established. An investment bank is engaged to ascertain the company's and its shares' worth prior to the stock's public offering and listing on an exchange. Analyzing a company whose stock has just been issued and has never been traded on an exchange before can be difficult for an investor.

However, astute investors can attempt to ascertain whether the stock is priced fairly by examining the registration documents of the company and evaluating its financials. Furthermore, anyone interested in becoming an early investor should comprehend the various aspects of how an investment bank conducts a company's IPO valuation.

1.2.5. The Components of IPO Valuation

The demand from investors for the company's shares determines whether an IPO is successful. A high level of demand for the company's stock will raise its price. An IPO valuation is determined by a number of factors, including industry comparables, growth prospects, and the narrative of the company, in addition to the demand for the shares of the offering.

- **Demand:** A company's value is not always increased by strong demand for its shares. It does, however, imply that the company's valuation will increase. The method by which an analyst ascertains the fair value of a company's shares is called an IPO valuation. The IPO timing and market demand can result in significantly different IPO valuations for two identical companies. An IPO is typically reserved for companies that determine there is significant market demand for their stock.

At the height of the bubble in 2000, the IPO valuations of numerous technology companies were enormous. They were valued far higher than businesses that went public later on, and as a result, they attracted a lot more investment capital. This was not necessarily a reflection of these companies' superiority; rather, it was primarily caused by the trend of technology stocks and the particularly high demand in the early 2000s.

- **Industry Comparables:** An additional step in the IPO valuation process is the use of industry comparables. The IPO valuation will compare the valuation multiples being given to the IPO candidate's competitors if it operates in an industry with comparable publicly traded companies. The reasoning behind this is that investors will be prepared to pay a new player in the market the same amount they are now paying for established businesses.
- **Growth Prospects:** Future growth estimates for the company are a major factor in IPO valuations. An initial public offering's main goal is to raise money to support future expansion. An IPO's ability to be successfully sold frequently hinges on the company's expectations and capacity for rapid growth.
- **A Compelling Corporate Narrative:** An IPO valuation is determined by a

variety of non-quantitative factors. The narrative of a business can have just as much impact as its predicted sales figures. A company's offering of novel goods or services that have the potential to transform an industry or be at the forefront of a brand-new business model may be taken into account during the valuation process. The businesses that helped establish the Internet in the 1990s are a prime example of this. Even though some of them were not making any money at the time, they were valued at several billions of dollars because they were pushing innovative and exciting technologies.

In an attempt to project the image of a developing company with seasoned management, some businesses may bolster their corporate narrative by hiring consultants and veterans of the field. The marketing campaign of a company can sometimes overshadow its actual fundamentals. For this reason, early investors should carefully examine the financials of a company and understand the risks associated with investing in a company without a track record of consistent trading.

A leveraged buyout (LBO) is a business acquisition in which the primary form of consideration is debt. In these kinds of deals, a private equity (PE) firm usually borrows as much as possible—up to 70 or 80% of the purchase price—from different lenders and uses their own equity to cover the remaining amount.

Financial models that include debt schedules and are more sophisticated than standard financial models are usually needed for an LBO transaction. Because an LBO requires cash flow waterfalls and has multiple layers of financing that create circular references, it is frequently one of the most complex and difficult financial model types. These models are uncommon outside of investment banking and private equity (Figure 1.11).

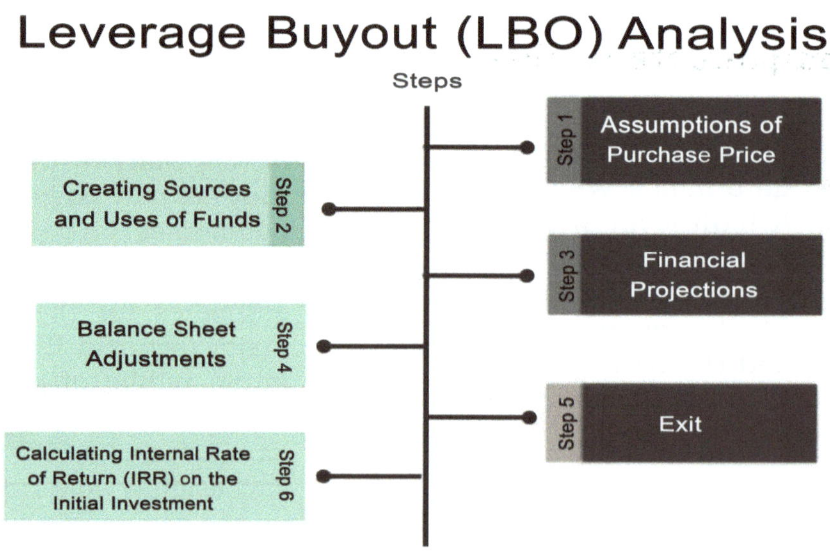

Figure 1.11. *Leveraged buyout (LBO).*

Source: https://cdn.wallstreetmojo.com/wp-content/uploads/2015/07/Leverage-Buyout-main.jpg.

When it comes to an LBO transaction, the required financial modeling can get complex. The added complexity comes from the following unique elements of an LBO:

- High degree of leverage
- Multiple tranches of debt financing
- Complex bank covenants
- Issuing of Preferred shares
- Management equity compensation
- Operational improvements targeted in the business

1.2.6. Sum of the Parts Model

This model is another kind of financial model that falls under the valuation category. It is created by adding various DCF financial models for consideration.

Additionally, the value of the business is increased by any other incidental elements that might not be appropriate for a DCF analysis.

To find the NAV for the company, you could, for instance, sum up the value of business units A, B, and investments C less liabilities D. This is known as the "Sum of the Parts." The sum of the parts (SOTP) method of business valuation involves valuing each of the company's subsidiaries or business segment separately and then adding them all up to determine the firm's overall value.

The majority of big businesses are involved in multiple industries. It is necessary to value a diversified company's corporate headquarters and each of its businesses separately. Stock market analysts and businesses alike frequently employ the process known as SOTP, or full form Sum of the Parts valuation, which involves breaking down a company's value into its component parts and then adding them all up.

1.2.7. Consolidation Model

The Reporting Model category of financial models includes the Consolidation Model. It combines multiple business units into a single model so that additional analysis and financial modeling can be done. Usually, there is a consolidation tab that merely summarizes the other business units, and each business unit has its own tab.

This is comparable to an exercise called Sum of the Parts, in which Division A and Division B are combined to create a single, new worksheet. The financial outcomes are combined to create a consolidation model. The income statement, balance sheet, and statement of cash flows are the three financial statements. These three central claims combine several business divisions into a single model.

1.2.7.1. Building a Consolidation Model

In order to fully explain the details, we will now take you step-by-step through the modeling process. The primary "business units" in this sample model are projects, each of which has its own expenses and income. This is a very basic model with few inputs; however, consolidation models can be highly complex in real-world business settings, involving multiple data sources and extensive computations.

1. **Create Workbooks with Labels Corresponding to the Projects:** FP&A analysts, managers, and directors are responsible for providing executives with the analysis and information they need starts building the consolidation model in Excel by creating multiple workbooks. Each project is assigned to a specific workbook.

2. **Identify column and Row Labels from Highest- to Lowest-Level Granularity:** For each project, the FP&A analyst identifies the columns and rows needed. In this model, time (i.e., months) is the main column and the financial metrics (total revenues, total costs, profits, etc.) are the main rows. Starting with the highest-level metrics, the analyst will insert rows for lower-level numbers such as various expenses. Besides the individual months, there is also often a column showing the full-year results or the monthly averages.
3. **Insert Relevant Data into the Tables:** Once all columns and rows are identified, the FP&A analyst inputs the corresponding information collected from financial statements or obtained from developing queries on raw data. They are data that needs to be manually filled into the table, so an analyst should use a different color font (blue is used in this sample model) to distinguish the numbers from those that will be calculated.
4. **Calculate Financial Figures Using the Data Tables:** With all the desired information in place, the FP&A analyst can calculate metrics that are not readily available from financial statements or other sources. The metrics may be figures such as total costs for each project, profit margins, and productivity rates. Formulas such as SUM, AVERAGE, and SUMPRODUCT are commonly used in the calculations. The analyst should always include cell references in their formulas to better track calculation errors. The numbers should be shown in black or other colors to distinguish them from the manually-encoded data.
5. **Validate Data with the Financial Statements:** After completing the data tables, the analyst should always validate the data with the numbers in the financial statements to ensure accuracy. This is a very crucial step in building consolidation models—one that must be completed before proceeding to the last few steps.
6. **Create a Summary or Consolidation Tab:** When all individual project analyzes are completed, the FP&A analyst creates a summary or consolidation worksheet as the first tab of the model. This is a page to summarize all the project financial metrics and present the highest-level information that is important to managers and corporate decision-makers. Analysts can create tables to display figures such as total revenue, total costs, profit margins, and margin percentages of the entire business. They can also include information that is helpful to managers in improving operating efficiencies such as employee productivity rates.
7. **Fill in the Cells by Using Cell References from Individual Project Data:** The next step is to insert numbers into the summary tables by using formulas. In the formulas, the analyst should always use cell references from individual project tabs instead of simply plugging in the numbers. This is to make sure the right figures are used in the calculations and to enable the analyst to return to, and check, the reference cells if variances exist.

8. **Generate Charts and Graphs to Visualize the Summary Data:** Using the data in the summary tables, the analyst inserts charts and graphs to present information in meaningful and easy-to-interpret formats. There are several types of charts utilized by FP&A analysts to visualize the data, so simply choose the types that would best represent the data characteristics and analytical trends.
9. **Present the Model in a Professional and Tidy Format:** Lastly, clean up, format, and embellish the consolidation model to make it look professional. This is very important because the management team does not want to see an unorganized dashboard where they will find the financial figures difficult to understand.

1.2.8. Budget Model

The budget for the following few years—typically one, three, or five years—is created using the Budget model, which is used to perform financial modeling in financial planning and analysis (FP&A). Budget financial models are designed to be heavily dependent on the income statement and should be based on monthly or quarterly data. This is an additional model that falls under the financial model category of reporting models. When a company wants to compare its projected future performance to an ideal one that includes its best estimates of revenue, costs, asset replacements, cash flows, and other variables, it creates a budget. A variety of substitute budgeting models are accessible. The salient features and drawbacks of each type of budgeting model are enumerated in the list below.

- **Static Budgeting:** This is the traditional method of budgeting, in which an organization models its anticipated financial position and results for the upcoming year and then makes every effort to ensure that actual results for that time period agree as closely as possible with the budget model. Usually, this budget structure is predicated on a single anticipated result, which can be very challenging to meet. Instead of enabling an organization to respond swiftly to continuous changes in its surroundings, it also has a tendency to instill a great deal of rigidity in it (Figure 1.12).

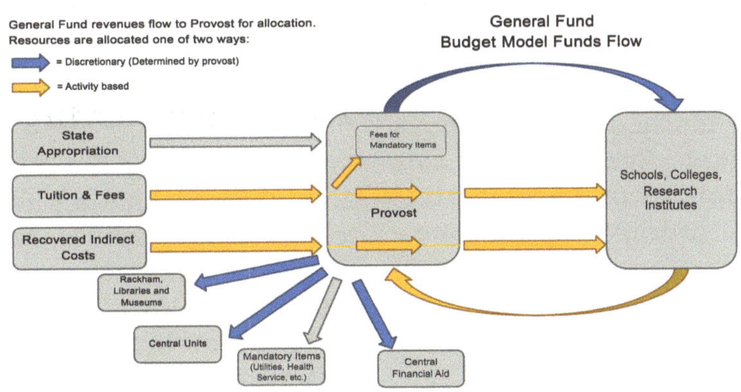

Figure 1.12. *Budget model.*

Source: https://obp.umich.edu/wp-content/uploads/2019/05/modelFlowChart.png.

- **Zero-Base Budgeting:** Establishing a set of expenses to support each of the outcomes that management has in mind is the first step in creating a zero-base budget. The different outcome-expenditure packages are combined to create a budget that should lead to a particular set of outcomes for the whole company. This strategy works best in organizations with a high service level, like governments, where providing services is crucial. However, compared to the static budget, it also requires a significant amount of time to develop.
- **Flexible Budgeting:** You can enter various sales levels into a flexible budget model, and the model will automatically modify the planned expense levels to reflect the entered sales levels. This method works well when it's hard to predict sales levels and a sizable amount of costs change in response to sales. While more complex to create than a static budget model, this kind of model typically produces a budget that is roughly equivalent to actual outcomes.
- **Incremental Budgeting:** Since incremental budgeting makes the assumption that past events can be carried over into the future, it is a simple method of updating a budget model. Even though this method simplifies budget updates, it doesn't prompt a thorough analysis of business expenses and efficiencies, which prevents it from helping to build a lean and effective organization.
- **The Rolling Budget:** A rolling budget necessitates the addition of a new budget period as soon as the previous one ends. This ensures that the budget covers a consistent amount of time in the future. However, in order to create the following incremental update, a significant amount of budgeting work must be done during each accounting period. Although it does draw continuous attention to the budget, it is the least effective budgeting option.
- **The Rolling Forecast:** A rolling forecast is an update to the sales forecast that is made on a regular basis, usually monthly, rather than a budget. The company then bases its short-term budget on the anticipated level of sales. The benefits of this strategy include its ease of updating and lack of infrastructure needed for budgeting.

Despite being cumbersome and infrequently reached, the static model of budgeting is by far the most popular of those displayed here. Using a rolling forecast, which enables managers to modify spending as needed to align with short-term sales targets, is a very different approach. Because of its great degree of flexibility, organizations may discover that the rolling forecast is a more effective type of budget model.

1.2.9. Forecasting Model

The forecasting model is also used in FP and A to produce a forecast that compares to the budget model, much like the budget model. It also falls under the Reporting model category of financial models because of its resemblance to the forecasting model. Sometimes they are entirely separate workbooks, but other times the budget and the forecast models are represented in one combined workbook (Figure 1.13).

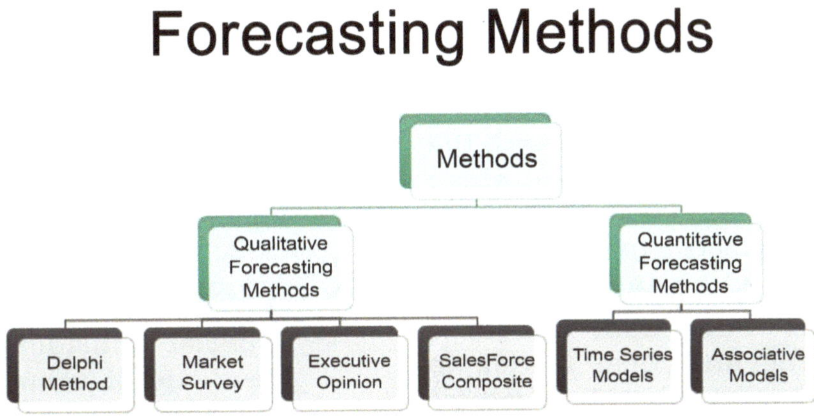

Figure 1.13. *The forecasting model.*

Source: https://cdn.wallstreetmojo.com/wp-content/uploads/2020/09/Forecasting-Methods.jpg.

1.2.10. Profitability Models for Forecasting

Using models, you can predict how profitable your business will be, but selecting the best model will yield the most accurate findings. The model you choose will depend on how your business is run, how well your finances have performed in recent years, where you stand in the market, and other factors. You can obtain the most accurate forecasts when you select the profitability model that best suits your needs.

You can forecast profitability using historical data if the market is stable and the financial results are changing gradually and predictably. Your model predicts future rates of change based on past rates. For instance, you can forecast that your profits will increase by 5% the following year if they have grown at a rate of 5% annually for the past three years. You can monitor associated variables, like income and expenses, to assess how well your model is working. To find out if the outcome matches your profitability forecast, extrapolate their historical rates of change into the future and compute profitability by deducting expenses from revenue.

- **Financial:** You cannot apply a historical model if your financial situation is changing. Your profitability will fluctuate, for instance, if you recently took out a loan to finance expansion or if the price of a crucial component of your production suddenly rises. In that scenario, estimating profitability can be done using financial computations. When projecting rising revenue from higher sales, you can compute interest charges or rising material costs and add them to expenditures. You can forecast company profitability and estimate profits with your calculations.
- **Trends.** Trends are sometimes observable, and your profitability model should account for them. To obtain an accurate forecast, you can use another model as a base and add the trend effects if you can isolate the trend's effects. You can begin by utilizing a historical model, for instance, if a low-cost rival has been stealing market share from your business for the past two years but is declaring

bankruptcy and will shut down in six months. You combine the effects of growing market share as a result of the competitor's bankruptcy in six months with the effect of decreasing market share over a two-year period. Your model correctly predicts a gradual drop in sales followed by an increase.

- **Analytic:** The least accurate model, the analytical model, is the only one that can be used for new product launches or quickly evolving markets in the absence of pertinent financial or historical data. Utilizing your understanding of the industry, past experience in related circumstances, and cost projections, analyze the company. To obtain all the information you require, it might be necessary for you to engage professionals with industry expertise. Compute the anticipated costs of product development and marketing, add overhead, project sales and revenue, and use the analytic model's output to forecast your profitability.

1.2.11. Option Pricing Model

This model belongs to the Pricing model category of financial models, as its name implies.

The two primary option pricing financial models are Binomial tree and Black-Sholes. They are based solely on mathematical financial modeling, not on particular standards, and as a result, they are Excel's built-in upfront calculators. According to option pricing theory, an options contract's value is determined by allocating a premium, or price, based on the probability that the contract will expire in the money (ITM). In essence, traders use the assessment of an option's fair value provided by option pricing theory to inform their strategy. In order to theoretically value an option, pricing models take into consideration factors like the current market price, strike price, volatility, interest rate, and time to expiration. Monte-Carlo simulation, binomial option pricing, and Black-Scholes are a few popular models for valuing options.

- **Special Considerations:** Different methods of valuation are needed for marketable and non-marketable options. The open market determines the price of real traded options, and just like with other assets, the value may differ from the theoretical value. But knowing the theoretical value helps traders determine how likely it is that they will make money if they trade those options.

Fischer Black and Myron Scholes' 1973 pricing model is credited with helping to shape the modern options market. For financial instruments with a known expiration date, a theoretical price is obtained using the Black-Scholes formula. This model is not the only one, though. The Monte-Carlo simulation and the Cox, Ross, and Rubinstein binomial option pricing model are also frequently employed.

- Using the Black-Scholes Option Pricing Theory: Five input variables were needed for the original Black-Scholes model: volatility, time to expiration, risk-free rate of return, strike price of an option, and current stock price. Future volatility cannot be directly observed; instead, it must be inferred or estimated. Therefore, historical or realized volatility is not the same as implied volatility.

CASE STUDY

FINANCIAL MODELING FOR INVESTMENT DECISION

Background

ABC Company, a technology startup, is seeking investment to expand its operations. The company specializes in AI-driven software solutions and has shown promising growth in its initial market. The management team believes that with additional funding, they can accelerate product development and enter new markets.

Objective

To create a financial model that assesses the viability of investing in ABC Company and provides insights into the potential return on investment (ROI) for potential investors.

Steps in Financial Modeling

1. **Business Analysis:**

- Understand ABC Company's current financial position, market strategy, revenue streams, and cost structure.
- Identify key assumptions such as growth rates, market size, pricing strategy, and operational expenses.

2. **Forecasting:**

- Project future revenues based on market demand forecasts, pricing strategy, and expected market penetration.
- Estimate costs including operating expenses, cost of goods sold, and capital expenditures required for expansion.

3. **Financial Statements Preparation:**

- Build a detailed income statement, balance sheet, and cash flow statement based on the forecasts.
- Ensure alignment between the three statements and validate the model for consistency and accuracy.

4. **Sensitivity Analysis:**

- Conduct sensitivity analysis to assess the impact of changes in key assumptions (e.g., revenue growth rate, gross margin, funding costs) on financial outcomes.
- Identify critical assumptions that significantly affect the financial viability of the investment.

5. **Valuation:**
- Determine the valuation of ABC Company using appropriate valuation methods (e.g., discounted cash flow analysis, comparable company analysis).
- Calculate key financial metrics such as NPV (Net Present Value), IRR (Internal Rate of Return), and payback period to evaluate the attractiveness of the investment.

6. **Investment Decision:**
- Present the financial model and analysis to potential investors, highlighting the projected financial performance, risks, and opportunities.
- Make a recommendation on whether to invest in ABC Company based on the financial analysis and valuation results.

Conclusion

Based on the financial modeling and analysis, investors can make informed decisions regarding the investment in ABC Company. The financial model serves as a tool to quantify the potential returns and risks associated with the investment, enabling stakeholders to assess the feasibility and profitability of the opportunity.

CLASS ACTIVITY

In a class activity focused on financial modeling, students collaborate to construct and analyze models that simulate real-world financial scenarios. They learn to incorporate historical data, make informed assumptions, and project future financial performance. Through spreadsheet software and mathematical formulas, they explore the impact of variables like revenue growth, expenses, and capital expenditures on financial outcomes. The activity emphasizes critical thinking, problem-solving, and communication skills as students interpret results and present their findings to peers. Ultimately, it prepares them for roles where accurate forecasting and strategic financial decision-making are essential in corporate finance and beyond.

SUMMARY

- Financial modeling is interpreting numbers of features of a company's operations. Financial modeling is the task of building an abstract representation, called financial models, of a real-world financial situation.
- Financial Modeling is a core skill that is almost mandatory for anyone who wants to build a career in finance. It is also important for anyone who wants to start his or her own business and even useful for sales/marketing professionals as it comes in handy in bidding for projects, determining payback/utility of campaigns etc.
- The IPO model is also a Valuation model. Financial professionals like investment bankers develop IPO financial models in Excel to value their business just before going public.
- A leveraged buyout (LBO) is a transaction where a company is acquired using debt as the main source of consideration.
- Another type of financial model that belongs to the Valuation category of financial models, this model is developed by taking in account a number of DCF financial models and adding them together.
- Similar to the budget model, the forecasting model is also used in FP&A to come up with a forecast that compares to the budget model.
- Models used to price options account for variables such as current market price, strike price, volatility, interest rate, and time to expiration to theoretically value an option.

REVIEW QUESTIONS

1. What is financial modeling, and why is it important in corporate finance?
2. Explain the difference between forecasting and budgeting in the context of financial modeling.
3. What are the key components of a financial model? Describe each briefly.
4. What are the common types of financial models used in practice? Provide examples where each type is appropriate.
5. Describe the steps involved in building a financial model from scratch.
6. What are the key assumptions that typically need to be made when constructing a financial model? How do these assumptions affect the outcomes?
7. Explain sensitivity analysis and scenario analysis. How are these techniques useful in financial modeling?
8. Discuss the importance of error-checking and auditing in financial modeling. What are some common errors that can occur?

9. How does financial modeling assist in decision-making within a company? Provide examples of decisions that can be supported by financial models.
10. What are the best practices for presenting and communicating the results of a financial model to stakeholders?

REFERENCES

1. Benninga, S. (2006). *Principles of Finance with Excel*. New York, NY: Oxford University Press.
2. Fabozzi, F. J. (2012). *Encyclopedia of Financial Models*. Hoboken, NJ: Wiley.
3. Ho, T., & Lee, S. B. (2004). *The Oxford Guide to Financial Modeling*. New York, NY: Oxford University Press.
4. Sengupta, C. (2009). *Financial Analysis and Modeling Using Excel and VBA* (2nd ed.). Hoboken, NJ: John Wiley & Sons.
5. Winston, W. (2014). *Microsoft Excel 2013 Data Analysis and Business Modeling*. Redmond, WA: Microsoft Press.
6. Yip, H. (2005). *Spreadsheet Applications to Securities Valuation and Investment Theories*. Milton, QLD: John Wiley & Sons Australia Ltd.

CHAPTER 2

Excel for Financial Modeling

LEARNING OBJECTIVES

After studying this chapter, you will be able to:

- Describe advanced excel functions
- Understand the data validation and conditional formatting
- Discuss circular reference
- Explain visual basic for applications (VBA).

KEY TERMS FROM THIS CHAPTER

Accounting skills
Financial analysis
INDEX function
LOOKUP function
Data validation
Financial skills
Logical values
Macros
Data validation
HLOOKUP function
Lookup array

INTRODUCTION

Excel financial modeling is widely available online. Numerous articles have been written about financial modeling education. Nonetheless, the majority of the training materials for financial modeling are the same. Beyond the typical jargon, it delves into the useful financial modeling that research analysts and investment bankers employ. In order to evaluate and assess the future of the business with regard to its profitability, cost, revenue, sales, and overall financial performance, financial modeling uses both historical and current data. It serves as a roadmap for decision-making, giving management the right course of action to propel the company toward expansion and success.

Excel is a frequently utilized tool for this particular practice. But despite the fact that building financial models in Excel is very valuable and has countless applications across industries, its full potential is not being realized. This skill, which is a component of financial analysis, involves using data analysis, accounting, and financial knowledge to achieve the goal of future forecasting. Financial statements, including balance sheets, cash flow statements, profit and loss statements, and all other supporting documentation, are used in Microsoft Excel to create the ideal foundation for this analysis. The availability of data, the veracity of the information, and the expertise of the experts who built the model will all have a major impact on how accurate the projections are.

2.1. ADVANCED EXCEL FUNCTIONS

Excel is a versatile and powerful tool widely used for data analysis, financial modeling, and many other applications. While basic functions like SUM, AVERAGE, and VLOOKUP are commonly used, Excel also offers a plethora of advanced functions that can significantly enhance your productivity and analytical capabilities.

2.1.1. LOOKUP Function

The LOOKUP function in Excel can perform the simplest types of vertical and horizontal lookups.

There are two forms of LOOKUP in Excel: Vector and Array.

- Vector Form

The vector form looks for a value in a specified column or row.

Syntax: LOOKUP(lookup_value,lookup_vector,result_vector)

Example:

Consider the following Master table.

Emp ID	Last Name	First Name	Dept	E-mail	Phone Ext	Location	Hire Date	Pay Rate
1054	Smith	Howard	AT	howards	148	Building 1	16-Apr-91	$ 11.25
1056	Gonzales	Joe	AT	joeg	121	Building 1	25-Oct-79	$ 12.25
1067	Scole	Gail	AT	gails	123	Building 1	20-Sep-87	$ 14.55
1075	Kane	Sheryl	AD	sherylk	126	Building 2	07-Aug-92	$ 11.25
1078	Hapsbuch	Kendrick	AC	kendrickh	101	Building 2	01-Apr-86	$ 10.20
1152	Henders	Mark	AD	markh	118	Building 2	21-Jan-90	$ 12.25
1196	Atherton	Katie	HR	katiea	289	Building 3	01-Apr-98	$ 9.95
1284	Bellwood	Frank	MK	frankb	124	Building 1	04-Jan-85	$ 12.30
1290	Cooper	Linda	AD	lindac	113	Building 2	03-Jan-85	$ 13.25
1293	Cronwith	Brent	HR	brentc	205	Building 3	14-Sep-84	$ 10.20
1299	Simpson	Sandrae	MF	sandraes	127	Building 1	21-Dec-89	$ 12.20
1302	Sindole	Randy	MK	randys	139	Building 1	06-Aug-84	$ 14.25
1310	Smith	Ellen	MF	ellens	137	Building 1	04-Oct-86	$ 11.50
1329	Vuanuo	Tuome	AC	tuomev	151	Building 2	22-Feb-89	$ 10.35
1333	Szcznyck	Tadeuz	HR	tadeuzs	122	Building 3	16-Apr-90	$ 10.15
1368	Wu	Tammy	AD	tammyw	132	Building 2	11-Mar-83	$ 12.25
1509	Kegler	Pam	AT	pamk	135	Building 1	19-Jun-85	$ 13.25
1516	Bell	Tom	AC	tomb	105	Building 2	06-Mar-85	$ 9.50

We will fetch the Dept corresponding to Emp ID using vector form of Lookup

Emp ID	Last Name	First Name	Dept	Pay Rate
1054	Smith			
1056	Gonzales			
1067	Scote			
1075	Kane			
1078	Hapsbuch			
1152	Henders			
1196	Atherton			
1284	Bellwood			

From the Lookup & Reference option, select LOOKUP. The following window will appear.

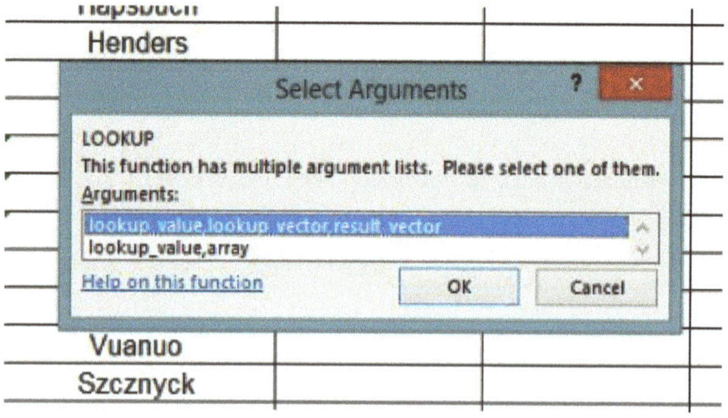

Select the vector form.

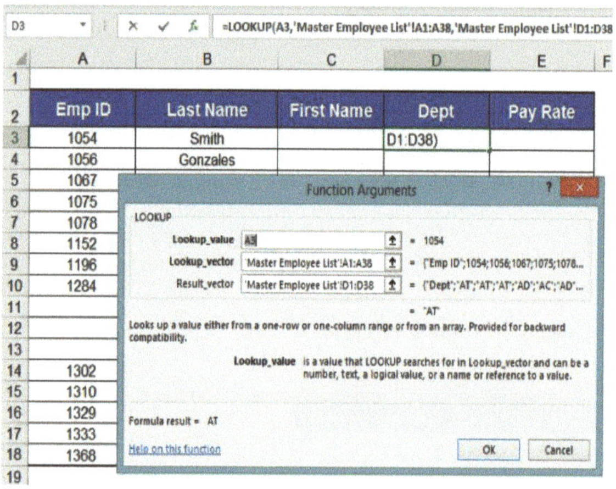

Lookup_value is the value that LOOKUP function searches in an array. It can be a number, text, a logical value, or a name or even a reference to a value.

Lookup_vector is a range that contains only one row or one column of a text, numbers, or logical values, placed in ascending order.

Result_vector is a range that contains only one row or column, the same size as Lookup_vector.

You will get the Department corresponding to the Employee ID.

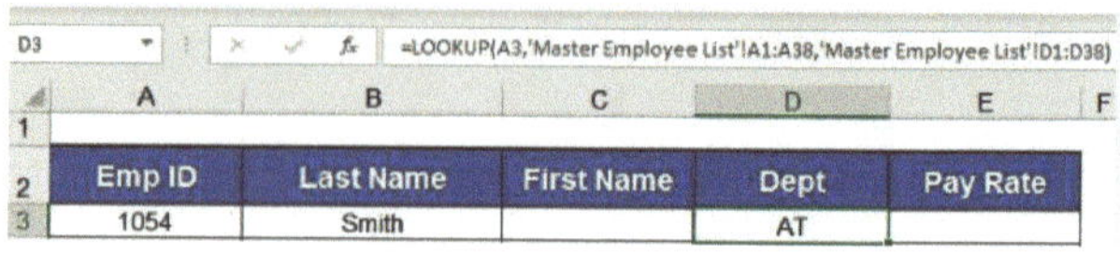

- **Array Form**

The array form looks for the value in the first row or column of an array.

Syntax: LOOKUP(lookup_value,array)

Example:

From the Lookup & Reference option, select LOOKUP. The following window will appear.

Select the array form.

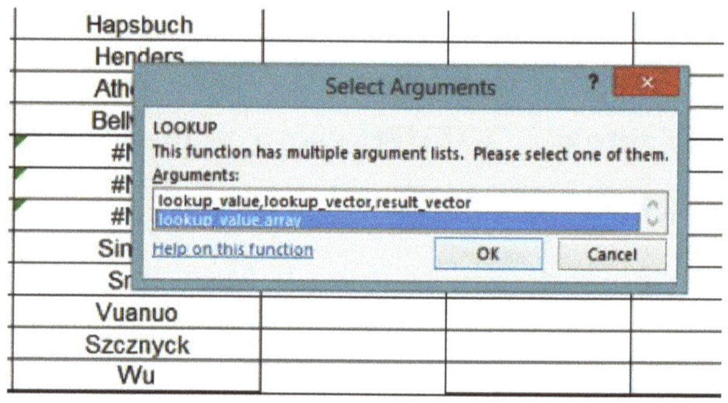

The argument window will appear.

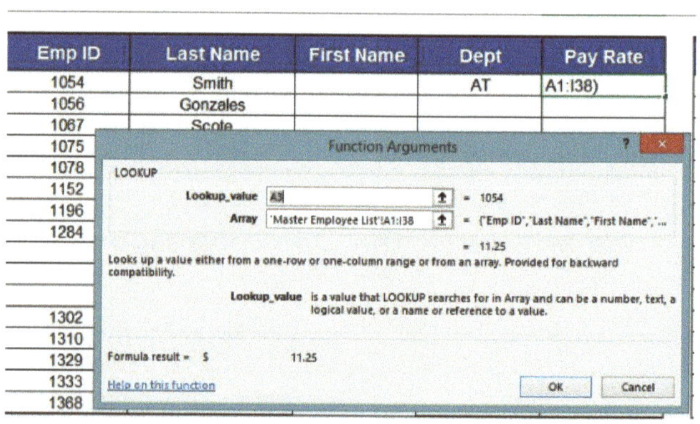

Lookup_value is a value that LOOKUP searches for in an array and can be a number, text, a logical value, or a name or reference to a value.

An array is a range of cells that contains text, number, or logical values that you want to compare with Lookup_value.

The Pay Rate is fetched from the master table.

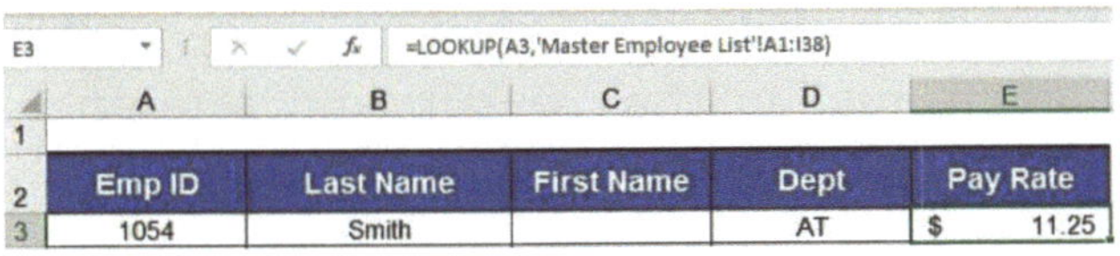
E3 =LOOKUP(A3,'Master Employee List'!A1:I38)

Emp ID	Last Name	First Name	Dept	Pay Rate
1054	Smith		AT	$ 11.25

2.1.2. VLOOKUP Function

The VLOOKUP function in Excel is a powerful function used to lookup data in a table organized vertically. It looks down the left column of a range to find a value.

Syntax: =VLOOKUP(lookup_value, table_array, col_index_num, [range_lookup])

Consider the master employee dataset.

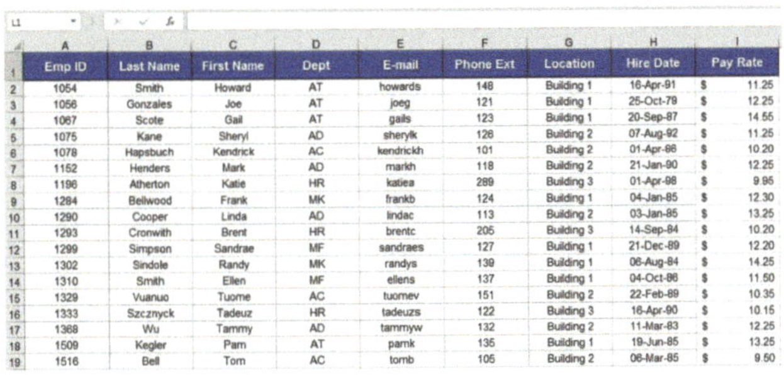

Emp ID	Last Name	First Name	Dept	E-mail	Phone Ext	Location	Hire Date	Pay Rate
1054	Smith	Howard	AT	howards	148	Building 1	16-Apr-91	$ 11.25
1056	Gonzales	Joe	AT	joeg	121	Building 1	25-Oct-79	$ 12.25
1067	Scote	Gail	AT	gails	123	Building 1	20-Sep-87	$ 14.55
1075	Kane	Sheryl	AD	sherylk	126	Building 2	07-Aug-92	$ 11.25
1078	Hapsbuch	Kendrick	AC	kendrickh	101	Building 2	01-Apr-86	$ 10.20
1152	Henders	Mark	AD	markh	118	Building 2	21-Jan-90	$ 12.25
1196	Atherton	Katie	HR	katiea	289	Building 3	01-Apr-98	$ 9.95
1284	Bellwood	Frank	MK	frankb	124	Building 1	04-Jan-85	$ 12.30
1290	Cooper	Linda	AD	lindac	113	Building 2	03-Jan-85	$ 13.25
1293	Cronwith	Brent	HR	brentc	205	Building 3	14-Sep-84	$ 10.20
1299	Simpson	Sandrae	MF	sandraes	127	Building 1	21-Dec-89	$ 12.20
1302	Sindole	Randy	MK	randys	139	Building 1	06-Aug-84	$ 14.25
1310	Smith	Ellen	MF	ellens	137	Building 1	04-Oct-86	$ 11.50
1329	Vuanuo	Tuome	AC	tuomev	151	Building 2	22-Feb-89	$ 10.35
1333	Szcznyck	Tadeuz	HR	tadeuzs	122	Building 3	16-Apr-90	$ 10.15
1368	Wu	Tammy	AD	tammyw	132	Building 2	11-Mar-83	$ 12.25
1509	Kegler	Pam	AT	pamk	135	Building 1	19-Jun-85	$ 13.25
1516	Bell	Tom	AC	tomb	105	Building 2	06-Mar-85	$ 9.50

We will look for the Emp ID in the master dataset and fill the first name corresponding to the Emp ID.

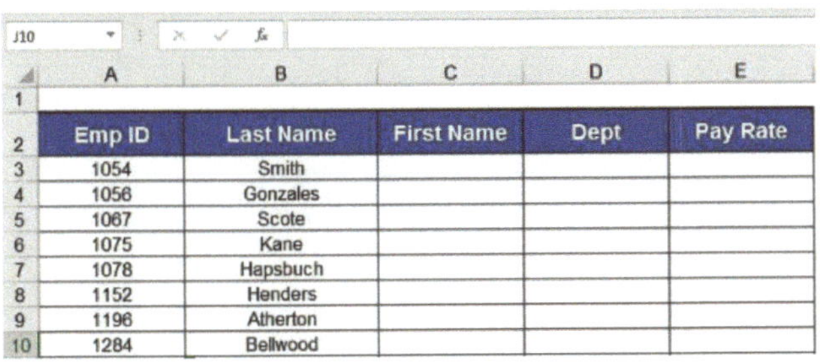

Emp ID	Last Name	First Name	Dept	Pay Rate
1054	Smith			
1056	Gonzales			
1067	Scote			
1075	Kane			
1078	Hapsbuch			
1152	Henders			
1196	Atherton			
1284	Bellwood			

To use the VLOOKUP function, follow the steps mentioned below.

Step 1. Click on the cell that you'd like the VLOOKUP formula to be calculated. In this case, the cell is C3.

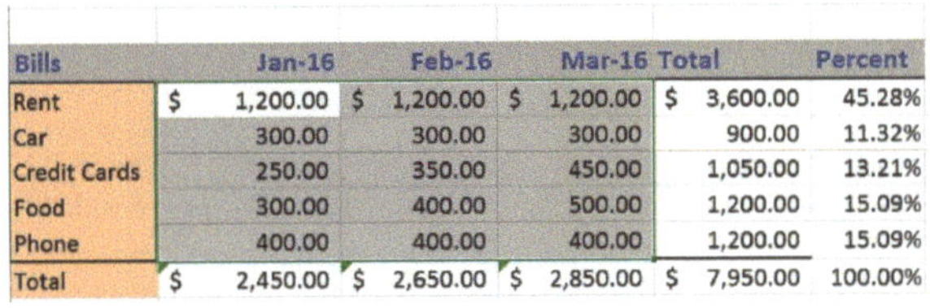

Bills	Jan-16	Feb-16	Mar-16	Total	Percent
Rent	$ 1,200.00	$ 1,200.00	$ 1,200.00	$ 3,600.00	45.28%
Car	300.00	300.00	300.00	900.00	11.32%
Credit Cards	250.00	350.00	450.00	1,050.00	13.21%
Food	300.00	400.00	500.00	1,200.00	15.09%
Phone	400.00	400.00	400.00	1,200.00	15.09%
Total	$ 2,450.00	$ 2,650.00	$ 2,850.00	$ 7,950.00	100.00%

Step 2. Click on the formula at the top of the screen, and in the lookup and reference, select VLOOKUP.

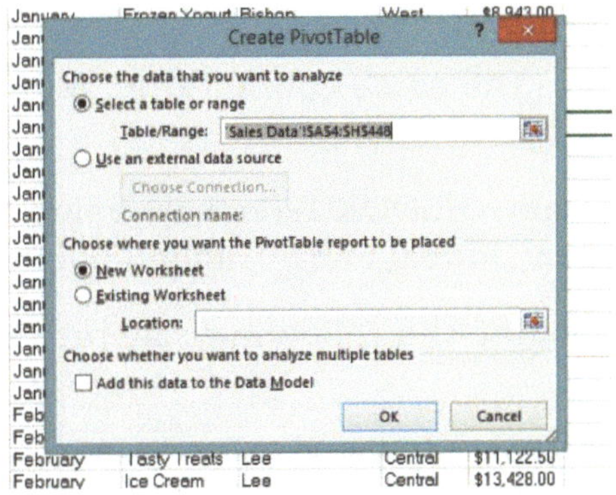

Step 3. Select the VLOOKUP option. The argument window will appear.

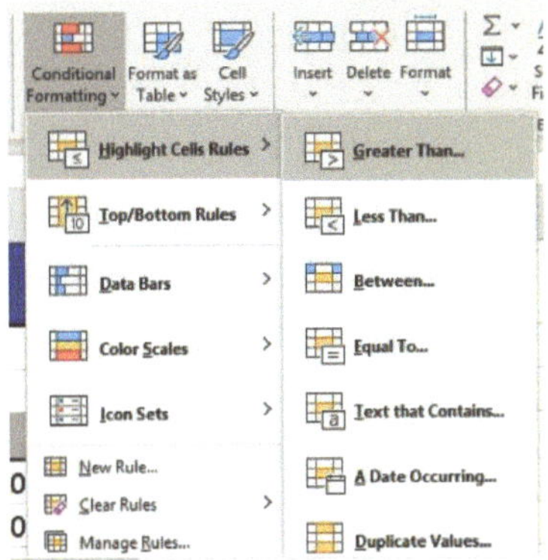

Step 4. Click the OK button.

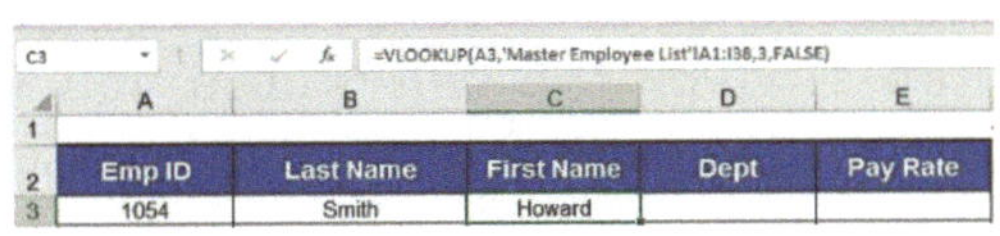
C3 =VLOOKUP(A3,'Master Employee List'!A1:I38,3,FALSE)

Emp ID	Last Name	First Name	Dept	Pay Rate
1054	Smith	Howard		

There is another way you can implement the VLOOKUP function. Use the formula bar and enter the required fields there.

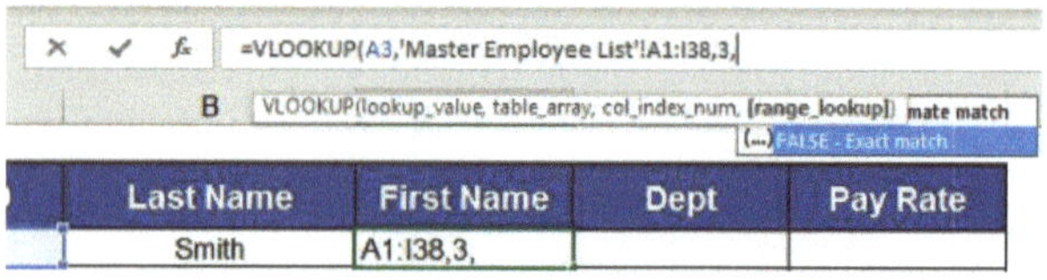

You will get the same result.

2.1.3. HLOOKUP Function

The HLOOKUP function looks up for a value in the first row of a given range and gives a value in the same column from a row that you specified.

Syntax: =HLOOKUP(lookup_value, table_array, row_index_num, [range_lookup])

Consider the following master table.

	A	B	C	D	E	F	G
1							
2	Product Code:	XP100	XP200	XP300	AX10	AX25	AX50
3	Warehouse 1	120	150	135	90	95	140
4	Warehouse 2	55	110	75	95	75	55
5	Warehouse 3	70	115	65	55	85	65
6							

We will get the warehouse 2 inventory details from the master table where the product code is XP200.

Inventory Status Check	
Enter Product Code Here:	XP200
Warehouse 1 Inventory:	150
Warehouse 2 Inventory:	
Warehouse 3 Inventory:	

To use the HLOOKUP function, follow the steps mentioned below.

Step 1. Click the cell where you want the HLOOKUP formula to be calculated.

Inventory Status Check	
Enter Product Code Here:	XP200
Warehouse 1 Inventory:	150
Warehouse 2 Inventory:	
Warehouse 3 Inventory:	

Step 2. Click formula at the top of the screen, and in the Lookup and reference, select HLOOKUP.

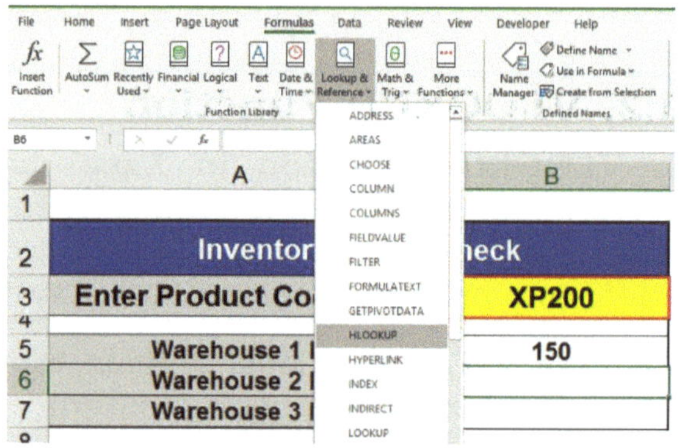

Step 3. Select the HLOOKUP option. The argument window will appear.

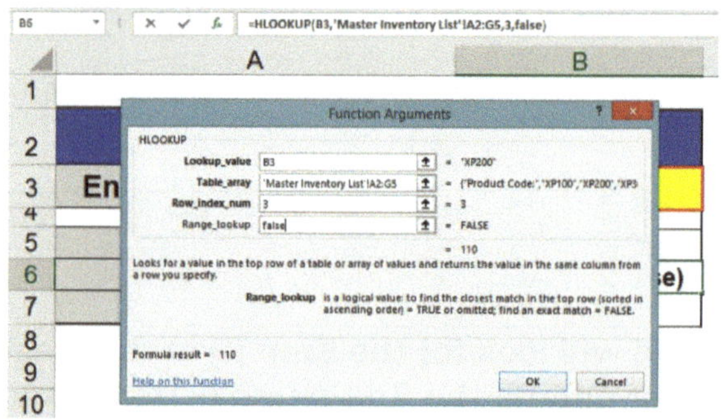

Step 4. Click OK.

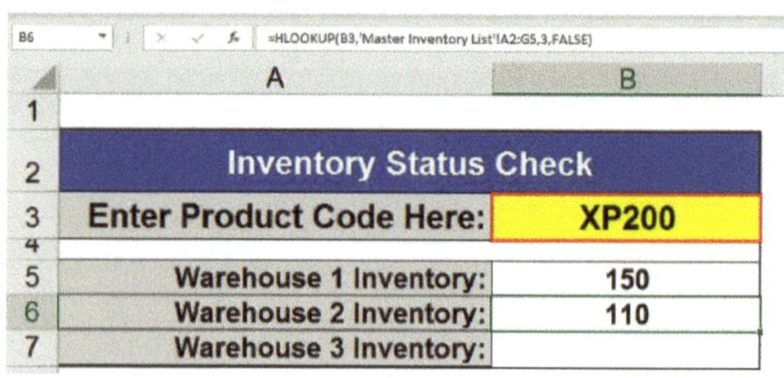

To use the formula bar for HLOOKUP, go to the formula bar and enter =HLOOKUP

After entering the formula, hit Enter. You will get the same result.

2.1.4. Index Match

A creative workaround for VLOOKUP's limitations in Excel is INDEX MATCH, which allows for two-way lookups. VLOOKUP, for instance, only functions when the lookup value is in the lookup array's first column.

It is also unable to return values that are to the left of the lookup value and to accept lists sorted in descending order. You may have encountered these issues if you frequently use VLOOKUP and have likely chosen to accept them. A great workaround is to become familiar with INDEX MATCH.

INDEX MATCH consists of two parts. The lookup value in a range of cells can be located using the MATCH function. Next, the value or cell reference from within a table or range is returned by the INDEX function.

2.1.4.1. How to Use the MATCH Function

The MATCH function is used to determine the position number of a known value within a range of cells. The MATCH function in Excel has three possible arguments, with the following syntax:

=MATCH(lookup_value,lookup_array,[match_type])

- Lookup_value is the known value that you will be using to conduct a lookup, or search. This can be a value or cell reference.
- Lookup_array is the range of cells where the lookup value will be found.
- Match_type is a setting that tells Excel whether you will accept a near-match if the lookup_value is not found in the lookup array.

Array Type	MATCH formula match_type
0	Exact match
1	Approximate match, to closest value smaller than lookup value
–1	Approximate match, to closest value larger than lookup value

For instance, if we wanted to know the position number of the word "matte" within the range B2 to B9 below.

=MATCH("matte,"B2:B9,0)

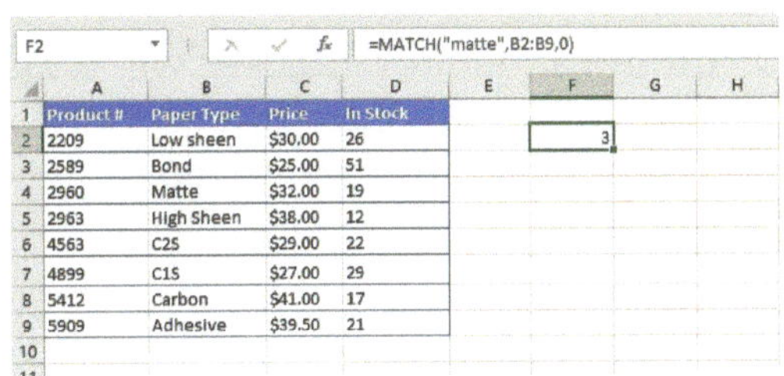

Note that in the example above, the value "matte" was typed directly into the formula between double quotation marks. If the lookup value is a cell reference, no double quotes are used.

2.1.4.2. How to use the INDEX Function

The Excel INDEX function returns a value or cell reference from within a table or range. The INDEX function has two formats – the array format and the reference format. The array format is used when we want to return the value that is found in the result cell. The reference format is used when we want Excel to return the cell reference of the result cell (e.g., D17). We'll focus on the array format, since this is the format you'll need to learn for the INDEX/MATCH combo.

The syntax of the INDEX array function is

=INDEX(array, row_num, [column_num])

- Array refers to the range or array containing the data to be indexed. This argument is required.
- Row_num is the row number where the cell containing the return value is to be found. Row_num can be omitted if the array consists of only one row. If row_num is omitted, column_num is required.
- Column_num is the column number where the cell containing the return value is to be found. Column_num is optional, but is required if row_num is omitted.

In the spreadsheet below, we want to display the value which is in the third row, second column of the array by using the INDEX function.

=INDEX(A2:D9,3,2)

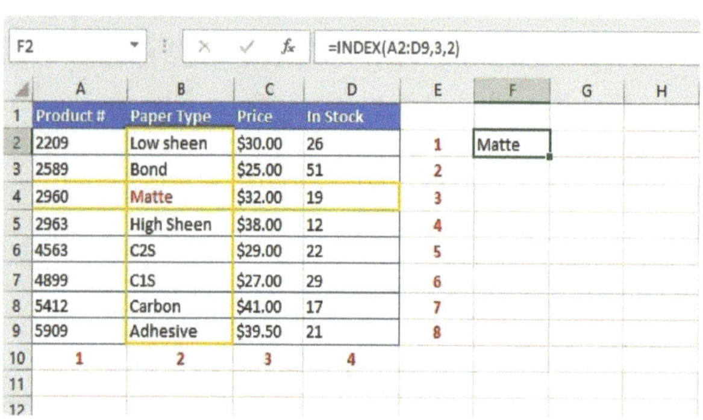

F2 =INDEX(A2:D9,3,2)

	A	B	C	D	E	F	G	H
1	Product #	Paper Type	Price	In Stock				
2	2209	Low sheen	$30.00	26	1	Matte		
3	2589	Bond	$25.00	51	2			
4	2960	Matte	$32.00	19	3			
5	2963	High Sheen	$38.00	12	4			
6	4563	C2S	$29.00	22	5			
7	4899	C1S	$27.00	29	6			
8	5412	Carbon	$41.00	17	7			
9	5909	Adhesive	$39.50	21	8			
10	1	2	3	4				
11								
12								

The third item in column 2 is identified as the value "Matte" and returned as the output in cell F2.

2.1.4.3. Combining the INDEX and MATCH Functions

The INDEX and MATCH formulas, when nested, can perform a lookup that accomplishes what the VLOOKUP does and more. Nesting a formula means using one entire formula as an argument of another function.

We can apply that to our simple query which extracts values from a dataset using the Product Number as an input or lookup value.

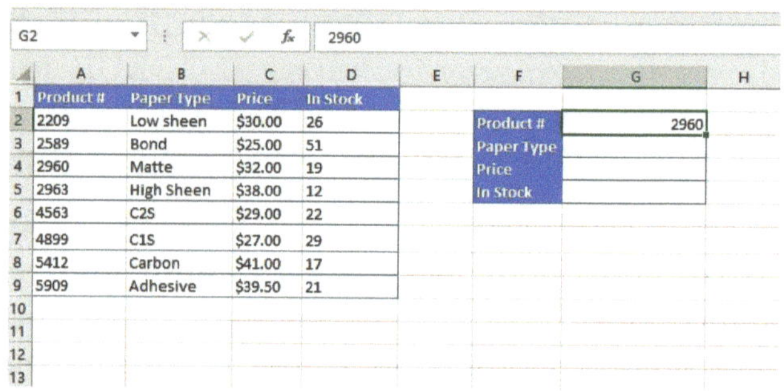

G2 2960

	A	B	C	D	E	F	G	H
1	Product #	Paper Type	Price	In Stock				
2	2209	Low sheen	$30.00	26		Product #	2960	
3	2589	Bond	$25.00	51		Paper Type		
4	2960	Matte	$32.00	19		Price		
5	2963	High Sheen	$38.00	12		In Stock		
6	4563	C2S	$29.00	22				
7	4899	C1S	$27.00	29				
8	5412	Carbon	$41.00	17				
9	5909	Adhesive	$39.50	21				
10								
11								
12								
13								

We will use MATCH to determine where in the list the product number falls (position number), and we will use INDEX to return the values from the corresponding columns (Paper Type, Price, or In Stock,) by their column numbers.

Shown separately, each function would read as follows:

=MATCH(G2, A2:A9,0)

This performs a search for the value in cell G2 within the A2 to A9 range, and requires an exact match. It returns the position number of that value.

=INDEX(A2:D9, row_num, 2)

This returns the value from the array A2 to D9 which intersects the row number found in the MATCH formula, and column number 2 (Paper Type). The MATCH formula will be used as the **row_num** argument.

=INDEX(A2:D9,MATCH(G2,A2:A9,0),2)

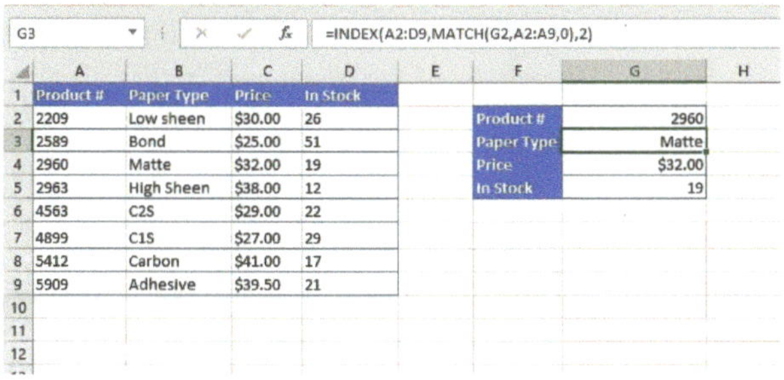
G3 =INDEX(A2:D9,MATCH(G2,A2:A9,0),2)

	A	B	C	D	E	F	G
1	Product #	Paper Type	Price	In Stock			
2	2209	Low sheen	$30.00	26		Product #	2960
3	2589	Bond	$25.00	51		Paper Type	Matte
4	2960	Matte	$32.00	19		Price	$32.00
5	2963	High Sheen	$38.00	12		In Stock	19
6	4563	C2S	$29.00	22			
7	4899	C1S	$27.00	29			
8	5412	Carbon	$41.00	17			
9	5909	Adhesive	$39.50	21			

The formula in G4 and G5 are identical, except for the last argument, which are 3 and 4 respectively, to represent each column number. To be fair, this does seem quite complicated when we consider that VLOOKUP already does this in a much more straightforward way, and with only four arguments. However, at the outset, we pointed out that VLOOKUP could not return a value that was located to the left of the lookup value. If we change the known value so that the Paper Type is now our lookup_value, VLOOKUP returns a #NA (Value Not Available) error. Let's see how INDEX MATCH handles this.

=INDEX(A2:D9, MATCH(G2, B2:B9,0),1)

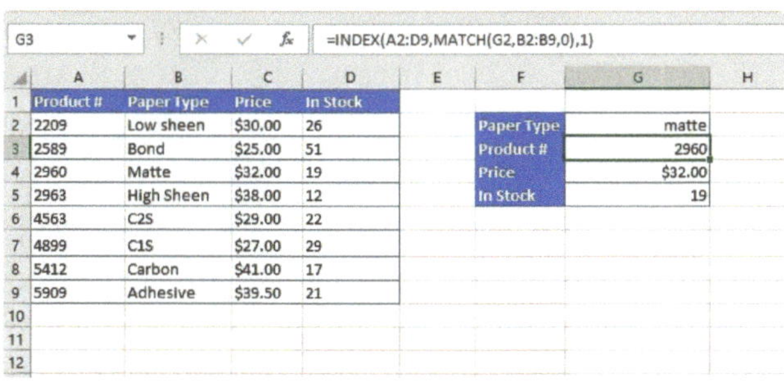
G3 =INDEX(A2:D9,MATCH(G2,B2:B9,0),1)

	A	B	C	D	E	F	G
1	Product #	Paper Type	Price	In Stock			
2	2209	Low sheen	$30.00	26		Paper Type	matte
3	2589	Bond	$25.00	51		Product #	2960
4	2960	Matte	$32.00	19		Price	$32.00
5	2963	High Sheen	$38.00	12		In Stock	19
6	4563	C2S	$29.00	22			
7	4899	C1S	$27.00	29			
8	5412	Carbon	$41.00	17			
9	5909	Adhesive	$39.50	21			

Lookups to the left or right are no problem for INDEX MATCH because the MATCH lookup_array stands on its own, and is not connected to the INDEX array.

In this way, INDEX MATCH can also be used as a substitute for HLOOKUP, which is the horizontal version of the VLOOKUP function.

Let's look at a more advanced application of the INDEX MATCH solution.

2.1.5. Logical Functions

Excel offers several logical functions that you can use to give your formulas simple to fairly complex decision-making abilities. You use an IF function to tell Excel to do one thing if the condition or logical test you specify in it is satisfied (that is, evaluates to TRUE) and do a different thing if the condition is not satisfied (that is, evaluates to FALSE). The other logical functions AND and OR let you create more complex conditions to include in the IF function.

2.1.5.1. The IF Function

The structure of the IF function is:

IF(logical_test,value_if_true,value_if_false)

The logical_test can be any value or expression that can be evaluated to TRUE or FALSE (for example, F33>100). Value_if_true and value_if_false can be simple or complex expressions (including other functions). Excel evaluates one of the expressions depending on the result of the logical test and enters the result in the cell.

Try this simple example. In cell B1 of an empty worksheet, enter the formula =IF(A1<=0,"Negative,""Positive"). Now if you enter a negative number or zero in cell A1, cell B1 will read Negative; for numbers greater than zero in cell A1, it will read Positive.

(Note that you use <= for less than or equal to, >= for greater than or equal to, and <> for not equal to.)

2.1.5.2. Nested IF Functions

In the two expressions (the second and third arguments) in an IF function you can include additional IF functions to create more sophisticated decision structures. This is called using nested IF statements. Suppose the interest rate on a loan will be 6% if the loan amount is less than $1 million, 5% for loan amounts between $1 and $2 million, and 4% for loans above $2 million. You want the appropriate interest rate to be entered in cell B1 depending on the size of the loan in cell A1. To do this, enter the following formula in B1:

=IF(A1<1000000,0.06,IF(A1<2000000,0.05,0.04))

Now if A1 is less than 1000000, the condition of the outer IF function will be satisfied and the interest rate will be 0.06 or 6%. If the condition is not satisfied, however, then Excel will evaluate the condition in the inner (nested) IF function and act on its result. See how this works by entering different values in A1.

Note two things. First, as with all functions, the result of an IF function is entered in its own cell. In this case you can use the interest rate in B1 (that is, use the cell address B1) in other calculations in your model that need to use the interest rate. Second, you have to make sure that the conditions you set up exactly reflect your intentions. For example, when you look at it closely, this formula says interest rate will be 5% for a loan size equal to or greater than 1,000,000 but less than 2,000,000. The problem says "between $1 and $2 million," which is somewhat vague. In this case the exact interpretation does not matter, but in other cases it may.

You can, of course, include additional IF functions in both the TRUE and FALSE legs of the IF function, and you can nest IF functions in up to 7 layers. But you should avoid more than two or three layers of nesting, because at that point the formulas start to get difficult to read and interpret and your chances of making a mistake go up.

2.1.5.3. AND and OR Functions

The AND and OR functions are used to create more complex conditions. The AND function has the structure AND(logical1,logical2,...) where the arguments are conditions. The AND function returns TRUE only if all its arguments are TRUE; otherwise it returns FALSE. For example, the formula =AND(A1>0,B1>0,C1>0) will return TRUE only if A1, B1, and C1 are all greater than 0.

The OR function has the same structure, but it returns TRUE as long as at least one of its arguments is TRUE. So the formula =OR(A1>0,B1>0,C1>0) will be TRUE as long as A1, B1, or C1 is greater than 0. You can enter formulas like the ones I just showed in a cell and the cell will say TRUE or FALSE depending on the result of the statement. These are called logical values, which you can then use in other formulas. If one of the formulas using AND or OR is in A2, you can write an IF function (say, in B2) such as =IF(A2=TRUE,0,1). More often, you will use AND or OR functions within IF functions to create more complex conditions.

There is one more logical function: NOT. It reverses the logic of its argument—that is, if the argument is TRUE, the result of the NOT function will be FALSE and vice versa.

2.2. DATA VALIDATION

Excel has a feature called data validation that lets you manage the kinds of data that are entered into a worksheet in order to increase the accuracy of the data. With Excel data validation, for instance, users can restrict specific data entries—like dates or numbers that fall outside of a predefined range—and limit data entries to a drop-down list selection. Formulas and the input that comes from them can both be controlled with the aid of data validation. When a user reaches a limit, you can even create personalized Excel data validation messages to assist in directing them toward the proper data entry. Therefore, Excel data validation aids in lowering the quantity of inconsistent data, mistakes, or extraneous information in worksheets.

Here are just a few examples of what Excel's data validation can do:

- Allow only numeric or text values in a cell.
- Allow only numbers within a specified range.
- Allow data entries of a specific length.
- Restrict dates and times outside a given range.
- Restrict entries to a selection from a drop-down list.
- Validate an entry based on another cell.
- Show an input message when the user selects a cell.
- Show a warning message when incorrect data has been entered.
- Find incorrect entries in validated cells.

For instance, you can set up a rule that limits data entry to 4-digit numbers between 1000 and 9999. If the user types something different, Excel will show an error alert explaining what they have done wrong:

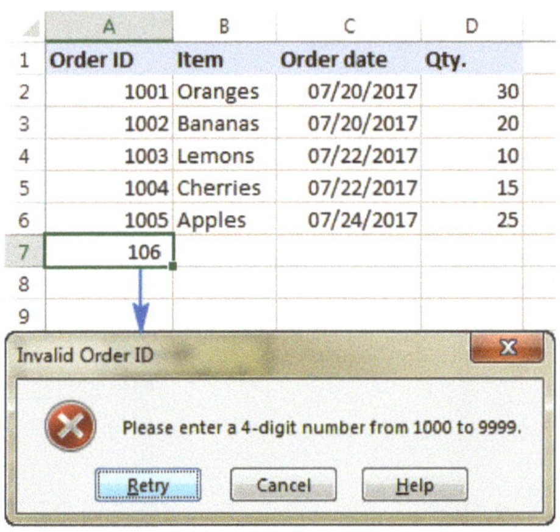

2.2.1. How to Do Data Validation in Excel

To add data validation in Excel, perform the following steps.

1. **Open the Data Validation Dialog Box:** Select one or more cells to validate, go to the *Data* tab > *Data Tools* group, and click the Data Validation button.

You can also open the Data Validation dialog box by pressing Alt > D > L, with each key pressed separately.

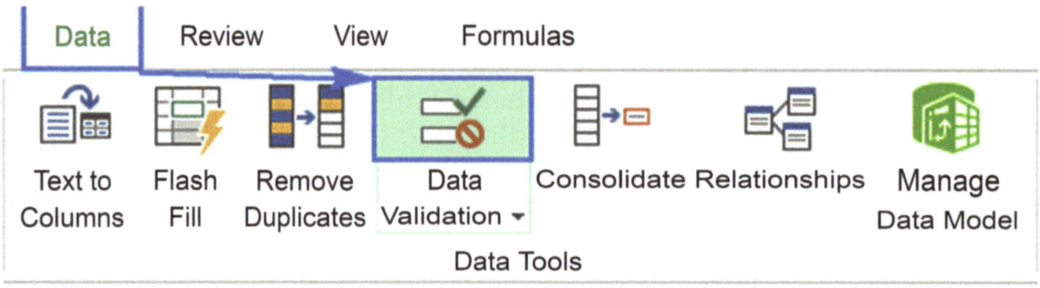

2. **Create an Excel Validation Rule:** On the Settings tab, define the validation criteria according to your needs. In the criteria, you can supply any of the following:

- **Values:** type numbers in the criteria boxes like shown in the screenshot below.
- **Cell References:** make a rule based on a value or formula in another cell.
- **Formulas**: allow to express more complex conditions like in this example.

As an example, let's make a rule that restricts users to entering a whole number between 1000 and 9999:

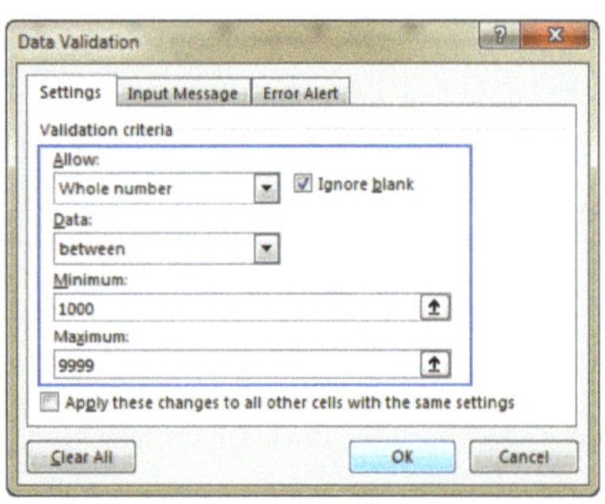

With the validation rule configured, either click OK to close the Data Validation window or switch to another tab to add an input message or/and error alert.

3. **Add an Input Message (Optional):** If you want to display a message that explains to the user what data is allowed in a given cell, open the *Input Message* tab and do the following:

- Make sure the Show input message when cell is selected box is checked.
- Enter the title and text of your message into the corresponding fields.
- Click *OK* to close the dialog window.

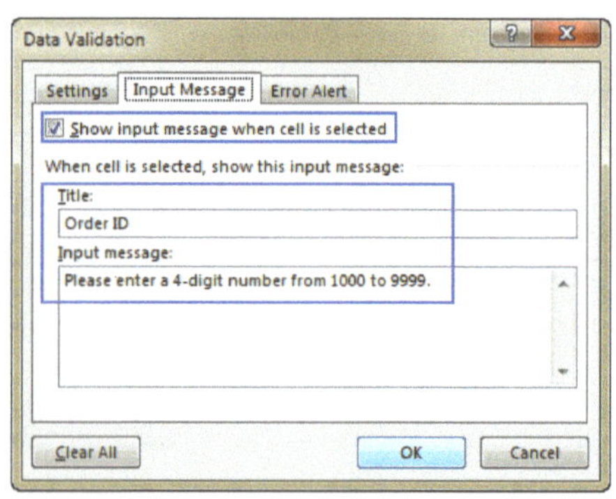

As soon as the user selects the validated cell, the following message will show up:

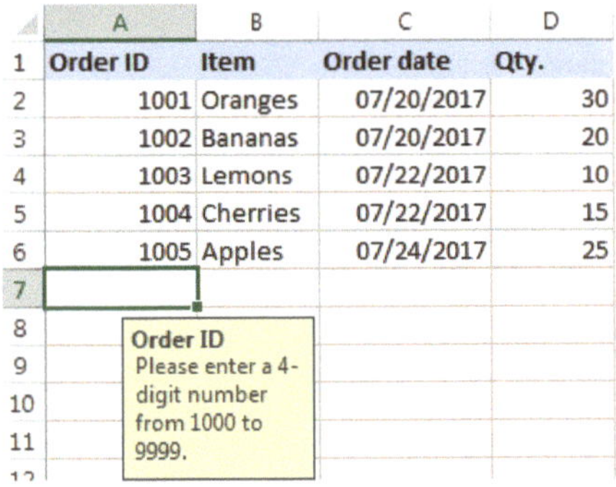

4. **Display an Error Alert (Optional):** In addition to the input message, you can show one of the following error alerts when invalid data is entered in a cell.

Alert type	Description
Stop (default)	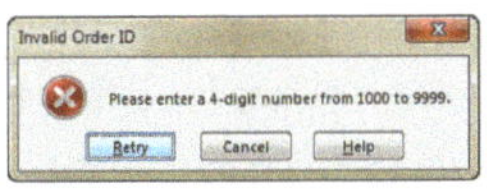 The strictest alert type that prevents users from entering invalid data. You click *Retry* to type a different value or *Cancel* to remove the entry.
Warning	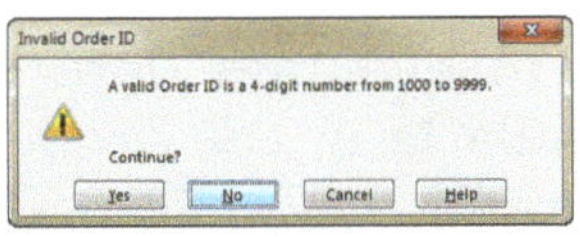 Warns users that the data is invalid, but does not prevent entering it. You click *Yes* to input the invalid entry, *No* to edit it, or *Cancel* to remove the entry.
Information	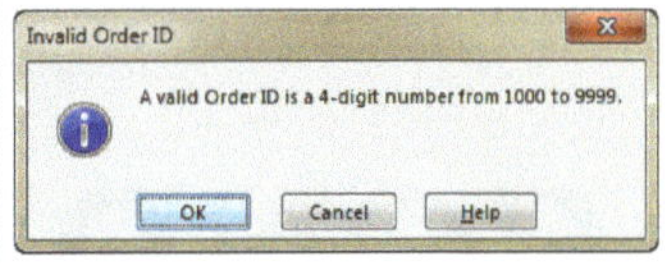 The most permissive alert type that only informs users about an invalid data entry. You click *OK* to enter the invalid value or *Cancel* to remove it from the cell.

To configure a custom error message, go to the *Error Alert* tab and define the following parameters:

- Check the Show error alert after invalid data is entered box (usually selected by default).
- In the *Style* box, select the desired alert type.
- Enter the title and text of the error message into the corresponding boxes.
- Click *OK*.

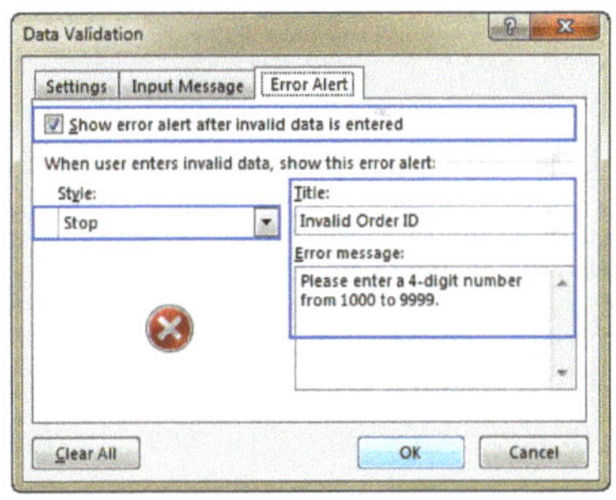

2.3. CONDITIONAL FORMATTING

On occasion, you might want to draw attention to a cell if certain requirements are met. For instance, you might want to highlight a financial ratio by making it bold and using a different color if it surpasses a particular threshold. Up to three conditions can be specified using conditional formatting, and the cell will be highlighted in the format of your choice under each condition.

2.3.1. Specifying Conditional Formatting

You can base the condition that will trigger the special format either on the value in the cell or a formula you specify. If you use a formula, it must evaluate to TRUE or FALSE, and the special format will be applied when it evaluates to TRUE. To set up conditional formatting, select the cells you want to highlight and choose Format ⊠ Conditional Formatting to open the dialog box for it. To use the value in the selected cells as the formatting criterion, click Cell Value Is in the dropdown list on the left, select the comparison phrase you want, and specify the value(s) in the appropriate box(es). You can enter a constant value or formula starting with an equals sign.

To use a formula as a formatting criterion, that is, to evaluate data or condition other than the values in the cells themselves, click Formula Is in the dropdown list on the left, and then enter the formula in the box on the right. Click Format and select the font, style, and so on, you want to apply when the condition is satisfied. (Note that you are limited to the choices available in this dialog box. For example, you cannot specify a different number format.) To add another condition, click Add and repeat the previous steps. You can add up to three conditions and a different formatting for each of them. If none of the specified conditions is satisfied then the cell keeps its existing formatting, which effectively creates a fourth condition.

To copy a format (including any conditional format) to another cell, select a cell that has the conditional format, click the Format Painter on the format toolbar, and select the cells you want to format. To copy only the conditional format to another cell, select the cells you want to format and include at least one cell in the selection that has the conditional format you want to copy. On the Format menu, click Conditional Formatting and then click OK. Note that copying and pasting a value into a cell wipes out any conditional formatting in it. Conditional formatting works only for data that is entered into the cell manually or is calculated by a formula.

2.4. CIRCULAR REFERENCE

The values in other cells whose values do not, either directly or indirectly, depend on the value of H32 will, for the most part, determine the value of any given cell in your model, such as H32. Put differently, Excel assumes that the values of every cell it references in the formula are known before calculating the formula in H32. But occasionally, a formula in a cell might make reference to the cell it's in—either directly or indirectly. We refer to this as circular reference. This can occur as a result of an error you made along the way, but it can also happen when you purposefully include one or more circular references in your model because they are a useful tool for solving specific kinds of issues.

2.4.1. Unintentional Circular

Reference If you accidentally create a circular reference, and if Iteration is not turned on (see later), you will see a long message on circular reference and you will also see the word Circular in the status bar at the bottom of your screen. Click OK and Excel will show a Help screen with information on how to track down and fix the problem.

2.4.2. Using Circular Reference Intentionally

You can use circular reference intentionally as a tool to solve a certain type of problems. It will be easiest to understand how by working through an example. Before we begin, select Tools ⇨ Options. Then in the Calculation tab of the Options dialog box, make sure that the check box for Iteration is not selected. (If it is selected, deselect it.) For our example, we will look at a company that has a policy of contributing 2% of its operating income to charity. Create a simple income statement for the company as shown in Figure 2.1 in the "No circular reference" column. Here, the formula in B8 is =B7*B14.

	A	B	C	D
1	Using Circular Reference			
2				
3		No circular reference	With circular reference	
4				
5	Revenue	$100,000	$100,000	
6	Costs	$70,000	$70,000	
7	Operating income	$30,000	$30,000	
8	Charitable contribution	$600	$356	
9	Income before tax	$29,400	$29,644	
10	Income tax	$11,760	$11,858	
11	Net income	$17,640	$17,787	
12				
13				
14	Contribution rate	2%	2%	
15	Tax rate	40%	40%	
16				
17				

Figure 2.1. *Example of circular reference.*

Source: Chandan Sengupta; Financial Modeling Using Excel and VBA; ISBN 0–471–26768–6.

Now suppose the company decides that it wants to contribute 2% of its net income (rather than operating income) to charity. In this case, you will have a circular reference when you try to model the company's income statement: The net income will depend on the charitable contribution because it is tax deductible and will affect taxes, but the charitable contribution itself will depend on the net income because of the new policy.

If you were doing the calculations manually, you could solve the problem using algebraic equations. You could also solve it using trial and error or iteration. For this last method, you would take a guess at the contribution (for example, start with the number from the previous version), calculate the net income, calculate a new contribution as 2% of the net income, calculate a new net income based on that, and so on until the values change very little in successive iterations and the charitable contribution becomes very close to 2% of net income.

To create the model reflecting the new policy, copy B5:B15 into C5:C15 and in C8 enter =C11*C14. You will immediately see a circular reference message. Click Cancel to continue. The message will go away, but you will notice that the answer is wrong because the charitable contribution amount does not equal 2% of net income. To have Excel solve it by iteration, go back to the Options dialog box as before and now select the check box for Iteration in the Calculation tab. Once you click OK to close the Options dialog box, Excel will do the iterations and come up with the right answers.

2.4.3. How to Set Up a Circular Reference

Some people have trouble understanding how to purposefully create a circular reference in order to solve the kind of problem we covered. As you can see, there is nothing special that needs to be done. Don't worry about circular references; just enter the formulas as normal. There won't be a notice if Iteration is already enabled. When you see the message, turn it on if it isn't already. That concludes it. But be sure to double-check (by hand-calculating if needed) that the iteration process yielded the correct answer, as it might not always. Is it necessary to always have the Iteration on? Probably not. Turning off Iteration will highlight any accidental circular references you may make unless you are purposefully creating them. Unintentional circular references could enter your models and cause errors if iteration is always on. If you intentionally use circular reference without turning it on, though, your model might not update correctly when you modify certain formulas or inputs. So use caution when turning it on or off.

2.4.4. Controlling the Accuracy of Your Answer

You can control the accuracy of the answer and how long you want Excel to try to produce an answer before stopping. To see how, select Tools ⊠ Options and then the Calculation tab. You can set two conditions here in the section for Iteration. In the box for Maximum iterations, specify the number of iterations that Excel should try before stopping (even if it does not reach an answer with the desired accuracy). The value you enter in the Maximum change box controls the accuracy of your answer. It says iteration should stop when the values of the variables involved change from one trial to the next by an amount smaller than this number. Iteration will stop as soon as one of the two conditions is satisfied. (If you leave these boxes blank, Excel uses default values of 100 and 0.001 respectively.)

Unless you have a huge model, each iteration takes almost no time on a modern PC. You can therefore set the Maximum iteration quite high. Nonetheless, you should set a reasonable number (100 or so to start with) just in case there is a bug in your program or some other problem that keeps the iterations going without getting closer to the answer. In the Maximum change box you should put a fairly small number to get an accurate answer, again because in most cases the time that it takes to get there will be miniscule. However, if you are working with a computation-intensive model, you will probably want to play around with these specifications to get the level of accuracy you need without wasting too much time.

2.5. VISUAL BASIC FOR APPLICATIONS (VBA)

VBA is an abbreviation for Visual Basic for Application. VBA is a programming language that was developed by Microsoft Corp., and it is integrated into the major Microsoft Office applications, such as Word, Excel, and Access.

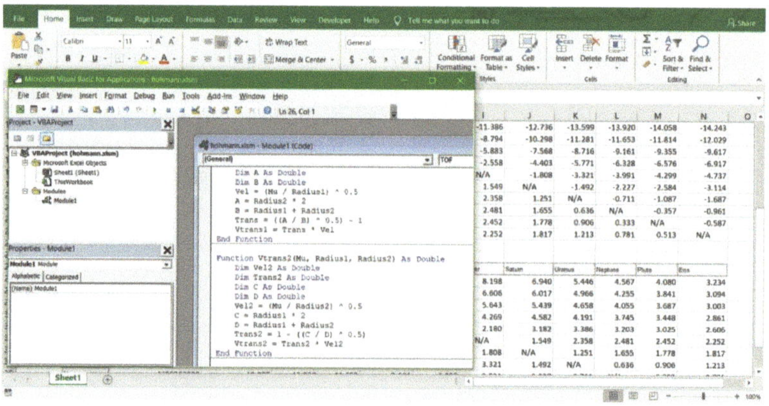

The VBA programming language allows users to access functions beyond what is available in the MS Office applications. Users can also use VBA to customize applications to meet the specific needs of their business, such as creating user-defined functions, automating computer processes, and accessing Windows APIs.

2.5.1. How Is VBA Used?

VBA is used to perform different functions, and different types of users use the programming language for various functions. The following are the different parties that use VBA:

1. **General Users:** Most users regularly use MS Office applications such as Excel in their routine. VBA language is included in the MS Office package at no cost to the user. VBA is used to automate tasks and perform several other functions beyond creating and organizing spreadsheets.

For example, users need to automate some aspects of Excel, such as repetitive tasks, frequent tasks, generating reports, etc. The user can create a VBA program (macro) within Excel that generates, formats, and prints monthly sales reports with graphical representation such as bar charts. They can execute the program with a single click, and Excel will automatically generate the reports with ease as per the needs of the company.

2. **Computer Professionals:** Computer professionals can use VBAs to perform more complex tasks that would otherwise take longer time and more resources to complete. For example, they can use VBAs to create custom add-ins for Excel that provide additional functionality to the application by introducing new functions that are not available in Excel.

   VBA also helps computer professionals perform complex functions, such as replicating large lines of code, designing languages within MS Office applications, and merging the functions of two or more different programs.

3 **Corporate Users:** VBA is not only useful to individuals, but also to corporate users. Companies can use the VBA programming language to automate key business procedures and internal processes. Functions such as accounting procedures, tracking minutes, processing of sales orders in real-time, calculating complex data, etc., can be implemented using VBA.

   VBA can automate the above-mentioned tasks to increase the efficiency of internal business processes. It also allows corporations to consolidate their data in the cloud to make it accessible from any location around the world.

2.5.2. Common uses of VBA among Finance Professionals

The following are some of the ways in which finance professionals use VBA in their work:

1. **Analyze Huge Amounts of Data:** Finance professionals, such as portfolio managers, financial analysts, traders, and investment bankers, often need to deal with large volumes of data. They are required to review all the data and use the information to make critical buy or sell decisions. The professionals can use VBA to create macros that facilitate speedy analysis of the data. Once the logic is defined and the important variables are specified, the finance professionals should feed the large volumes of data into the relevant cells and get results with a click of a button. Also, as long the correct data is added to the program, the data output will be more accurate compared to the output obtained manually since humans are bound to make mistakes.
2. **Create and Maintain Complex Models:** Finance professionals can also use VBA to create trading, pricing, and risk management models. The models can be used to track the performance of stocks in the securities exchange market in real-time, forecast the trend of each stock, and provide signals on when to buy or sell and the appropriate pricing at each stage. The VBA program can also be used to generate financial ratios that allow analysts to evaluate the financial performance of publicly traded companies, as well as compare the trends and performance of two or more entities over a defined period of time.
3. **Create Investment Scenarios:** Investment bankers and financial analysts often need to make decisions by comparing two or more investment scenarios. For example, in mergers and acquisitions, finance professionals must consider the financial impact of the merger to determine if it is feasible. The professionals can use VBA to create macros that simulate the investment scenarios to get an overview of the expected results/effects.

CLASS ACTIVITY

Assessment: Students will construct a dynamic financial model for a hypothetical company. This will include projecting income statements, balance sheets, and cash flow statements over a five-year period. The exercise will emphasize sensitivity analysis, scenario planning, and the use of financial functions to evaluate profitability and liquidity.

SUMMARY

- Financial modeling in Excel is all around the web. There has been a lot written about learning financial modeling. However, most of the financial modeling pieces of training are the same. It goes beyond the usual gibberish and explores practical financial modeling used by Investment Bankers and Research Analysts.
- Excel is a versatile and powerful tool widely used for data analysis, financial modeling, and many other applications. While basic functions like SUM, AVERAGE, and VLOOKUP are commonly used, Excel also offers a plethora of advanced functions that can significantly enhance your productivity and analytical capabilities.
- The LOOKUP function in Excel can perform the simplest types of vertical and horizontal lookups.
- The VLOOKUP function in Excel is a powerful function used to lookup data in a table organized vertically. It looks down the left column of a range to find a value.
- The HLOOKUP function looks up for a value in the first row of a given range and gives a value in the same column from a row that you specified.
- INDEX MATCH is a clever way to do a two-way lookup in Excel, and it can be used as a workaround for the limitations of VLOOKUP.
- INDEX MATCH is made up of two functions. The MATCH function is used to figure out where the lookup value is located in a range of cells. The INDEX function then returns the value or cell reference from within a table or range.
- The Excel INDEX function returns a value or cell reference from within a table or range. The INDEX function has two formats – the array format and the reference format. The array format is used when we want to return the value that is found in the result cell.
- Data validation in Excel is a feature that allows you to control the type of data entered into a worksheet to improve the accuracy of the data. For example, Excel data validation enables users to limit data entries to a selection from a drop-down list and to restrict certain data entries, such as dates or numbers outside of a predetermined range.

REVIEW QUESTIONS

1. What is the difference between the VLOOKUP and HLOOKUP functions? Provide an example of when you might use each.
2. Explain how the INDEX and MATCH functions can be combined to perform more flexible lookups than VLOOKUP.
3. Explain how to set up a data validation rule to restrict user input to a list of predefined values. What are the benefits of using data validation in Excel?
4. What is a circular reference in Excel, and why is it generally advised to avoid them? How can you identify and resolve a circular reference in your workbook?
5. Explain the difference between a Sub procedure and a Function procedure in VBA. Provide an example of each.

REFERENCES

1. Alshowishin, A. (2021). Financial analysis. *International Journal of Scientific and Research Publications (IJSRP), 11*(4), 208–211. http://dx.doi.org/10.29322/ijsrp.11.04.2021.p11226.
2. Bala, B. K., Arshad, F. M., & Noh, K. M. (2016). *System Dynamics Modeling and Simulation*. Springer.
3. Bodie, Z., Kane, A., & Marcus, A. J. (2017). *Essentials of Investments* (10th ed., international ed.). New York, NY: McGraw-Hill Education.
4. Brealey, R. A., Ian, C. A., & Habib, M. A. (1996). Using project finance to fund infrastructure investments. *Journal of Applied Corporate Finance, 9*(3), 25–39.
5. Collan, M. (2004). *Ciga-Investments: Modeling the Valuation of Very Large Industrial Real Investments* (Doctoral dissertation, Institute of Academic Research).
6. Fairhurst, D. S. (2022). *Financial Modeling in Excel for Dummies*. John Wiley & Sons.
7. K., Dr. Siva Nageswararao. (2020). Financial performance analysis of Andhra Bank. *International Journal of Psychosocial Rehabilitation, 24*(5), 65–75. http://dx.doi.org/10.37200/ijpr/v24i5/pr201668.
8. Palepu, K. G., Healy, P. M., Peek, E., & Bernard, V. L. (2007). *Business Analysis and Valuation: Text and Cases*. Cengage Learning EMEA. ISBN 978-1-84480-492-4.
9. Low, R. K. Y., & Tan, E. (2016). The role of analysts' forecasts in the momentum effect. *International Review of Financial Analysis, 48*, 67–84. https://doi.org/10.1016/j.irfa.2016.09.007.
10. Mbona, R. M., & Yusheng, K. (2019). Financial statement analysis. *Asian Journal of Accounting Research, 4*(2), 233–245. http://dx.doi.org/10.1108/ajar-05-2019-0037.

CHAPTER 3

Financial Statements and Ratio Analysis

LEARNING OBJECTIVES

After studying this chapter, you will be able to:

- Discuss about the financial statements
- Define other statements
- Describe the goals of financial analysis
- Explain financial statement analysis
- Know about the ratio analysis
- Elaborate the significance of ratio analysis in financial statement analysis for startup.

KEY TERMS FROM THIS CHAPTER

Amortization	Balance sheet	Cash flow statement
Depreciation	Equity	Financial health
Financial stability	Fixed asset	Income statement
Market value	Net profit	Profit and loss statement
Retained Earnings	Shareholder equity	Short-term assets
Short-term liabilities		

INTRODUCTION

Financial statements are essential documents that provide a comprehensive summary of a company's financial performance and position. These statements, including the balance sheet, income statement, and cash flow statement, offer critical insights into a company's operations, financial health, and profitability. They are crucial for stakeholders, including investors, creditors, management, and regulatory bodies, to make informed decisions.

The balance sheet, also known as the statement of financial position, outlines a company's assets, liabilities, and shareholders' equity at a specific point in time. It provides a snapshot of what the company owns and owes, and the amount invested by shareholders. The income statement, or profit and loss statement, details the company's revenues, expenses, and profits over a particular period. It highlights the company's ability to generate profit from its operations, making it a key indicator of financial performance. The cash flow statement provides a detailed view of the cash inflows and outflows from operating, investing, and financing activities. It helps stakeholders understand how well a company manages its cash position, ensuring it has sufficient liquidity to meet its obligations and invest in growth opportunities.

Ratio analysis is a powerful tool used to interpret financial statements, allowing for a deeper understanding of a company's financial health and performance. By calculating various financial ratios, such as liquidity, profitability, and leverage ratios, stakeholders can assess the company's operational efficiency, profitability, and financial stability. For example, the current ratio evaluates a company's ability to cover short-term liabilities with its short-term assets, while the debt-to-equity ratio assesses the company's financial leverage and long-term solvency.

3.1. THE FINANCIAL STATEMENTS

The balance sheet, income statement, and statement of cash flows are the three financial statements that are essential to understanding financial statements. We give a succinct synopsis of each statement and explain the data it includes.

3.1.1. The Balance Sheet

The balance sheet provides the details of the accounting identity.

Assets = Liabilities + Owners' equity

or

Investments = Investments paid for with debt + Investments paid for with equity

The balance sheet, which is typically created at the conclusion of the fiscal year, is a financial snapshot of the company. In other words, it offers details regarding the state of the company at a specific moment in time. Through an examination of multiple balance sheets from various years, the analyst can discern shifts within the company over time. A sample balance sheet is displayed in Table 3.1, and its contents are covered in the video.

Table 3.1. Sample Balance Sheet

Assets	**Liabilities and Equity**
Current Assets	Current Liabilities
Cash	Accounts payable
Marketable securities	Accrued expenses
Accounts receivable	Short-term notes
Inventories	
Total current assets	Total current liabilities
Fixed Assets	Long-Term Liabilities
Machinery and equipment	Long-term notes
Buildings	Mortgages
Land	
Total fixed assets	Total long-term liabilities
Other Assets	Equity
Investments	Preferred shares
Patents	Common shares
	Par value
	Paid in capital
	Retained earnings
Total other assets	Total equity
Total Assets	**Total Liabilities and Equity**

Source: https://www.pearsoncanada.ca/media/highered-showcase/multi-product-showcase/corporate-ch02.pdf.

A balance sheet is a quick view of a company's financial situation, as opposed to the income statement, which is a financial movie. A balance statement shows the financial standing of a business as of a particular date (the business's year end). The balance sheet may fluctuate throughout the year due to changes in sales, assets, and receivables. A company that engages in seasonal business, like Toro (lawnmowers and snowblowers), will see significant annual fluctuations in its inventory levels, sales, and receivables.

Liabilities and equity are on the right side of the balance sheet, while assets are on the left. All assets, including cash and accounts receivable and investments, are listed on the left side. Liabilities of the company, including debts and accounts payable, are listed on the right side. Retained earnings and shareholder equity, or the value of the company owned by its stockholders, are also shown on the right side.

The order of items on the balance sheet is determined by their liquidity, or how long it takes to turn them into cash. Since they are the least liquid, items with the longest terms are listed last. Because they are the least liquid and will only be compensated in the event of bankruptcy after all other debts have been paid, stockholders are listed last on the right side. A balance sheet's values are book values, which are determined by the purchase price. The market value, or current fair market values, may differ significantly from book values, or the purchase price.

3.1.1.1. Assets

Liquidity separates assets into two groups: current assets and fixed assets. Cash, accounts receivable, and inventory are the three types of current assets. It is anticipated that these items will be converted to cash in less than a year. Raw materials, work-in-progress, and finished goods are all included in inventory. When a business sells a product to a customer and then has to wait for payment, it creates accounts receivable. Intangible assets like patents and tangible assets like buildings, machinery, and land are both considered fixed assets. Businesses may also own stakes in securities or other businesses. These assets are shown in order of liquidity on the balance sheet as well. The total asset number of a company is the sum of all of these assets.

3.1.1.2. Liabilities and Equity

Liabilities and equity are shown on the right side of the balance sheet, arranged according to liquidity. Money owed is listed first under liabilities.

Payments for current liabilities are due in a year. When a business purchases advertising or raw materials but delays paying for them, accounts payable are created. Longer-term obligations like accruals and notes payable are listed next. Wages owed to workers and taxes owed to the government are referred to as accruals. Notes payable are company-incurred loans. These could also be classified as long-term debt and have a longer term.

Retained earnings and shareholder equity are included in the equity component. The total amount of profits a company has made since its founding that have not been distributed as dividends is known as retained earnings. Retained earnings are earnings that are used to fund business operations rather than cash. A stockholder's claim on the company is known as stockholder equity. Equity, or "common equity," is the total of retained earnings and common stock. Common equity can also be referred to as net worth, which is the assets of a business less its liabilities (Figure 3.1).

Balance Sheet

All figures in '000 unless otherwise stated

Assumptions (<< Click to Open)

	2018	2019	2020	2021	2022	2023
ASSETS						
Current Assets						
Cash/Checking's	1,477	1,372	4,495	9,439	15,114	21,328
Inventory (WIP)	-	31	54	59	63	57
Inventory (Finished Goods)	-	12	22	22	22	22
Accounts Receivable	-	-	-	-	-	-
Prepaid Expense	-	4	9	10	10	10
Tax Asset	82	-	-	-	-	-
Other Assets	-	9	19	20	20	21
Total Current Assets	1,560	1,428	4,598	9,550	15,228	21,437
Fixed Assets						
PP&E	1,640	3,440	3,440	3,440	3,440	3,440
Accumulated Depreciation	(26)	(257)	(551)	(845)	(1,139)	(1,433)
Total Fixed Assets	1,614	3,184	2,890	2,596	2,302	2,008
Total Assets	3,174	4,612	7,488	12,146	17,530	23,444
LIABILITIES						
Accounts Payable	13	16	16	17	17	18
Interest Payable	-	-	-	-	-	-
Accrued Payroll	-	11	13	13	14	14
Total Current Liabilities	13	27	29	30	31	32
Long-term Liabilities						
Convertible Debt	-	-	-	-	-	-
Long-term Debt						
Capital Lease	-	600	200	(0)	(0)	(0)
Total Liabilities	1,013	1,253	229	30	31	32
EQUITY						
Capital Account	2,000	2,000	2,000	2,000	2,000	2,000
Owner's Investment	355	355	355	355	355	355
Retained Earnings	(194)	1,004	4,903	9,760	15,144	21,057
Total Equity	2,161	3,359	7,258	12,115	17,499	23,412
Total Equity + Liabilites	3,174	4,612	7,488	12,146	17,530	23,444

Figure 3.1. *Pro-forma balance sheet.*

Source. https://cfoshare.org/wp-content/uploads/2022/06/Pro-forma-balance-sheet-eaxmple-pdf.jpg.

It is crucial to remember that assets are only owned in relation to the revenue they can generate for the company. Owners' equity and liabilities supply the money needed to buy these assets.

1. **Assets Generate Income (the Left-Hand Side):** The asset side of a company's balance sheet showcases its resources. A company maintains assets solely for the purpose of generating revenue. These company assets serve as the source of its income. There's no justification for a company to possess an asset if it fails to yield income.
2. **Financing the Assets (the Right-Hand Side):** On the right side of the balance sheet, there will be a dollar of equity or a dollar of

liability for every dollar of assets the company has. The balance sheet's right side illustrates how the company finances its assets. The lowest financing cost can be attained by modifying the ratio of debt to equity.

In conclusion, the assets that generate income are listed on the left side of the balance sheet, and the financing for these assets is listed on the right.

3.1.2. Income Statement

The income statement is the first financial statement we look at. Revenues received, costs incurred, and the final figure that matters to investors—net income—are all listed on an income statement. Similar to a movie, the income statement presents a company's financial picture over time. It is a dynamic representation of the company's financial performance over a specified time frame, usually a year, though quarterly and monthly financial statements are also generated. Furthermore, companies frequently choose different dates for the end of their fiscal year based on their industry or selling cycle, even though the calendar year ends on December 31.

An income statement's revenue line, sometimes known as the top line or sales revenue, is what appears first. This represents the total amount of money sold in products and services over the specified time frame. Cost of goods sold (COGS) is the amount from which the direct costs incurred to make the good are subtracted. Gross profit, or Earnings Before Interest, Taxes, Depreciation, and Amortization (EBITDA), is the outcome of this. What the business made from producing and selling its goods is known as its gross profit. We must pay operating, financial (interest), and tax expenses out of gross profit. Operating expenses are the usual costs associated with running a business and include leasing costs, depreciation, amortization, and selling, general, and administrative (SG&A) expenses.

While a machine or building will eventually wear out and need to be replaced, fixed assets are not directly "used up" over time. The annual charges of amortization and depreciation represent the allowable portion of the costs of the assets that can be written off. For tangible assets like machinery, depreciation is used, and for intangible assets like patents, amortization is used.

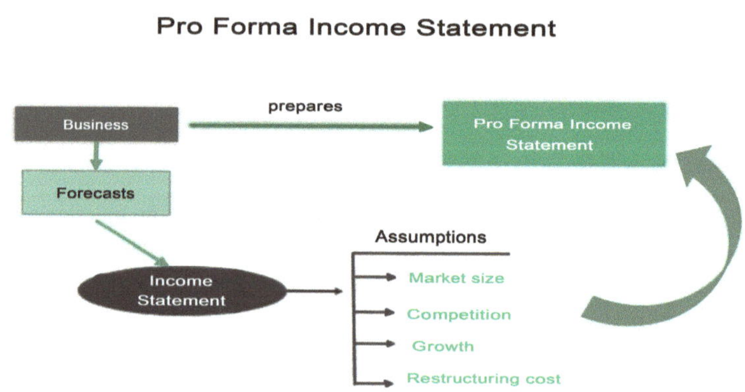

Figure 3.2. *Pro-forma income statement.*

Source. https://www.wallstreetmojo.com/wp-content/uploads/2023/02/What-Is-A-Pro-Forma-Income-Statement.jpg.

Earnings before interest and taxes is what remains after deducting operating expenses from gross profit (EBIT). EBIT demonstrates the company's capacity to produce cash flow. Taxes and interest costs are examples of external factors that we deduct from EBIT. Net profit before taxes, or Earnings Before Taxes (EBT), is what remains after deducting interest. We have to pay the tax man at the end. Net income, also called profit, is what's left over after taxes are deducted.

The income statement shows us how the company has done over time, as opposed to the balance sheet, which describes the company's status at a specific moment in time (Figure 3.2).

Typically, income statements consist of two sections. The operating income or results of operating activities are reported in the first section. This sums up sales less operating costs. The financing activities are reported in the second section. Net income is calculated by deducting taxes, interest expense, and preferred dividends. A sample income statement is given in Table 3.2, and the video goes over the information on it.

Table 3.2. Sample Income Statement

Sales	Operating Activities
− Cost of goods sold	
Gross Profit	
− Selling expense	
− Administrative expense	
− Depreciation expense	
Earnings Before Interest and Taxes (EBIT)	
− Interest expense	Financing Activities
Earnings Before Taxes	
− Taxes	
Net Income Before Preferred Dividends	
− Preferred share dividends	
Net Income Available to Common Shareholders	

Source: https://www.pearsoncanada.ca/media/highered-showcase/multi-product-showcase/corporate-ch02.pdf.

3.1.3. Cash Flow Statement

A company's capacity to make money is essential to its success. A summary of the cash flows for the reported period is provided in the statement of cash flows. The difference between an organization's revenue and expenses is known as cash flows. Businesses must make enough money from their operations to finance their expansion, any upcoming capital or security investments, and to remain a reliable source of investment for investors (Figure 3.3).

Cash flows from investments, financing, and operations are all included in the cash flow statement. Cash flows derived from regular business operations are known as operating cash flows. Depreciation and changes in working capital are examples of non-cash items that are taken into account by operating cash flows.

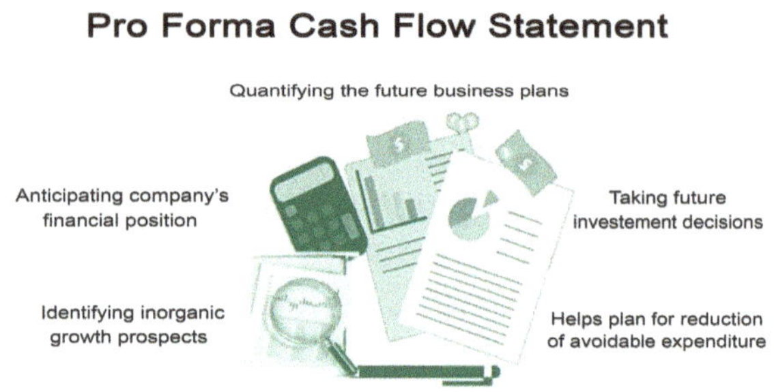

Figure 3.3. *Pro-forma statement of cash flows.*

Source: https://www.wallstreetmojo.com/wp-content/uploads/2021/02/Pro-Forma-Cash-Flow-Statement.jpg.

Cash flows from investments, such as the purchase and sale of fixed assets within our company or financial investments in other companies, are referred to as investing cash flows. Cash flows from financing activities are referred to as financing cash flows. This includes debt from selling investments, equity, or loan principal payments. Stock repurchases and dividend payments are also included in this section.

Operating activity cash flow can be either positive or negative. A company's cash flow is positive when it generates revenue and negative when it pays its bills. The company's capacity to produce positive cash flow is crucial to investors. If not, your chances of surviving will be slim.

The income statement and balance sheet are more familiar to most people than the statement of cash flows. It does, however, offer information that the other statements do not immediately provide. Cash flows are of greater importance to us in finance than accounting earnings. A sample statement of cash flows can be found in Table 3.3.

Table 3.3. Sample Statement of Cash Flows

Cash Flow from Operations
Net profit after taxes
+ Depreciation
+ Decrease in accounts receivable
+ Decrease in inventories
+ Increase in accounts payable
+ Decrease in accruals
Cash provided by operations
Cash Flow from Investments
Increase in fixed assets
Change in business ownership
Cash provided by investment activities
Cash Flow from Financing Activities
+ Decrease in notes payable
+ Increase in long-term debt
+ Changes in shareholders' equity
− Dividends paid
Cash provided by financing activities
Net increase/decrease in cash and marketable securities

Source: https://www.pearsoncanada.ca/media/highered-showcase/multi-product-showcase/corporate-ch02.pdf.

3.2. OTHER STATEMENTS

3.2.1. Statement of Shareholder Equity

The changes to a company's equity section of the balance sheet over a year are described in the statement of shareholder equity. This covers all transactions involving equity accounts, including retained earnings, common and preferred stock, and other sources of income. It displays the starting balance, any additions or subtraction, and the final shareholder equity balance.

3.2.2. Statement of Retained Earnings

Retained earnings change over a year is reported in the statement of retained earnings. It is essentially the statement of shareholders' equity condensed. The retained earnings from net income (or loss) and any dividends over a given period of time are explained in this statement.

3.3. THE GOALS OF FINANCIAL ANALYSIS

Analyzing a company's financials can help us achieve a number of goals. Financial analysis is a useful tool that can influence management and investment choices. We won't, however, come across many definitive answers. We might discover several warning signs that assist in concentrating our attention.

It is evident that insiders have access to information that is not available to other market participants, so outsiders will conduct financial analysis differently than managers, also known as insiders.

They benefit from this when ratios cause concern. Assume, for instance, that a company finds its profit margin is decreasing. Additionally, it has discovered that its inventory is not moving as quickly as it used to. Insiders can request an analysis to find out which particular products aren't selling well. Regarding the quality of the inventory mix, outsiders can only conjecture. Nonetheless, the objective shared by insiders and outsiders is to try to determine the firm's advantages and disadvantages.

3.3.1. Identify Company Weaknesses

Finding issues that the company is experiencing is one of the objectives of financial analysis. Early problem detection allows managers to make adjustments that enhance company performance. Certain issues might be difficult to pinpoint. Financial analysis can be used to determine why a company appears to be making money but is continuously cash strapped.

Early detection of troubled companies is of interest to investors as well. Nobody wants to spend more time than necessary on a sinking ship. In order to sell their shares before the price declines, analysts hope to spot troublesome companies before other investors do.

3.3.2. Identify Company Strengths

Financial analysis also serves the equally important goal of identifying a company's strengths so those strengths can be maximized and extended. For instance, declining inventory turnover ratios and return on equity ratios in the early 1970s informed JCPenney that, while it could sell high-quality clothing, it could not effectively compete with large volume discount stores. Following this discovery, the company underwent a significant realignment that included upscaling its apparel lines and discontinuing its furniture, appliance, and car divisions. These adjustments allowed it to succeed where many of its rivals had failed.

3.4. FINANCIAL STATEMENT ANALYSIS

Many of the more popular financial ratios are introduced and briefly discussed in this section. By any measure, this is not an exhaustive list. Numerous ratios are available for use. As a matter of fact, analysts frequently develop customized ratios to examine a characteristic unique to a company or sector. For instance, airlines frequently calculate their revenues and costs per kilometer flown.

The ratio formulas shown here might not match those found elsewhere. This section attempts to find the most widely accepted definition for each formula; however, reporting agencies cannot agree on some of them. This means that you need to ensure that ratios calculated from various sources are comparable when comparing them.

3.4.1. Cross-Sectional Analysis

In isolation, most financial ratios don't really mean anything. An inventory turnover ratio, for instance, indicates how frequently the company sells its inventory annually; we will talk more about this ratio later in the chapter. Until we find out that other companies in the sector have an inventory turnover ratio of 3, a value of 20 is not particularly intriguing. Similarly, depending on the industry, gross profit margins, liquidity ratios, and activity ratios all differ significantly. It goes without saying that a grocery store will change out its stock more often than an auto dealer.

Comparing one company to other similar companies is known as cross-sectional analysis. The firm's numbers are compared to a cross-section of the industry. There are numerous places to find cross-sectional data. Industry average ratio statistics are published by Mergent, Value Line, and the Risk Management Association. An industry can be determined, for example, by a company's Standard Industrial Classification (SIC) code. The government assigns businesses four-digit SIC codes for the purpose of statistical reporting.

Many companies, like conglomerates that operate in dozens of different industries, lack a distinct industry to compare against. For these kinds of businesses, there are no suitable standards for selecting comparison numbers. In other instances, the industry ratios are just a reflection of how dominant the company under investigation is in the sector. Take a look at General Motors (GM). Because there are so few companies in the auto industry, the industry is affected by what happens to GM.

Developing your own list of rivals is one way to address the challenge of locating reliable comparison data. Examine the firm in question in relation to the averages on this list. This method frequently produces comparison numbers that are far better than those in the published reference materials.

3.4.2. Time-Series Analysis

Time-series analysis is another equally important method of financial analysis. It compares the performance of the company to previous periods. The analyst can find trends—changes over time that are more or less consistent in one direction—by using this method. Previous period numbers are almost a perfect comparison with current figures, unless the company has experienced some kind of significant restructuring.

Both cross-sectional and time-series analyzes are important. For this reason, analysts should use both.

3.4.3. The Ratios

The ratios are presented in groups to facilitate understanding. We have grouped the ratios into 5 categories:

- Profitability ratios
- Liquidity ratios
- Activity ratios
- Financing ratios
- Market ratios

The categories are given varying degrees of importance by different companies. For instance, since inventory is typically a small cost factor, service companies are more concerned with how quickly they collect accounts receivable than they are with how much inventory they use. On the other hand, manufacturing companies need to monitor their inventory closely, while collections are frequently not an issue.

Consider the ratio's intended use and whether a higher or lower ratio is generally preferable as you go over this section. Observe the unit of measurement as well as any modifications that could make the ratio better.

3.4.4. Profitability Ratios

Since profitability ratios are ultimately the most important, we start our discussion of ratio analysis with them. Analysts are generally more tolerant of variations in other ratios if a company is making respectable profits. For instance, high prices might be the cause of low inventory turnover. Investors are unlikely to protest if this corporate strategy generates large profits. On the other hand, low inventory turnover is seen as a severe weakness if profits are not high.

Ratios of profitability indicate how well a company uses its resources to turn a profit. Of all the financial ratios, the first three that are listed here are most likely the most well-known and frequently utilized. Investor satisfaction increases as profitability ratios rise.

When combined, these profitability ratios provide the analyst with information about the firm's performance. For instance, you can check the different profit margin accounts to see if the issue is with the cost of goods sold, operating costs, or financing costs if the return on equity is unacceptable.

3.5. RATIO ANALYSIS

Ratio analysis is another tool. If used correctly (as Jim's father does), they can be very helpful; if not, as Jim does, they can be dangerous. While some are somewhat more complex, others are easily understood. This section focuses on the financial manager's toolkit and the items within, as opposed to the toolbox from the newspaper ad. One of the most crucial instruments for assessing the financial health of a business is ratio analysis, which can also be entertaining. Ratio interpretation and the identification of opportunities, threats, and changes go beyond simple ratio calculation. When it comes to analysis, ratios are only as good as the mind (yours). Ratios are classified into groups based on the objects they evaluate. Liquidity Ratios is the first category.

3.5.1. Liquidity Ratios

The ability of a company to satisfy its short-term financial obligations is gauged by liquidity ratios. These ratios are connected to the working capital of a company.

3.5.2. Current Ratio

The current ratio is the name of our first ratio. By dividing current assets by current liabilities, this can be calculated. A company's capacity to pay back its current liabilities is gauged by its current ratio.

$$\text{Current Ratio} = \frac{\text{Total Current Assets}}{\text{Total Current Liabilities}}$$

3.5.3. Quick Ratio (Acid Test)

Another liquidity ratio that's sometimes referred to as the "acid test" is the Quick Ratio. The term "acid test" was derived from a technique employed by gold miners to verify the authenticity of their nuggets.

The gold nuggets that the miners found were dipped in acid. With the exception of gold, most metals dissolve in acid and fail the test. Financially speaking, the "acid test" assesses a company's capacity to settle its debts with actual money. The acid test determines whether a business can cover its current obligations without needing to sell any inventory.

Inventories are subtracted from current assets in the acid test, and the result is divided by current liabilities. Industry-specific factors determine the acceptable range for the real value, although a quick ratio larger than 1 is typically advised. When a company's inventory cannot be swiftly turned into cash, the quick ratio is a more appropriate metric to use. The current ratio is favored when a company has liquid inventory.

$$\text{Quick Ratio} = \frac{\text{Total Current Assets} - \text{Inventories}}{\text{Total Current Liabilities}}$$

3.5.4. Asset Management Ratios

Asset management ratios, also known as activity ratios, fall into the second category and indicate how well a company manages its assets.

Let's talk about averages first. We use an average for many of the asset management ratios. Average purchases, average inventory, or average sales can occur occasionally. We are searching for an average for these figures per day. In each of these cases, divide the annual number (year end) by 365 to find the average daily. While some textbooks use 360 to make the math simpler, we use 365 in this case. Here is an example of a sales average calculation:

$$\text{Average Sales} = \frac{\text{Annual Sales}}{365}$$

That's it! So any time you see an average in the next section remember to divide the annual number by 365.

3.5.5. Inventory Turnover Ratio

The number of times the company's inventory is bought and sold annually is indicated by the inventory turnover ratio. Again, this ratio varies by industry, but it is better if it is relatively high. This result can be influenced by technology and distribution strategies, and it is most significant when compared to competitors.

$$\text{Inventory Turnover Ratio} = \frac{\text{Cost of Goods Sold}}{\text{Average Inventory}}$$

The average age of inventory is another important metric.

By simply dividing the inventory turnover ratio by 365, one can easily convert it to this. Please take note that this computation differs from the averages that were made previously.

$$\text{Average Age of Inventory} = \frac{365}{\text{Inventory Turnover Ratio}}$$

3.5.6. Average Payment Period

The length of time it takes a business to pay its suppliers is gauged by the average payment period. Accounts payable is divided by the daily average of purchases to arrive at this figure. As the average payment period rises, cash should also rise. Businesses typically pay their largest suppliers first, though some will pay quicker to benefit from trade discounts.

$$\text{Average Payment Period} = \frac{\text{Accounts Payable}}{\text{Average Purchases per Day}}$$

3.5.7. Receivables Turnover Ratio

The other side of the equation is the receivables turnover ratio. It gauges how well a business extends credit and gathers debts, or how successful it is at collecting money that is owed to them.

It is calculated by dividing total revenue by average receivables. It goes without saying that we would prefer to receive our money as soon as possible.

$$\text{Receivables Turnover Ratio} = \frac{\text{Sales}}{\text{Average Receivables}}$$

3.5.8. Total Asset Turnover Ratio

The total asset turnover ratio helps us understand how well a company uses its resources to produce revenue. By dividing total revenues by total assets for the same time period, it is calculated. A high asset turnover ratio indicates that the company is making effective use of its assets to drive revenue. If it is low, the company is not making the most of its assets and, should sales not rise, it might want to think about selling some of them.

$$\text{Total Asset Turnover} = \frac{\text{Sales}}{\text{Total Assets}}$$

3.5.9. Fixed Asset Turnover Ratio

We occasionally also compute the turnover using only our fixed assets, like machinery and plants. These costs have varying effects on financial statements since they are variable costs—that is why they are called such. Our long-term assets are the subject of fixed asset turnover, which is computed by dividing sales by net fixed assets (keep in mind that net means depreciation removed).

$$\text{Fixed Asset Turnover} = \frac{\text{Sales}}{\text{Net Fixed Assets}}$$

3.5.10. Debt Management Ratios

Debt management ratios quantify a company's level of debt financing. When a business employs debt financing, it borrows money from others to fund its operations. While debt carries a higher risk, it also offers a higher potential return. The financial statements of a company are impacted by debt. The financial leverage of a company increases with its debt utilization. Because debt allows investors to keep control over the company, higher debt levels are associated with higher financial leverage and higher returns to investors. We attempt to gauge the firm's level of debt using debt ratios, which helps us determine how risky the company is to invest in. There are two different kinds of debt usage metrics. The first is the business's capacity to repay its debts. The second is the extent of the company's debt. The debt ratio is the first indicator of a company's level of debt.

3.5.10.1. Debt Ratio

The ratio of debts to assets, or more accurately, total liabilities to total assets, is known as the debt ratio. It calculates the proportion of funds contributed by long-term debt and current liabilities. Low debt ratios are preferred by creditors because they show that the company has sufficient assets to cover its obligations. Stated differently, the company possesses a financial safety net that serves as a safeguard against the losses incurred by creditors in the event of insolvency. However, a higher ratio can be preferred by investors since it shows that the company is using leverage wisely, which increases the return to the investors. The debt ratio is expressed as a percentage. It is a measure of financial leverage and represents the percentage of funding in the form of liabilities.

$$\text{Debt Ratio} = \frac{\text{Total Liabilities}}{\text{Total Assets}}$$

3.5.10.2. Debt-Equity Ratio

The debt-equity ratio is a close relative of the debt ratio and a different measure of a company's level of debt. The information is presented slightly differently in the debt-equity ratio. In the denominator, total liabilities are subtracted from total assets. Because this calculation shows us dollars of debt for every dollar of equity, it is simple to understand.

$$\text{Debt-Equity Ratio} = \frac{\text{Total Liabilities}}{(\text{Total Assets} - \text{Total Liabilities})}$$

3.5.11. Times-Interest-Earned (TIE, or the Ability to Pay Interest or Interest Coverage Ratio)

The first indicator of a company's ability to repay debt is the time-interest-earned, or TIE. TIE calculates how much operating income can drop before a business can no longer pay its yearly interest expenses. By dividing earnings before interest and taxes by interest expense, it can be calculated. Creditors may pursue a company if it doesn't make interest payments on schedule. The greater the figure, the more capable the company is of repaying its loans. It is desirable to have a value of at least 3 points, but preferably closer to 5 points. (Leave in?) The percentage that the TIE number gives us represents the amount that EBIT could drop by and the company would still be able to pay interest.

$$\text{Times-Interest-Earned} = \frac{\text{EBIT}}{\text{Interest Expense}}$$

- **EBITDA Coverage Ratio:** EBITDA coverage ratio serves as an additional indicator of a company's capacity to repay debt. Since it accounts for lease payments and has more cash available for debt than just EBIT, the EBITDA Coverage ratio outperforms the TIE ratio. Because money can be used to pay off debt after the short-term depreciation, short-term lenders can benefit most from this ratio.

$$\text{EBITDA Coverage Ratio} = \frac{(\text{EBITDA} + \text{Lease Payments})}{(\text{Interest} + \text{Principal Payments} + \text{Lease Payments})}$$

- **Fixed Payments Coverage Ratio:** An additional metric to assess risk and the company's capacity to reimburse its debts is the fixed-payments coverage ratio. This ratio assesses the company's capacity to repay all of its fixed-rate debt, including loans and leases. The greater the value, the better, since it shows how much the company can pay its fixed expenses. Lenders and owners are at greater risk when the ratio is lower.

$$\text{overage Ratio} = \frac{\text{EBIT} + \text{Lease Payments}}{\text{Interest} + \text{Lease Payments} + \{ (\text{Principal Payments} + \text{Preferred Stock Divid}}$$

3.5.12. Profitability Ratios

The "bottom line," or profit, is what we love to concentrate on. We can better understand our profit figure by using ratio analysis. When combined, these ratios can provide a clear picture of a company's profitability.

- **Profit Margin:** The amount of profit that remains after expenses are deducted from each dollar of sales is known as the profit margin. The better the number, the more money the company keeps from each dollar of sales.

$$\text{Profit Margin} = \frac{\text{Sales} - \text{Cost of Goods Sold}}{\text{Sales}}$$

- **Operating Profit Margin:** Operational profit margin is computed solely using operating expenses. Taxes, interest, and depreciation are not taken into account. Higher is also preferable in this situation.

$$\text{Operating Profit Margin} = \frac{\text{Operating Profits}}{\text{Sales}}$$

- **Net Profit Margin:** The portion of every dollar in sales that is left over after all costs have been paid is known as the net profit margin. Interest, taxes, and dividends on preferred stock are among the costs. This can also be expressed as net profits divided by sales after taxes. Higher is also preferable in this case, although industry-specific standards for what constitutes a "good" profit margin are very different.

$$\text{Net Profit Margin} = \frac{\text{Earnings Available for Common Stockholders}}{\text{Sales}}$$

- **Earnings Per Share:** The amount of earnings produced by each share of stock is known as earnings per share. It may not always correspond to the actual earnings distributed to each share (dividends per share). The amount of money made for every share of stock is known as earnings per share.

$$\text{Earnings Per Share} = \frac{\text{Earnings Available for Common Stockholders}}{\text{Number of Shares of Common Stock Outstanding}}$$

- **Basic Earning Power (BEP):** Basic Earning Power displays the company's actual earning potential prior to the effects of leverage and taxes. An analysis of this is useful because the financing and tax situations of firms vary greatly.

$$\text{Basic Earning Power} = \frac{\text{EBIT}}{\text{Total Assets}}$$

3.5.13. Return on Equity (ROE)

ROE and ROA are two of our favorite (and most well-known, if ratios can be famous) ratios. These ratios represent return on investment. The ratio of net income to total equity is known as return on equity. This ratio indicates the rate of return on investment for investors. A higher ratio is preferable.

$$\text{Return on Equity} = \frac{\text{Net Income}}{\text{Common Equity}}$$

3.5.14. Return on Assets (ROA)

The ratio of net income to total assets is known as return on assets. This gauges how well a manager uses the resources of the company to generate profits overall. The better the ratio, the higher it is.

$$\text{Return on Assets} = \frac{\text{Net Income}}{\text{Total Assets}}$$

3.5.15. Market Value Ratios (Investment Valuation Ratios)

Market Value Ratios establish a connection between the stock price of a company and other accounting metrics like cash flow and earnings. These allow you to compare the value of one company's stock to that of another.

- **Price/Earnings Ratio:** Price/Earnings ratio is used to show how much investors are willing to pay per dollar of profits.

$$\text{Price/Earnings Ratio} = \frac{\text{Price per share of stock}}{\text{Earnings per share of stock}}$$

- **Price/Cash Flow Ratio:** Cash is king, as we've already mentioned. The ability of a company to create and manage cash is reflected in the price of its stock. Price/Cash Flow is a helpful ratio that assesses the company's cash-generating capacity.

$$\text{Price/Cash Flow Ratio} = \frac{\text{Price Per Share}}{\text{Cash Flow Per Share}}$$

3.5.16. Market Book Ratio

The market book ratio is a gauge used by investors to assess the success of a company. It connects the company's book value to its market value. The book value is an accounting metric, whereas the market value represents the company's current worth. The book value per share of stock is determined first.

$$\text{Book Value Per Share of Stock} = \frac{\text{Common Stock Equity}}{\text{Number of Shares of Stock Outstanding}}$$

This is then substituted in to calculate the Market/Book ratio

$$\text{Market Book Ratio} = \frac{\text{Market Value per share of common stock}}{\text{Book Value per share of common stock}}$$

If a firm is expected to earn a high return relative to its risk will most often sell at a higher Market/Book multiple.

3.5.17. DuPont Equation

The DuPont equation, which combines the balance sheet and income statement using profitability metrics, is a useful tool for evaluating a company's financial situation. DuPont combines ROE with ROA. The two additional ratios we computed—net profit margin and total asset turnover—are now used to define ROA. Divided by total assets, net income was used to compute ROA.

$$\text{Return on Assets} = \frac{\text{Net Income}}{\text{Total Assets}}$$

ROE was calculated as net income divided by earnings available to shareholders (common equity).

$$\text{Return on Equity} = \frac{\text{Net Income}}{\text{Common Equity}}$$

The DuPont equation defines ROA as follows:

$$\text{ROA} = \text{Net Profit Margin} \times \text{Total Asset Turnover}$$

Remembering that net profit margin is earnings available for shareholders divided by sales and total asset turnover is sales divided by total assets, we can make the following substitutions:

$$\text{ROA} = \frac{\text{earnings available for shareholders}}{\text{sales}} \times \frac{\text{sales}}{\text{total assets}}$$

From this we see that sales will cancel out and ROA will become earnings available for shareholders divided by total assets.

$$\text{ROA} = \frac{\text{earnings available for shareholders}}{\text{total assets}}$$

This will give us the same number for ROA that was calculated using the original formula. However, the DuPont equation breaks it down into two components: profit on a company's sales and return to the use of a company's assets.

3.5.18. Trend Analysis, Comparative Ratios and Benchmarking

The value of the numbers over time is just as significant as the numbers themselves.

Ratio trends can reveal a lot about a business and show us whether it is trending positively or negatively. Cross-sectional data is equally important as time series data. Even though we think our ratio is excellent, it might be low for our industry.

Ratios are especially helpful when comparing to rival businesses and other companies. Industries can view available ratios and a business can compare itself to its rivals.

3.5.19. Uses and Limitations of Ratio Analysis

Ratios are only as good as the head who analyzes them. They can be incredibly helpful tools when used properly and create horrible mistakes if misused.

1. A single ratio is generally not enough to judge the overall performance of the firm.
2. Ratios should be used at the same time for each year.
3. Be sure to use audited financial statements.
4. Be aware of different accounting treatments behind the financial data and ratios.

3.6. THE SIGNIFICANCE OF RATIO ANALYSIS IN FINANCIAL STATEMENT ANALYSIS FOR STARTUP

Ratio analysis is an effective technique for analyzing financial statements for startups since it offers important information about the performance and health of a business's finances. Ratio analysis is a useful tool that startups can use to evaluate their overall financial stability, make well-informed decisions, and pinpoint areas for improvement. Let's explore the significance of ratio analysis in financial statement analysis for startups in detail:

1. **Assessing Financial Performance:** Through the use of ratio analysis, startups can assess their financial performance by comparing various financial ratios over time. These ratios are useful for calculating solvency, profitability, liquidity, and efficiency. Startups are better able to assess their financial progress and pinpoint areas that need attention by looking for trends and patterns in these ratios.
2. **Benchmarking Against Industry Standards:** Startups can compare their financial performance to industry norms by using ratio analysis. Analyzing ratios against comparable businesses in the sector offers important information about how a startup is doing in comparison to its rivals. By highlighting strengths and weaknesses, these comparisons can assist startups in establishing strategies and goals that are doable.
3. **Identifying Financial Strengths and Weaknesses:** Startups can evaluate their financial strengths and weaknesses with the use of ratios. For instance, profitability ratios that show how well a startup makes money include gross profit margin, net profit margin, and return on equity. The ability to meet short-term obligations is indicated by liquidity ratios such as the quick and current ratios. Debt-to-equity ratios and other solvency ratios evaluate a startup's long-term financial viability. Startups can identify areas for improvement and leverage their strengths by examining these ratios.
4. **Evaluating Financial Health:** Ratio analysis helps startups evaluate the stability and health of their finances. It assists in figuring out whether the startup's assets exceed its liabilities. Through the examination of solvency ratios such

as debt ratio and interest coverage ratio, startups can ascertain if they possess sufficient financial means to fulfill their committed obligations. Having this knowledge is essential for controlling risk and choosing appropriate financing options.

5. **Monitoring Operational Efficiency:** Through the analysis of ratios such as inventory turnover, receivables turnover, and asset turnover, startups can keep an eye on how efficiently their operations are running. By identifying inefficiencies in the use of resources and assets, these ratios assist startups in streamlining their operations and increasing profitability. Startups can evaluate the success of their operational strategies by monitoring these ratios over time.
6. **Planning and Forecasting:** For startups, ratio analysis is essential to financial planning and forecasting. Startups can forecast future performance and make well-informed decisions about budgeting, investment, and growth strategies by examining historical financial ratios. Ratios are also useful for establishing attainable goals and realistic financial projections.

To sum up, ratio analysis is crucial to the examination of startup financial statements. Startups can use it to analyze their financial performance, compare it to industry norms, pinpoint their advantages and disadvantages, assess their financial stability, track operational effectiveness, and make long-term plans. Startups can maximize financial resources, make well-informed decisions, and succeed over the long run by employing ratio analysis effectively.

3.6.1. The Key Considerations When Conducting Vertical and Horizontal Analysis in Financial Statement Analysis for Startup

Both vertical and horizontal analysis are crucial tools for evaluating the performance and financial health of a startup when doing financial statement analysis. These two techniques can offer insightful information about the company's financial standing, market trends, and possible growth areas. Here are the key considerations to keep in mind when conducting *vertical and horizontal analysis* for a startup:

1. **Understanding Vertical Analysis:** *Vertical analysis* involves analyzing the individual line items of *financial statements* in relation to a common base. This base is typically *the total revenue* or net sales for the period under consideration. It helps in assessing the composition and proportion of various expenses, assets, and liabilities in relation to the revenue generated.
2. **Reviewing Income Statement Through Vertical Analysis:** When conducting vertical analysis on the income statement, it is important to review the various expense categories as a percentage of net sales. This analysis provides insights into the cost structure and efficiency of the startup. For example, if the cost of goods sold (COGS) is increasing as a percentage of net sales, it may indicate issues with procurement or pricing strategies. Similarly, if selling and administrative expenses are growing rapidly, it may suggest

the need for cost control measures.

3. **Analyzing Balance Sheet Through Vertical Analysis:** Vertical analysis of the balance sheet involves reviewing the composition of assets and liabilities as a percentage of total assets or total liabilities, respectively. This analysis helps in understanding the capital structure and liquidity position of the startup. For example, if accounts payable are increasing as a percentage of total liabilities, it may indicate *potential cash flow issues* or *strained relationships* with suppliers.
4. **Interpreting Horizontal Analysis:** Horizontal analysis involves comparing financial statement data over multiple periods to identify trends and patterns. It helps in understanding the growth rate, stability, and consistency of various line items. By comparing historical data, startups can identify areas of improvement or *potential risks*.
5. **Assessing Income Statement Trends Through Horizontal Analysis:** When conducting horizontal analysis on the income statement, it is important to compare revenue, expenses, and profitability measures over multiple periods. This analysis can reveal growth rates, seasonality, and potential issues such as declining margins or increasing expenses. For example, if the cost of goods sold is consistently increasing at a higher rate than revenue, it may indicate pricing or cost control issues.
6. **Examining Balance Sheet Trends Through Horizontal Analysis:** *Horizontal analysis* of the balance sheet involves comparing assets, liabilities, and equity over time. This analysis can highlight changes in working capital, leverage, and *overall financial health*. For instance, if accounts receivable days are consistently increasing, it may suggest issues with *customer collections* or *credit policies*.
7. **Considering Industry Benchmarks:** In addition to conducting vertical and horizontal analysis, it is crucial to compare the startup's financial performance against industry benchmarks. This helps in understanding how the startup is performing relative to its peers and identifying areas of strength or weakness. Industry benchmarks can provide insights into *key financial ratios*, *profitability measures*, and *operating metrics*.
8. **identifying Key Performance Indicators:** To conduct effective vertical and horizontal analysis, startups should identify and track key performance indicators (KPIs) that are relevant to their industry and business model. KPIs such as gross margin, net profit margin, return on investment, and asset turnover ratio provide valuable insights into the financial performance and efficiency of the startup.
9. **Considering External Factors:** When conducting *financial statement analysis* for a startup, it is important to consider external factors that may impact the financial results. These factors may include changes in the economy, *industry trends*, regulatory environment, or competitive landscape. By considering these *external factors*, startups can gain a holistic understanding of their financial performance and make *informed decisions*.

Understanding these techniques and how to apply them thoroughly is necessary to conduct both vertical and horizontal analysis in financial statement analysis for startups. Start-ups can obtain important insights into their financial health, performance, and possible areas for improvement by taking into account the important factors mentioned above.

3.6.2. How Can Trend Analysis Be Used in Financial Statement Analysis for Startup?

When analyzing a startup's financial statement, trend analysis is a useful tool. Analysts can learn a lot about the financial performance and health of a startup by looking at trends in financial data over time.

Here are several ways in which trend analysis can be used in financial statement analysis for startups:

1. **Identifying Patterns and Trends:** Trend analysis allows analysts to identify patterns and trends in financial data. By looking at the historical performance of a startup, analysts can determine whether certain financial metrics are improving or deteriorating over time. This can help identify areas of strength and weakness within the startup's financials.
2. **Assessing Growth Potential:** Trend analysis can help assess the growth potential of a startup. By examining the growth rate of key financial metrics such as revenue, net income, and cash flow over time, analysts can determine whether the startup is on a growth trajectory. This information can be crucial for investors and stakeholders looking to evaluate the startup's potential for future profitability and success.
3. **Monitoring Financial Stability:** Trend analysis can also be used to monitor the financial stability of a startup. By analyzing trends in financial ratios such as liquidity ratios, solvency ratios, and profitability ratios, analysts can assess the startup's ability to meet its short-term and long-term financial obligations. This can help identify any potential financial risks and vulnerabilities that may exist within the startup.
4. **Benchmarking Against Industry Peers:** Trend analysis can be used to benchmark a startup's financial performance against its industry peers. By comparing the startup's financial ratios and trends to industry averages, analysts can gain insights into how the startup is performing relative to its competitors. This can help identify areas where the startup may be underperforming or outperforming its peers, and inform strategic decision-making.
5. **Identifying Seasonality and Cyclical Trends**: trend analysis can help identify seasonality and cyclical trends within a startup's financial data. By examining the historical performance of key financial metrics on a quarterly or annual basis, analysts can determine whether certain financial metrics exhibit recurring patterns or fluctuations. This information can be useful for forecasting future financial performance and planning for potential fluctuations in revenue and expenses.
6. **Evaluating the Effectiveness of Financial Strategies:** Trend

analysis can also be used to evaluate the effectiveness of financial strategies implemented by a startup. By examining trends in financial metrics such as return on investment, return on equity, and gross margin over time, analysts can assess the impact of strategic decisions on the startup's financial performance. This information can help management make informed decisions regarding the allocation of resources and the implementation of future financial strategies.

For startups, trend analysis is a useful tool for financial statement analysis. Analysts can learn about a startup's financial health, growth potential, stability, and efficacy of financial strategies by looking for patterns and trends in financial data. In order to make wise decisions and propel the startup's success, investors, stakeholders, and management may find this information to be extremely helpful.

3.6.3. Financial Statement Analysis for Startup and Why Is It Important

Financial statement analysis for startups is the process of looking over financial statements to evaluate the performance and health of a business, including the cash flow, income, and balance sheets. Through a thorough examination of these financial statements, lenders, investors, and other relevant parties can obtain important knowledge about the profitability, liquidity, solvency, and general sustainability of a startup.

Here are several key reasons why financial statement analysis is crucial for startups:

1. **Evaluating Profitability:** Financial statement analysis helps investors and lenders assess a startup's profitability. By analyzing the income statement, which shows the company's revenue, expenses, and net profit, stakeholders can determine whether the startup is generating consistent profits or facing losses. Understanding the profitability of a startup is essential for making informed investment or lending decisions.
2. **Assessing Liquidity:** Liquidity refers to a company's ability to meet its short-term obligations. Financial statement analysis allows stakeholders to evaluate a startup's liquidity by examining its current assets and liabilities. For example, by analyzing the balance sheet, which shows a company's assets, liabilities, and equity, stakeholders can determine if a startup has sufficient cash and other liquid assets to cover its immediate financial needs. This analysis is crucial for assessing a startup's ability to pay its bills, repay loans, and fund its operations.
3. **Analyzing Solvency:** Solvency refers to a company's ability to meet its long-term obligations. Financial statement analysis helps stakeholders gauge a startup's solvency by examining its long-term debt and equity. By reviewing the balance sheet and cash flow statement, stakeholders can evaluate a startup's ability to generate enough cash to meet its long-term debt obligations. This analysis is crucial for assessing a startup's financial stability and its ability to sustain its operations and repay its debts in the long run.
4. **Identifying Financial Trends:**

Financial statement analysis allows stakeholders to identify financial trends that may impact a startup's future performance. By comparing financial statements over multiple periods, stakeholders can identify patterns or changes in revenue, expenses, profitability ratios, or working capital ratios. This analysis helps stakeholders understand how a startup's financial performance has evolved and predict its future trajectory. For example, a declining profitability trend may indicate underlying issues that need to be addressed.

5. **Comparing Performance to Industry Benchmarks:** Financial statement analysis enables stakeholders to compare a startup's financial performance to industry benchmarks or competitors. By benchmarking key financial ratios such as profitability ratios, liquidity ratios, and solvency ratios against industry averages or similar companies, stakeholders can assess how a startup's financial performance stacks up. This analysis helps identify areas of strength or weakness and allows stakeholders to make informed decisions accordingly.
6. **Supporting Decision-Making:** Financial statement analysis provides stakeholders with valuable information to support decision-making. Whether it's evaluating an investment opportunity, deciding to lend money to a startup, or assessing the financial health of a potential business partner, financial statement analysis helps stakeholders make informed decisions. By understanding a startup's financial position, performance, and trends, stakeholders can assess risks and opportunities, allocate resources effectively, and make strategic decisions that align with their goals.

Analyzing financial statements is essential for evaluating startups' performance and financial health. It supports decision-making by assisting stakeholders in identifying financial trends, assessing profitability, assessing liquidity and solvency, and comparing performance to industry benchmarks. Lenders, investors, and other stakeholders can help startups succeed in the long run by making well-informed decisions based on thorough financial statement analysis.

3.6.4. Benchmarking Used in Financial Statement Analysis for Startup

For startups, benchmarking is a useful tool for financial statement analysis. It entails assessing a startup's financial performance in comparison to competitors or peers in the industry to determine its strengths and weaknesses. Startups can obtain important insights into their financial health and make well-informed decisions to enhance their performance by benchmarking their financial statements. Here are several ways benchmarking can be used in *financial statement analysis* for startups:

1. **Identifying Industry Norms and Standards:** benchmarking allows startups to compare their financial ratios and performance metrics against industry averages. This helps them understand how they stack up against their competitors and identify areas where they

may be underperforming or outperforming.

2. **Assessing Financial Stability and Liquidity:** By benchmarking liquidity ratios such as the current ratio and quick ratio, startups can determine their ability to meet short-term obligations and determine if they have an optimal level of cash and working capital.
3. **Evaluating profitability:** Benchmarking profitability ratios, such as gross profit margin, operating profit margin, and net profit margin, helps startups gauge their profitability compared to industry peers. This analysis can highlight areas where the startup may need to improve cost control or pricing strategies.
4. **Analyzing Efficiency and Operational Performance:** By benchmarking efficiency ratios such as asset turnover and inventory turnover, startups can determine how effectively they are utilizing their assets and managing their inventory. This analysis helps identify areas where the startup can improve operational efficiency and reduce costs.
5. **Identifying Areas for Improvement:** Benchmarking financial statements not only helps startups identify areas of strength but also areas where they can improve. By comparing their financial performance with industry peers, startups can identify specific weaknesses or inefficiencies and develop strategies to address them.
6. **Setting Realistic Financial Goals:** Benchmarking can help startups set realistic financial goals by providing them with a benchmark or standard to strive for. By comparing their financial performance against industry averages, startups can set targets that are achievable and realistic.
7. **Attracting Investors and Lenders:** benchmarking financial performance against industry standards can be a powerful tool for startups seeking funding. By demonstrating that their financial performance is in line with or better than industry averages, startups can increase their credibility and attractiveness to investors and lenders.
8. **Monitoring Progress Over Time:** By regularly benchmarking their financial statements, startups can track their progress over time. This allows them to see if their financial performance is improving or deteriorating and take necessary actions accordingly.

For startups, benchmarking is a useful tool for financial statement analysis. It enables startups to assess their strengths and weaknesses by comparing their financial performance to industry averages. Startups can use benchmarking to improve their financial health by attracting investors and lenders, setting reasonable financial goals, and making well-informed decisions.

3.6.5. Limitations of Financial Statement Analysis for Startup

Lenders, investors, and other stakeholders use financial statement analysis as a critical tool to evaluate a company's performance and financial health. On the other hand, there are some restrictions that must be taken into account when handling startups. The main drawbacks of financial statement analysis for startups will be covered in this response.

1. **Limited Historical Data:** Startups often have a limited operating history, making it difficult to analyze their financial statements. Traditional financial ratios and benchmarks may not be applicable or meaningful for startups with only a few years of data. This makes it challenging to evaluate their financial performance and predict future trends based on historical financial statements.
2. **Lack of Comparability:** Startups operate in unique and dynamic business environments, often with innovative business models. As a result, it can be challenging to find comparable companies or industry benchmarks for financial statement analysis. Without reliable benchmarks, it becomes difficult to assess the startup's financial performance relative to its peers and industry standards.
3. **Volatility and Uncertainty:** Startups are more susceptible to market fluctuations and economic uncertainties compared to established companies. Their financial statements may reflect significant fluctuations in revenue, expenses, and cash flows, making it challenging to identify trends or assess their stability. Startups may also face uncertainties related to their product/service demand, market penetration, and competition, which can impact their financial performance unpredictably.
4. **Non-Traditional Metrics:** Startups often use non-traditional metrics to measure their performance, such as customer acquisition cost, lifetime value of a customer, and churn rate. These metrics may not be reflected in the financial statements or may require additional data to calculate accurately. Therefore, relying solely on financial statement analysis may not provide a complete picture of a startup's performance and value.
5. **Limited Disclosure:** Startups may not disclose all relevant financial information due to competitive or strategic reasons. They may choose to keep certain metrics confidential or provide limited details in their financial statements. This lack of transparency can hinder the effectiveness of financial statement analysis, as analysts may not have access to key information necessary to make informed decisions.
6. **Accounting Challenges:** Startups often face unique accounting challenges, especially related to revenue recognition, valuation of intangible assets, and equity-based compensation. These challenges may result in inconsistencies or complexities in their financial statements, making it difficult to accurately assess their financial position and performance.
7. **Rapid Growth and Scalability:** Startups aim to achieve rapid growth and scalability, which can impact their financial statements. Growth-oriented startups may prioritize revenue growth over profitability, leading to negative net income and cash flow in the initial years. This can make it challenging to evaluate their financial viability and sustainability based on traditional financial ratios.
8. **Limited Liquidity and Capital Constraints:** Startups often face liquidity and capital constraints, which can impact their financial

statements. Cash flows may be irregular or negative due to high investments in research and development, marketing, and expansion activities. These constraints can affect their ability to meet short-term obligations, resulting in a weaker financial position.

Applying financial statement analysis to startups has certain drawbacks. These restrictions include the following: insufficient historical data, incompatibility, volatility, and uncertainty; non-traditional metrics; restricted disclosure; difficulties with accounting; rapid expansion; and capital limitations. To obtain a thorough grasp of a startup's financial situation and future prospects, investors and analysts must take these limitations into account and complement financial statement analysis with other assessment techniques.

3.6.6. Break-Even Analysis Play in Financial Statement Analysis for Startup

An important tool for evaluating a startup's financial health and viability is break-even analysis, which is a critical part of financial statement analysis. A startup's profitability, risk, and potential growth can all be understood by using break-even analysis, which calculates the point at which total revenue plus total costs equals the startup. This comprehensive and educational response will go over the many uses and advantages of break-even analysis for new businesses.

1. **Definition and Calculation:** Break-even analysis is a financial tool that helps identify the point at which a startup experiences neither a profit nor a loss due to its total revenue equaling its total costs. The difference between the selling price per unit and the variable cost per unit is divided by fixed costs to determine the break-even point. The number of units a startup must sell to pay its expenses is determined by this calculation.
2. **Assessing Profitability:** Break-even analysis determines the lowest quantity of sales necessary to cover costs, which aids startups in understanding their profitability. Startups can assess whether they are making money or not by comparing their actual sales volume to the break-even point. A startup is profitable if its sales volume surpasses its break-even point. Conversely, the startup is losing money if the sales volume is less than the break-even point.
3. **Risk Assessment:** Startups can evaluate the amount of risk involved in their operations with the help of break-even analysis. Through the analysis of the break-even point, startups can ascertain the lowest sales volume necessary to meet their expenses. This data aids in determining how susceptible the startup is to variations in expenses or sales volume. High break-even point startups carry a higher risk because they are more vulnerable to market volatility and economic downturns.
4. **Establishing Pricing Strategies:** Break-even analysis helps new businesses determine the best prices to offer. Startups can ascertain the effect of varying pricing levels on their break-even point by comprehending the relationship among costs, sales volume, and

pricing. As an example, raising the unit selling price could lead to a higher break-even point but also higher profit margins. On the other hand, cutting the selling price per unit might result in a lower break-even point but lower profit margins. Startups can find the ideal balance between pricing and profitability with the aid of break-even analysis.

5. **Planning Growth and Expansion:** In order to plan for growth and expansion, startups must perform break-even analysis. Startups can achieve profitable growth by setting realistic sales targets by understanding the break-even point. Additionally, startups can assess how different growth strategies—like raising production levels or entering new markets—affect the break-even point. In order to make sure growth plans are financially viable, this analysis helps determine the timing and viability of the plans.
6. **Evaluating Cost structure and Efficiency:** Startups can assess their efficiency and cost structure with break-even analysis. Startups can find areas of inefficiency and possible cost savings by examining the fixed and variable costs. To reduce the break-even point, for instance, startups with high fixed costs might think about outsourcing some functions or putting cost-cutting measures in place. Break-even analysis aids in the cost structure optimization and general efficiency improvement of startups.
7. **Benchmarking and Performance Comparison:** Startups can use break-even analysis to compare their performance to competitors and industry norms. Startups can evaluate their competitiveness and relative position by comparing their break-even point to industry averages. Additionally, by comparing break-even points, profit margins, and pricing strategies, startups can use break-even analysis to assess how they are performing in relation to their competitors. This data aids in pinpointing areas in need of development and prospective advantages over competitors.

An essential component of financial statement analysis for startups is break-even analysis. It offers insightful information about the profitability, risk, pricing policies, growth strategy, cost structure, and performance comparison of a startup. Startups can increase their odds of long-term success, optimize their operations, and make well-informed financial decisions by learning and applying break-even analysis.

3.6.7. Financial Statement Analysis for Startup help in Evaluating the Company's Performance

A startup's financial statement analysis is an essential tool for assessing the performance of the business. Investors, lenders, and other stakeholders can obtain important insights into the company's financial health and make well-informed decisions by looking over various financial statements, including the cash flow statement, income statement, and balance sheet. This response will go over a number of methods that financial statement analysis can help assess a startup's performance.

1. **Assessing Profitability:** Financial statement analysis allows stakeholders to analyze a startup's

profitability. By examining the income statement, investors can identify the company's revenue, expenses, and net income. This helps determine whether the startup is generating profits or incurring losses. Additionally, analyzing profitability ratios such as gross profit margin, operating profit margin, and net profit margin provides further insights into the company's ability to generate profits from its operations.

2. **Evaluating Liquidity:** Liquidity is a vital aspect of a startup's financial health. Financial statement analysis helps assess the company's ability to meet its short-term obligations. By examining the balance sheet and cash flow statement, investors can calculate liquidity ratios such as the current ratio and quick ratio. These ratios provide insights into the startup's ability to pay off its current liabilities using *its current assets*. A higher ratio indicates better liquidity, which is crucial for the company's survival and growth.
3. **Analyzing Solvency:** Solvency analysis is essential to determine a startup's long-term financial viability. By examining the balance sheet and related ratios, stakeholders can assess the company's ability to meet its long-term debt obligations. Debt ratios such as debt-to-equity ratio and interest coverage ratio provide insights into the startup's solvency. A lower debt ratio indicates lower financial risk, while a higher interest coverage ratio suggests the company can comfortably meet its interest payments.
4. **Understanding Cash Flow:** cash flow analysis is crucial for evaluating a startup's ability to generate cash and manage its cash flows effectively. The cash flow statement provides information on the company's operating, investing, and financing activities. By analyzing the cash flow statement, stakeholders can assess the startup's ability to generate positive cash flows from its core business operations. It also allows them to evaluate the company's investing and financing activities, such as capital expenditures, debt repayments, and *equity financing*.
5. **Identifying Growth Potential:** Financial statement analysis helps identify a startup's growth potential. By examining the income statement and related ratios, stakeholders can assess the company's revenue growth rate, profit growth rate, and return on investment. These indicators provide insights into the startup's ability to increase its sales, expand its market share, and generate attractive returns for investors. Additionally, analyzing trends in key financial metrics over time can provide insights into the company's historical performance and its growth trajectory.
6. **Benchmarking Against Industry Peers:** Financial statement analysis allows stakeholders to compare a startup's performance with industry peers. By benchmarking key financial ratios against industry averages, stakeholders can assess the company's relative performance and competitive positioning. This comparison provides insights into the startup's strengths and

weaknesses compared to its competitors, helping investors and lenders make more informed investment decisions.

An analysis of the financial statements is essential for assessing the performance of a startup. Through evaluation of the startup's profitability, liquidity, solvency, cash flow, growth potential, and comparison with industry peers, stakeholders can obtain significant understanding of the financial well-being and make well-informed decisions. This analysis aids in determining the startup's long-term viability, risk assessment, and strengths and weaknesses.

3.6.8. Some Common Red Flags to Look for in Financial Statement Analysis for Startup

A startup's financial statements should always be examined carefully for any warning signs that point to possible problems or hazards. These warning signs can provide important information about the financial stability of the business and assist stakeholders or investors in making defensible choices. The following are typical warning signs for startups to watch out for in their financial statement analysis:

1. **Negative or Declining Cash Flow:** Cash flow is one of the most critical indicators of a company's financial health. Negative or declining cash flow can be a red flag, as it may indicate that the startup is not generating enough cash to cover its operating expenses or invest in growth. This could signal potential liquidity issues or an unsustainable business model.
2. **High Burn Rate:** The burn rate refers to the rate at which a company is using up its cash reserves to finance its operations. A high burn rate could be a red flag, especially if it exceeds the company's revenue growth rate. It suggests that the startup is spending more money than it is generating, which can lead to a rapid depletion of its cash reserves and potential financial instability.
3. **Increasing Debt Levels:** A startup that relies heavily on debt financing can be a cause for concern. While debt can be used strategically to finance growth, excessive debt levels can become problematic, especially if the company is unable to generate sufficient cash flow to service its debt payments. Increasing debt levels may indicate that the startup is struggling to fund its operations or expand without relying on debt, which can increase its financial risk.
4. **Lack of Profitability or Declining Margins:** Profitability is a key metric that investors often look for when evaluating startups. A lack of profitability or declining profit margins can be a red flag, as it suggests that the business is not generating enough revenue to cover its costs and make a profit. This could indicate pricing pressures, increased competition, or an inefficient cost structure, all of which may hinder the company's long-term sustainability.
5. **Inconsistent or Unreliable Financial Reporting:** Inaccurate or unreliable financial statements can make it difficult to assess the true financial position of a startup. Red flags in this area may include frequent restatements of

financial results, inconsistencies in accounting practices, or a lack of transparency in reporting. These issues can erode investor confidence and raise concerns about the integrity of the company's financial reporting.

6. **Overreliance on a Single Customer or Few Customers:** Startups that depend heavily on one or a few customers for a significant portion of their revenue are at risk if they lose those customers. This concentration of revenue can be a red flag as it exposes the company to a high level of customer dependency. If the key customer(s) decide to reduce or terminate their business relationship, the startup's revenue could decline significantly, putting its financial stability at risk.
7. **Poor Working Capital Management:** Working capital is the measure of a company's short-term liquidity and its ability to meet its current obligations. Red flags in this area may include consistently high levels of accounts payable, slow collections of accounts receivable, or excessive inventory levels. These issues can indicate poor working capital management, which can strain the startup's ability to pay its bills, invest in growth, or respond to unexpected expenses.
8. **Lack of Transparency or Disclosure:** Startups that are not transparent in their financial reporting or provide limited disclosures can raise concerns. It is important for stakeholders to have access to sufficient information to evaluate the company's financial performance and assess the risks associated with their investment. A lack of transparency may indicate that the startup has something to hide or that it may not be following appropriate accounting practices.

It's important to take these typical warning signs into careful consideration when doing a comprehensive financial statement analysis for startups.

Investors and stakeholders can reduce potential risks and make better decisions by recognizing and resolving these issues early on. To fully comprehend the startup's financial situation and future prospects, financial statement analysis should be utilized as a tool in conjunction with other types of due diligence.

CASE STUDY

FINANCIAL STATEMENTS OF APPLE INC.

Let's now consider the financial statements of Apple Inc. shown in Exhibits 2.7 to 2.10. Apple's financial statements are more complex than Fashion Company's financial statements. For example, Apple's income statement includes more accounts than Fashion Company's. Yet, both companies' income statements show revenues and expenses, and the resulting net income. Apple's income statement, entitled "Consolidated Statements of Operations," is shown in Exhibit 2.7.

Exhibit 2.7. Apple Inc. Consolidated Statements of Operations (Adapted)

	Years ended September 25,		
	20Y3 ($ Millions)	20Y2 ($ Millions)	20Y1 ($ Millions)
Net sales	$65,225	$42,905	$37,491
Cost of goods sold	39,541	25,683	24,294
Gross margin	25,684	17,222	13,197
Operating expenses:			
Research and development	1,782	1,333	1,109
Selling, general and administrative	5,517	4,149	3,761
Total operating expenses	7,299	5,482	4,870
Operating income	18,385	11,740	8,327
Other income and expenses	155	326	620
Income before income tax expense	18,540	12,066	8,947
Income tax expense	4,527	3,831	2,828
Net income	$14,013	$8,235	$6,119

https://demo.webassign.net/smifinacct2/2-exhibit-07–10.pdf.

Apple is a parent firm, which means it owns other firms called "subsidiaries." To provide a full accounting of all of the resources that Apple controls, the amounts shown on the financial statements include figures for both Apple and its subsidiaries. The financial statements for most companies show the consolidation of the parent firm and its subsidiary firms and use the word "consolidated" in financial statement titles. You will note that Apple's income statement shows three years' data for comparative purposes. What is the trend? Apple has experienced dramatic increases in net income each year. The other financial statements should be reviewed to further understand how this income was generated and used.

Apple's Statement of Shareholders' Equity is shown in Exhibit 2.8. Having an increase in retained earnings for three years in a row is also a good sign for Apple. Retained earnings went from $9.1 billion in the beginning of 20Y1 to over $37 million in 20Y3.

Exhibit 2.8. Apple Inc. Consolidated Statements of Retained Earnings (Adapted)

	Years ended September 25,		
	20Y3 ($ Millions)	20Y2 ($ Millions)	20Y1 ($ Millions)
Beginning retained earnings	$23,353	$15,129	$9,111
Net income	14,013	8,235	6,119
Dividends	(197)	(11)	(101)
Ending retained earnings	$37,169	$23,353	$15,129

Apple's balance sheet includes data for two years, as shown in Exhibit 2.9. Apple's assets are categorized into current assets and long-term assets. Current assets are those that will be used up, sold, or converted to cash within the year, or the normal operating cycle if longer than one year. All other assets are referred to as "long-term assets."

Apple's liabilities are also categorized into current and long-term. Current liabilities are those debts that are payable within one year, or within the firm's normal operating cycle if more than one year. All other debts are referred to as "long-term liabilities." Categorizing assets and liabilities into current and long-term is necessary for all companies.

Did the company's financial position improve or decline? From 20Y2 to 20Y3, Apple's total assets increased by approximately $27.7 million. Total liabilities increased by $11.5 million. Stockholders' equity decreased by over $16 million. This information, along with the large increases in income has made Apple an appealing investment for many.

Exhibit 2.9. Apple Inc. Consolidated Balance Sheets (Adapted)

	Years ended September 25,	
	20Y3 ($ Millions)	20Y2 ($ Millions)
ASSETS		
Current assets:		
Cash and cash equivalents	$11,261	$5,263
Short-term marketable securities	14,359	18,201
Accounts receivable, net	5,510	3,361
Inventories	1,051	455
Other current assets	9,497	4,275
Total current assets	41,678	31,555
Long-term marketable securities	25,391	10,528
Property, plant and equipment, net	4,768	2,954
Goodwill	741	206
Acquired intangible assets, net	342	247
Other assets	2,263	2,011
Total assets	$75,183	$47,501
LIABILITIES AND STOCKHOLDERS' EQUITY		
Current liabilities:		
Accounts payable	$12,015	$5,601
Accrued expenses	5,723	3,852
Deferred revenue	2,984	2,053
Total current liabilities	20,722	11,506
Deferred revenue — non-current	1,139	853
Other non-current liabilities	5,531	3,502
Total liabilities	27,392	15,861
Stockholders' Equity:		
Common Stock	10,668	8,210
Retained earnings	37,169	23,353
Accumulated other comprehensive income	(46)	77
Total stockholder's equity	47,791	31,640
Total liabilities and stockholder's equity	$75,183	$47,501

Apple's statement of cash flows provides data for multiple years, as shown in Exhibit 2.10. Apple has experienced an increase in cash flow from operations each year. The company's overall cash balance has fluctuated over the three years due primarily to investing decisions. The statement illustrates the company's ability to use its cash to continue ongoing operations and to consider new ventures. By reviewing the statement of cash flows, along with the other financial statements, the top management of Apple can assess the company's financial situation. They can make plans to achieve company goals, such as increasing sales and reducing expenses. For external users, such as investors and lenders, financial statements help them assess the likelihood of a good return on their investment or repayment of their loans.

Exhibit 2.10. Apple Inc. Consolidated Statements of Cash Flows (Adapted)

	Years ended September 25,		
	20Y3 ($ Millions)	20Y2 ($ Millions)	20Y1 ($ Millions)
Net cash provided by operating activities	$ 18,595	10,159	9,596
Net cash used in investing activities	(13,854)	(17,434)	(8,189)
Net cash provided by financing activities	1,257	663	1,116
Net increase (decrease) in cash	5,998	(6,612)	2,523
Cash and cash equivalent at beginning of year	5,263	11,875	9,352

Preparing financial statements requires entering data, making calculations, and presenting information in a readable format. To help with this formidable task, spreadsheet software, such as Microsoft Excel, is extremely useful. The boxed insert, "Focus on Technology," shows how to prepare an income statement using *Microsoft Excel.*

CLASS ACTIVITY

Students will report on how the company performs as compared to the industry norms and where the company stands relative to its competitors in the industry. The company's weak and/or strong areas of performance must be identified and recommendations for improvement presented.

SUMMARY

- The balance sheet is a financial snapshot of the firm, usually prepared at the end of the fiscal year. That is, it provides information about the condition of the firm at one particular point in time.
- Assets are divided by liquidity into two categories: current assets and fixed assets. Current assets consist of cash, accounts receivable and inventories.
- Accounts payable are generated when a company makes a purchase for raw materials or advertising but does not pay for it immediately.
- An income statement includes revenues earned, expenses paid, and the bottom line to the investors: net income. The income statement is like a movie: it provides a financial film of a firm over a period of time.
- The statement of cash flows is a summary of cash flows over the period of time reported. Cash flows are the difference between what a company brings in and what it pays out.
- The statement of shareholder equity describes the changes to a company's equity section of the balance sheet over a year.
- The statement of retained earnings reports the change in retained earnings over a year. In essence it is an abbreviated form of the statement of shareholders equity.
- Cross-sectional analysis is the comparison of one firm to other similar firms. A cross- section of an industry is used as a comparison for the firm's numbers.
- Another equally important method of financial analysis is time-series analysis, which involves comparing the firm's current performance to prior periods.
- Profitability ratios measure how effectively the firm uses its resources to generate income. The first three of the ratios reported here are probably the best known and most widely used of all financial ratios.
- Liquidity ratios measure the ability of a business to meet its short-term financial obligations.
- The inventory turnover ratio tells how many times during a year the firm's inventory is bought and sold.
- Total asset turnover ratio gives us an idea how effectively a firm uses its assets to generate sales.
- Debt management ratios measure how much a firm uses debt as a source of financing. When a company uses debt financing, they use other people's money to finance their business activities
- Profit margin is the amount of profit left over from each dollar of sales after expenses are paid.

REVIEW QUESTIONS

1. What is the balance sheet?
2. What is statement of retained earnings?
3. What are the goals of financial analysis?
4. How to analyze financial statement?
5. What is the role of ratio analysis in financial statement?

REFERENCES

1. Abdel-Khalik, A. R. (1974). On the usefulness of financial ratios to investors in common stock: A comment. *The Accounting Review, 49*(3), 547–550.
2. Adiel, R. (1996). Reinsurance and the management of regulatory ratios and taxes in the property-casualty insurance industry. *Journal of Accounting and Economics, 22*(1–3), 207–240.
3. Altman, E. I. (1976). Capitalization of leases and the predictability of financial ratios: A comment. *The Accounting Review, 51*(2), 408–412.
4. Baber, W. R., Roberts, A. A., & Visvanathan, G. (2001). Charitable organizations' strategies and program-spending ratios. *Accounting Horizons, 15*(4), 329–343.
5. Barlas, S. (2017). SEC changes ahead for reporting compensation ratios? *Strategic Finance, 98*(11), 17.
6. Beaver, W. H. (1966). Financial ratios as predictors of failure. *Journal of Accounting Research, 4*(Empirical Research in Accounting: Selected Studies), 71–111.
7. Beaver, W. H. (1968). Market prices, financial ratios, and the prediction of failure. *Journal of Accounting Research, 6*(2), 179–192.
8. Beaver, W. H., Carreia, M., & McNichols, M. F. (2012). Do differences in financial reporting attributes impair the predictive ability of financial ratios for bankruptcy? *Review of Accounting Studies, 17*(4), 969–1010.
9. Beaver, W. H., McNichols, M. F., & Rhie, J. (2005). Have financial statements become less informative? Evidence from the ability of financial ratios to predict bankruptcy. *Review of Accounting Studies, 10*(1), 93–122.
10. Biddle, G. C. (1988). Discussion of "Inventory accounting and earnings/price ratios: A puzzle". *Contemporary Accounting Research, 5*(1), 389–396.
11. Bildersee, J. S. (1978). Discussion of the impact of price-level adjustment in the context of risk assessment and the effect of general price-level adjustments on the predictive ability of financial ratios. *Journal of Accounting Research, 16*(Studies on Changes in General and Specific Prices), 285–292.
12. Bonsack, R. A. (1985). Inventory performance ratios–Fact or fiction? *Journal of Accountancy and EDP, 3*(3), 61–65.
13. Bunker, R. B., Cagle, C., & Harris, D. (2019). A liquidity ratio analysis of lean vs. not-lean operations. *Management Accounting Quarterly, 20*(2), 10–16.

14. Burrell, O. K. (1928). A teaching device in ratios and turnovers. *The Accounting Review, 3*(3), 274–277.

15. Casey Jr., C. J. (1980). The usefulness of accounting ratios for subjects' predictions of corporate failure: Replication and extensions. *Journal of Accounting Research, 18*(2), 603–613.

16. Cashwell, K., Copley, P., & Dugan, M. (2019). Using ratio analysis to manage not-for-profit organizations. *The CPA Journal, 89*(5), 52–57.

17. Chue, T. K. (2015). Understanding cross-country differences in valuation ratios: A variance decomposition approach. *Contemporary Accounting Research, 32*(4), 1617–1640.

18. Crandell, J. C. (1936). Ratios available for financial analysis. *N.A.C.A. Bulletin, 17*(15), 1349–1382.

19. Davis, H. Z., & Peles, Y. C. (1993). Measuring equilibrating forces of financial ratios. *The Accounting Review, 68*(4), 725–747.

20. Deakin, E. B. (1976). Distributions of financial accounting ratios: Some empirical evidence. *The Accounting Review, 51*(1), 90–96.

21. Derstine, R. P., & Huefner, R. J. (1974). LIFO-FIFO, accounting ratios and market risk. *Journal of Accounting Research, 12*(2), 216–234.

22. Ding, K., Peng, X., & Wang, Y. (2019). A machine learning-based peer selection method with financial ratios. *Accounting Horizons, 33*(3), 75–87.

23. Drum, J., Stangle, B., & Starfield, R. (2018). Keeping covenants: Getting debt ratios right. *Journal of Accountancy, 225*(6), 34–38.

24. Easton, P. D. (2004). PE ratios, PEG ratios, and estimating the implied expected rate of return on equity capital. *The Accounting Review, 79*(1), 73–95.

25. Elam, R. (1975). The effect of lease data on the predictive ability of financial ratios. *The Accounting Review, 50*(1), 25–43.

26. Elam, R. (1976). Capitalization of leases and the predictability of financial ratios: A reply. *The Accounting Review, 51*(2), 413–414.

27. Ford, H. C. (1968). Ratios to standard direct cost. *Management Accounting, 49*(1), 34–35.

28. Frecka, T. J., & Hopwood, W. S. (1983). The effects of outliers on the cross-sectional distributional properties of financial ratios. *The Accounting Review, 58*(1), 115–128.

29. Gibson, C. H. (1982). How industry perceives financial ratios. *Management Accounting, 63*(10), 13–19.

30. Gombola, M. J., & Ketz, J. E. (1983). A note on cash flow and classification patterns of financial ratios. *The Accounting Review, 58*(1), 105–114.

31. Greenlee, J. S., Randolph, D. W., & Richtermeyer, S. B. (2011). Better analytical reviews of charitable organizations: Using financial ratios and benchmarks. *The CPA Journal, 81*(7), 32–36.

32. Grove, H., & Clouse, M. (2014). Using fraud models and ratios to improve cross-border forensic analysis: Examples with Chinese IPO and RTO companies. *Journal*

of Forensic & Investigative Accounting, 6(3), 189–235.

33. Gupta, M. C., & Huefner, R. J. (1972). A cluster analysis study of financial ratios and industry characteristics. *Journal of Accounting Research, 10*(1), 77–95.
34. Halkos, G. E., & Salamouris, D. S. (2004). Efficiency measurement of the Greek commercial banks with the use of financial ratios: A data envelopment analysis approach. *Management Accounting Research, 15*(2), 201–224.
35. Harvard Business Review. (1925). Summaries of business research: The use of financial ratios. *Harvard Business Review, 4*(1), 79–93.
36. Heilman, E. A. (1933). Comments and questions on the use of ratios. *The Accounting Review, 8*(3), 246–247.
37. Hill, J. A. (1940). Basic standard cost accounting employing the use of cost ratios. *N.A.C.A. Bulletin, 21*(10), 693–704.
38. Hopwood, W. S., & Schaefer, T. F. (1988). Incremental information content of earnings- and nonearnings-based financial ratios. *Contemporary Accounting Research, 5*(1), 318–342.
39. Horrigan, J. (1966). The determination of long-term credit standing with financial ratios. *Journal of Accounting Research, 4*(Supplement), 44–62.
40. Joehnk, M. D., & McGrail, G. R. (1977). Benefit-cost ratios for family practice residency centers. *Management Accounting, 58*(8), 41–46.
41. Justin, W. H. (1924). Operating control through scientific analysis. *Journal of Accountancy, 38*(3), 183–195.
42. Kallapur, S. (1994). Dividend payout ratios as determinants of earnings response coefficients: A test of the free cash flow theory. *Journal of Accounting and Economics, 17*(3), 359–375.
43. Kaminski, K. A., & Wetzel, T. S. (2004). Financial ratios and fraud: An exploratory study using chaos theory. *Journal of Forensic Accounting, 5*, 147–172.
44. Kennedy, H. A. (1975). A behavioral study of the usefulness of four financial ratios. *Journal of Accounting Research, 13*(1), 97–116.
45. Ketz, J. E. (1978). The effect of general price-level adjustments on the predictive ability of financial ratios. *Journal of Accounting Research, 16*(Studies on Changes in General and Specific Prices), 273–284.
46. Koot, R. S., & Walker, D. A. (1972). A reconsideration of the 'great ratios' of economics. *Decision Sciences, 3*(3), 115–123.
47. Kraten, M. (2016). Reimaging the financial ratios. *The CPA Journal, 86*(6), 14.
48. Lai, C. (2020). A note on a framework for valuation ratios on fundamentals. *Contemporary Accounting Research, 37*(4), 2213–2223.
49. Larcker, D. F. (1989). Discussion of accounting measurement, price-earnings ratios, and the information content of security prices. *Journal of Accounting Research, 27*(Studies on The Information Content of Accounting Earnings), 145–152.
50. Lee, C. J. (1984). The speed of adjustment of financial ratios: An error-in-variable problem. *Journal of Accounting Research, 22*(2), 776–781.

51. Lee, C. J. (1988). Inventory accounting and earnings/price ratios: A puzzle. *Contemporary Accounting Research, 5*(1), 371–388.
52. Lee, R. T. (2014). How cost ratios can destroy value. *Journal of Corporate Accounting & Finance, 25*(2), 13–18.
53. Lev, B. (1969). Industry averages as targets for financial ratios. *Journal of Accounting Research, 7*(2), 290–299.
54. Lev, B., & Sunder, S. (1979). Methodological issues in the use of financial ratios. *Journal of Accounting and Economics, 1*(3), 187–210.
55. Libby, R. (1975). Accounting ratios and the prediction of failure: Some behavioral evidence. *Journal of Accounting Research, 13*(1), 150–161.
56. Linares-Mustaros, S., Coenders, G., & Vives-Mestres, M. (2018). Financial performance and distress profiles: From classification according to financial ratios to compositional classification. *Advances in Accounting, 40*, 1–10.
57. Lueg, R., Punda, P., & Burkert, M. (2014). Does transition to IFRS substantially affect key financial ratios in shareholder-oriented common law regimes? Evidence from the UK. *Advances in Accounting, 30*(1), 241–250.
58. Manes, R. P., & Schaefer, T. F. (1986). Relating financial leverage to annual report ratios. *Issues in Accounting Education, 1*(2), 261–267.
59. McLeay, S., & Trigueiros, D. (2002). Proportionate growth and the theoretical foundations of financial ratios. *Abacus, 38*(3), 297–316.
60. Mears, P. K. (1966). Discussion of financial ratios as predictors of failure. *Journal of Accounting Research, 4*(Empirical Research in Accounting: Selected Studies), 119–122.
61. Mecimore, C. D. (1968a). Classifying and selecting financial ratios. *Management Accounting, 49*(8), 11–17.
62. Mecimore, C. D. (1968b). Some empirical distributions of financial ratios. *Management Accounting, 50*(3), 13–16.
63. Morrison, D. G. (1970). On forming confidence intervals for certain Poisson ratios. *Decision Sciences, 1*(1–2), 234–236.
64. Mucklow, W. (1924). Financial and operating ratios in management. *Journal of Accountancy, 37*(2), 152–154.
65. Mulford, C. W. (1985). The importance of a market value measurement of debt in leverage ratios: Replication and extensions. *Journal of Accounting Research, 23*(2), 897–906.
66. Neter, J. (1966). Discussion of financial ratios as predictors of failure. *Journal of Accounting Research, 4*(Empirical Research in Accounting: Selected Studies), 112–118.
67. Nezlobin, A., Rajan, M. V., & Reichelstein, S. (2016). Structural properties of the price-to-earnings and price-to-book ratios. *Review of Accounting Studies, 21*(2), 438–472.
68. Nissim, D., & Penman, S. H. (2003). Financial statement analysis of leverage and how it informs about profitability and price-to-book ratios. *Review of Accounting Studies, 8*(4), 531–560.

69. Norgaard, R. L., & Pettway, R. H. (1966). Evaluating average ratios used in capital budgeting. *Management Accounting, 48*(6), 16–20.

70. O'Connor, M. C. (1973). On the usefulness of financial ratios to investors in common stock. *The Accounting Review, 48*(2), 339–352.

71. O'Connor, M. C. (1974). On the usefulness of financial ratios to investors in common stock: A reply. *The Accounting Review, 49*(3), 551–556.

72. Ohlson, J. A. (1980). Financial ratios and the probabilistic prediction of bankruptcy. *Journal of Accounting Research, 18*(1), 109–131.

73. Ohlson, J. A. (1983). Price-earnings ratios and earnings capitalization under uncertainty. *Journal of Accounting Research, 21*(1), 141–154.

74. Patell, J. M. (1978). Discussion of the impact of price-level adjustment in the context of risk assessment and the effect of general price-level adjustments on the predictive ability of financial ratios. *Journal of Accounting Research, 16*(Studies on Changes in General and Specific Prices), 293–300.

75. Paton, W. A. (1928). Limitations of financial and operating ratios. *The Accounting Review, 3*(3), 252–260.

76. Peck, L. G. (1966). Discussion of the determination of long-term credit standing with financial ratios. *Journal of Accounting Research, 4*(Empirical Research in Accounting: Selected Studies), 63–66.

77. Peles, Y. C., & Schneller, M. I. (1979). Liquidity ratios and industry averages–New evidence. *Abacus, 15*(1), 13–22.

78. Penman, S. H. (1996). The articulation of price-earnings ratios and market-to-book ratios and the evaluation of growth. *Journal of Accounting Research, 34*(2), 235–259.

79. Quosigk, B. M., & Forgione, D. A. (2018). The association of program ratios and consolidation choices: Evidence from nonprofit hospitals. *Accounting Horizons, 32*(4), 147–162.

80. Rickey, K. R. (1963). How accountants can help management manage. *N.A.A. Bulletin, 45*(9), 25–36.

81. Sharp, D. (1970). The effect of direct costing on the relative size of financial ratios. *Management Accounting, 52*(5), 14–18.

82. Tosi, H., & Patt, H. (1967). Administrative ratios and organizational size. *The Academy of Management Journal, 10*(2), 161–168.

83. Tucker, S. A. (1962). A system of managerial control using "live" ratios and control charts. *N.A.A. Bulletin, 43*(8), 5–24.

84. Valencia, A., Smith, T. J., & Ang, J. (2013). The effect of noisy fair value measures on bank capital adequacy ratios. *Accounting Horizons, 27*(4), 693–710.

85. Von Rosen, U. F. (1924). Operating ratios and costs as guides to management. *National Association of Cost Accountants Official Publications, 6*(12), 4–11.

86. Wallace, W. A. (1996). Editor's addendum: Ratios for your use in extending internationalization in accounting courses. *Issues in Accounting Education, 11*(2), 337–343.

87. Watson, C. J. (1990). Multivariate distributional properties, outliers, and transformation of financial ratios. *The Accounting Review, 65*(3), 682–695.

88. West, R. R. (1966). Discussion of the determination of long-term credit standing with financial ratios. *Journal of Accounting Research, 4*(Empirical Research in Accounting: Selected Studies), 67–70.

89. Westerdahl, W. E. (1961). Comparing the company with its industry by ratios. *N.A.A. Bulletin, 43*(3), 29–42.

90. Wilcox, J. W. (1971). A simple theory of financial ratios as predictors of failure. *Journal of Accounting Research, 9*(2), 389–395.

91. Williamson, R. W. (1984). Evidence on the selective reporting of financial ratios. *The Accounting Review, 59*(2), 296–299.

92. Wyman, H. E. (1977). Standardized debt coverage ratios. *The Accounting Review, 52*(2), 503–507.

93. Youell, H. D. (1967). Inventory management through inventory ratios. *Management Accounting, 49*(2), 43–48.

CHAPTER

4 Forecasting Financial Statements

LEARNING OBJECTIVES

After studying this chapter, you will be able to:

- Understand the need and importance forecasting
- Learn about financial forecasting
- Know about revenue forecasting models
- Learn about a typical one-year projection
- Discuss on sensitivity analysis with projected financial statements.

KEY TERMS FROM THIS CHAPTER

Account targeting	Balance sheet	Budgeting
Capital expenditure	Cash flow	Depreciation
Financial forecasting	Financial risk	Forecasting
Income statement	Marketing	Prediction
Product forecasting	Sales forecasting	Sales territories
Revenue forecasting		

INTRODUCTION

While analyzing a company's current financial statements can be informative, doing so is not as insightful as analyzing its financial statements for the future. After all, a company's stock value is based on its projected earnings and dividends, and credit quality is determined by the likelihood that future debt service payments will be made on time. Investors do, in fact, look to the past for some indication of the future. However, examining already-reported financials won't probably give you a substantial advantage over rival investors because they are publicly accessible. The analyst needs to take action on the earnings and credit quality metrics that will show up on future statements in order to capture fundamental value that is not currently reflected in securities prices.

Naturally, an analyst cannot predict with absolute certainty the details of a company's future financial statements. However, financial projections are not just conjecture. The procedure is a continuation of past trends and connections, predicated on forecasts for market dynamics, economic circumstances, and managerial decisions.

The accuracy of the assumptions will determine how closely financial projections match actual future results. For this reason, analysts ought to actively seek out information beyond the statements. By growing their network among the suppliers, consumers, and rival businesses of the companies they study, they must continuously aim to increase the caliber of their assumptions.

4.1. NEED AND IMPORTANCE FORECASTING

Everybody is curious about what lies ahead. Some concerning themselves. Some in regard to others—their loved ones. Some in reference to their rivals. Not many people are merely inquisitive. If others are aware of future contingencies in advance, they should prepare themselves (PLAN). It's interesting to observe that we can't precisely predict the future. People save money for the future, for instance, to cover unexpected costs such as major illnesses and large bills, or to support their families and children in the event of an unexpected death. These backup plans might not materialize, or if they do, their impact might be so great that the overall savings fall short. That means that plans can be made and carried out to better handle contingencies if it is accurately known in advance.

Managers and decision-makers deal with the same issue in their respective fields of expertise. Since it takes time to finish an action, its purpose might not be achieved once it is finished if it takes a long enough amount of time.

- **Example:** As a manager, you must now acknowledge that the demand for your product exceeds the combined output of all producers. In order to capitalize on the significant supply gap and boost production, you choose to establish an additional plant. The plant's impact and production won't be felt for several years. By then, there might not be a significant demand gap because either the market has shrunk or more producers have begun to produce. Thus, by the time your plant is finished, it serves no purpose for which it was intended. Had you been aware of this circumstance sooner, you would have begun building the plant with the intention of finishing it today, which would have fulfilled the original intent behind its construction.

Every manager wants to know the precise nature of what is going to happen so they can plan ahead and take appropriate action when there is enough time to carry out the plan. The precision with which he predicts future events will determine how successful his plan will be. However, regardless of how precisely future events are known, every manager makes plans for them. That suggests that, to the best of his ability, discretion, and experience, he does attempt to predict the future.

4.1.1. Concept of Forecast

The process of making predictions about the future by taking into account past and present events is known as forecasting. In essence, it is a tool for making decisions that uses past data and trends to assist businesses in managing the impact of future uncertainty. It's a planning tool that helps companies map out their next course of action and make budgets that should account for any unforeseen circumstances (Figure 4.1).

Figure 4.1. *Forecasting.*

Source: https://cdn.corporatefinanceinstitute.com/assets/forecasting.jpeg.

Usually forecasting and predicting are used interchangeably in general usage. Adam and Ebert in their book Production and operation management have defined and distinguished the two as follows:

- **Forecasting**: "Is a process of estimating a future event by casting forward past data. The past data are systematically combined in a predetermined way to obtain the estimate of the future."
- **Prediction**: "Is a process of estimating a future event based on subjective considerations other than just past data; these subjective considerations need not be combined in a predetermined way."

A forecast, then, is an estimation of the future values of a few designated indicators in relation to a situation involving decision-making or planning. There are circumstances in which a single indicator forecast suffices, and others in which a multiple indicator forecast is required. Depending on how the forecast will be used, the quantity of indicators and level of detail needed will vary.

How far into the future is a matter of context. It should be sufficiently ahead of time to give the decision maker enough time to make a decision or plan and implement it by the time the anticipated situation materializes (Figure 4.2).

Thus;

Forecast (Time in future) ≥Time taken for preparation of plan + Time taken to implement the plan

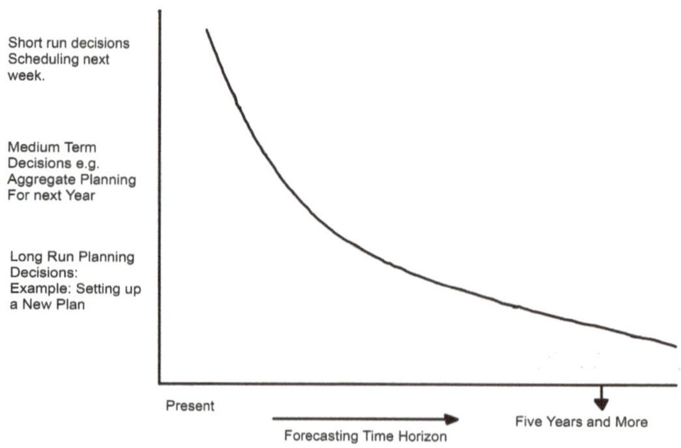

Figure 4.2. *Forecast time horizon indication for various categories of decision situations.*

Source: https://egyankosh.ac.in/bitstream/123456789/10803/1/Unit-4.pdf.

What methodology is to be used for projecting the past data into future? – depends on:

a. Type of past data
b. Pattern of past data
c. Time horizon of forecast

This method of projecting the past into future is termed as forecasting model. A large many statistical forecasting models are available suitable to different decisions.

4.1.2. Need of Forecast in Production/Operations Management

There are two basic reasons for the need of forecast in any field more so in production/ operation management.

4.1.2.1. Purpose

Every plan or action is thought out or developed in the present to address a contingency arising from a circumstance, state, or combination of conditions established in the future. These future circumstances provide a goal to strive for in order to maximize the benefits of these fixture conditions or, in the event that the conditions are unfavorable, to lessen their negative effects.

A plan or an action cannot be developed or carried out in void—that is, without a goal, objective, or target. Every strategy or course of action has an objective. The function "this something" is derived from a future condition (s).

Example: The process of establishing a second plant in order to boost output. Future demand-supply gaps will determine how much more output is needed and how big the new plant should be. A goal of higher production is determined in order to benefit from this future demand-supply gap. A strategy is created and implemented in order to meet this goal.

4.1.2.2. Time

Time is a resource that is needed for the preparation of a plan, the organization of resources for its implementation, plan implementation, and plan completion. Certain scenarios require very little time, while others require years. Therefore, appropriate actions can be planned and carried out "in-time" if future forecasts are available in advance.

- **Example:** Consider the same example discussed earlier -to take advantage of future demand – supply gap:

a. Plan or decision is to be taken. Through exploration several alternatives are considered and one of them chosen. In the above case, the alternative chosen is setup an additional plant.' This takes time suppose this is t1.

b. Location of the additional plant is to be chosen. This again takes time. Suppose this is Q.

c. i) Technology negotiations if any have to be conducted. ii) Land purchase negotiations, acquisition activities i.e., registration etc., have to be completed. iii) Permissions and clearances from various authorities as required under the law have to be applied for and obtained. iv) Provision for adequate finances is to be made. Suppose all this takes time t3.

d. Actual erection, construction, testing is to be completed and commercial production is to be started.

Suppose this takes time 0.

Thus, minimum time required to plan and implement is = t1 + t2 + t3 + t4 If as and when a situation arises, and planning and action can be completed immediately-without taking any time; perhaps forecasting would not be needed at all.

4.1.3. Budgeting vs. Forecasting

Budgeting and forecasting are both tools that help businesses plan for their future. However, the two are distinctly different in many ways:

- Financial statements, including anticipated revenue, expenses, cash flow, and investments, are created for a given period as part of the budgeting process. Since it takes input from several departments to produce a comprehensive and in-depth report, it is typically carried out with input from numerous departments. As a result, finishing the budgeting process takes time. The budget serves as a guide for the business's financial operations. A budget is, in other words, a plan for the future of a business.
- Forecasts are typically updated on a monthly or quarterly basis, whereas budgets are typically created for the full year. A business can use forecasting to project its future and, based on that projection, modify its budget and devote more or less money to a particular project. To sum up, forecasts influence budgets.

4.1.4. Forecasting Methods

When attempting to forecast potential future events, businesses can choose between qualitative and quantitative methods.

1. **Qualitative Method:** Qualitative forecasting, also referred to as the judgmental method, is based on the subjective opinions of experts or forecasters and produces subjective results. Because forecasts are non-mathematical and rely on the expertise, experience, and intuition of the forecaster, they are frequently skewed. One instance is when someone predicts the result of an NBA Finals game primarily out of interest and self-motivation. One drawback of this approach is that it is subject to bias and inaccuracy.
2. **Quantitative Method:** Because the quantitative approach to forecasting is based on mathematics, it is impartial and consistent. It uses a lot of interpreted data and figures rather than relying solely on opinion and intuition to arrive at its conclusions.

4.1.5. Features of Forecasting

Here are some of the features of making a forecast:

1. **Involves Future Events:** Forecasts are created to predict the future, making them important for planning.
2. **Based on Past and Present Events:** Forecasts are based on opinions, intuition, guesses, as well as on facts, figures, and other relevant data. All of the factors that go into creating a forecast reflect some extent what happened with the business in the past and what is considered likely to occur in the future.
3. **Uses Forecasting Techniques:** Most businesses use the quantitative method, particularly in planning and budgeting.

4.1.6. The Process of Forecasting

Forecasters need to follow a careful process in order to yield accurate results. Here are some steps in the process:

1. **Develop the Basis of Forecasting:** The first step in the process is investigating the company's condition and identifying where the business is currently positioned in the market.
2. **Estimate the Future Operations of the Business:** Based on the investigation conducted during the first step, the second part of forecasting involves estimating the future conditions of the industry where the business operates and projecting and analyzing how the company will fare in the future.
3. **Regulate the Forecast:** This involves looking at different forecasts in the past and comparing them with what actually happened with the business. The differences in previous results and current forecasts are analyzed, and the reasons for the deviations are considered.
4. **Review the Process:** Every step is checked, and refinements and modifications are made.

4.1.7. Sources of Data for Forecasting

1. **Primary Sources:** Information from primary sources takes time to gather because it is first-hand information, also considered the most reliable and trustworthy sort of information. The forecaster does the collection, and may do so through things such as interviews, questionnaires, and focus groups.
2. **Secondary Sources:** Secondary sources supply information that has been collected and published by other entities. An example of this type of information might be industry reports. As this information has already been compiled and analyzed, it makes the process quicker.

4.1.8. Importance of Forecasting

Accurately projecting future trends and events is helpful in a variety of situations, including business management. Forecasting is important because it can be used for:

- **Estimating the Success of a New Business Venture:** When launching a new company, accurate forecasting can provide important insights that could impact the success of the venture in the future. Forecasting can provide an entrepreneur with the necessary tools to foresee elements such as the strength of the competition, potential demand for a product or service, and future industry development. It also reveals some of the risks and uncertainties that a new business faces.
- **Estimating Financial Necessities:** One of the most crucial applications of forecasting is estimating a company's future financial needs. By projecting future sales, the funds required for future product development, the price of upcoming expansions, and other projected expenses that are used to project future costs, it can assist a business in determining its financial future.
- **Ensuring the Company's Operational Consistency:** Accurate forecasting can provide crucial

insights into future revenue and expenses. The management of the company can plan more effectively and accurately for the future if they have an estimate of the money coming in and going out of the organization over a specific time period.

- **Helping Managers Make the Right Decisions:** Relying on precise forecasting is a major factor in many management decisions. Depending on the precise nature and goal of the organization, most businesses, regardless of size, face a number of potential uncertainties. These include seasonal fluctuations in sales, staffing changes, and shifts in the price of raw materials. In order to give managers the knowledge they need to decide on the company's future course, forecasting is essential.
- **Increasing a Business Venture's Odds of Success:** Correct allocation of funds and fine margins are critical components of any business's success. Important metrics, such as the quantity of raw materials required, the appropriate budget for each department within the company, and the volume of future sales, can be predicted through forecasting. Depending on the type of business and the anticipated data, these numbers assist management in allocating funds and resources and giving one product or service priority over another.
- **Formulating Effective Plans for the Future:** Since forecasting is a necessary component of all planning, it plays a critical role in creating useful and realistic plans. Forecasting plays a critical role in all types of planning, from short-term to long-term, and there is a direct correlation between precise forecasting and sufficient planning.
- **Promoting Workplace Cooperation:** Coordination and cooperation between all of the department managers of the organization as well as other staff members are usually necessary for gathering and analyzing the data needed for forecasting. This fosters collaboration throughout the process, boosting cohesiveness and team spirit.
- **Helping an Organization Improve:** Managers can use the information provided by forecasting to identify any weaknesses in the organization's processes. The management of the company are better equipped to address any weaknesses before they have an impact on earnings since they are aware of potential issues before they arise.

4.1.9. Applications

Applications for forecasting can be found in many domains where projections of future conditions are valuable. The degree of accuracy varies greatly depending on the field. It is likely that the final value will be near to the forecast if the factors related to what is being forecast are well understood and known, and if there is a substantial amount of data that can be used. The forecasts' reliability may be much reduced if this is not the case or if the predictions have an impact on the actual result. The application of Egain Forecasting for buildings is a result of both climate change and rising energy costs. This aims to lower the amount of energy required to heat the structure and subsequently lower greenhouse gas emissions. Manufacturing and distribution companies use forecasting in their daily operations to plan for customer demand. Forecasting of general economic trends is common, but the accuracy of predictions for actual stock returns is contested using the efficient-market hypothesis as justification. Both for-profit private organizations and non-profit organizations offer this kind of analysis.The most common method for predicting changes in foreign exchange is to combine fundamental analysis with charts. A key distinction between chart analysis and fundamental economic analysis is that the former focuses only on a market's price action, while the latter seeks to identify the underlying causes of the movement (Allen & Taylor, 1990). Financial institutions combine the data from their chartist and fundamental researchers into a single note to provide a final estimate for the currency under consideration. Conflict situations have also been predicted to develop through forecasting (Chadefaux, 2014). Forecasters conduct studies that evaluate the efficacy of specific forecasting models using empirical data. However, studies have revealed that there isn't much of a difference in the accuracy of forecasts made by people with much less knowledge of the conflict situation and those made by experts (Kesten C. Greene & Armstrong, Scott, 2007). In a similar vein, researchers have found no evidence to support the claim that role thinking—putting oneself in other people's shoes to predict their actions—improves forecast accuracy (Green & Armstrong, 1975). The relationship between planning and forecasting is a significant, if frequently overlooked, aspect of forecasting. While planning predicts what the future should look like, forecasting can be defined as predicting what the future will look like. There isn't just one accurate forecasting technique to apply. The method you choose should be determined by your goals and the conditions (data, etc.) that you have. A selection tree is a good resource for finding a method. This is an illustration of a selection tree. Forecasting has application in many situations:

- **Supply Chain Management and Customer Demand Planning:** Supply chain management can use forecasting to make sure the right product is delivered at the right time and place. Retailers can boost their profit margin by reducing excess inventory with the aid of accurate forecasting. Moreover, accurate forecasting will enable them to satisfy customer demand. Demand planning, also known as supply chain forecasting, is a discipline that combines consensus-building with statistical forecasting. Research indicates that company earnings forecasts are the most reliable, and extrapolations are the least accurate (Scott Armstrong, 1983).
- Economic forecasting
- Earthquake prediction
- Egain forecasting
- Energy forecasting for renewable power integration
- Finance against risk of default via credit ratings and credit scores
- Land use forecasting
- Player and team performance in sports
- Political forecasting
- Product forecasting
- Sales forecasting
- Technology forecasting
- Telecommunications forecasting
- Transport planning and forecasting
- Weather forecasting, flood forecasting and meteorology

4.2. FINANCIAL FORECASTING

The process of projecting or estimating future statistics for an organization is known as financial forecasting, i.e., how the company will perform going forward based on historical data by examining the income statement, position statement, current circumstances, historical financial trends, and the external and internal environment. These analyzes are typically done with the aim of creating a budget and allocating resources to ensure the best possible use.

By using financial forecasting techniques, businesses can clearly define their goals based on their stage of growth and find direction. Additionally, it assists them in identifying areas of concern where optimization may lead to increased revenue and profits. On a larger scale, it also increases the allure of investing in a highly transparent company for investors (Figure 4.3).

Figure 4.3. *Financial forecasting.*

Source: https://www.wallstreetmojo.com/financial-forecasting/.

The process of creating estimates about how the business will perform in the future is known as financial forecasting. It aids in providing direction and identifying the business's weak points. It entails assessing the company's historical performance and carefully examining present trends. But it's crucial to recognize that depending on the type of business and why these projections are being made, the elements of the financial forecasting models may vary. Higher revenue, sales, and eventually profits are the ultimate goals of any organization, regardless of its size, type of business, or stage of growth. Predicting performance and analyzing it based on recent experiences to improve it for the next quarter or year provides a high level of clarity for all members of the organization. Furthermore, when a company and its management are transparent about not only their strong points but also their flaws, which are being actively and consciously worked upon, investors find the business more appealing to park their investments in.

4.2.1. Components of Financial Forecasting

Let us understand the components and financial forecasting tools through the discussion below. This will give us a detailed understanding of the concept and its related factors (Figure 4.4).

1. **Projected Income Statement:** This is an anticipated income statement that depicts the expected expenses and revenues for the future financial period, i.e., usually one year.
2. **Cash Budget**: This depicts total cash inflow and outflow expected in the future. Sources of cash inflow include cash sales, collection from accounts receivable, short-term borrowing, long term debt, cash sales, and equity capital. Sources of cash outflow include payments of accounts payable, salaries, wages, capital expenditure, repayment of loans, and debts. The cash budget does not include expenses like depreciation. The reflected surplus or deficit in the cash budget forms the base for investment and financing.
3. **Projected Balance Sheet**: This sheet reflects the expected assets, liabilities, and owner's equity at a particular date. To prepare this, inputs like initial balance sheet, capital expenditure budget, profit plan, investment, and financial plan are required.
4. **Projected Sources and Uses of Fund:** Sources of funds and its uses in the planning period are shown in this statement. The projected income statement, balance sheet, initial balance sheet are the inputs required for its preparation. Projected sources of funds are cash flow from operations, a decrease in fixed assets, an increase in long-term liabilities, and the issuance of share capital.

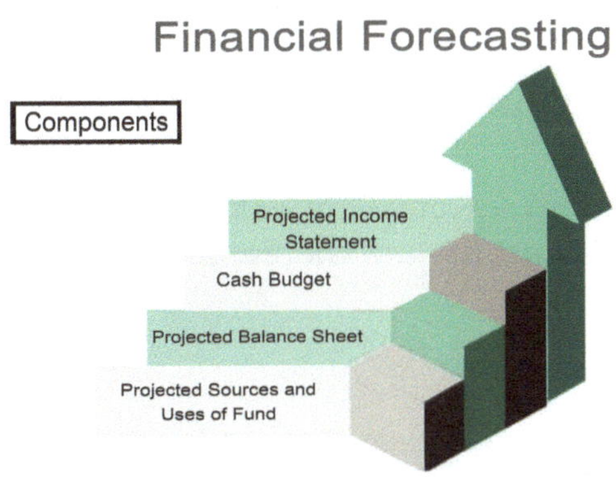

Figure 4.4. *Financial forecasting components.*

Source: https://www.wallstreetmojo.com/financial-forecasting/.

4.2.2. Examples

Let us understand the concept of using financial forecasting techniques with the help of a couple of examples. These examples will give us a practical understanding of the concept and its intricacies.

- **Example 4.1**

Orange Inc. has collected the following data for the future 5 years. You are requested to draw a comparative financial statement for the next 5 years and determine the company's growth potential.

Year	Sales	Operating Expenses	Non Operating Cost
1	1,000,000	600,000	200,000
2	1,120,000	630,000	224,000
3	1,400,000	787,500	291,200
4	1,960,000	1,102,500	407,680
5	2,195,200	1,234,800	456,602

Out of the above figures, cash sales are 80%, and cash expenses are 75% of the total figure. Assume opening cash as 50,000 and comment on the cash position of the company.

- **Solution**

Comparative Financial Statement

Particulars	YEAR 1	YEAR 2	YEAR 3	YEAR 4	YEAR 5
Sales	1,000,000	1,120,000	1,400,000	1,960,000	2,195,200
Operating Expenses	600,000	630,000	787,500	1,102,500	1,234,800
Non Operating Expenses	200,000	224,000	291,200	407,680	456,602
Net Profits	200,000	266,000	321,300	449,820	503,798

Comment – Company has good growth potential as profits are increasing at a good rate.

Cash Position

Particulars	YEAR 1	YEAR 2	YEAR 3	YEAR 4	YEAR 5
Opening	50,000	250,000	505,500	816,475	1,251,840
Add: - Cash Sales	800,000	896,000	1,120,000	1,568,000	1,756,160
Less: - Cash Expenses	600000	640500	809025	1132635	1268551
Cash Position	**250,000**	**505,500**	**816,475**	**1,251,840**	**1,739,449**

Comment – Since the company has a higher percentage of cash sales than cash expenses, the cash position is becoming stronger with the increasing sales year by year. Therefore, it can be said that the overall company has good growth potentials.

- **Example 4.2**

Leading company in the Baltic tourism market, Novaturas, had its best quarter ever this past quarter. They changed their EBITDA from EUR 3–5 million to EUR 4–6 million following the completion of a financial forecasting process.

The company's revenue for the first quarter of 2023 was EUR 39.6 million, which is 35% more than it was during the same time last year.

made the decision to increase the figures in their annual performance forecast after carefully reviewing their financial statements from the prior year and assessing the state of the market at the time. For the fiscal year 2023–2024, the experts who performed the analysis adjusted the numbers up by EUR 1–2 million based on the performance.

4.2.3. Process of Financial Forecasting

Using financial forecasting techniques is a multi-step process. These actions can differ between businesses and at different points in the same business's timeline. Let's examine the following explanation to gain an understanding of the process's key points.

- **Purpose:** It is vital to understand the purpose for which the elaborate process of analyzing, processing, making changes, and constant monitoring is being implemented.
- **Gathering Data:** Gathering historical sales and marketing data along with financial statements could allow the management to make more informed decisions based on past performance. Adjustments to strategies become easier with past performances in order.

- **Time Frame:** Creating clarity in terms of the length of this process can give the management and the other employees in the company a clear idea of what they are working towards in terms of daily actions supporting the plans.
- **Method:** Choosing a forecasting method that fits the best to the structure of the business and the purpose of the forecast and maintaining all documentation in the same format need to be clearly established to make analyzing more efficient.
- **Results:** Regular documentation of happening can help managers assess the results in real-time or at least in regular intervals, which makes the process less time-bound. Therefore, resources also could be mindfully spent.
- **Analysis:** The final data can be analyzed and it can be clarified if the strategies worked well for the company. Based on the results they can choose an interval after which these checks coulf be conducted again.

4.2.4. Importance of Financial Forecasting

Let us understand the importance of using financial forecasting tools through the points below.

- **New Business Promotion**: Financial forecasting helps businesses utilize their funds to promote new business ventures and initiatives. It also helps in determining the success rate of the business they are promoting.
- **Seamless Functioning**: Accurate and effective forecasting of the finances like current revenue, revenue potential, and other expenses helps in the organization's smooth running. The forecast also helps in anticipating future roadblocks.
- **Estimating Financial Requirements**: It helps determine sales and cost of customer acquisition, capital for a specific project, and other expenses required for further management of the business. This preemptive forecast helps in making sound business decisions.
- **Control Cash Flow**: It helps in controlling the cash flows of a business. Organizations with a good amount of cash/bank balance are more financially organized and better control their business operations.
- **Archive Overall Success:** Financial forecast is important in achieving overall success for the business as it forms a strong foundation for the complete budgeting of departments across the organization.

4.2.5. Advantages of Financial Forecasting

Let us understand the advantages of financial forecasting models through the explanation below.

The financial forecast allows businesses to predict future financial performance against set standards. It provides a benchmark against which performance, loopholes, and corrective actions of an organization are monitored.

- It helps in identifying the processes that are most capital consuming. Financial risk can be lowered by pumping out money from such processes and channelizing them towards the profitable ones.

- It helps in predicting the financial viability of new business ventures. It helps prepare the best model for figuring out how a business will perform when specific plans and strategies are worked out.

4.2.6. Disadvantages of Financial Forecasting

Despite the various advantages mentioned above and throughout the article, there are a few factors from the other end of the spectrum that prove to be a hassle for the management and employees. Let us understand the disadvantages of using financial forecasting techniques through the points below.

- Even if we have forecasting experts and a great process in place, predicting the future accurately is impossible. Markets have a high volatility level, and the number of factors influencing demand keeps changing with time.
- Data gathering, data organizing, and coordination are required for this process, which is very time-consuming. Also, substantial input from the marketing and sales team is required, making it a resource-intensive process.
- Hiring a team of advanced planners is a significant investment. Adding good-quality tools, high-quality talent, and software might prove a costly affair for the forecasting process.

4.2.7. Difference Between Financial Forecasting and Financial Modeling

Financial modeling and forecasting have both been extensively studied and are used interchangeably. There are a few variations in their core ideas and ramifications, though. Let's examine the comparison below to better understand the differences.

A company uses financial forecasting as a means of making predictions and getting ready for the future. While financial modeling is the process of financial forecasting, it involves a potential future outcome by analyzing its current financial statements and performance.

Financial modeling is used after the forecast assumptions are established and calculations are made using a financial statement. A predictive operating model is created through financial modeling to assist a business in making wise decisions. These financial models are mathematical constructs that establish connections between various variables. Preparing the company's future balance sheet is part of the process.

4.3. REVENUE FORECASTING MODELS

For any business, revenue forecasting is essential, but it becomes even more crucial for B2B SaaS. Due to the rapid advancement of this sector, it is imperative to stay abreast of emerging trends, consistently test out new distribution methods, and modify budgetary allocations in accordance with anticipated revenue growth. Reliable revenue projections assist businesses in making data-driven decisions about expansion. Everything you need to know about revenue forecasting models will be covered in this section.

4.3.1. Revenue Forecasting

The process of projecting future revenue for a business using qualitative insights, predictive modeling, and historical performance data is known as revenue forecasting. Revenue forecasts offer an approximation of the total expected revenues for a given time frame.

Forecast time horizons can be as short as one month, as short as one quarter, or as long as five years. While long-term projections adopt a more comprehensive market-based approach, short-term forecasts might concentrate on the immediate conversion of the sales pipeline.

The aim of revenue forecasting is to produce the most precise estimate of future revenue based on available data. Utilizing attribution data can also enhance these reports, giving you precise insight into which marketing and sales initiatives generate actual revenue.

Revenue forecasting helps answer questions like:

- How much revenue can we expect to generate in the next quarter/year?
- How seasonality trends and new product will launches impact revenue?
- How quickly are we expected to grow over the next 5 years?

When done right, revenue forecasting can power key business functions:

- **Financial planning**: Building P&L statements, budgets, valuation
- **Sales planning**: Setting quotas, territory mapping, compensation
- **Marketing planning**: Demand generation budgeting, growth modeling
- **HR planning**: Hiring goals, resource allocation across teams
- **Manufacturing planning**: Inventory needs, capacity expansion

- **Executive planning**: Strategy setting, investment decisions

While revenue forecasting attempts to predict future revenues, it differs from a revenue projection which is typically more aspirational.

4.3.2. Revenue Forecasting vs. Revenue Projections vs. Sales Forecasts

These three terms are used quite often when it comes to budgeting and strategic planning but they mean different things.

- **Revenue Forecasts** model the actual monetary revenue expected based on sales forecasts, historic performance, market conditions and statistical modeling. It provides the most likely, evidence-based scenario.
- **Revenue Projections** are what leadership desires to happen—an optimistic target rather than a data-driven expectation. Projections represent an aspirational revenue goal.
- **Sales Forecasts** predict expected sales bookings and pipelines based on leading indicators like open opportunities. They are an input into revenue forecasts.

4.3.3. Key Types of Revenue Forecasts

There are also different types of revenue forecasts based on methodology and time span:

- **Short-term vs. Long-Term**" Short-term forecasts focus on immediate pipeline conversion, while long-term forecasts take a broader market-based view.
- **Top-down vs. Bottom-Up**: Top-down forecasting starts with macro assumptions and allocates them across business units. Bottom-up rolls-up forecasts built from ground realities.
- **Operational vs. Financial**: Operational forecasts model near-term revenue streams. Financial forecasts take a holistic P&L view including costs and expenses.
- **Deterministic vs. Probabilistic**: Deterministic forecasts provide a single expected outcome. Probabilistic forecasts model a range of outcomes and probabilities.

4.3.4. Importance of Revenue Forecasting

Precise revenue projections possess the potential to distinguish a prosperous enterprise from one that fails. The following are some ways that forecasting influences planning throughout the company:

1. **Budgeting with Realistic Precision:** Building organizational-wide budgets is the single biggest use of forecasts for finance teams. Spending on everything from payroll and marketing initiatives to R&D investments is determined by budgets. Budgets become arbitrary when revenue projections aren't dependable. For instance, let's say a business made $5 million in sales the previous year. Next year's budget needs to be built by the CFO.

i. With intelligent forecasts, finance can model that based on new product launches, a 10% industry growth rate, and sales team expansions, revenues are likely to reach around $7.5M next year.

ii. The CFO can now budget for expenses accordingly – say $1M for new engineering hires, $500K for more marketing, $150K for sales operations software etc.

iii. Without forecasts, the CFO is flying blind. Maybe she pads the budget with a 20% increase to $6M. But if actual revenues only end up at $5.5M, suddenly there's a multi-hundred-thousand dollar budget shortfall, requiring drastic cuts.

Conversely, if revenues actually reach $8M but budgets are based on last year's numbers, the company is now missing key growth opportunities due to under-investment.

2. **Optimize Operations Management:** Beyond budgets, forecasts guide operational decisions across departments:

i. **Sales**: Forecasts feed territory assignments, quota setting, compensation planning, and capacity modeling whereas under-forecasting leaves money on the table.

ii. **Marketing**: Forecasts dictate digital and outbound campaign budgets and funnel targets where bad forecasts can waste spending and lead to missed opportunities.

iii. **Product**: Prioritizing the roadmap requires expected revenues from new features so bad forecasts can result in misplaced priorities.

iv. **HR**: Hiring and workforce planning requires expected growth rates and flimsy forecasts risk talent shortages or bloat.

Across the board, teams depend on forecasts to optimize operational management for future success amid constraints.

3. **Fuel Strategic Decisions:** Forecasts also provide the quantified confidence executives need to drive growth through major strategic moves:

i. **Funding rounds**: Forecasts build credibility on growth potential to establish valuations. Weak forecasts undermine bids for capital.

ii. **M&A valuation**: Pre-transaction due diligence depends on target revenue forecasts. Bad forecasts lead to overpayment or lost deals.

iii. **Market expansion**: Breaking into new regions or verticals requires quantifying addressable revenues and investment payback.

iv. **New product prioritization**: High-impact opportunities are identified by revenue potential under constrained resources.

v. **Executive recruitment**: Attracting star senior talent requires painting a compelling growth.

Creating reliable revenue forecasts empowers executives to place decisive strategic bets amid uncertainties, as opposed to shooting blind.

4. **Track Performance to Plan:** Revenue projections additionally offer a benchmark for tracking actual outcomes. Real revenue performance is contrasted with. Forecasted expectations then make it simple to identify deviations. With this knowledge at hand, teams can make necessary corrections before minor errors turn into significant mishaps.

It is impossible to consistently monitor progress in relation to potential without using forecasts as the benchmark. Without context, revenue figures cannot indicate whether performance is on track or not.

4.3.5. Types of Revenue Forecast Model

Now that we are familiar with the principles of revenue forecasting, let's look at some of the most widely used models and methods. In general, forecasting techniques belong to one of two families:

- **Quantitative models** take a data-driven statistical approach to identifying trends and patterns in historical data that can be used for future predictions.
- **Qualitative models** incorporate expert perspectives, market analyzes and contextual business insights to predict future revenues.

Four popular forecasting models are time series, bottom-up, top-down, and linear regression. To get the most out of each model, it is best to combine them to perform revenue forecasting.

Let's explore some of these popular models.

1. **Linear Regression Models:** In order to model how changes in important variables affect revenue, linear regression examines historical data. Regression offers a data-supported perspective on the factors that influence revenue expansion and contraction. Regression models, however, are only as good as the data they are fed. They might overlook intricate real-world dynamics that historical data does not capture. It's crucial to treat them as useful guides rather than as infallible truths (Figure 4.5).

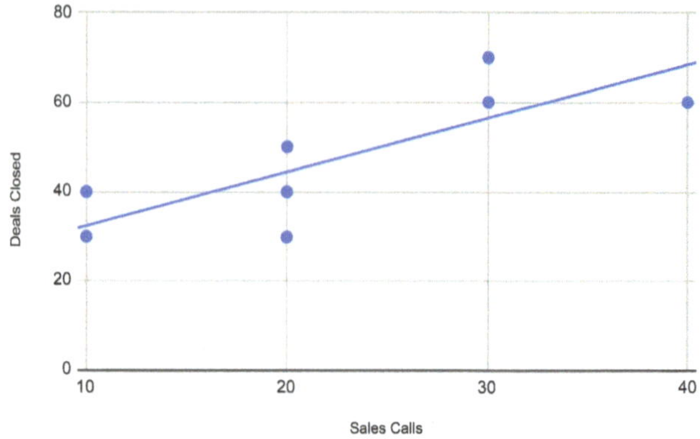

Figure 4.5. *Linear regression models.*

Source: https://www.factors.ai/blog/revenue-forecasting-models.

- **Key Benefits**
  - Quantifies the relationship between revenue drivers and outcomes
  - Calculates the impact of each variable on revenues
  - Models complex interactions between multiple variables
  - Provides data-driven revenue projections
- **How It Works:** One variable is frequently used in simple linear regression to forecast revenue. For instance, it can assist a company in estimating the extra revenue that, historically, each $1 increase in marketing expenditure has brought in. This knowledge can be applied to revenue forecasting in various contexts.

Multiple linear regression takes into account other variables at the same time, such as market dynamics, sales activity, and marketing budget. The model uses past data to compute coefficients that indicate the particular relationship between each variable and revenue. The predictive model uses these insights to forecast expected revenue under various scenarios.

- **Considerations**
  - Regression modeling requires large volumes of accurate historical data
  - Predictive power diminishes beyond modeled relationships
  - Difficult to model nonlinear variable interactions

A data-supported understanding of the factors influencing revenue growth and contraction is offered by regression. It adds statistical rigor to estimating the impact of decisions on hiring, pricing, product launches, geographic expansion, and other areas on both the top and bottom lines. These models, however, are limited by the quality of the input data. They might overlook intricate real-world dynamics that historical data does not capture. It's crucial to treat them as useful guides rather than as infallible truths.

2. **Time Series Forecasting:** Time series analysis looks for patterns in data that have existed in the past. This makes it easier to distinguish seasonal and cyclical patterns from noise and more general growth trajectories. It decomposes revenue time series into:

- **Trend:** Overall upward/downward trajectory
- **Seasonality:** Cyclical patterns
- **Noise:** Random unexplained variations

Time series models are used to generate sophisticated revenue projections that are specific to the business by maximizing signals and minimizing noise in historical data. These models can take into account recent data, allowing you to extract useful insights for reporting and forecasting while balancing responsiveness to change with noise reduction (Figure 4.6).

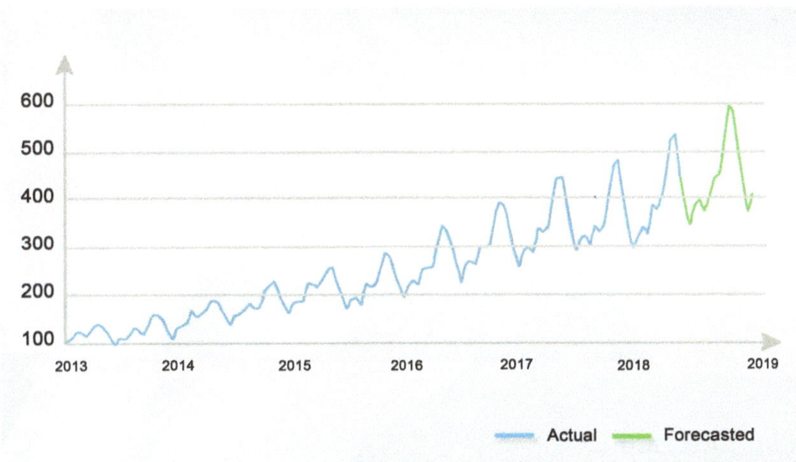

Figure 4.6. *Time series forecasting.*

Source: https://www.factors.ai/blog/revenue-forecasting-models.

- **Key Benefits**
  - Models trends and seasonality specific to the business
  - Highlights time-based nuances impacting revenue
  - Provides granular, frequently updating forecasts

- **How It Works:** In order to maximize the predictive modeling of a revenue time series, time series techniques such as moving averages, exponential smoothing, and ARIMA modeling are utilized to analyze the data. For instance, a year-end budget flush may cause enterprise software revenues to spike every fourth quarter. When travel is at its peak during the summer, media subscriptions may decline. Comprehending these subtleties facilitates the creation of more precise and relevant forecasts.

The growth curve can then be smoothed using the insights gleaned from the time series forecasts, providing you with more predictable revenue.

- **Considerations:** For time series models to identify trustworthy patterns, there must be enough historical data. Unlike in the past, they might overlook completely new market dynamics or unique occurrences. Therefore, it's crucial to combine them with human judgment.

3. **Bottom-Up Forecasting:** In order to create projections, bottom-up forecasting uses information from frontline teams like account management and sales. In addition to historical data, they take into account pipeline health, competitive threats, and market sentiment (Figure 4.7).

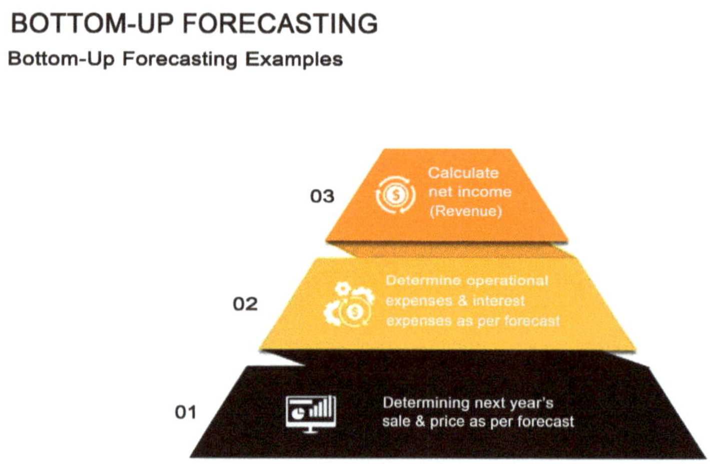

Figure 4.7. *Bottom-up forecasting.*

Source: https://www.factors.ai/blog/revenue-forecasting-models.

- **How It Works:** Let's take an example organization with sales, marketing, finance, and leadership teams. Here's how bottom-up forecasting would work:
  - **The sales team starts by analyzing the health** of its current pipeline and expected deal cycles to forecast expected conversion rates by product line and region.
  - **Meanwhile, marketing examines recent campaign performance** and lead generation trends to estimate new MQLs by campaign channel. They apply

conversion rates to project new SQLs.

  - **Finance consolidates these detailed bottom-up forecasts** from each department. They identify and resolve any inconsistent methodologies or assumptions between teams.
  - **Leadership reviews the consolidated forecast** and makes final top-down adjustments to determine the official revenue projection.

- **Key Benefits**
  - Incorporates insights from sales, account management, and other frontline teams
  - Reflects pipeline health, competitive dynamics, and micro-market nuances
  - Promotes buy-in through the inclusion of cross-functional inputs
- **Considerations:** The forecast as a whole may be distorted by teams making inconsistent assumptions. Aligning assumptions and methodologies is facilitated by leadership guidance on industry outlook, macroeconomic factors, and growth objectives.

4. **Top-Down Forecasting:** The big picture of the entire addressable market, growth trajectories, economic conditions, and business strategy are the first things that top-down forecasting starts with. The leadership assigns targets for revenue and divides them among the functions. This guarantees that short-term operations and long-term goals are strategically aligned. But, without a clear explanation of the reasoning behind the targets, teams may become demotivated. For this reason, when using top-down forecasting, it's important to guarantee open and honest communication between leadership and team members (Figure 4.8).

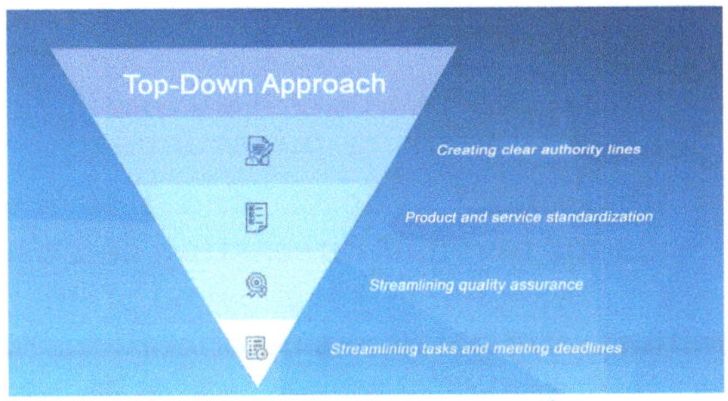

Figure 4.8. *Top-down forecasting.*

Source: https://www.factors.ai/blog/revenue-forecasting-models.

- **How It Works:** Let's look at top-down revenue forecasting through an example.
  - The executive/leadership team starts with the overall revenue growth target based on market outlook and strategic goals. They divide this target across sales, marketing and customer success based on revenue impact capacity.
  - Each team gets their individual revenue target along with guidance on growth assumptions like pricing, conversions, expansions etc.
  - Teams build goal-aligned execution plans around sales territories, campaigns, and account targeting to meet their top-down number.
  - Leadership reviews department plans to ensure coordination and consistent assumptions are in place.

- **Considerations**
  - Teams lack insights into the rationale behind seemingly arbitrary targets
  - Overlooks micro-market nuances and competitive dynamics
  - Requires reconciliation of opposing projections

Combining top-down and bottom-up methods for revenue forecasting can assist in setting reasonable goals based on market conditions and coordinating operations with expansion goals.

4.3.6. Best Method for Revenue Forecasting

The best forecasting method depends on your use case. Let's understand this with two examples.

1. A SaaS company with recurring subscription revenue may find time series analysis to be very effective. That's because, studying historical revenue patterns over time, seasonal cycles and trends become apparent. Statistical time series models can help quantify these patterns to accurately predict recurring revenues.
2. On the other hand, for a retail chain opening new store locations, a bottom-up approach could prove more useful. Each new store manager could prepare detailed forecasts for their location based on demographics, nearby competitors, marketing plans etc. Aggregating these bottom-up projections provides a realistic the overall revenue forecast.

The point is, every business is situated differently. The ideal approach depends on:

- **Data Availability**: length of revenue history, presence of relevant drivers/ variables
- **Revenue Characteristics:** recurring/ seasonal patterns, level of variability
- **Business Structure**: centralized/ decentralized, product diversity
- **Strategic Context**: expanding to new markets/geographies, introducing major new offerings

In order to customize the forecasting methodology to their unique circumstances and goals, leaders must have a thorough understanding of the revenue drivers in their industry and company.

Combining approaches has its advantages as well. Time series analysis can be used, for instance, to leverage recent revenue trends in a short-term quarterly forecast.

Additionally, a bottom-up strategy could include local market viewpoints for the annual budget to provide a comprehensive picture. The secret is to modify forecasting methodologies to align with business realities, as this yields the precision and understanding needed for secure decision-making throughout the enterprise.

4.3.7. Revenue Forecasting Models: Best Practices

What are some of the best practices for ensuring accurate revenue forecasting when using these revenue forecasting models? Let's look at 4 of the best practices that you should consider following.

1. **Start with High-Quality Data**: Remember this—garbage in,

garbage out. Even the most advanced model cannot compensate for poor-quality data. Invest in processes and systems to collect accurate, complete revenue data, with proper change logs and auditing.

2. **Eliminate Outdated Information**: Stale data loses relevance quickly. Establish mechanisms to continually gather the latest data on revenue drivers. This could involve surveys, sales team feedback, customer interviews etc.
3. **Reduce the Length of Planning Cycles**: Annual plans using old assumptions miss market shifts. Re-forecast more frequently using the latest data to stay agile. Quarterly or even monthly cycles are preferable.
4. **Avoid a Futile Bid for Perfection**: Obsessing over tiny accuracy improvements is counterproductive beyond a point. Focus on balancing usefulness and cost when selecting model sophistication.

4.4. A TYPICAL ONE-YEAR PROJECTION

The impact of the analyst's assumptions on each of the three fundamental financial statements is examined in the ensuing one-year projection. To understand how the income statement, cash flow statement, and balance sheet are related to each other, there's probably no better way to look at the numbers than this. The current financial statements of Colossal Chemical Corporation, a fictional company, are shown in Exhibit 4.1. The projection's foundation is provided by the historical statements, which validate the plausibility of the predictions made about future financial performance. Throughout the commentary on the Colossal Chemical projection, we will assume that the analyst has looked at the company's performance over the previous year as well as the previous few years.

Exhibit 4.1. Financial Statements of Colossal Chemical Corporation Year Ended December 31, 2010 ($000,000 Omitted)

Income Statement	
Sales	$1,991
Cost of goods sold	1,334
Selling, general, and administrative expense	299
Depreciation	119
Research and development	80
Total costs and expenses	1,832
Operating Income	159
Interest expense	36
Interest (income)	(6)
Earnings before income taxes	129
Provision for income taxes	44
Net income	$ 85

Statement of Cash Flows	
Sources	
Net income	$ 85
Depreciation	119
Deferred income taxes	20
Working capital changes, excluding cash and borrowings	(8)
Funds provided by operations	216
Uses	
Additions to property, plant, and equipment	125
Dividends	28
Reduction of long-term debt	60
Funds used by operations	213
Net increase in funds	$ 3

Balance Sheet			
Cash and marketable securities	$ 69	Notes payable	$ 21
Accounts receivable	439	Accounts payable	263
		Current portion of long-term debt	32
Inventories	351	Total current liabilities	316
Total current assets	859	Long-term debt	379
Property, plant, and equipment	895	Deferred income taxes	70
	$1,754	Shareholders' equity	989
			$1,754

Source: Martin S. Fridson, Fernando Alvarez. Financial Statement Analysis. Wiley. ISBN: 9780470635605.

4.4.1. Projected Income Statement

An earnings forecast is presented first in the financial projection (Exhibit 4.2). A projected statement of cash flows will eventually include net income and depreciation, two important numbers from the projected income statement. In turn, the cash flow statement will provide information needed to create a projected balance sheet. The analyst will have to make more assumptions at each level that follows. However, a projection of earnings sets the stage for the logical flow and will have a major impact on how all three statements appear.

Exhibit 4.2. Earnings Forecast

Colossal Chemical Corporation Projected Income Statement ($000 omitted)

	2002
Sales	$2,110
Cost of goods sold	1,393
Selling, general, and administrative expense	317
Depreciation	121
Research and development	84
Total costs and expenses	1,915
Operating Income	195
Interest expense	34
Interest (income)	(5)
Earnings before income taxes	166
Provision for income taxes	56
Net income	$ 110

Source: Martin S. Fridson, Fernando Alvarez. Financial Statement Analysis. Wiley. ISBN: 9780470635605.

The assumptions underlying each line in the income statement—which are shown from top (sales) to bottom (net income)—are discussed immediately after.

4.4.1.1. Sales

Activities pertaining to selling or the quantity of goods sold within a specified time frame are referred to as sales. A sale can also occur when a service is provided in exchange for payment. A sale could also refer to a time when products are offered for a lower price.

The estimated $2.110 billion for 2011 indicates an approximate 6% increase over the actual amount for 2010 as displayed in Exhibit 4.1. 2% of this increase will come from higher shipments, and 4 percent from higher prices.

Utilizing the historical segment data displayed in Exhibit 4.3, the analyst constructs a forecast from the ground up to arrive at these numbers. The company's business, which consists of basic chemicals, plastics, and industrial chemicals, can generate sales projections with the assistance of trade publications, trade associations, and companies that offer econometric forecasting models. All such forecasts are predicated on specific assumptions regarding economic growth, or an increase in the gross domestic product, in the upcoming year. It is important for the analyst to carefully determine the forecaster's underlying assumptions and assess their plausibility.

Exhibit 4.3. Sales Forecast

Colossal Chemical Corporation Results by Industry Segment ($000 omitted)

	2001	2002	2003	2004	2005
Sales					
Basic chemicals	$ 975	$ 921	$ 878	$ 807	$ 786
Plastics	433	422	399	370	373
Industrial chemicals	583	546	531	475	461
Total	$1,991	$1,889	$1,808	$1,652	$1,620
Operating Income					
Basic chemicals	$ 94	$ 82	$ 65	$ 52	$ 59
Plastics	24	16	25	41	26
Industrial chemicals	41	35	28	31	28
Total	$ 159	$ 133	$ 118	$ 124	$ 113
Depreciation					
Basic chemicals	$ 55	$ 51	$ 50	$ 46	$ 46
Plastics	27	25	22	20	19
Industrial chemicals	37	36	35	31	31
Total	$ 119	$ 112	$ 107	$ 97	$ 96
Identifiable Assets					
Basic chemicals	$ 813	$ 772	$ 741	$ 676	$ 674
Plastics	390	369	352	314	309
Industrial chemicals	551	530	510	457	456
Total	$1,754	$1,671	$1,603	$1,447	$1,439

Source: Martin S. Fridson, Fernando Alvarez. Financial Statement Analysis. Wiley. ISBN: 9780470635605.

In order to ensure that the analyst's earnings projection aligns with the internal economic forecast, it is imperative to establish a historical correlation between key performance indicators and the shipments of the company's diverse business segments. For instance, shipments within a specific segment may have historically increased at a rate 1.5 times faster than industrial production or have varied nearly directly with housing starts. In a similar vein, price increases ought to be connected to the anticipated rate of inflation. This will be shown by the Producer Price Index or the Consumer Price Index, depending on the product.

Basic industries that are best suited for the macroeconomic-based strategy outlined here include chemicals, paper, and capital goods.

Sales and the overall economic trend typically have a looser relationship in technology-driven industries and hit-driven businesses like toys and movies. In such cases, establishing contacts within the industry under study is crucial to forecasting. Making educated guesses about the likelihood of a company's new products succeeding is the goal.

Exhibit 4.4, which shows the sales history by geographic area, adds another source of information to the sales projection. The figures derived from industry segment forecasts can be adjusted by an analyst to account for the possibility of exceptionally strong or exceptionally weak economic performance in a specific global region. Similarly, a business in a particular area might be dealing with an odd issue, like a disagreement with a foreign government. The breakdown of geographic sales can provide some understanding of the expected impact of such events.

Exhibit 4.4. Colossal Chemical Corporation Results by Geographic Area ($000,000 Omitted)

	2006	2007	2008	2009	2010
Sales					
North America	$ 873	$ 896	$ 968	$1,019	$1,077
Europe	526	551	601	622	649
Latin America	103	99	90	87	102
Far East	118	106	149	161	163
Total	$1,620	$1,652	$1,808	$1,889	$1,991
Operating Income					
North America	$ 25	$ 32	$ 29	$ 36	$ 43
Europe	52	47	61	62	77
Latin America	17	24	17	16	26
Far East	19	21	11	19	13
Total	$ 113	$ 124	$ 118	$ 133	$ 159

Source: Martin S. Fridson, Fernando Alvarez. Financial Statement Analysis. Wiley. ISBN: 9780470635605.

4.4.1.2. Cost of Goods Sold

Exhibit 4.2's cost-of-goods-sold of $1.393 billion corresponds to 66% of expected sales. This translates to a gross margin of 34%, which is marginally higher than the 33% from the previous year. A company's expected gross margin, in turn, represents expectations regarding shifts in labor and material costs. The expected level of industry competition, which impacts a company's capacity to pass cost increases through to customers or hold onto cost reductions, also has an impact on the gross margin forecast.

A crucial factor in a capital-intensive industry like basic chemicals is the anticipated capacity utilization percentage for both the business and the sector. Unit costs are minimized at full capacity because fixed costs are distributed over the highest volume that can be achieved. Furthermore, none of the producers will be motivated to raise volume by lowering prices if demand surpasses capacity and they are all operating at full capacity. Cost increases will be fully (or more than fully) passed on and gross margins will expand under such circumstances. That will be the outcome, at the very least, until new industrial capacity is developed and supply and demand are balanced again. On the other hand, Exhibit 4.2's predicted gross margin would likely be lower than in 2010 rather than higher if demand were predicted to decrease rather than increase in 2002, resulting in a drop in capacity utilization.

The analyst can project the cost of goods sold segment by segment, starting from the bottom up, just like with sales. The analyst must add segment depreciation to operating income because Exhibit 4.3's segment information only displays operating income and not gross margin.

They must also make assumptions regarding the distribution of research and development (R&D) and selling, general, and administrative (SG&A) expenses by segment. For example, if SG&A and R&D expenses are distributed according to segment sales, operating income by segment for 2010 is displayed in Exhibit 4.5.

Exhibit 4.5. Colossal Chemical Corporation Operating Income by Segment ($000,000 Omitted)

	Basic Chemicals	Plastics	Industrial Chemicals	Total
Operating income	$ 94	$ 24	$ 41	$ 159
Plus: Depreciation	55	27	37	119
Plus: SG&A	146	65	88	299
Plus: R&D	39	17	24	80
Equals: Gross Margin	$ 334	$ 133	$ 190	$ 657
Sales	$ 975	$ 433	$ 583	$1,991
Gross Margin Percentage	34.3%	30.7%	32.6%	33.0%
Memo: Segment Sales as Percentage of Total:	49.0%	21.7%	29.3%	100.0%

Source: Martin S. Fridson, Fernando Alvarez. Financial Statement Analysis. Wiley. ISBN: 9780470635605.

The analyst can create models for segment-by-segment gross margin percentage forecasting by gathering the necessary data over a number of years.

4.4.1.3. Seling, General, and Administrative Expense

Exhibit 4.2's forecast is based on the assumption that the steady relationship that has historically seen SG&A expenses roughly equal 15% of sales will continue. If, for instance, recent quarterly income statements or remarks from reputable industry sources suggested a trend to a higher or lower level, the analyst would adjust this percentage for forecasting purposes.

4.4.1.4. Depreciation

The amount of a company's fixed assets and the typical number of years over which it writes them off determine the depreciation expense. The company will write off one-eighth (12.5%) of its property, plant, and equipment (PP&E) annually on a straight-line basis if the property, plant, and equipment (PP&E) classes are depreciated over an average of 8 years.

The base of depreciable assets will increase yearly until PP&E additions surpass depreciation charges. Exhibit 4.2 projects depreciation costs to be 13.5% of PP&E at year-end, based on a consistent ratio between the two items over a long period of time. A projection should, of course, account for any anticipated departures from past trends. For instance, a business may decide to increase or decrease its average write-off period due to shifts in its accounting policies, which may be justified by variations in the rate at which equipment becomes obsolete. Additionally, a company's asset mix could alter. When relatively short-lived assets, like data processing equipment, rise as a percentage of capital expenditures and long-lived assets, like bricks and mortar, decrease, the average write-off period should progressively shorten.

4.4.1.5. Research and Development

R&D is another expense that is usually budgeted on a percentage-of-sales basis, along with advertising.

If the company, for instance, makes a large acquisition in an industry that is either significantly more or significantly less research-intensive than its current operations, the percentage of research and development may change.

Furthermore, a company's perception of the proportion of sales it needs to devote to research in order to stay competitive may change in response to shifting incentives for research, such as longer or shorter patent protection periods.

If such things don't happen, the analyst can reasonably confidently predict that R&D spending will account for roughly the same portion of sales as it did in the previous year. An assumption of this kind (4 percent of sales) is included in Exhibit 4.2.

4.4.1.6. Operating Income

The total costs and expenses are calculated by adding the four projected expense lines. The total ($1,915 million) is deducted from anticipated sales to arrive at a projected $195 million operating income.

4.4.1.7. Interest Expense

Information from the financial statements' notes is shown in Exhibit 4.6, which can be used to project the interest expense for the upcoming year. (The level of detail displayed here is not included in every annual report. When the information is less clear, more assumptions must be made.).

Exhibit 4.6. Details of Long-Term Debt, Short-Term Debt, and Interest Expense

Colossal Chemical Corporation
($000 omitted)

Long-Term Debt (Excluding Current Maturities)	2001	2000
10.0% notes payable 2003	$ 52	$ 78
8.1% notes payable 2007	77	111
9.5% debentures due 2010	75	75
8.875% debentures due 2014	125	125
6.5% industrial development bonds due 2017	50	50
	$379	$439

Long-Term Debt	2001
Average interest rate for year	8.50%
Average annual amount outstanding	$29
Annual maturities of long-term debt for the next five years are as follows:	
2002	$27 million
2003	$13 million
2004	$22 million
2005	$18 million
2006	$31 million

Interest Expense	2001
Interest incurred	41
Capitalized interest	5
Interest expense	36

Source: Martin S. Fridson, Fernando Alvarez. Financial Statement Analysis. Wiley. ISBN: 9780470635605.

Estimating Colossal Chemical's embedded cost of debt, or the weighted average interest rate on the company's current long-term debt, is crucial to the forecasting methodology used here. Projected interest charges of $22.32 million are obtained by applying the embedded cost of 5.43 percent to Colossal's 2010 year-end long-term debt (including current maturities, which are assumed to carry the same average interest rate). The 2011 cash flow projection, as displayed in Exhibit 4.6, indicates that there was no appreciable decrease in the amount of debt outstanding in 2011. As a result, even though this approach is only approximative, it shouldn't prove to be too inaccurate. The forecaster has to add interest charges for the short-term debt (notes payable) to the $22.32 million figure. These estimates are based on the $30.0 million average of the outstanding balances at year-end 2010 and projected year-end 2011 outstanding balances. Assuming slightly higher interest rates in 2011, the assumed average interest rate is 1.75%. Keep in mind that the strategy presented for calculating interest expense incorporates certain degrees of simplification. Using this technique in a backward-looking manner may not deliver the exact interest expense figures presented in the historical financial reports. This discrepancy can be attributed to the non-uniform occurrence of debt paydowns at midyear, which is an assumption made in the estimation process for the average amounts of long-term debt outstanding. Analysts should acknowledge and account for significant, upcoming changes in interest expenses, such as the refinancing of high-interest bonds with more affordable borrowings. In addition, forecasters should avoid becoming overly fixated on achieving absolute precision in this area. For instance, for Colossal Chemical, projected interest for 2011 constitutes only 1% of sales, meaning a 10% error in estimation will have negligible impact on the forecasted net income. Analysts should focus their efforts on estimating interest expense for companies with substantial debt loads, as their financial stability may depend on their ability to manage these expenses.

4.4.1.8. Interest Income

A projection of an unaltered cash balance for 2011 is included in Exhibit 4.2. The average balance of $69 million will yield (in round numbers) $1 million in interest income based on the assumption of an average money market rate of return of 1.5 percent on corporate cash.

4.4.1.9. Provision for Income Taxes

Earnings before income taxes are $166 million after deducting interest expense and adding interest income. Because Colossal's effective rate has historically approximated the statutory rate, the forecast lowers this amount by the 35% statutory tax rate.

Exhibit 4.7. Projected Statement of Cash Flows, 2011

Colossal Chemical Corporation ($000 omitted)		
Sources		
Net income	$110	
Depreciation	121	
Deferred income taxes	25	
Working capital changes, excluding cash and borrowings	(43)	
Cash provided by operations	213	
Uses		
Additions to property, plant, and equipment	165	
Dividends	37	
Repayment of current maturities of long-term debt	32	
Cash used by operations	234	
Net cash provided (used) by operations	(21)	
Increase in notes payable	$ 21	
Changes in Working Capital		
Decrease (increase) in accounts receivable		$ (25)
Decrease (increase) in inventories		(29)
Increase (decrease) in accounts payable		11
		$ (43)

Source: Martin S. Fridson, Fernando Alvarez. Financial Statement Analysis. Wiley. ISBN: 9780470635605.

Effective rates may differ significantly for other businesses due to various factors, such as investment tax credits and tax loss carryforwards. Changes in the statutory rate are generally well-publicized by media coverage of federal tax legislation, and management will typically be able to offer some guidance regarding significant changes in the effective rate.

4.4.2. Projected Statement of Cash Flows

The first two lines of the projected statement of cash flows (Exhibit 4.7) are supplied by the completed income statement projection. Exhibit 4.2 directly provides the net income of $114 million and the depreciation of $121 million, which together account for most of the total sources (funds provided by operations) figure. The projections are largely unaffected by the other two items.

4.4.2.1. Deferred Income Taxes

Changes in the difference between tax and book depreciation, as well as other factors like leases, installment receivables, and unremitted earnings of foreign subsidiaries, can cause this number to fluctuate somewhat year over year. This number may be forecast with assistance from the company management. A trend-line projection is used to arrive at the $25 million figure displayed in Exhibit 4.7.

4.4.2.2. Working Capital Changes (Excluding Cash and Borrowings)

The $43 million projection's derivation is explained in detail at the bottom of Exhibit 4.7. According to Exhibit 4.1's historical statements, every working capital item is assumed to remain at the same percentage of sales in the forecast. As sales increase from $1,991 million in 2010 to a projected $2,110 million in 2011, accounts receivable, for instance, at 22% of sales, increase from $439 million to $464 million (an increase of $25 million). The analyst needs to confirm that the ratios from the most recent year are indicative of the experience over a number of years before assuming a constant-percentage relationship. Future variations from past norms must also be taken into account. In an attempt to boost sales, the company might increase accounts receivable or forcefully accumulate inventory in response to a sharp decline in sales by providing more lenient credit terms.

4.4.2.3. Additions to Property, Plant, and Equipment

Capital expenditures are the primary and most significant use of this cash flow projection. A business may include a detailed capital expenditure forecast in its annual report, and as the year goes on, it may revise that estimate in press releases, quarterly statements, and 10-Q reports. The company's investor-relations officer will typically reply to inquiries regarding the range or at least the direction (up, down, or flat) for the upcoming year, even if the company does not release a precise figure.

4.4.2.4. Dividends

The $37 million figure represents the assumption that Colossal will stick to its declared dividend policy, which calls for paying out roughly one-third of its sustainable earnings (exceptional gains and losses excluded). This kind of rule is usually understood as an average payout over time, meaning that the dividend rate does not change as much during a typical business cycle as earnings do. Even after a year or more of losses, a company may decide not to reduce its dividend by borrowing money if needed to keep the payout going. The board of directors, which has the power to declare dividends, may debate and often criticize this practice.

When attempting to project future dividends, an analyst can only make an educated estimate until the board formally announces its decision. Furthermore, in a challenging earnings climate, there is no guarantee that the board will decide in favor of maintaining the dividend three months later.

4.4.2.5. Repayment of Current Maturities of Long-Term Debt

The $32 million amount displayed is taken straight from Exhibit 4.1's current liabilities section of the balance sheet.

4.4.2.6. Increase in Notes Payable

A net use of $17 million is obtained by deducting the $234 million in cash utilized in operations from the $217 million generated by operations. Any net cash generated is expected to be used for debt retirement in this projection. Conversely, a net cash use will be compensated for by using short-term bank lines. The management's stated goals and some understanding of how consistently management has followed plans in the past serve as the foundation for these assumptions about the company's actions. In other situations, different presumptions might be more appropriate. For instance, a decrease or increase in cash and marketable securities may balance out a net provision or use of cash. If management has expressed a desire to purchase stock and has been given permission by the board of directors to do so, a sizeable net cash provision may be assumed to be intended for share repurchase, lowering shareholders' equity. Rather than using short-term debt to cover a significant cash shortfall, a business may choose to fund the borrowings as soon as possible, which would increase its long-term debt. As an alternative, a business might finance any significant cash requirement by utilizing a mix of long-term debt and equity, utilizing the amounts of each that are necessary to maintain a certain debt to equity ratio.

4.4.3. Projected Balance Sheet

No additional assumptions are needed when building the projected balance sheet (Exhibit 4.8); all assumptions are already made when projecting the income statement and statement of cash flows. Using data from the other statements, the analyst merely updates the historical balance sheet in Exhibit 4.1.

Exhibit 4.8. Colossal Chemical Corporation Projected Balance Sheet December 31, 2011 ($000,000 Omitted)

Cash and marketable securities	$ 69	Notes payable	$ 42
Accounts Receivable	464	Accounts payable	274
		Current portion of	
Inventories	380	long-term debt	27
Total Current Assets	913	Total Current Liabilities	343
		Long-term debt	352
		Deferred income taxes	95
Property, plant, and equipment	939	Shareholders' equity	1,062
	$1,852		$1,852

Source: Martin S. Fridson, Fernando Alvarez. Financial Statement Analysis. Wiley. ISBN: 9780470635605.

Shown in Exhibit 4.7, the projected statement of cash flows contains the majority of the necessary data. The anticipated changes in working capital, for instance, are reflected in accounts payable, inventories, and accounts receivable. The cash flow projection would also reflect changes in marketable securities and cash, which in this instance is not changing. Property, plant, and equipment increased by $165 million after depreciation of $121 million, compared to the previous year's $895 million level. The changes in notes payable, deferred income taxes, and shareholders' equity (net income less dividends) are also provided by the projected cash flow statement.

The figures required to finish the long-term debt projection are found in the historical balance sheets (Exhibit 4.6) details of long-term debt. The balance sheet now shows the $27 million 2011 current maturities of long-term debt, as the $32 million 2010 current maturities have been settled. The new amount of $352 million is obtained by deducting the $27 million amount from the $379 million long-term debt (noncurrent) in 2010. (Any additional long-term debt adjustments—of which there are none in these projections—would show up in the anticipated cash flows statement.).

4.5. SENSITIVITY ANALYSIS WITH PROJECTED FINANCIAL STATEMENTS

Under certain assumptions, creating a set of projected financial statements offers a peek at the financial state of a business in the future. Colossal Chemical's credit quality measures are expected to improve in 2011 (Exhibit 4.9), based on historical and projected data presented in Exhibits 4.1 through 4.8. The total debt will decrease from 29.0% to 26.5% of total capital, both in absolute terms and as a percentage. Likewise, the amount of cash provided will increase from 50.8% to 62.2% of the total debt. (Alternatively, the reciprocals show debt as a cash-provided multiple that decreases from 1.97X to 1.61X). These two patterns point to lower financial risk. The projected statements that produced these ratios are only as reliable as the underlying assumptions. Despite their apparent logic, the assumptions rely largely on macroeconomic forecasting, which is, to put it mildly, far from an exact science. Usually, when business activity deviates from anticipated levels, the analyst has to adjust the projections and the underlying economic assumptions multiple times a year.

Exhibit 4.9. Trend of Credit Quality Measures—Base Case

Colossal Chemical Corporation ($000,000 omitted)		
	2010 (Actual)	2011 (Projected)
Total Debt		
Notes payable	$ 21	$ 42
Current portion of long-term debt	32	27
Long-term debt	379	352
	432	421
Deferred income taxes	70	95
Shareholders' equity	989	1,062
Total Capital	$1,491	$1,578
Total debt as a percentage of total capital	29.0%	26.7%
Cash provided by operations (before working captial charges)	224	256
Total Debt	432	421
Cash Provided as a Percentage of Total Debt	51.9%	60.8%

Source: Martin S. Fridson, Fernando Alvarez. Financial Statement Analysis. Wiley. ISBN: 9780470635605.

A single set of projections, or point forecast, is not going to be the sole basis for decisions made by prudent lenders and investors, who understand that conditions can, and almost certainly will, change. Rather, they will evaluate the possible outcomes in light of a variety of risks and rewards.

The analyst can adjust the underlying assumptions and then see how much the projected ratios change, as shown in Exhibit 4.10. The term "sensitivity analysis" refers to this procedure. In the given instance, the analyst forecasts a mere 3% increase in sales compared to the previous year. That is half of the growth rate that is anticipated in the most likely scenario, or the base case, as shown in Exhibit 4.2. The base case's assumption of a robust economy is not supported by the less optimistic sales forecast. For instance, the analyst might predict a 3% inflation rate and no real growth. The analyst's revised scenario is predicated on the assumption that chemical producers will not have any chance to improve their gross margins from the previous year. Assuming no changes to the other factors, the updated estimates indicate somewhat lower increases in net income, shareholders' equity, and funds provided by operations as compared to the base case. According to the revised assumptions, long-term debt decreases more slowly.

Exhibit 4.10. Sensitivity Analysis Projected Financial Statements

Colossal Chemical Corporation
Year Ended December 31, 2001
($000 omitted)
Base Case (Exhibit 12.2) Sales Growth Assumption Reduced from 6% to 3%
(No improvement in gross margin over preceding year)

Income Statement	
Sales	$2,051
Cost of goods sold	1,374
Selling, general, and administrative expense	308
Depreciation	121
Research and development	82
Total costs and expenses	1,885
Operating Income	166
Interest expense	34
Interest (income)	(5)
Earnings before income taxes	137
Provision for income taxes	47
Net income	$ 90

Statement of Cash Flow	
Sources	
Net income	$ 90
Depreciation	121
Deferred income taxes	25
Working capital changes, excluding cash and borrowings	(26)
Cash provided by operations	$ 210
Uses	
Additions to property, plant, and equipment	165
Dividends	30
Repayment of current maturities of long-term debt	32
Cash provided by operations	227
Net cash provided (used) by operations	(17)
Increase in long-term debt	17
Net change in cash	$ 0

Balance Sheet

Cash and marketable securities	$ 69	Notes payable	$ 21
Accounts receivable	451	Accounts payable	267
Inventories	369	Current portion of long-term debt	27
		Total current liabilities	$ 315
Total current assets	889	Long-term debt	369
		Deferred income taxes	95
Property, plant, and equipment	939	Shareholders' equity	1,049
	$1,828		$1,828

Source: Martin S. Fridson, Fernando Alvarez. Financial Statement Analysis. Wiley. ISBN: 9780470635605.

The analyst can recalculate the credit quality measures from Exhibit 4.9, as displayed in Exhibit 4.11, using the updated statements from Exhibit 4.10. Projected funds from operations will account for 56.1% of total debt under the revised, more conservative gross margin and sales growth assumptions. Compared to the 62.2% ratio predicted in the base case, the implied improvement over 2011 is less. The adjusted assumptions result in a slight increase in total debt as a percentage of total capital, from 26.5% in the base case to 27.1%. In the pessimistic scenario, there is less growth in shareholders' equity due to retained earnings addition, but there is also less need for additional working capital to support higher sales. This lowers the need for borrowing, somewhat offsetting the slower rate of equity growth.

Exhibit 4.11. Trend of Credit Quality Comparison

Colossal Chemical Corporation
Year Ended December 31, 2002 (Projected)
($000 omitted)

	Pessimistic Case*	Base Case†
Total debt		
Notes payable	$ 21	$ 42
Current portion of long-term debt	27	27
Long-term debt	369	352
	417	421
Deferred income taxes	95	95
Shareholders' equity	1,049	1,062
Total capital	$1,541	$1,578
Total debt as a percentage of total capital	26.7%	26.7%
Funds provided by operations (before working capital changes)	236	256
Total debt	417	421
Cash provided as a percentage of total debt	56.6%	60.8%

Source: Martin S. Fridson, Fernando Alvarez. Financial Statement Analysis. Wiley. ISBN: 9780470635605.

An investor or lender will want to project financial statements on an optimistic, or best-case, scenario in order to finish the analysis. Sample assumptions for a three-scenario sensitivity analysis might be:

	Assumed Sales Growth	Assumed Gross Margin
Optimistic case (best realistic scenario)	8%	36%
Base case (most likely scenario)	6%	34%
Pessimistic case (worst realistic scenario)	3%	33%

Take note that symmetry is not required among the assumptions. In this case, the pessimistic case lowers base case sales by 3 percentage points, while the optimistic case assumes sales that are only 2 percentage points higher than the base case. The analyst merely thinks that there are more negative aspects than positive ones in the most likely scenario.

In order to acknowledge the interplay between the different accounts, additional presumptions can also be changed. In the short term, Colossal Chemical may have a lot of room to reduce its capital spending if its operating revenue declines. A forecast that disregarded this financial flexibility might come out as unduly negative. On the other hand, assuming that a business will use any extra money to pay down debt could result in an unrealistic capital structure estimate. In a multiyear projection for a strong cash generator, in particular, the ratio of debt to capital may decline in the later years to an extent that the business would deem unduly cautious. In these situations, changing the assumption from debt retirement to the maintenance of a given leverage ratio might be appropriate. Therefore, excess funds will be used for stock repurchases to the extent that delaying them would result in a reduction of the debt component of capital below a predetermined threshold.

Sensitivity analysis can be used to generate a variety of scenarios and determine the relative effects of altering a projection's various underlying assumptions. Compare the effects of a 1 percent change in the tax rate and a 1 percent change in gross margins, for instance, on Colossal Chemical's income statement. Exhibit 4.12, with all other assumptions held constant, illustrates how these two changes in assumptions affect the projected income statement in Exhibit 4point 2. When all other factors remain constant, net income is sensitive to a 1% change in gross margins by $13 million ($114 million minus $101 million). Conversely, assuming all other factors remain constant, a 1% change in the tax rate has a mere $1 million impact on net income.

Exhibit 4.12. Sensitivity Analysis: Impact of Changes in Selected Assumptions on Projected Income Statement

Colossal Chemical Corporation
Year Ended December 31, 2002
($000 omitted)

	Base Case	1% Decline in Gross Margin	1% Rise in Tax Rate
Sales	$2,110	$2,110	$2,110
Cost of goods sold	1,393	1,414	1,393
Selling, general, and administrative expense	317	317	317
Depreciation	121	121	121
Research and development	84	84	84
Total costs and expenses	1,915	1,936	1,915
Operating Income	195	174	195
Interest expense	34	34	34
Interest (income)	(5)	(5)	(5)
Earnings before income taxes	166	145	166
Provision for income taxes	56	49	58
Net income	$ 110	$ 96	$ 108

Source: Martin S. Fridson, Fernando Alvarez. Financial Statement Analysis. Wiley. ISBN: 9780470635605.

Among investors, this kind of analysis is quite common. For instance, they could calculate the effect of a 10-cent increase in the price of a pound of copper on a mining company's earnings and, consequently, on the value of its stock. Finding out which businesses will react most sharply to a certain anticipated economic development, like a decline in interest rates, is another use. A business where interest costs make up a small portion of total expenses will be less affected by a rate decrease. A company that has a high interest cost component and a large portion of its debt at floating rates will be more affected. (This presupposes that the asset return of the business is not likewise rate-sensitive.).

Sensitivity analysis is a technique that needs to be used carefully, despite its allure. As implied, it typically focuses on a single premise and works under the supposition that everything else stays the same. This is rarely the case in real life. Usually, when sales decline, so do gross margins. The rationale is that prices are under pressure to decline due to declining capacity utilization. Similarly, interest income and expense are not the only things impacted by rising interest rates. Increased rates discourage investment in the economy, which may ultimately result in a decline in sales for the business.

CASE STUDY

DEMAND FORECASTING

Mr. Ali has recently joined a fast paced growing pharmaceutical company as a "Demand Planner" for broad range of products. He is responsible for making consolidated demand forecast on monthly basis for an organization that used to have separate demand-planners for each product-line using his own tools and techniques.

In his previous employment, he was considered a person with strong analytical skills in demand forecasting, he looked after several beverage product lines, planning about their future demands. His formula for demand forecasting proved to be a success as it produced close-to-accurate results. He also had a very supportive team working under his supervision that used to maintain the data in state-of-the-art demand forecasting software. The software was capable of handling a large variety of SKUs on the basis of customized forecasting formula set by the demand planner.

Mr. Ali, through the software, was able to forecast demand and supply needs for beverages with a single customized formula, as the company was dealing in cold beverages only.

In his new position at Perfect Pharmacy, he feels overwhelmed by the complexity and variation found in the industry. There are primarily four types of product lines to forecast for:

- Products having stable demand and consistent in trends – generally on-the-counter medicines.
- Products showing seasonal shifting and variation – like cough syrup, etc.
- Products that are only for specific need emergency cases.

Mr. Ali has only one week to develop a forecast for all product ranges of the company. Being the demand-planner, he has called an urgent meeting to determine the single basis of forecasting for all the product lines.

As the meeting commenced, Mr. Ali has a very clear agenda in his mind – 'Decision on the basis of forecasting.' He was sure all product-planners would agree on simplicity and this would also bring efficiency in the system while removing extra workload from the product-planners.

He put forward a simple question, to start with, before his product-planners on how they forecast for their product lines. It was an open forum, so each product-planner shared his views and argued in its favor. Meeting went on and the team had a heated discussion and lot of idea sharing. Each product-planner presented before the demand-planner sound rationale for his own formula. He started noting down all the suggested formulae on a piece of paper. Till the half time, Mr. Ali was even more confused than before. He quickly adjourned the meeting and moved back to his office. As he approached his desk he saw a car in front of him that he did not notice before.

This was your visiting card; you closely worked with him in his last organization as a supply-chain consultant. You happened to be an expert in demand planning. In desperation to meet his deadline, he picked up your visiting card and called you to help him come out of the dilemma he was facing.

You agreed to help him find out the best mechanism for the demand planning in an organization with such a wide variety of product line.

- **Questions**

1. What forecasting method would you recommend to Mr. Ali?
2. Explain the nature and relevance of your recommended forecasting method to his current problem.

CLASS ACTIVITY

What is the distinction between forecasting and planners? How can organizations become confused one forecasting when this distinction is not clear?

SUMMARY

- Forecasting refers to the practice of predicting what will happen in the future by taking into consideration events in the past and present. Basically, it is a decision-making tool that helps businesses cope with the impact of the future's uncertainty by examining historical data and trends. It is a planning tool that enables businesses to chart their next moves and create budgets that will hopefully cover whatever uncertainties may occur.
- Budgeting involves creating financial statements for a specific period, such as projected revenue, expenses, cash flow, and investments. It is usually conducted with input from many different departments, because it requires input from multiple departments in order to come up with a holistic and detailed report. Therefore, the budgeting process takes time to complete. The company uses the budget to guide it in its financial activities. In other words, a budget is a plan for a company's future.
- Qualitative forecasting offers subjective results, as it is comprised of personal judgments by experts or forecasters. Forecasts are often biased because they are based on the expert's knowledge, intuition and experience, making the process non-mathematical.
- The quantitative method of forecasting is a mathematical process, making it consistent and objective. It steers away from basing the results on opinion and intuition, instead utilizing large amounts of data and figures that are interpreted.
- Financial forecasting refers to the process of drafting projections relating to the future performance of the business. It helps with direction and finding problem areas of the business. It includes analyzing the business's past performance and thoroughly studying current trends. It is however important to acknowledge the fact that the components of the financial forecasting models might differ based on the nature of the business and the purpose of conducting these projections.
- Revenue forecasting is the process of predicting future revenue for a company using historical performance data, predictive modeling, and qualitative insights. Revenue forecasts provide an estimated projection of the total revenues expected in a future period.
- Linear regression analyzes historical data to model how changes in key variables impact revenue. Regression provides a data-backed view into drivers of revenue growth and contraction. However, regression models are only as good as the input data. They may miss complex real-world dynamics that are not reflected in historical data.
- Time series analysis detects historical patterns in data over time. This helps tease out seasonal and cyclical trends from broader growth trajectories and random noise.
- Bottom-up forecasting taps insights from sales, account management and other frontline teams to build projections. They incorporate pipeline health, competitive threats, and market mood along with historical data.
- Top-down forecasting starts with the big-picture view of the total addressable

market, growth trajectories, economic conditions and business strategy. Leadership sets goals and divides revenue targets across functions. This ensures strategic alignment between long-term goals and short-term operations.

- Sales are activities related to selling or the number of goods sold in a given targeted time period. The delivery of a service for a cost is also considered a sale. A period during which goods are sold for a reduced price may also be referred to as a "sale."

REVIEW QUESTIONS

1. What is forecasting?
2. What are the two basic methods of forecasting?
3. Why is forecasting important?
4. Explain the process of forecasting.
5. List the sources of data for forecasting.
6. What is financial forecasting?
7. What is revenue forecasting?
8. List the different types of revenue forecasts.
9. Name the four common forecasting models.
10. What do you mean by sales?

REFERENCES

1. Armstrong, J. S. (2001). *Principles of Forecasting: A Handbook for Researchers and Practitioners*. Kluwer Academic Publishers.
2. Allen, H., & Taylor, M. P. (1990). Charts, noise and fundamentals in the London foreign exchange market. *The Economic Journal, 100*(400), 49–59. https://doi.org/10.2307/2234183.
3. Armstrong, J. S. (1983). Relative accuracy of judgmental and extrapolative methods in forecasting annual earnings. *Journal of Forecasting, 2*(4), 437–447. https://doi.org/10.1002/for.3980020411.
4. Green, K. C., & Armstrong, J. S. (2019). Role thinking: Standing in other people's shoes to forecast decisions in conflicts. *International Journal of Forecasting, 39*, 111–116. https://doi.org/10.1016/j.ijforecast.2018.07.003.
5. Kress, G. J., & Snyder, J. (1994). *Forecasting and Market Analysis Techniques: A Practical Approach*. Quorum Books.
6. Makridakis, S., Wheelwright, S., & Hyndman, R. J. (1998). *Forecasting: Methods and Applications* (3rd ed.). John Wiley & Sons.
7. Rescher, N. (1998). *Predicting the Future: An Introduction to The Theory of Forecasting*. State University of New York Press.
8. Chadefaux, T. (2014). Early warning signals for war in the news. *Journal of Peace Research, 51*(1), 5–18. https://doi.org/10.1177/0022343313511997.

CHAPTER

5

Time Value of Money

LEARNING OBJECTIVES

After studying this chapter, you will be able to:

- Explain the role of time value in finance
- Define present value and future value
- Discuss mixed streams
- Understand the net present value (NPV) and internal rate of return (IRR).

KEY TERMS FROM THIS CHAPTER

Annuity
Discount Rate
Financial values
Interest rate
Present value
Cash flow
Financial tables
Future Value
Mixed Streams
Time Value of Money (TVM)

INTRODUCTION

The Time Value of Money (TVM) is a fundamental financial concept that asserts the value of money changes over time. It is based on the principle that a specific amount of money today is worth more than the same amount in the future due to its potential earning capacity. This core idea underlies the operations of interest, inflation, and investment returns. TVM is crucial for making informed financial decisions, whether for personal finance or corporate investments. It encompasses several components: present value (PV), future value (FV), interest rate (r), and the number of periods (n). The present value represents the current worth of a sum to be received in the future, discounted at a specific interest rate. Conversely, the future value is the amount a present sum will grow to after earning interest over a specified period. The relationship between these variables is captured through equations such as PV = FV/(1 + r)n and FV = PV * (1 + r)n, which allow for the calculation of one variable when the others are known. This relationship highlights how money's potential to earn interest affects its valuation. Higher interest rates or longer time periods increase the future value of a given amount of money. The TVM principle is applied in various financial scenarios, including loan amortizations, retirement planning, investment appraisals, and bond pricing. For instance, when evaluating investment opportunities, understanding TVM helps in comparing the profitability of projects with different time horizons and cash flows. Moreover, TVM plays a critical role in assessing the impact of inflation, which erodes purchasing power over time. Financial instruments such as annuities, perpetuities, and savings accounts are also analyzed using TVM principles to determine their value. Overall, the Time Value of Money is a cornerstone of financial theory and practice, emphasizing the importance of time in the valuation of money and guiding prudent financial decision-making.

5.1. THE ROLE OF TIME VALUE IN FINANCE

Opportunities to earn positive rates of return on their investments are always present for financial managers and investors, whether they choose to invest in interest-bearing securities or deposits or in appealing projects. Therefore, financial managers clearly recognize the time value of money, which has significant economic implications depending on when cash is taken in and out. The idea behind time value is that a dollar now is more valuable than a dollar that you will receive later. The two perspectives of time value—future value and present value—as well as the computational tools that make time value calculations more efficient and the fundamental cash flow patterns are all taken into consideration as we start our investigation of time value in finance.

5.1.1. Future Value Versus Present Value

Either present value or future value techniques can be used to evaluate financial values and decisions. These methods will arrive at the same conclusions, but they have different perspectives on the matter. Cash flows are usually measured at the end of a project's life using future value techniques. Cash flows are measured at the beginning of a project's life (time zero) using present value techniques. Present value is the same as having cash on hand right now, while future value is the money you will receive at a specific future date. The cash flows connected to a specific investment can be shown using a timeline. It is a horizontal line with future periods indicated from left to right and time zero at the leftmost end. Figure 5.1 shows a line spanning five periods, in this case years. Above the line are the cash flows that occur at time zero and at the end of each year; the negative values signify cash outflows ($10,000 at time zero), and the positive values signify cash inflows ($3,000 at year's end, $5,000 at year's end, and so forth).

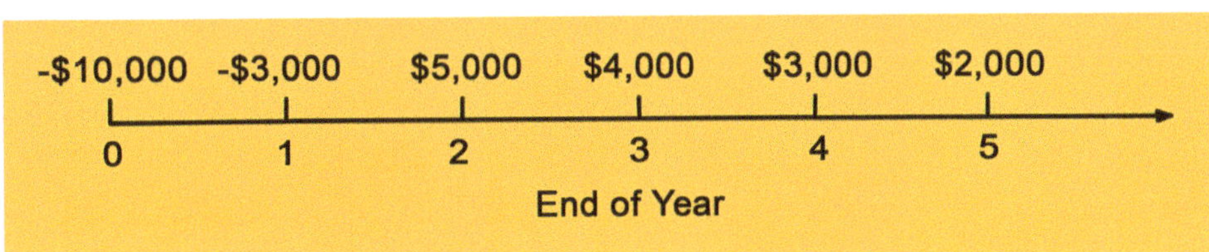

Figure 5.1. *Time line depicting an investment's cash flows.*

Source: https://www.studocu.com/row/document/university-of-the-punjab/financial-management/chapter-4-time-value-of-money/57173142.

All of the cash flows connected to an investment, like those shown in Figure 5.1, must be measured at the same time because money has a time value. That is usually the point at which the investment's life ends or begins. Compounding is used in the future value technique to determine the future value of each cash flow at the end of the investment's life. The investment's future value is then calculated by adding these values. Figure 5.2 shows this method above the timeline. The figure illustrates how each cash flow's future value is calculated at the conclusion of the investment's five-year life. The present value technique, on the other hand, finds the investment's current value by first calculating the present value of each cash flow at time zero through the use of discounting. This value is then added up. The use of this strategy is shown in Figure 5.2 the timeline. Financial managers typically rely on present value techniques because they make decisions at time zero, even though future value and present value lead to the same decisions.

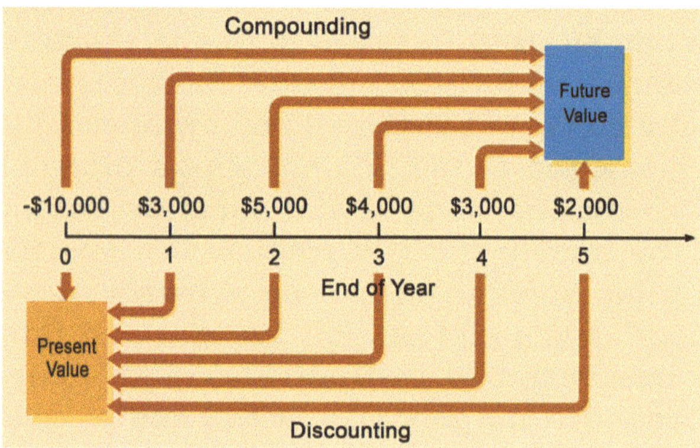

Figure 5.2. *Time line showing compounding to find future value and discounting to find present value.*

Source: https://www.studocu.com/row/document/university-of-the-punjab/financial-management/chapter-4-time-value-of-money/57173142.

5.1.2. Computational Tools

Determining present and future values frequently requires laborious computations. Time value techniques can be applied more efficiently, even though you should understand the underlying concepts and mathematics of these calculations. We concentrate on the use of financial tables, spreadsheets, computers, and handheld financial calculators as computational tools.

5.1.2.1. Financial Tables

Time value calculations are made simpler by the inclusion of multiple future and present value interest factors in financial tables. With varying degrees of rounding, the values displayed in these tables are easily derived from formulas. Usually, the interest rate (in columns) and the number of periods (in rows) are used to index the tables. This general layout is shown in Figure 5.3. The dark blue box indicates the intersection of the 20% column and the 10-period row, which is where the interest factor at a 20% interest rate for 10 years would be found.

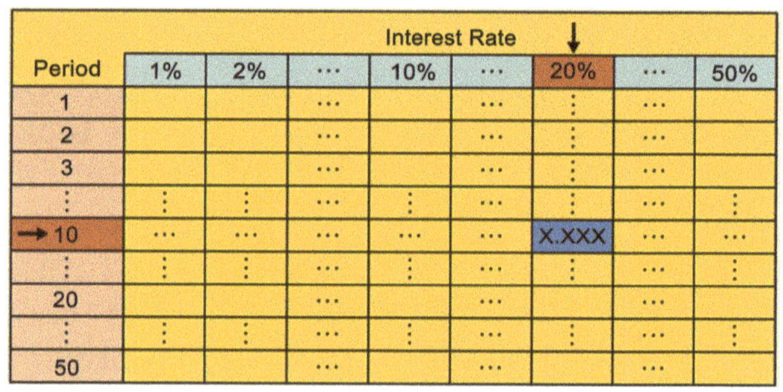

Figure 5.3. *Layout and use of a financial table.*

Source: https://www.studocu.com/row/document/university-of-the-punjab/financial-management/chapter-4-time-value-of-money/57173142.

5.1.2.2. Financial Calculators

Time value calculations can also be performed with financial calculators. Financial calculators typically come with a large number of pre-programmed financial operations. We utilize the crucial financial keys, which are labeled in a way that is compatible with the majority of large financial calculators, for convenience. Our main focus is on the keys that are illustrated and defined in Figure 5.4.

In addition to the compute (CPT) key, we usually use four of the first five keys listed in the left column. For each of the four keys, there is an unknown value that needs to be calculated. (On rare occasions, one key is used to represent the unknown value while the other five are utilized. Some of the more advanced calculators require menu-driven keystrokes; once you choose the appropriate routine, the calculator asks you to enter each value; a compute key is not required to get a solution on these calculators. Financial tables can be replaced with any calculator that has the fundamental future and present value functions. The reference guides that come with other financial calculators provide an explanation of their keystrokes. You'll probably want to use a calculator to expedite regular financial calculations once you grasp the fundamental ideas. You can improve your financial computations' accuracy and speed with a little practice. Be aware that values determined by using financial tables and those obtained with a financial calculator are likely to differ slightly due to the greater precision of the calculator. Recall that the goal is to grasp the content conceptually. Don't accept answers just because you can use a calculator to solve problems; this does not always indicate that you understand the material. Work with the material until you are certain that you comprehend the ideas as well.

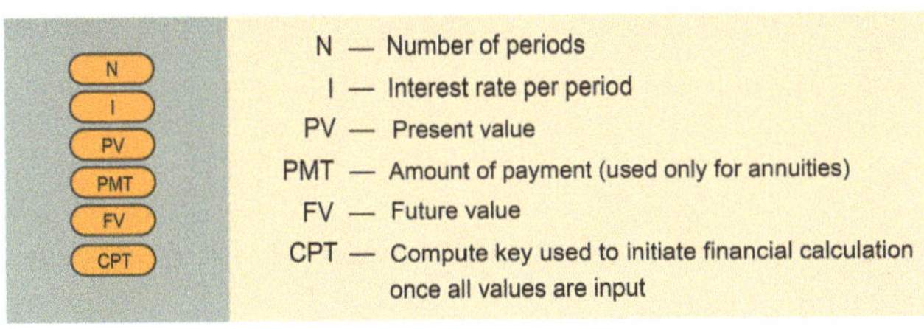

Figure 5.4. *Calculator keys.*

Source: https://www.studocu.com/row/document/university-of-the-punjab/financial-management/chapter-4-time-value-of-money/57173142.

5.1.2.3. Computers and Spreadsheets

Spreadsheets and computers both have built-in routines that make time value calculations easier, just like financial calculators do. Throughout the text, we offer several spreadsheet solutions that pinpoint the cell entries needed to compute time values. The spreadsheet's cells are used to record the values for each variable, and an equation connecting the cells is used to program the calculation. Because of the equation connecting the cells, the solution automatically adjusts when the values of the variables change. At the bottom of the spreadsheet is the equation that drives the computation.

It is important that you become familiar with the use of spreadsheets for several reasons.

Spreadsheets are far more computationally capable than calculators. They provide numerous routines for significant statistical and financial relationships. For instance, they carry out intricate analyzes that assess the chances of success and failure for managerial choices.

Spreadsheets have the ability to program logical decisions. They enable the process of automatically selecting the best option among two or more options to be automated. We provide multiple instances of this capacity to determine the best alternative investment to choose from and the appropriate amount of credit to offer clients.

Spreadsheets display not only the calculated values of solutions but also the input conditions on which solutions are based. Sensitivity analysis, or assessing how changes in conditions affect the values of the solutions, is made possible by the connections between the cells in a spreadsheet. After all, managers are rarely just interested in finding one value under a specific set of circumstances. Situations evolve, and managers who are not ready to act swiftly to capitalize on these shifts will have to bear the repercussions.

Spreadsheets encourage teamwork. They compile information from various business units and combine it into the cash budgets and financial statements of a company. To assess capital investments, they combine data from manufacturing, marketing, and other functional organizations. The ability to carry these skills and use spreadsheets with ease is made possible by laptop computers, regardless of where the user is—at the company headquarters for a crucial meeting or visiting a far-off client or supplier.

Spreadsheets enhance learning. Making spreadsheets advances a person's knowledge of a subject. Spreadsheets are interactive, so changes you make are immediately responded to. Many find the interaction between the user and the computer to be both entertaining and educational, as it becomes a game. Finally, spreadsheets communicate as well as calculate. Tables and charts that can be included in reports are among their outputs. They interact with the massive databases that businesses use to plan and manage their international operations. They are the closest thing we have to a global language for business.

5.1.3. Basic Patterns of Cash Flow

- The cash flow—both inflows and outflows—of a firm can be described by its general pattern. It can be defined as a single amount, an annuity, or a mixed stream.
- **Single Amount:** A lump-sum amount either currently held or expected at some future date. Examples include $1,000 today and $650 to be received at the end of 10 years.
- **Annuity:** A level periodic stream of cash flow. For our purposes, we'll work primarily with annual cash flows. Examples include either paying out or receiving $800 at the end of each of the next 7 years.
- **Mixed Stream:** A stream of cash flow that is not an annuity; a stream of unequal periodic cash flows that reflect no particular pattern. Examples include the following two cash flow streams A and B.

	Mixed cash flow steam	
End of year	A	B
1	$ 100	–$ 50
2	800	100
3	1,200	80
4	1,200	– 60
5	1,400	
6	300	

Note that neither cash flow stream has equal, periodic cash flows and that A is a 6-year mixed stream and B is a 4-year mixed stream.

5.2. PRESENT VALUE

The idea of present value asserts that a sum of money is worth more now than it will be in the future. Stated differently, the value of money received in the future is not equivalent to the same amount received today. In five years, $1,000 is worth more than $1,000 if it is received now. The reason for this is that an investor can put that $1,000 into the market now and hopefully earn a rate of return over the next five years. Any potential interest rate that an investment might earn is factored into present value. If an investor receives $1,000 today and can earn a 5 percent annual rate of return, for instance, that $1,000 is undoubtedly worth more than $1,000 five years from now. There would be an opportunity cost or a loss of the five-year rate of return if an investor waited five years to receive $1,000.

5.2.1. Present Value Formula and Calculation

$$\text{Present Value} = \frac{\text{Future Value}}{(1 + i)^n}$$

Where; FV is the Future Value; r is the Rate of return; and n=Number of periods

1. Input the future amount that you expect to receive in the numerator of the formula.
2. Determine the interest rate that you expect to receive between now and the future and plug the rate as a decimal in place of "r" in the denominator.
3. Input the time period as the exponent "n" in the denominator. So, if you want to calculate the present value of an amount you expect to receive in three years, you would plug in the number three.
4. A number of online calculators are available, including this present value calculator.

5.2.2. Determining the Discount Rate

The investment rate of return used in the present value computation is called the discount rate. To put it another way, the discount rate represents the rate of return that would be lost if an investor decided to accept a sum of money now rather than the same amount in the future. Because the discount rate is the expected rate of return you would have received if you had invested today's dollars for a certain amount of time, it is highly subjective when determining present value.

In many cases, a risk-free rate of return is determined and used as the discount rate, which is often called the hurdle rate. The rate represents the rate of return that the investment or project would need to earn in order to be worth pursuing. A U.S.

Treasury bond rate is often used as the risk-free rate because Treasuries are backed by the U.S. government. So, for example, if a two-year Treasury paid 2% interest or yield, the investment would need to earn more than 2% to justify the risk.

The time value plus an appropriate interest rate that increases future value in nominal or absolute terms mathematically is the sum of the discount rate. On the other hand, a lender can determine the reasonable amount of any future earnings or obligations in relation to the present value of the capital by using the discount rate to calculate future value in terms of present value. When future value is reduced to present value, it is referred to as a discount. In many financial computations, the discounted or present value computation is crucial. Discounted or present value, for instance, is used to calculate net present value, bond yields, and pension obligations. Making present value calculations with an Excel spreadsheet or financial calculator can help you determine whether to accept offers like a cash rebate, 0 percent financing for a car purchase, or pay points on a mortgage.

5.2.3. Importance

- **Important for Analysis**: Understanding future cash inflow or outflow from the company is crucial for any kind of business; when you anticipate a specific level of future cash flow, a PV calculation is required.
- **Fundamental Concept:** PV calculations are required in order to determine the value of different investments, such as stocks, bonds, bank deposits, insurance, and pension funds.
- **Time-Value of Money:** The amount of interest rate, inflation, and time periods all play a role in determining the expected future return on your investment. What is the present value of the future worth that influences the choice of investments?
- **Inflation Effect:** They ensure that, over time, the impact of inflation on money is computed by taking into account the inflation rate or by discounting the expected rate of return on future cash flow.

5.2.4. Benefits of Present Value

- Financial and investment decision-making by corporations and investors can benefit from the use of present value. When deciding which investments to prioritize over others, it can offer insightful information.
- If an investment's estimated rate of return is insufficient to justify the investment's future outcome, its present value can shed light on the matter.
- Furthermore, it can function as an essential comparative instrument in the process of choosing investments.
- The economic effects of the fluctuating value of money during periods of high inflation can be better understood by applying the formula for present value.

5.2.5. Limitations of Present Value

- A discount rate (rate of return) assumption is made when calculating present value. In order to get the results they require, those making decisions about corporate projects or creating financial analysis reports can change that assumption. A company's performance or the integrity of its decision-making process will suffer from this.

- To be useful, rates of return in a present value calculation must be reasonable. Unfortunately, estimated rates of inflation and return are just that—projections. There is no way to get exact values.
- It's critical to remember that no investment decision is guaranteed to yield a profit, and inflation can also deplete value.

5.2.6. Examples of Present Value

- **Example 1**

After three years, Mr. X requests $10,000. He is interested in a particular investment, and the interest rate on it is 4% annually. How much money he needs to put in today to get the desired amount.

- Solution

Given;

- Future Value = $10,000
- Interest = 4% per annum
- Period = 3 years

Calculation of Present Value can be done as follows:

B6 | =B3/(1+B4)^B5

Present Value = Future Value / (1+i) ^ n

	A	B
2	Particulars	Amount
3	Future Value (FV)	$10,000
4	Interest Rate (i)	4%
5	Period (n)	3
6	Present Value	$8,889.96
7		

- $= \$10,000/(1+0.04)^3$
- = $8,889.96

i.e., Mr. X should invest $8,889.96 amount today to get the desired amount in 3 years.

- **Example 2**

Mr. A has $100,000 in hand from his savings; he wants $200,000 after 10 years. He has three options, i.e., either.

1. Bank deposit at a rate of 4% per annum compounded quarterly.
2. Government bonds at 3.85% for 10 years.
3. Invest in a Hedge fund with expected returns of a minimum of 8% per annum. Which investment option is best to achieve his goals?

Calculation of Present Value for Option A can be done as follows:

B6 | =B3/(1+B4)^B5

Present Value = Future Value / (1+i) ^ n

	A	B	C
2	Particulars	A	
3	Future Value	$200,000.00	
4	Interest Rate (i)	1%	
5	Periods (n)	40	
6	Present Value	134330.63	
7			

$=\$200000.00/(1+1\%)^{40}$

= 134330.63

Similarly, we can calculate PV for Option B and Option C

	A	B	C	D
2	Particulars	A	B	C
3	Future Value	$200,000.00	$200,000.00	$200,000.00
4	Interest Rate (I)	1%	3.85%	8%
5	Periods (n)	40	10	10
6	Present Value	134330.63	$137,077.12	$92,638.70
7				

Looking at the table above, the answer seems quite simple: an investment in option C, i.e., hedge funds give more returns, which help Mr. A to achieve his future investment returns. In contrast, investment options of bank deposits and government bonds will need an additional investment of $34,330.64 and $37,077.12 on the current amount in hand to achieve the desired return of $200,000.

Mr. A initially believes that choosing investment option C is an easy decision. However, it should be noted that investing in hedge funds carries a risk of loss, so there's no assurance that investors will realize the anticipated returns in the future. Although there is very little risk involved in investing in options A and B—bank deposits and government bond purchases—they might not yield the anticipated returns. Risk capacity decisions can be made based on Mr. A's financial situation. An aggressive investor will choose Option C if he is prepared and has the financial means to take the risk, while a conservative investor would prefer Option A or B.

5.3. FUTURE VALUE

The value of a current asset at a future date, calculated using an assumed growth rate, is known as future value, or FV. It is used by financiers and investors to project future values of investments made today. The future value of an asset can be negatively impacted by external factors like inflation. One can compare present value (PV) with future value.

5.3.1. Future Value Formula

Investors can forecast the potential profit margin from assets by using the future value computation. The kind of investment determines an asset's future value. A constant rate of growth is assumed in the future value formula. Accurately estimating the future value is simple when funds are deposited into a savings account that offers a guaranteed interest rate. Investments in securities with a volatile rate of return, such as stocks, can, however, produce varying outcomes.

5.3.1.1. Simple Annual Interest

The future value calculation is predicated on a steady growth rate and a single upfront payment that is held in reserve for the duration of the investment. If an investment earns simple interest compounded annually, then the FV formula is:

$$FV = I \times (1 + (R \times T))$$

Where; I is the Investment amount; R=Interest rate; and T=Number of years

If a $1,000 investment is held for five years in a savings account with 10% simple interest paid annually, the FV of the $1,000 equals $1,000 × [1 + (0.10 x 5)], or $1,500.

5.3.1.2. Compounded Annual Interest

The rate is applied to the total account balance at the end of each period when compound interest is used. In the aforementioned example, the initial year's investment yields interest of 10% × $1,000, or $100. But instead of $1,000, the account balance is $1,100 the next year. For second-year interest earnings of 10% × $1,100, or $110, compound interest is calculated by applying the 10% interest rate to the entire balance.

FV of an investment earning compounding interest is:

$$FV = I \times (1 + R)^T$$

Where; I is the investment amount; R is the interest rate; and T is the number of years

Using the above example, the same \$1,000 invested for five years in a savings account with a 10% compounding interest rate would have an FV of $\$1,000 \times [(1 + 0.10)^5]$, or \$1,610.51.

5.3.2. Using FV Calculations

- **Future Value Allows for Planning:** When people are aware of their financial situation, they can make plans for the future. For instance, using future value, a homebuyer hoping to save \$100,000 for a down payment can determine how long it will take to reach these savings.
- **Future Value Makes Comparisons Easier:** An investor can compare options by computing future values and comparing outcomes. A \$5,000 investment is needed, and over the following three years, it will yield a 10% return. In the other, a \$3,000 investment will yield a return of 5% in year one, 10% in year two, and 35% in year three.
- **Future Value Is Easy to Calculate Due to Estimates:** Anyone can use future value in hypothetical situations because it is based on estimates. For instance, the homebuyer who is attempting to save \$100,000 can use their estimated monthly savings, estimated interest rate, and estimated savings period to determine the future value of their savings.

5.3.3. Limitations

- **Future Value Usually Assumes Constant Growth:** Growth may not always be linear or consistent year-over-year.
- **Future Value Assumptions May Not Happen:** When the market fails to produce the estimated return, the calculated value proves worthless.
- **Future Value May Fail at Comparisons:** Future value gives an estimate of an item's ultimate monetary value. Consequently, there are certain restrictions when comparing projects. When considering only future value, one option might seem better because it has a higher starting point, but it doesn't account for the initial investment.

5.3.4. Future Value Pros and Cons

- **Pros**
  - Relies on readily available estimates
  - Lump sum or simple cashflows may be easy to calculate
  - Future value helps determine whether an investor meets a target or goal.
  - The concept of future value can be applied to any cashflow, return, or investment structure.
- **Cons**
  - Estimates may be quickly invalidated
  - Future value of annuities or irregular cashflow may be difficult to calculate
  - Future value cannot be used to compare and choose between two mutually exclusive projects
  - Future value models assume constant rate growth

5.3.5. Difference Between Present Value vs Future Value

Let's now look at the head to head difference between Present Value vs Future Value (Table 5.1)

Table 5.1. Present Value vs Future Value

Basis – Present Value vs Future Value	Present Value	Future Value
Meaning	The present value is defined as the current value of the cash flow in the future. It is basically the amount of cash in hand on today's date.	It is defined as the value of the future cash flow after a certain future period. This is the amount of cash that will be received at a specified future date.
Time Frame	It is the current value of an asset or investment at the starting of a particular time period.	It is the value of the asset or investment at the end of a particular time period.
Inflation Effect	For the present value, inflation is considered.	For future value, inflation is not considered.
Rates Applicable	While calculating present value, both the discount rate and interest rate are taken into account.	While calculating future value, only the interest rate is taken into account.
Decision Making	Present value is very much important for the investors as it helps to decide whether to invest or not.	Since this reflects the future profits from an investment, it has lesser importance in decision making regarding investments.
Calculation Method	While calculating present value, the discount is applied to find out the present value of every cash flow, and then all these values are added up to find the investment's value on today's date.	Future value calculation uses the compounding technique to arrive at the future value of every cash flow after a certain time period, and then all these values are added up to get the investment's future value.
Nature	The present value is the amount that is required to obtain the future value.	Future value is the amount that an individual will get from cash on hand.

Source: https://www.wallstreetmojo.com/present-value/.

5.4. MIXED STREAMS

An annuity or a mixed stream are the two main forms of cash flow streams that are feasible. A mixed stream is a stream of unequal periodic cash flows that do not follow any specific pattern, in contrast to an annuity, which is a pattern of equal periodic cash flows. Financial managers often have to assess opportunities that should yield a variety of cash flow streams. Here, we take into account mixed streams' present and future values.

5.4.1. Future Value of a Mixed Stream

It is simple to calculate the future value of a mixed stream of cash flows. To find the total future value, we first calculate the future value of each cash flow at the given future date. We then add up all of the individual future values.

- **Example**

A small customer of Shrell Industries, a cabinet manufacturer, is expected to provide a mixed stream of cash flows over the next 5 years.

End of year	Cash flow
1	$11,500
2	14,000
3	12,900
4	16,000
5	18,000

If Shrell invests these cash flows as soon as it receives them, with an expected return of 8%, how much will it have amassed by the end of year five?

This situation is depicted on the following time line (Figure 5.5):

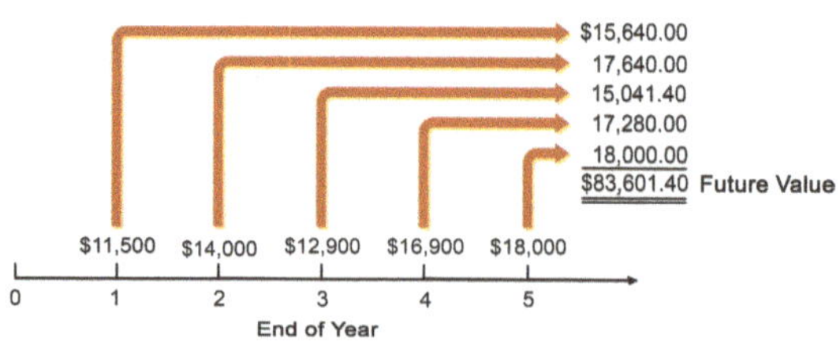

Figure 5.5. *Time line for future value of a mixed stream (end-of-year cash flows, compounded at 8% to the end of year 5).*

Source: https://www.studocu.com/row/document/university-of-the-punjab/financial-management/chapter-4-time-value-of-money/57173142.

- **Table Use:** We calculate each cash flow's future value, compounded at an 8 percent rate for the appropriate number of years, in order to solve this problem. The first cash flow, $11,500, received at the end of the first year, will earn interest for four years (from the end of the first year to the end of the fifth year); the second cash flow, $14,000, received at the end of the second year, will earn interest for three years (from the end of the second year to the end of the fifth year); and so on. The future value of the mixed cash flow stream is equal to the sum of the individual end-of-year-5 future values. The computations required to determine the cash flow stream's future value are shown in Table 5.2, and the result is $83,601.40.

Table 5.2. Future Value of a Mixed Stream of Cash Flows

Year	Cash flow (1)	Number of years earning interest (n) (2)	$FVIF_{8\%,n}$ [a] (2)	Future value [(1) x (3)] (4)
1	$11,500	5 - 1= 4	1.360	$15,640.00
2	14,000	5 - 2= 3	1.260	17,640.00
3	12,900	5 - 3= 2	1.166	15,041.40
4	16,000	5 - 4= 1	1.080	17,280.00
5	18,000	5 - 5 = 0	1.000[b]	18,000.00
			Future value of mixed stream	$83,601.40

Source: https://www.studocu.com/row/document/university-of-the-punjab/financial-management/chapter-4-time-value-of-money/57173142.

- **Calculator Use:** To determine the future value of the stream, you can utilize a calculator to calculate the future value of each individual cash flow and then add up all of the future values. Unfortunately, most calculators don't have a feature that lets you enter all of the cash flows, set the interest rate, and figure out the future value of the entire cash flow stream—that is, unless you can program your calculator. The future value of Shrell Industries' cash flow stream at the end of year five would have been $83,608.15 if you had used your calculator to find each future cash flow value and then added them up. This is a more accurate estimate than the one you would have obtained by using a financial table.
- **Spreadsheet Use:** The following Excel spreadsheet can be used to calculate the mixed stream's future value.

	A	B
1	FUTURE VALUE OF A MIXED STREAM	
2	Interest rate, pct/year	8%
3	Year	Year-End Cash Flow
4	1	$11,500
5	2	$14,000
6	3	$12,000
7	4	$16,000
8	5	$18,000
9	Future value	$83,608,15

Entry in Cell B9 is
=-FV(B2,A8.0,NPV(B2,B4:B8))
The minus sign appears before FV to convert the future value to a positive amount.

Shrell Industries will have roughly $83,600 by the end of year five if it invests the cash flows it receives from customers at an 8% interest rate for the next 5 years.

5.4.2. Present Value of a Mixed Stream

Determining the future value of a mixed stream of cash flows bears similarities to determining its present value. To find the total present value, we first calculate the present value of each future amount and then add up all of the individual present values.

- **Example**

Frey Company, a shoe manufacturer, has been offered an opportunity to receive the following mixed stream of cash flows over the next 5 years:

End of year	Cash flow
1	$400
2	800
3	500
4	400
5	300

If the firm must earn at least 9% on its investments, what is the most it should pay for this opportunity? This situation is depicted on the following time line (Figure 5.6):

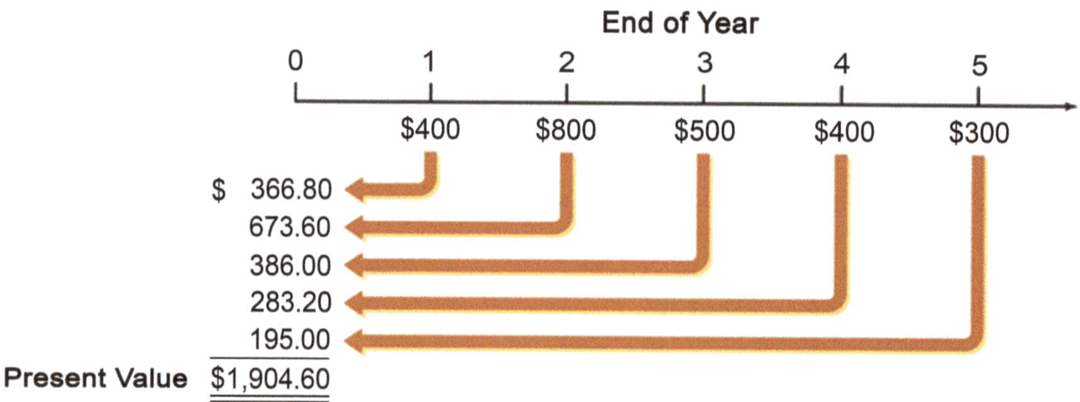

Figure 5.6. *Time line for present value of a mixed stream (end-of-year cash flows, discounted at 9% over the corresponding number of years.*

Source: https://www.studocu.com/row/document/university-of-the-punjab/financial-management/chapter-4-time-value-of-money/57173142.

- **Table Use:** Find the present value of each cash flow discounted at 9% for the appropriate number of years in order to solve this problem. The present value of the entire stream is the sum of these individual values. The computations required to determine the cash flow stream's present value are shown in Table 5.3, and the result is $1,904.60.

Table 5.3. Present Value of a Mixed Stream of Cash Flows

Year (n)	Cash flow (1)	$PVIF_{9\%,n}$[a] (2)	Present value [(1) × (2)] (3)
1	$400	0.917	$ 366.80
2	800	0.842	673.60
3	500	0.772	386.00
4	400	0.708	283.20
5	300	0.650	195.00
		Present value of mixed stream	$1,904.60

Source: https://www.studocu.com/row/document/university-of-the-punjab/financial-management/chapter-4-time-value-of-money/57173142.

- **Calculator Use:** The present value of the stream can be calculated by adding the present values of each individual cash flow, which can be done with a calculator. The majority of financial calculators, however, include a feature that lets you enter all cash flows, choose the discount rate, and instantly determine the present value of the total cash flow stream. Calculators yield more accurate results than rounded table factors, so the present value of the cash flow stream for Frey Company found with a calculator is $1,904.76, which is not too dissimilar from the previous calculation of $1,904.60.
- **Spreadsheet Use:** The present value of the mixed stream of future cash flows also can be calculated as shown on the following Excel spreadsheet.

	A	B
1	PRESENT VALUE OF A MIXED STREAM OF FUTURE CASH FLOWS	
2	Interest Rate, pct/year	9%
3	Year	Year-End Cash Flow
4	1	$400
5	2	$800
6	3	$500
7	4	$400
8	5	$300
9	Present Value	$1,904.76
	Entry in Cell B9 is =NPV (B2,B4:B8)	

Paying about $1,905 would provide exactly a 9% return. Frey should pay no more than that amount for the opportunity to receive these cash flows.

5.5. NET PRESENT VALUE (NPV)

The future profitability of an investment, project, or business is ascertained using net present value. The total future cash flows over the investment's lifetime, discounted to the present value, is the net present value (NPV) of the investment. When deciding how and where to allocate capital, businesses frequently use net present value in their budgets. Finance professionals can make better decisions if they set the value of each investment option or potential project to the same level, or what it will ultimately be worth.

5.5.1. Who Uses Net Present Value?

Net present value is a tool often used by corporate finance professionals. Investment bankers, for instance, compare net present values to decide which merger or acquisition is cost-effective. Furthermore, when managing budgets and setting project priorities, certain accountants—like certified management accountants—may rely on net present value (NPV). Knowing how to compute net present value (NPV) can also help business owners make better budgetary decisions and get a better idea of the future worth of their company.

5.5.2. NPV Formula

The cash flows for each period of the project or investment must be found, discounted to present value, and the initial investment must be deducted from the total of the project's discounted cash flows in order to arrive at net present value.

The NPV formula is:

$$\text{NPV} = \frac{\text{Cash Flow}_1}{(1+r)^1} + \frac{\text{Cash Flow}_2}{(1+r)^2} + \frac{\text{Cash Flow}_n}{(1+r)^n} - \text{Initial Investment}$$

In this formula:

- Cash Flow is the sum of money spent and earned on the investment or project for a given period of time.
- n is the number of periods of time.
- r is the discount rate.

5.5.3. Components of NPV

- **Cash Flow:** Cash flows encompass all financial outflows and inflows related to an investment, such as interest, loan payments, and capital expenses. Both outflows for expenses and inflows for revenue, profits, or dividends are included in the cash flow for each period.

- **Number of Periods (n):** The number of periods is equivalent to the project or investment's duration in months or years. The number of periods will occasionally default to 10, or 10 years, as that is the typical duration of a business. Different investments, businesses, and projects, however, might have more precise deadlines.
- **Discount Rate (r):** The weighted average cost of capital (WACC) of the company is typically the discount rate. The amount of money a business must make in order to cover its operating expenses is known as its WACC. The company's interest rate, loan payments, and dividend payments are all included in WACC. The idea of the time value of money requires that cash flows be discounted. This is the idea that money obtained now is more valuable than money obtained later. For instance, you can invest the money you receive now to earn interest over the course of the next year, so $10 today is worth more than $10 in a year. We can more precisely evaluate and contrast investment options by discounting future cash flows to their present value because inflation and interest rates have an impact on the value of $1.
- **Initial Investment:** The project or investment's upfront costs are known as the initial investment. The initial $5 million cost of a project, for instance, will be deducted from the total discounted cash flows.

5.5.4. Advantages of Net Present Value Method

- **Time Value of Money:** The net present value method is a tool used to examine a project's profitability. The time value of money is taken into account. The future cash flows will be worth less than the current cash flows. Therefore, the value will decrease the further the cash flows. The NPV approach appropriately takes this significant factor into account. This enables the company to compare two projects that are reasonably similar. For example, if Project A has a three-year life and Project B has a three-year life and has higher cash flows in the later period, the company can use net present value (NPV) to make a sensible decision to choose Project A because inflows now are worth more than inflows later.
- **Comprehensive Tool:** The total amount of inflows, outflows, time span, and risk are all taken into account by net present value. As a result, net present value (NPV) is a thorough tool that accounts for all investment-related factors.
- **Value of Investment:** The Net Present Value method provides the total profit value in addition to indicating whether or not a project will be profitable. Similar to the example above, the project will profit $361,05 after the cash flows are discounted. The tool calculates the investment's gains or losses.

5.5.5. Limitations of the Net Present Value Method

- **Discounting Rate:** Determining the rate of return is the primary constraint on net present value. A higher rate of return may give a false negative net present value (NPV), and a lower rate of return may indicate a project's false profitability and lead to poor decision-making.

- **Different Projects Are Not Comparable:** When comparing two projects that are not from the same time period, NPV cannot be used. Because many businesses have a fixed budget and occasionally have two project options, it is not possible to compare two projects that differ in terms of duration or level of risk by using net present value (NPV).
- **Multiple Assumptions:** In addition, the NPV approach makes numerous assumptions about inflows and outflows. It's possible that significant costs won't be realized until the project really takes off. The inflows might also not always be what is anticipated. The majority of software available today does NPV analysis and helps management make decisions. Despite all of its drawbacks, the NPV approach to capital budgeting is popular because it is highly beneficial.

5.5.6. Interpreting Net Present Value

Net present value has three potential outcomes:

- **Positive NPV:** A project or investment may be profitable and worthwhile to pursue if the monetary amount is positive.
- **Negative NPV:** A negative dollar amount means the project or investment is unlikely to be profitable and should probably not be pursued.
- **Zero NPV:** When an investment or project has a net present value of zero, it is neither costly nor profitable. A company may still consider projects and investments with an NPV of zero if the project has significant intangible benefits, such as strategic positioning, brand equity, or increased consumer satisfaction.

5.5.7. Net Present Value Example

Assume for the moment that your business has two possible projects it could begin. How can we determine which project is the better choice? Since the weighted average cost of capital for your company is 7%, the discount rate for both projects will be 7%. A project has a five-year lifespan.

The initial investment and cash flows for the two projects are:

- Project A
  - **Initial investment:** $15 million
  - **Cash Flow Year 1:** $3 million
  - Cash Flow Year 2: $3 million
  - **Cash Flow Year 3:** $5 million
  - Cash Flow Year 4: $5 million
  - Cash Flow Year 5: $5 million
- Project B
  - **Initial investment:** $20 million
  - **Cash Flow Year 1:** $2 million
  - **Cash Flow Year 2:** $4 million
  - **Cash Flow Year 3:** $6 million
  - **Cash Flow Year 4:** $8 million
  - **Cash Flow Year 5:** $10 million

Discounting these cash flows using the 7% weighted average cost of capital, the annual discounted cash flows for each project are:

Year	Project A	Project B
1	$2,803,738	$1,869,159
2	$2,620,316	$3,493,755
3	$4,081,489	$4,897,787
4	$3,814,476	$6,103,162
5	$3,564,931	$7,129,862
Cash Flow Sum	$16,884,950	$23,493,725

Note: Numbers are rounded to the nearest whole dollar amount.

Once we have the total of the discounted cash flows for the duration of the project, we can find the net present value for each by subtracting the initial investment:

Project A's NPV = $16,884,950 – $15,000,000

NPV = $1,884,950

Project B's NPV = $23,493,725 – $20,000,000

NPV = $3,493,725

Any project will turn a profit. Based on its apparent profitability, Project B appears to be superior due to its higher net present value (NPV). Still, it's critical to take other aspects into account.

When deciding which project is a better investment, financial professionals also take into account intangible benefits like brand equity and strategic positioning. For instance, is the net present value of Project B high enough to justify a bigger initial investment?

5.6. INTERNAL RATE OF RETURN (IRR)

The profitability of an investment is gauged by the internal rate of return, or IRR. The rate of return on an investment is determined by calculating its internal rate of return (IRR), which is internal because it ignores external factors like inflation and risk. By completing a discounted cash flow (DCF) analysis, investors can choose between different investment options by calculating the internal rate of return (IRR), which is the discount rate that would cause an investment's net present value (NPV) to be zero. The investment breaks even when the net present value (NPV) is zero, which is achieved when the total investment amount, related expenses, and generated revenue are equal to the present value of all future cash flows. As such, IRR gives the yield rate, or the expected return on investment, shown as a percentage of the investment. For instance, a $10,000 investment yielding a 20% internal rate of return would profit $2,000. But since IRR is a form of compound annual growth rate, the investment's yearly yield is compounded or reinvested.

5.6.1. Why Internal Rate of Return Is Important?

Investors can determine an investment's expected profitability with the use of IRR. An investment might be said to have a 10% IRR, for example. This means that over the course of its life, an investment will yield an annual rate of return of 10%. In particular, internal rate of return (IRR) is a discount rate that results in a net present value (NPV) of zero when applied to projected cash flows from an investment. Analyzing the internal rate of return (IRR) of various investments can assist investors in selecting which to make. IRR does have certain restrictions, though, so investors must exercise caution when choosing investments. Financial analysts utilize both NPV and IRR, as they are related concepts. The distinction is that, although NPV represents the investment's present value (in, say, dollars), IRR provides the yield on an investment (as a percentage).

5.6.2. What Is IRR Used For?

IRR is a tool used by businesses to choose which investments or projects to fund. For example, IRR could assist a manager in making a decision about investing more in product development or upgrading equipment. Companies frequently impose a hurdle rate, or minimum required rate of return, on investments. A project proposal is doomed to failure if it is unable to generate an IRR greater than the hurdle rate. The interest paid on a loan taken out to finance the investment, or the cost of capital, should also be less than the project's internal rate of return (IRR). The project will probably fail if the IRR is lower than the capital cost. IRR is a tool that investors can use to determine their expected return on a stock purchase. It can also be used to calculate the yield to maturity of a bond. It can even be useful in real estate transactions to balance risk and reward. IRR is a metric used by venture capitalists and private equity investors to assess their company investments. IRR is appropriate for situations where there is an initial financial investment and one or more subsequent financial returns over time.

5.6.3. How to Calculate Internal Rate of Return

The formula for computing internal rate of return is the same as that for calculating net present value (NPV) or discounted cash flow (DCF). The net present value, however, must be set to zero in this computation. Our equation's "x" is the discount rate, which is what we are solving for rather than NPV (usually denoted as "r" in a DCF or NPV formula). It is crucial to bear in mind that this particular compound annual growth rate implies that the investment returns are reinvested on an annual basis.

Internal Rate of Return Formula

$$NPV(0) = \frac{\text{Cash Flow}_1}{(1+IRR)^1} + \frac{\text{Cash Flow}_2}{(1+IRR)^2} + \frac{\text{Cash Flow}_n}{(1+IRR)^n} - \text{Initial Investment}$$

In this formula:

- *NPV* is set to zero.
- *Cash flows* are the sums of money spent and earned on the investment for a given period of time (e.g., monthly or annually).
- *1, 2, and n* are the periods of time, with n being the number of time intervals.
- *IRR* is the internal rate of return.
- *Initial investment* is how much the investment costs upfront.

5.6.3.1. Components of IRR Formula

1. **Net Present Value (NPV):** A sum of future cash flows discounted to present value is called net present value, or NPV. In order to find the rate of return (IRR) that brings the investment to a break-even point (when NPV equals zero), this is set to zero for the purposes of this calculation.
2. **Cash Flow:** Any money received or spent on an investment is referred to as cash flows. This covers cash inflows for earnings, sales, or dividends as well as cash outflows for costs, interest, or loan repayments.
3. **Number of Periods:** The length of the investment is indicated by the number of periods. A five-year project, for instance, would consist of five time periods. Because that is the typical lifespan of a company, in certain cases the number of periods defaults to 10. Because the internal rate of return (IRR) is an average over all periods and cannot be readily adjusted to differentiate for time frames of different sizes, these time periods needed for the IRR calculation must be steady intervals, such as monthly, quarterly, or annual.
4. **IRR:** This is the discount rate, or how much the cash flows need to be adjusted to bring them to present value. In this formula, the "x" we must solve for is also the IRR.
5. **Initial Investment:** The upfront expense incurred to begin a project or investment is known as the initial investment. The initial investment of $10 million, for instance, must be

deducted from the total discounted cash flows if the company spends that amount on new machinery for a limited run of goods.

5.6.4. Example IRR Calculation

In the end, figuring out which percentage rate yields a zero net present value when calculating IRR by hand is essentially a guessing game. Let's go through a simple calculation by hand using the following details:

- Initial investment: $4,115
- Cash flow for first year: $1,000
- Cash flow for second year: $1,100
- Cash flow for third year: $1,200
- Net present value: 0

So, with this information, we have this for a formula:

$$0(\text{NPV}) = \frac{1000}{(1-\text{X}\%)^1} + \frac{1100}{(1-\text{X}\%)^2} + \frac{1200}{(1-\text{X}\%)^3} - \$4,115$$

Since the initial investment is small and only lasts for three years, it generally cannot have a very high rate of return. The IRR cannot be zero since the discounted cash flow periods (years one, two, and three) must each be greater than $1,000 in order to balance out the initial investment. We need to enter various percentages and view each NPV in order to determine the true IRR.

- If the IRR is 5%, the NPV for this equation would be –443. So, the IRR is not 5%.
- If the IRR is 15%, the NPV for this equation would be 537. So, the IRR is not 15%.
- If the IRR is 10%, the NPV for this equation would be 0. So, the IRR is 10%.

Fortunately, IRR calculations by hand are rare because they require a laborious process of trial and error. Instead, to calculate an investment's internal rate of return (IRR), finance professionals usually use a proprietary or online calculator. They could also use the XIRR or IRR functions in Excel.

5.6.5. The Limitations of IRR

IRR, in its broadest sense, is just one of many metrics that investors and businesses use to analyze potential investments. IRR may have the drawback of favoring smaller investments over larger ones. Additionally, it could give the impression that investments with lower short-term returns are better than those with higher long-term returns. This can cause an investor to pass up more lucrative opportunities. An investment of $100 yielding a $300 annual return, for instance, has a better internal rate of return (IRR) than one of $10,000 yielding a $20,000 annual return. However, the $10,000 investment would significantly increase the investor's value. Investors consider NPV in addition to IRR in order to overcome its limitations. Combined, the two will aid in identifying investments that offer both higher rates of return and a greater impact on wealth.

CASE STUDY

INTERNAL RATE OF RETURN: A CAUTIONARY TALE

Our own research underlined this proclivity to risky behavior. In an informal survey of 30 executives at corporations, hedge funds, and venture capital firms, we found only 6 who were fully aware of IRR's most critical deficiencies. Our next surprise came when we reanalyzed some two dozen actual investments that one company made on the basis of attractive internal rates of return. If the IRR calculated to justify these investment decisions had been corrected for the measure's natural flaws, management's prioritization of its projects, as well as its view of their overall attractiveness, would have changed considerably.

So why do finance pros continue to do what they know they shouldn't? IRR does have its allure, offering what seems to be a straightforward comparison of, say, the 30% annual return of a specific project with the 8 or 18% rate that most people pay on their car loans or credit cards. That ease of comparison seems to outweigh what most managers view as largely technical deficiencies that create immaterial distortions in relatively isolated circumstances.

Admittedly, some of the measure's deficiencies are technical, even arcane, but the most dangerous problems with IRR are neither isolated nor immaterial, and they can have serious implications for capital budget managers. When managers decide to finance only the projects with the highest IRRs, they may be looking at the most distorted calculations—and thereby destroying shareholder value by selecting the wrong projects altogether. Companies also risk creating unrealistic expectations for themselves and for shareholders, potentially confusing investor communications and inflating managerial rewards.

We believe that managers must either avoid using IRR entirely or at least make adjustments for the measure's most dangerous assumption: that interim cash flows will be reinvested at the same high rates of return.

- **The Trouble with IRR**

Practitioners often interpret internal rate of return as the annual equivalent return on a given investment; this easy analogy is the source of its intuitive appeal. But in fact, IRR is a true indication of a project's annual return on investment only when the project generates no interim cash flows—or when those interim cash flows really can be invested at the actual IRR.

When the calculated IRR is higher than the true reinvestment rate for interim cash flows, the measure will overestimate—sometimes very significantly—the annual equivalent return from the project. The formula assumes that the company has additional projects, with equally attractive prospects, in which to invest the interim cash flows. In this case, the calculation implicitly takes credit for these additional projects. Calculations of net present value (NPV), by contrast, generally assume only that a company can earn its cost of capital on interim cash flows, leaving any future incremental project value with those future projects.

IRR's assumptions about reinvestment can lead to major capital budget distortions. Consider a hypothetical assessment of two different, mutually exclusive projects, A and B, with identical cash flows, risk levels, and durations—as well as identical IRR values of 41%. Using IRR as the decision yardstick, an executive would feel confidence in being indifferent toward choosing between the two projects. However, it would be a mistake to select either project without examining the relevant reinvestment rate for interim cash flows. Suppose that Project B's interim cash flows could be redeployed only at a typical 8 percent cost of capital, while Project A's cash flows could be invested in an attractive follow-on project expected to generate a 41% annual return. In that case, Project A is unambiguously preferable.

Even if the interim cash flows really could be reinvested at the IRR, very few practitioners would argue that the value of future investments should be commingled with the value of the project being evaluated. Most practitioners would agree that a company's cost of capital—by definition, the return available elsewhere to its shareholders on a similarly risky investment—is a clearer and more logical rate to assume for reinvestments of interim project cash flows.

When the cost of capital is used, a project's true annual equivalent yield can fall significantly—again, especially so with projects that posted high initial IRRs. Of course, when executives review projects with IRRs that are close to a company's cost of capital, the IRR is less distorted by the reinvestment-rate assumption. But when they evaluate projects that claim IRRs of 10% or more above their company's cost of capital, these may well be significantly distorted. Ironically, unadjusted IRRs are particularly treacherous because the reinvestment-rate distortion is most egregious precisely when managers tend to think their projects are most attractive. And since this amplification is not felt evenly across all projects, managers can't simply correct for it by adjusting every IRR by a standard amount. How large is the potential impact of a flawed reinvestment-rate assumption? Managers at one large industrial company approved 23 major capital projects over five years on the basis of IRRs that averaged 77%. Recently, however, when we conducted an analysis with the reinvestment rate adjusted to the company's cost of capital, the true average return fell to just 16%. The order of the most attractive projects also changed considerably. The top-ranked project based on IRR dropped to the 10th-most-attractive project. Most striking, the company's highest-rated projects—showing IRRs of 800, 150, and 130%—dropped to just 15, 23, and 22%, respectively, once a realistic reinvestment rate was considered. Unfortunately, these investment decisions had already been made. Of course, IRRs this extreme are somewhat unusual. Yet even if a project's IRR drops from 25% to 15%, the impact is considerable.

- **What To Do?**

The most straightforward way to avoid problems with IRR is to avoid it altogether. Yet given its widespread use, it is unlikely to be replaced easily. Executives should at the very least use a modified internal rate of return. While not perfect, MIRR at least allows users to set more realistic interim reinvestment rates and therefore to calculate a true annual equivalent yield. Even then, we recommend that all executives who review projects claiming an attractive IRR should ask the following two questions.

1. What are the assumed interim-reinvestment rates? In the vast majority of cases, an assumption that interim flows can be reinvested at high rates is at best overoptimistic and at worst flat wrong. Particularly when sponsors sell their projects as "unique" or "the opportunity of a lifetime," another opportunity of similar attractiveness probably does not exist; thus interim flows won't be reinvested at sufficiently high rates. For this reason, the best assumption—and one used by a proper discounted cash-flow analysis—is that interim flows can be reinvested at the company's cost of capital.
2. Are interim cash flows biased toward the start or the end of the project? Unless the interim reinvestment rate is correct (in other words, a true reinvestment rate rather than the calculated IRR), the IRR distortion will be greater when interim cash flows occur sooner. This concept may seem counterintuitive, since typically we would prefer to have cash sooner rather than later. The simple reason for the problem is that the gap between the actual reinvestment rate and the assumed IRR exists for a longer period of time, so the impact of the distortion accumulates.

CLASS ACTIVITY

Using a Time Line: The financial manager at Starbuck Industries is considering an investment that requires an initial outlay of $25,000 and is expected to result in cash inflows of $3,000 at the end of year 1, $6,000 at the end of years 2 and 3, $10,000 at the end of year 4, $8,000 at the end of year 5, and $7,000 at the end of year 6.

a. Draw and label a time line depicting the cash flows associated with Starbuck Industries' proposed investment.
b. Use arrows to demonstrate, on the time line in part a, how compounding to find future value can be used to measure all cash flows at the end of year 6.
c. Use arrows to demonstrate, on the time line in part b, how discounting to find present value can be used to measure all cash flows at time zero.
d. Which of the approaches—future value or present value—do financial man- agers rely on most often for decision making? Why?

SUMMARY

- Financial managers and investors are always confronted with opportunities to earn positive rates of return on their funds, whether through investment in attractive projects or in interest-bearing securities or deposits.
- Discounting is the procedure used to calculate the present value of an individual payment or a series of payments that will be received in the future based on an assumed interest rate or return on investment.
- The interest rate, r, is the required rate of return; r is also called the discount rate or opportunity cost.
- An interest rate can be viewed as the sum of the real risk-free interest rate and a set of premiums that compensate lenders for risk: an inflation premium, a default risk premium, a liquidity premium, and a maturity premium.
- The future value, FV, is the present value, PV, times the future value factor, $(1 + r)^N$.
- The interest rate, r, makes current and future currency amounts equivalent based on their time value.
- The stated annual interest rate is a quoted interest rate that does not account for compounding within the year.
- The periodic rate is the quoted interest rate per period; it equals the stated annual interest rate divided by the number of compounding periods per year.
- There are two types of annuities, the annuity due and the ordinary annuity. The annuity due has a first cash flow that occurs immediately; the ordinary annuity has a first cash flow that occurs one period from the present (indexed at $t = 1$).
- On a time line, we can index the present as 0 and then display equally spaced hash marks to represent a number of periods into the future. This representation allows us to index how many periods away each cash flow will be paid.
- Annuities may be handled in a similar approach as single payments if we use annuity factors rather than single-payment factors.
- The present value, PV, is the future value, FV, times the present value factor, $(1 + r)^{-N}$.
- The present value of a perpetuity is A/r, where A is the periodic payment to be received forever.
- The cash flow additivity principle can be used to solve problems with uneven cash flows by combining single payments and annuities.

REVIEW QUESTIONS

1. What is the difference between future value and present value? Which approach is generally preferred by financial managers? Why?
2. Define and differentiate among the three basic patterns of cash flow: (1) a single amount, (2) an annuity, and (3) a mixed stream.

3. How are present value and future value calculations related?
4. How is the future value of a mixed stream of cash flows calculated? How is the present value of a mixed stream of cash flows calculated?
5. Define Net Present Value (NPV) and explain its significance in financial decision-making.
6. Define Internal Rate of Return (IRR) and describe its role in evaluating investment projects.

REFERENCES

1. Achmad, N., & Muda, I. (2017). Economic activities of Karo older adults in Linga Village, Tanah Karo Regency, North Sumatera, Indonesia. *International Journal of Economic Research, 14*(16), 365–379.
2. Ahamed, N. (2020). Time value of money: Concepts and applications. *Indian Journal of Finance, 14*(5–7), 37.
3. Al Ghanem, K., Al Qubaisi, N., Al Zaabi, H., Al Dhahmani, L., Al Naqbi, A., Al Dhanhani, H., Al Shamisi, F., & Nobanee, H. (2021). Financial analysis of AstraZeneca. *SSRN Electronic Journal*. DOI: 10.2139/ssrn.3895292.
4. Badaruddin, R., Ermansyah, E., & Muda, I. (2017). Village governance with implementation of Law Number 6 of 2014 on the village and village administration. *International Journal of Economic Research, 14*(16), 350–363.
5. Chen, J. K. (2009). Time value of money and its applications in corporate finance: A technical note on linking relationships between formulas. *American Journal of Business Education, 2*(6), 77.
6. Gollier, C. (2010). Expected net present value, expected net future value, and the Ramsey rule. *Journal of Environmental Economics and Management, 59*, 2142–2148.
7. Hamza, H., & Jedidia, K. B. (2017). Money time value and time preference in Islamic perspective. *Turkish Journal of Islamic Economics, 4*(2), 19–35.
8. Hsieh, T. P., Dye, C. Y., & Ouyang, L. Y. (2008). Determining optimal lot size for a two-warehouse system with deterioration and shortages using net present value. *European Journal of Operational Research, 191*, 182–192.
9. Khorrami, B. (2001). Static and dynamic inventory models under inflation, time value of money and permissible delay in payment. Morgantown, WV: West Virginia University Libraries.
10. López Rousseau, A., & Ketelaar, T. (2021). Time value of money and happiness. *Revita de Psicología, 17*(33), 22–35.
11. McGowan, C. B., & Joyner, D. T. (2015). Computing bond values to teach time value of money principles. *Applied Finance and Accounting, 1*(2), 64.
12. Muda, I., & Hasibuan, M. (2018). Public discovery of the concept of time value of money with economic value of time. *Proceedings of MICoMS 2017*, 251–257.

13. Nordström, M. (2020). *Is Time Money? Philosophical Perspectives on the Monetary Valuation of Travel Time*. Licentiate thesis, KTH, Filosofi.
14. Osborne, M. J. (2010). *The Use and Meaning of All Solutions (interest rates) to the Time Value of Money Equation.* Thesis, Middlesex University.
15. Smitizsky, G., Liu, W., & Gneezy, U. (2021). On the value(s) of time: Workers' value of their time depends on mode of valuation. *Proceedings of the National Academy of Sciences, 118*(34), e2105710118.
16. Syahyunan, et al. (2017). The effect of learner index and income diversification on the general bank stability in Indonesia. *Banks and Bank Systems, 12*(4), 56–64.
17. Weiss, A. (2006). *Value for Money: Defining and Measuring 'Value' in MoD's Acquisition Policy of Obtaining best Value for Money.* Thesis, University College London (University of London).
18. Zaman, M., & Movassaghi, H. (2002). Interest-free Islamic banking: Ideals and reality. *The International Journal of Finance, 14*(4), 2428–2443.

CHAPTER 6

Financial Valuation Techniques

LEARNING OBJECTIVES

After studying this chapter, you will be able to:

- Understand comparable company analysis (CCA)
- Describe concept of precedent transaction analysis
- Define adjusted present value (APV)
- Discuss the basics of asset-based valuation
- Explain the valuation using discounted cash flows
- Define price–earnings ratio.

KEY TERMS FROM THIS CHAPTER

- Accounting standards
- Balance sheet
- Comparable company analysis
- Competitive dynamics
- Corporate finance
- DCF valuation
- Enterprise value-to-ebitda (EV/EBITDA)
- Enterprise value-to-sales (EV/S)
- Financial distress
- Financial metrics
- Financial subsidies
- Leveraged buyouts (LBOs)
- Merger and acquisition (M&A)
- Precedent transaction analysis
- Valuation multiples

INTRODUCTION

The process of figuring out the worth of a (potential) investment, asset, or security is known as valuation in the finance industry. Three methods are typically used: relative valuation, contingent claim valuation, and discounted cash flow valuation.

Liabilities (such as bonds issued by a company) and assets (such as investments in marketable securities like companies' shares and related rights, business enterprises, or intangible assets like patents, data, and trademarks) can both be valued. Since valuation is a subjective process, the value of the asset under consideration may also be impacted by the valuation procedure itself.

Financial reporting, merger and acquisition activities, capital budgeting, investment analysis, and taxable events to ascertain the correct tax liability are just a few of the situations in which valuations may be required. Analysts use stock valuation in the context of portfolio management to ascertain the price at which a stock is fairly valued in relation to its projected and historical earnings and, consequently, to profit from related price movement. In the context of business valuation, various techniques are employed to determine the (hypothetical) price that a third party would pay for a given company.

6.1. COMPARABLE COMPANY ANALYSIS (CCA)

Comparable company analyzes, or CCAs, are methods for assessing a company's worth based on the metrics of other companies in the same industry that are of a comparable size. The foundation of comparable company analysis is the idea that comparable businesses will have comparable valuation multiples, such as EV/EBITDA.

6.1.1. Comparable Company Analysis: An Overview

The process of valuing a business using the market multiples of comparable businesses in the same sector or industry is known as comparable company analysis, or CCA. CCA is sometimes referred to as public market multiples, equity comps, trading multiples, or peer group analysis. When valuing a target company for mergers and acquisitions, initial public offerings, or private equity deals, investors, analysts, and bankers frequently use CCA (Bowman & Graves, 2004). The foundation of CCA is the notion that businesses with comparable size, growth, profitability, risk, and competitive advantage should trade at comparable multiples of their financial metrics, which include book value, cash flow, earnings, and revenue. One can determine a range of valuation multiples that can be applied to the target company in order to estimate its value by comparing its metrics to those of its peers.

There are several steps involved in conducting a CCA, which are:

1. **Select a Peer Group of Comparable Companies:** Since the selection of peers has a substantial impact on the valuation outcomes, this is the most crucial and subjective step in the CCA process. Companies in the same industry with comparable business models, growth prospects, profitability, risk profiles, and capital structures as the target company should ideally make up the peer group. Nevertheless, in practice, it is frequently challenging to locate the ideal fit for the target organization, so one must exercise some discretion and judgment when choosing the peers. Some of the criteria that can be used to select the peers are:

- **Industry Classification:** To find the businesses that are in the same industry as the target company, one can utilize industry codes like SIC or NAICS. These codes, however, might not adequately represent the subtleties and variations within a sector, so it's important to take into account the goods and services, clientele, regional markets, and business rivalry.
- **Size:** The target company should be compared to peers with comparable sizes, as determined by market capitalization, enterprise value, earnings, or revenue. Larger companies may benefit from economies of scale, market dominance, or diversification, whereas smaller companies may have greater growth potential, innovation, or niche markets. These factors can all have an impact on valuation multiples.

- **Growth:** The target company should be compared to peers with comparable growth rates, as determined by past or anticipated growth in cash flow, earnings, or revenue. Growth can have an impact on valuation multiples; companies with greater growth may be valued at higher multiples, while those with slower growth may be valued at lower multiples.
- **Profitability:** Comparing the target company to competitors with comparable profitability in terms of margins, return on equity, return on assets, or return on invested capital is a good idea. The valuation multiples are influenced by profitability; companies that are more profitable tend to trade at higher multiples, while those that are less profitable may trade at lower multiples.
- **Risk:** The target company should be compared to peers with comparable risk profiles, as determined by credit rating, interest coverage ratio, beta, and debt-to-equity ratio measurements. The valuation multiples can be impacted by risk; companies with higher levels of risk may trade at lower multiples, while those with lower levels of risk may trade at higher multiples.
- **Competitive Advantage:** It is advisable to contrast the target company with its competitors who possess comparable competitive advantages, like cost leadership, network effects, customer loyalty, intellectual property, and brand recognition. Companies with stronger competitive advantages may trade at higher multiples, while those with weaker competitive advantages may trade at lower multiples. This means that competitive advantage can have an impact on valuation multiples.

For instance, if the target company is a rapidly expanding online retailer of consumer electronics, peers with comparable sizes, growth rates, profitability, risk, and competitive advantages may be chosen. Alternatively, peers may be online retailers of other products.

2. **Gather Financial Data and Calculate Valuation Multiples:** Gathering the target company's and its competitors' financial information, including revenue, earnings, cash flow, book value, market capitalization, and enterprise value, is the next stage. These details are available from a number of places, including websites, databases, analyst reports, and company filings. Next, the valuation multiples for each company must be determined.

   These multiples include enterprise value-to-ebitda (EV/EBITDA), price-to-sales (EV/S), price-to-earnings (P/E), price-to-sales (P/S), price-to-cash flow (P/CF), price-to-book (P/B), and so on. These multiples, which show how much the market is willing to pay for each unit of the metric, are ratios that contrast a company's market value with its financial metric. The selection of multiples is contingent upon various industry and company characteristics, including growth stage, profitability, capital intensity, and accounting practices. Multiples that are meaningful, consistent, and comparable for the target company and its peers should generally be used.

Multiples like P/S or EV/S, for instance, can be used if the target company and its competitors are online retailers with strong growth, low profitability, and low capital intensity. These multiples are more reliable and comparable than multiples based on earnings or cash flow, which can be unstable or negative. On the other hand, multiples like P/E, P/CF, or EV/EBITDA, which are more meaningful and reflect the earnings and cash flow generation of the companies, may be used if the target company and its peers are established, profitable, and capital-intensive. (Fama, E. and K. French, 1996)

3. **Analyze and Adjust the Valuation Multiples:** In order to ensure that the multiples are reliable and comparable, the third step involves analyzing and adjusting the valuation multiples of the target company and its peers. The distribution, average, median, minimum, and maximum of the multiples must all be examined in order to spot any trends or outliers that could distort the findings. Aside from accounting policies, growth rates, profitability, risk, competitive advantage, and non-recurring items, other factors that could cause the multiples to deviate from the norm include non-operating assets and liabilities and growth rates. Regression analysis, industry benchmarks, historical averages, and analyst estimates can all be used to make the necessary adjustments. Normalizing the multiples and making them as comparable and representative as feasible are the objectives.

For instance, if the target company is growing faster than its competitors, its multiples might be adjusted lower because companies with faster rates of growth typically trade at higher multiples. On the other hand, since lower profitability companies typically trade at lower multiples, one may raise the multiples if the target company has a lower profitability than its peers. Comparably, since riskier companies typically trade at lower multiples, one may reduce the target company's multiples if it poses a greater risk than its peers. Alternatively, one may raise the target company's multiples if it has a greater competitive advantage than its rivals, as these companies typically trade at higher multiples.

4. **Apply the Valuation Multiples to the Target Company:** Applying the valuation multiples to the target company in order to estimate its value is the last step. Depending on the analyst's judgment and preference, one may use a combination of the multiples' minimum, maximum, median, average, and/or minimum. Additionally, one can employ various multiples and weight them based on their dependability and relevance. Based on the market values of its competitors, a range of values for the target company are produced as a result. The estimated value can then be contrasted with the target company's current market value to see if it is undervalued or overvalued.

For instance, if the target company's revenue is $10 billion and the average P/S multiple of the peer group is 5, one can calculate the target company's value by multiplying the revenue by the multiple to arrive at $50 billion. The target company is undervalued if its market value of $40 billion is greater than its peer group value. This is because the target company's value is higher than its market value. To validate the valuation result, one should also take into account additional factors like the target company's competitive advantage, profitability, growth prospects, and risk.

6.1.2. Selecting Comparable Companies

Comparable company analysis is a widely used technique for determining a company's value (CCA).

Finding a collection of comparable publicly traded businesses that are involved in the same industry and share comparable financial characteristics is the first step in this technique. We can determine the target company's fair value by comparing the valuation multiples of these businesses, such as price-to-earnings (P/E), price-to-sales (P/S), or enterprise value-to-EBITDA (EV/EBITDA). Selecting similar businesses is not an easy task, though. There are many factors that need to be considered, such as:

1. **Industry Classification:** Finding the sector or industry that the target company operates in is the first step. Standard industry codes, like SIC or NAICS, or industry-specific resources, like trade associations or market research reports, can be used for this. In order to fully capture the distinctive qualities and risks of the target company, the industry classification needs to be as detailed as possible. Comparing the target company with other technology companies is insufficient, for instance, if it is a software company. The industry must be limited to software, and then software type must be specified, such as enterprise, consumer, or cloud-based software.
2. **Geographic Location:** The target company's and the comparable companies' geographic locations are taken into account as the second factor. For the purpose of accounting for variations in competitive landscapes, consumer preferences, regulatory environments, and economic conditions, the comparable companies should ideally operate in the same or similar markets as the target company. For instance, since the US and China have different consumer behaviors, growth prospects, and competitive dynamics, it might not be appropriate to compare a US retail chain with a Chinese retail chain. However, it might be required to use regional or global averages of valuation multiples, or to include comparable companies from other nations, if the target company is a multinational corporation with operations in several regions.
3. **Size and Scale:** The target company's and comparable companies' sizes and scales should be taken into account as the third factor. Numerous metrics, including revenue, earnings, assets, market capitalization, and workforce size, can be used to quantify size and scale. Comparable businesses should, in general, be of a similar size and scope to the target business in order to account for variations in market power, profitability, growth potential, and risk. Comparing the target company to a large established company with low growth prospects may not be meaningful, for instance, if the target is a small start-up with high growth prospects. On the other hand, it could be helpful

to compare the target company with bigger rivals or to modify the valuation multiples to account for size variations if it is a niche player in a big market.

4. **Financial Performance and Outlook:** The target company's and comparable companies' financial performance and outlook are taken into account as the fourth factor. A number of indicators, including revenue growth, profit margins, return on equity, earnings per share, and free cash flow, can be used to evaluate the financial performance and outlook. To capture the variations in value drivers, profitability, risk, and growth opportunities, the comparable companies should have comparable financial performance and outlook to the target company. It might not be comparable to a company with low revenue growth and high profit margins, for instance, if the target company is seeing high revenue growth but low profit margins. Nonetheless, the target company might be compared to one that has already attained high profitability if it is anticipated to increase its profitability in the future.

5. **Business Model and Strategy:** The target company's and comparable companies' business models and strategies should be taken into account as the fifth factor. A business's product or service offerings, customer segments, distribution channels, pricing strategies, capacity for innovation, and competitive advantages are just a few of the factors that can affect its business model and strategy. To account for the variations in value creation, differentiation, and sustainability, the comparable companies should have a business model and strategy similar to that of the target company. A transaction-based business that depends on one-time sales from price-conscious customers may not be comparable to the target company if it is a subscription-based business that receives recurring revenue from devoted clients. On the other hand, the target business might be similar to one that has already done so if it intends to increase its customer base or diversify its sources of income.

These are a few of the most important things to take into account when choosing similar businesses. Nevertheless, there's no hard-and-fast method for choosing similar businesses. Analysts may differ in their assessments of which companies are most similar to the target company, as well as in their preferences. Consequently, in order to assess the robustness of the valuation results, it is crucial to employ a variety of information sources, exercise good judgment, and carry out sensitivity analysis. By doing this, we can make sure that the comparable company analysis we use to determine a company's value is the most appropriate and trustworthy one.

6.1.3. Gathering Financial Data

Obtaining financial information about the target company and its competitors is one of the most crucial phases in the comparable company analysis (CCA) process. Utilizing this data, a number of valuation multiples and ratios are computed that facilitate the comparison of the relative values of various businesses operating in the same sector or industry. But obtaining financial information isn't always simple or easy. This process involves numerous sources, techniques, and obstacles. Here, we will discuss some of the key aspects of gathering financial data for CCA, such as:

1. **Sources of Financial Data:** Analysts have access to a wide range of financial data sources, including investor presentations, company filings, annual reports, websites, databases, and outside sources. There are some of these sources that are more trustworthy, thorough, and up to date than others. For instance, because they are subject to government regulation and auditing, corporate filings and annual reports are regarded as the most reliable sources of financial information. They might not, however, be updated regularly or have all the data necessary for CCA. Press releases and investor presentations, on the other hand, might offer more precise and up-to-date information, but they might also be inaccurate or biased. As a result, analysts should use a variety of financial data sources and double-check their findings for accuracy and consistency.
2. **Methods of Gathering Financial Data:** For CCA, there are primarily two ways to collect financial data: automated and manual. With manual methods, information is gathered and manually entered into a database or spreadsheet from a variety of sources. Because analysts can select the data they require and modify it in accordance with their presumptions and preferences, this approach offers greater flexibility and customization. But manual methods are also more laborious, error-prone, and time-consuming. Using software tools or platforms that can automatically extract, process, and organize data from multiple sources is what is meant by automated methods. Because it can save time and cut down on human error, this method is more accurate and efficient. Nevertheless, automated techniques are also more expensive, inflexible, and reliant on the reliability and accessibility of the data sources. Thus, depending on their resources, goals, and limitations, analysts should combine manual and automated methods to collect financial data for CCA.
3. **Challenges of Gathering Financial Data:** There are many challenges that analysts may face when gathering financial data for CCA, such as:

i. **Data Availability:** Not all businesses, particularly private businesses or businesses in developing nations, regularly or publicly disclose their financial information. As a result, analysts may have fewer and lower-quality comparable companies to choose from when performing CCA. Furthermore, it might be challenging to compare a company's financial data with that of the target company because different companies may report their financial data in different formats, standards, or currencies. As a result, analysts ought to make an effort to locate as many comparable businesses as they can, then modify their financial data for consistency and comparability.

ii. **Data Reliability:** Since financial data sources can include mistakes, omissions, or inconsistencies, not all of them are equally trustworthy. For instance, distinct definitions, computations, or modifications may be employed by various sources for identical financial metrics, like earnings, cash flow, or revenue. The validity and accuracy of the valuation multiples and ratios derived from them may be impacted by this. As a result, analysts ought to confirm and validate the sources of their financial data and employ the most suitable and reliable metrics for CCA.

iii. **Data Relevance:** Not all financial data is equally relevant since it might not accurately represent the companies' value or performance in the present or the future. Certain financial data, for instance, might be projected, historical, or out-of-date and might not accurately reflect the expectations, trends, or state of the market today. Furthermore, non-recurring or exceptional items like mergers, acquisitions, divestitures, or impairments may have an impact on some financial data and may distort the companies' normal operations or value. As a result, for CCA, analysts should use the most representative and comparable periods and items, as well as update and normalize their financial data.

Compiling financial data is a difficult but necessary step in comparable company analysis. The financial data of the target company and its competitors should be gathered, processed, and analyzed by analysts using a variety of tools, sources, and procedures. They will be able to gather more pertinent, dependable, and accurate data this way, which will enable them to carry out a more efficient and insightful CCA.

6.1.4. Adjusting Financial Statements

Making comparable adjustments to the target company's financial statements and those of the peer group companies is a crucial step in the comparable company analysis (CCA) process. This is due to the possibility that various businesses' non-recurring items, capital structures, reporting schedules, and accounting policies will have an impact on their valuation ratios and financial performance. We can get rid of these discrepancies and make sure we're comparing apples to apples by making adjustments to the financial statements. Here, we will discuss how to adjust the financial statements for CCA and what are the common adjustments that are made.

Some of the common adjustments that are made to the financial statements for CCA are:

1. **Adjusting for Different Fiscal Year Ends**: We must change the fiscal year end of the target company's financial statements to the same date as that of the peer group companies if they differ. The most recent quarterly or monthly data can be used for this, and they can be annualized to obtain an estimate for the entire year. An annualized estimate for the year ending December 31 can be obtained by multiplying the data from the peer company's first quarter by four, for instance, if the target company's fiscal year ends on December 31 and the peer company's fiscal year ends on March 31.
2. **Adjusting for Different Accounting Policies**: Accounting policies for revenue recognition, depreciation, inventory valuation, and lease accounting may vary amongst

companies. These regulations may have an impact on the companies' reported earnings, costs, assets, and liabilities, as well as their valuation ratios. We must determine the discrepancies and restate the financial statements of the companies using a common policy in order to account for various accounting policies. We must restate the depreciation expense and the net book value of the peer company's fixed assets using the straight-line method if, for instance, the target company employs the straight-line method of depreciation while the peer company uses the double-declining balance method.

3. **Adjusting for Non-Recurring Items**: One-time or exceptional occurrences that have an impact on a company's financial performance but are not anticipated to happen again are known as non-recurring items. Gains or losses from asset sales, impairments, restructuring charges, court settlements, and tax credits are a few examples of these items. We must recognize non-recurring items and remove them from the companies' balance sheets and income statements in order to account for them. This will provide us with a more realistic view of the companies' assets and normalized earnings. For instance, we must deduct the gain of $10 million from the target company's net income and equity if it made money from the sale of a subsidiary the year before.
4. **Adjusting for Capital Structure Differences**: Various businesses may have varying capital structures, which refer to varying debt to equity ratios in their funding. This may impact the companies' valuation ratios as well as their cost of capital, interest expense, tax rate, and earnings per share. We must compute the companies' unlevered free cash flow and enterprise value and use those figures to derive the valuation multiples in order to account for variations in capital structure. The cash flow generated by the business's operations before interest and taxes are paid is known as the unlevered free cash flow. The market value of the company's debt and equity is known as the enterprise value. Regardless of their capital structure, we can compare the companies using these metrics based on their overall value and operating performance. For instance, if the peer company's debt-to-equity ratio is 1 point0 and the target company's debt-to-equity ratio is 0.5, we must compute both companies' enterprise values and unlevered free cash flow in order to determine the EV/FCF multiple.

6.1.5. Calculating Valuation Multiples

Finding the valuation multiples for the target company and the peer group is a crucial step in comparable company analysis (CCA). Comparing a company's financial metrics (like revenue, earnings, cash flow, or book value) to its market value (like share price or enterprise value) yields valuation multiples. These multiples not only show a company's growth potential and profitability, but also how cheap or expensive it is in comparison to its peers.

Here, we will discuss how to calculate some of the most common valuation multiples used in CCA, such as:

- Price-to-earnings (P/E) ratio
- Enterprise value-to-EBITDA (EV/EBITDA) ratio
- Price-to-book (P/B) ratio
- Price-to-sales (P/S) ratio
- Price-to-free cash flow (P/FCF) ratio

We will also go over how to interpret and compare each multiple across various businesses and industries, as well as the benefits and drawbacks of each multiple. Lastly, we'll give some illustrations of how to use these multiples to determine a company's CCA value.

To calculate valuation multiples, we need to follow these steps:

1. **Select the Appropriate Multiple for the Analysis**: We may select one or more multiples that best fit the attributes of the peer group and the target company, depending on the goal and extent of the analysis. For instance, we can use the P/E ratio, which shows how much investors are willing to pay for a company's earnings, to compare the profitability and growth prospects of businesses in an established and stable industry. However, the EV/EBITDA ratio, which calculates the acquisition costs of a company's core business operations, can be used to compare the capital structure and operational efficiency of businesses in cyclical and capital-intensive industries. Some factors that may influence the choice of multiple include:

i. The accounting standards and practices of the companies and the industry. For example, some multiples may be affected by different depreciation methods, inventory valuation methods, or revenue recognition policies.

ii. The growth stage and life cycle of the companies and the industry. For example, some multiples may be more suitable for high-growth or low-growth companies, or for emerging or mature industries.

iii. The business model and competitive strategy of the companies and the industry. For example, some multiples may be more relevant for companies that have high margins or low margins, or for companies that have high market share or low market share.

2. **Gather the Required Data for the Multiple**: After choosing the multiple, we must gather market and financial information for both the peer group and the target company. The information can be obtained from a number of sources, including financial databases, stock exchanges, company reports, and trade journals. The information should represent the same time period and currency for each company, and it should be as current and consistent as feasible. These are a few of the data that we might require:

i. The share price and the number of shares outstanding for each company. These are used to calculate the market capitalization, which is the total value of a company's equity.

ii. The net debt and the minority interest for each company. These are used to calculate the enterprise value, which is the total value of a company's business operations.

iii. The earnings, EBITDA, book value, sales, and free cash flow for each company. These are the financial metrics that are used in the numerator or denominator of the multiples. They can be based on historical, current, or forecasted figures, depending on the type of multiple and the availability of data.

iv. The industry average or median values for the multiples. These are used as benchmarks to compare the target company and the peer group.

3. **Calculate the multiple for each company**: Once the information is gathered, we can divide the relevant financial metric by the relevant market value to determine the multiple for each company. For instance, we divide the earnings per share (EPS) by the share price to get the P/E ratio. We divide the enterprise value by EBITDA to get the EV/EBITDA ratio. The formulas for some of the common multiples are:

i. P/E ratio = EPS/Share price

ii. EV/EBITDA ratio = EV/EBITDA

iii. P/B ratio = Share price/Book value per share

iv. P/S ratio = share price/sales per share

v. P/FCF ratio = Share price/FCF per share

Depending on the availability and dependability of the data, the multiples can be calculated on a trailing (based on historical data), forward (based on forecasted data), or blended (based on a combination of historical and forecasted data) basis. To reflect the normalized or sustainable performance of the companies, the multiples can also be adjusted for non-recurring items like extraordinary gains or losses, impairments, or restructuring charges.

4. **Analyze and Compare the Multiples Across the Companies**: After calculating the multiples, we can examine and contrast them with respect to the peer group and the target company. The multiples can reveal information about a number of corporate characteristics, including:

i. **Their Relative Valuation:** In comparison to its peers or the industry average, a company with a higher multiple is thought to be more costly or overvalued, whereas one with a lower multiple is thought to be more affordable or undervalued. When two companies have different P/E ratios—for instance, Company A with a 20 and Company B with a 15—investors are willing to pay more for Company A's earnings than for Company B's, suggesting that Company A is more highly valued or has better growth prospects.

ii. **Their Growth Potential:** In comparison to its peers or the industry average, a company may have lower growth potential or expectations if its multiple is lower. Conversely, a higher multiple may also indicate a higher growth potential or expectation. Investors are paying more for Company A's sales than for Company B's sales, for instance, if Company A has a P/S ratio of 5 and Company B has a P/S ratio of 3. This suggests that Company A has greater sales growth potential or expectations than Company B.

iii. **Their Profitability:** In comparison to its peers or the industry average, a lower multiple may suggest that a company has lower profitability or margins. Conversely, a higher multiple may also suggest that a company has higher profitability or margins. For instance, if Company A has an EV/EBITDA ratio of 10 and Company B has a ratio of 8, then Company A has higher EBITDA margins than Company B, which suggests that Company A is more cost-effective or has higher operational efficiency.

iv. **Their Risk Profile:** In comparison to its peers or the industry average, a company may be implied to have lower risk or uncertainty by a lower multiple, or it may have higher risk or uncertainty by a higher multiple. For instance, if Company A's P/B ratio is two and Company B's is one, this indicates that Company A has more goodwill or intangible assets than Company B, which suggests that Company A is more vulnerable to impairment or write-down.

The quality of the financial data, the assumptions and projections made, the business models and strategies of the companies, the competitive environment and industry dynamics, and the macroeconomic and market conditions should all be taken into consideration when interpreting the multiples.

6.1.6. Applying Valuation Multiples to the Target Company

Using valuation multiples on the target company is one of the key steps in the comparable company analysis (CCA).

The financial performance, growth, and value of a company are compared to that of another similar company or the industry average using valuation multiples. Based on the market prices of similar companies, they are used to calculate the target company's fair value. A variety of data sources, including income statements, balance sheets, cash flow statements, and market capitalization, can be used to calculate valuation multiples.

There are many types of valuation multiples that can be used in CCA, but some of the most common ones are:

1. **Price-to-Earnings (P/E) Ratio**: This represents the proportion of a company's market price per share to its earnings per share (EPS). It gauges the price at which investors are prepared to pay for a given earnings unit. Greater valuation and growth potential are indicated by a higher P/E ratio. Investors are paying twice as much for Company A's earnings as they are for Company B's, for instance, if Company A has a P/E ratio of 20 and Company B has a ratio of 10. We must calculate the average P/E ratio of the comparable companies and multiply it by the EPS of the target company in order to apply the P/E ratio to the target company. This will provide us with the target company's estimated market price per share.
2. **Enterprise value-to-EBITDA (EV/EBITDA) Ratio**: The enterprise value (EV) to earnings before interest, taxes, depreciation, and amortization (EBITDA) ratio is this. EV is the total of a company's net debt and market value of equity. EBITDA is a gauge of a business's operational profitability. It does not include the impact of taxes, financing, or non-cash expenses. The amount that would be required to purchase the entire business,

including its debt, is indicated by the EV/EBITDA ratio. A lower valuation and higher cash flow generation are indicated by a lower EV/EBITDA ratio. For instance, if Business A's EV/EBITDA ratio is 8 and Business B's is 12, then Business A is more profitable and less expensive than Business B. We must calculate the average EV/EBITDA ratio of comparable companies and multiply it by the EBITDA of the target company in order to apply the EV/EBITDA ratio to the target company. This will provide us with the target company's estimated equity value.

3. **Price-to-book (P/B) Ratio**: This is the proportion between a company's book value per share and its market price per share. A company's book value is its net asset value, which is determined by subtracting all liabilities from all assets.

   It stands for the amount that would be distributed to shareholders in the event of a company liquidation. The price per unit of equity that investors are paying is indicated by the P/B ratio. Greater valuation and growth potential are indicated by a higher P/B ratio. Investors are paying twice as much for Company A's equity as they are for Company B's, for instance, if Company A has a P/B ratio of 2 and Company B has a ratio of 1. In order to apply the P/B ratio to the target company, we must multiply the target company's book value per share by the average P/B ratio of the comparable companies. This will provide us with the target company's estimated market price per share.

These are a few of the most popular valuation multiples in CCA, but there are a lot more that can be applied based on the business model, the industry, and the data's accessibility. As an illustration, consider the following ratios: enterprise value-to-sales (EV/S), enterprise value-to-free cash flow (EV/FCF), price-to-sales (P/S), price-to-cash flow (P/CF), price-to-free cash flow (P/FCF), etc. The following standards ought to guide the selection of valuation multiples:

i. **Relevance**: The main factors influencing the performance and value of businesses in the same sector should be reflected in the valuation multiples. For instance, P/E ratios are more pertinent to established, stable businesses, whereas P/S ratios are more pertinent to rapidly expanding, losing businesses.

ii. **Reliability**: The valuation multiples ought to be predicated on easily obtainable, consistent data that can be independently verified. For instance, earnings and market prices are more dependable than sales and cash flows, which are subject to the whims and assumptions of accounting.

iii. **Comparability**: Similar definitions and computations for the target company and the comparable companies should form the basis of the valuation multiples. For instance, any one-time or non-recurring items that could skew the results should be taken into account when adjusting EPS and EBITDA.

One of the most important steps in CCA is applying valuation multiples to the target company. This gives you a range of estimates for the target company's fair value based on comparable companies' market prices. It is crucial to remember that valuation multiples are not perfect measures of value because they might not account for all the elements that influence a company's value, such as risks, growth prospects, and competitive advantages. As a result, valuation multiples ought to be applied sparingly and in conjunction with other techniques, like precedent transaction analysis and discounted cash flow (DCF) analysis.

6.1.7. Interpreting the Results

In the valuation process, interpreting the findings of a comparable company analysis (CCA) is essential. CCA is a technique for valuing a business that compares it to other businesses of a similar kind in the same sector or industry using a range of financial ratios and metrics. Determining the target company's implied share price and fair value is the primary objective of CCA. The conclusions drawn from CCA, however, are not infallible and could change based on the criteria, assumptions, and data sources that are employed. It is crucial to comprehend how to interpret the findings and what they mean for the prospective investors as well as the target company. Here are some tips on how to interpret the results of CCA:

1. **Compare the Target Company's Valuation Multiples with the Peer Group's Multiples:** Ratios known as valuation multiples are used to express a company's value in relation to various financial performance metrics, including sales, earnings, and assets. Price-to-earnings (P/E), price-to-sales (P/S), price-to-book (P/B), and enterprise value-to-EBITDA (EV/EBITDA) are common valuation multiples used in CCA. One can determine whether the target company is overvalued or undervalued in relation to its peers by comparing its multiples with those of the peer group. The target company may be undervalued or have better growth prospects than its peers if, for instance, its P/E ratio is lower than that of the peer group.
2. **Consider the Quality and Reliability of the Data Sources:** Depending on the information's timeliness, accuracy, and availability, the quality and dependability of the data sources used in CCA may differ. The comparability of the financial metrics and ratios may be impacted, for instance, by the use of different accounting standards, reporting periods, or currency conversions in some data sources. To guarantee consistency and comparability, it is crucial to evaluate the caliber and dependability of the data sources and make any required adjustments. To lessen the impact of outliers or anomalies, one could, for instance, use the average or median of the peer group's multiples rather than the individual multiples.
3. **Adjust the Results for Any Differences or Discrepancies Between the Target Company and the Peer Group:** The size, growth, profitability, risk, capital structure, and business model of the target company may differ or diverge from those of the peer group, which could have an impact on the target company's valuation. In order to accurately represent the target company's true value, it is crucial to account for any variations or discrepancies between the target

company and the peer group in the results. The target company's multiples could be subject to a premium or discount, for instance, depending on its competitive advantage, growth potential, and relative performance in relation to its peers.

4. **Use Multiple Valuation Methods and Scenarios to Cross-Check the Results:** The difficulty of locating truly comparable companies, the sensitivity of the results to the choice of the peer group and the valuation multiples, and the potential to miss other factors that could affect the target company's value make CCA not the only valuation method available. It is therefore wise to employ a variety of valuation techniques and scenarios in order to cross-check the outcomes and derive a range of potential values for the target company. For example, to supplement CCA and verify the accuracy of the assumptions and estimations used in CCA, one may employ discounted cash flow (DCF) analysis, precedent transaction analysis, or market-based valuation techniques.

6.1.8. Limitations of Comparable Company Analysis

A popular technique for determining a company's worth based on the multiples of comparable businesses in the same sector or industry is comparable company analysis, or CCA.

Before using CCA to solve a valuation problem, it is important to be aware of its limitations. This section will address some of the primary disadvantages of CCA and how they may impact the dependability and precision of the valuation outcomes. OME of the limitations of CCA are:

1. **Selection Bias**: The process of choosing comparable businesses is frequently biased and subjective. Various analysts may select distinct groups of companies according to their own standards and inclinations. This may result in valuation outcomes that are inconsistent and non-comparable. Furthermore, the quality and accessibility of comparable company data can change based on the source and the time frame. For instance, some businesses might not disclose specific financial data or might use different accounting principles and procedures. This may complicate and skew the comparison.
2. **Differences in Growth, Risk, and Profitability**: The comparable companies may differ in terms of growth rates, risk profiles, and profitability margins even though they operate in the same industry or sector. The implied value of the target company and the valuation multiples may be impacted by these variables. For instance, even if two companies have the same earnings per share (EPS), the company with the higher growth rate may have a higher price-to-earnings (P/E) ratio than the company with the lower growth rate. Comparably, even if two companies have the same book value per share (BVPS), one with a higher risk may have a lower price-to-book (P/B) ratio than the other. As a result, it's critical to account for these variations in the valuation multiples or to utilize relative multiples that do so, like the PEG

ratio (P/E divided by growth rate) or the PEGY ratio (P/E divided by growth rate plus dividend yield).

3. **Market Inefficiencies and Anomalies**: CCA makes the assumptions that the market is efficient and rational and that the market prices of comparable companies reflect their intrinsic values. That might not always be the case, though. Market sentiment, speculation, hype, rumors, and manipulation are examples of irrational factors that can impact the market prices of comparable companies. These elements have the potential to produce anomalies and inefficiencies in the market, like bubbles, crashes, or mispricing. For instance, many internet companies had extraordinarily high valuation multiples during the.-com bubble in the late 1990s, multiples that were not supported by their fundamentals. It would be excessively valued and unrealistic to expect other internet companies to be valued using these multiples. Therefore, before using the valuation multiples and the market prices of the comparable companies for CCA, make sure they are valid and reasonable.

6.2. PRECEDENT TRANSACTION ANALYSIS

A valuation technique called precedent transaction analysis (PTA) compares a company's value to other similar businesses that have previously been sold. Before making any investment decisions, this method is frequently used in investment banking and other financial industries to ascertain a company's value.

Analyzing previous transactions is helpful when determining a company's prospective worth in relation to merger and acquisition (M&A) activity. It is employed to ascertain the worth of an organization by examining past dealings with analogous organizations. When there is a respectable amount of M&A activity in the sector and recent transaction data is accessible, it may be useful (Figure 6.1).

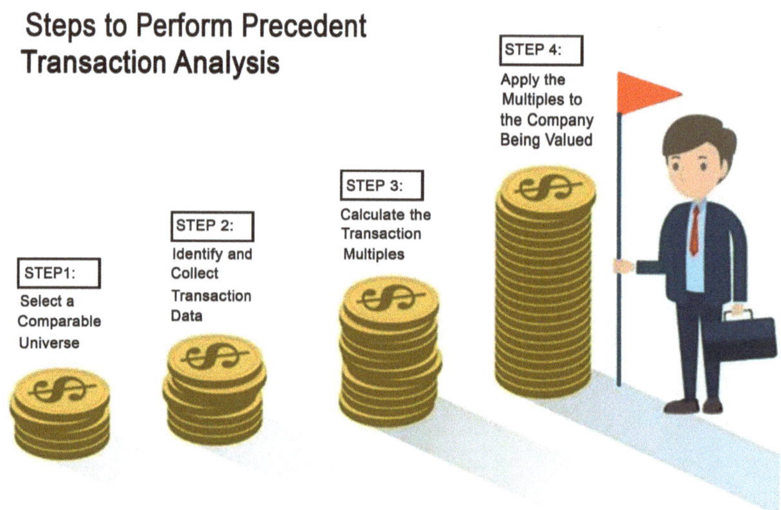

Figure 6.1. *Steps to perform precedent transaction analysis.*

Source: https://www.investmentbankingcouncil.org/blog/understanding-precedent-transaction-analysis-step-by-step-complete-guide.

- **Step 1: Select a Comparable Universe:** The initial step of Precedent Transaction Analysis involves the identification of a similar group of businesses. The universe of companies ought to be comparable to the enterprise under valuation with respect to its industry, scale, and potential for expansion. The purpose of this universe is to locate and contrast the transaction multiples of businesses that have previously been sold.

- **Step 2: Identify and Collect Transaction Data:** Finding and gathering transaction data for the comparable universe is the next step. The companies that have been sold, the transaction multiples, and any other pertinent transaction-related information should all be included in this data.
- **Step 3: Calculate the Transaction Multiples:** Finding each company's transaction multiple in the comparable universe is the third step. The enterprise value (EV) of a company is usually divided by its earnings before interest, taxes, depreciation, and amortization (EBITDA) to determine transaction multiples. You can also use other multiples, like price-to-earnings (P/E) and price-to-sales (P/S) ratios.
- **Step 4: Apply the Multiples to the Company Being Valued:** The company being valued can then use the transaction multiples that have been computed. The relevant transaction multiple is multiplied by the company's earnings or other financial metrics to achieve this. An estimated value for the business based on previous transactions is the outcome.

6.3. ADJUSTED PRESENT VALUE (APV)

Project and company valuation is done using Adjusted Present Value, or APV. It uses the net present value (NPV) in addition to the present value of the costs associated with debt financing, such as interest tax shields, debt issuance costs, financial distress costs, financial subsidies, and so forth.

- **How Debt and Equity Affect the Value of a Project?:** Since the cost of capital often falls with leverage, converting some projects with negative net present value (NPV) into positive ones, the value of a project financed with debt may be higher than that of a project financed entirely with equity. Accordingly, if a project is entirely financed with equity, it may be rejected by the NPV rule; however, if it is partially financed with debt, it may be approved (Booth, 2002).

While NPV ignores the advantages of increasing debt (such as an interest tax shield), the Adjusted Present Value approach does. For this reason, in highly leveraged transactions, APV analysis is preferred.

6.3.1. APV and Financial Modeling

In financial modeling, the unlevered value of a project or the enterprise value of the company is calculated using Net Present Value and the firm's Weighted Average Cost of Capital as the discount rate.

If equity value is desired, it is obtained by subtracting the present value of net debt.

6.3.2. Adjusted Present Value Assumptions

We make the following simplifying assumptions before using the APV approach in the valuation of a project:

- The project's risk is equivalent to the firm's overall risk, which is also the average risk of other projects within the company. Put another way, the project at hand is a "typical" project that the company generally undertakes. In this instance, the project's applicable discount rate is determined by the firm's risk.
- The only significant market imperfection at the selected debt level is corporate taxes. This means that the effects of debt issuance costs and financial distress are disregarded in favor of the interest tax shields alone.
- All debt is perpetual.

6.3.3. Unlevered Cost of Capital

Since the APV method initially assumes that the project is fully financed by equity, it uses the unlevered cost of capital to discount free cash flows.

We must first determine the project's unlevered beta in order to calculate the unlevered cost of capital. A measure of a company's risk compared to the market is called unlevered beta. Since a company's equity beta equals its asset beta in the absence of leverage, it is also known as asset beta.

We can search for a company's beta on financial resource websites like CapIQ or Bloomberg Terminal. We can locate a comparable listed company in its place if the company is not listed.

The unlevered cost of capital is calculated as:

Unlevered cost of capital (rU) = Risk-free rate + beta * (Expected market return – Risk-free rate).

6.3.4. The Adjusted Present Value for Valuation

The APV method to calculate the levered value (VL) of a firm or project consists of three steps:

- **Step 1:** Calculate the value of the unlevered firm or project (VU), i.e., its value with all-equity financing. To do this, discount the stream of FCFs by the unlevered cost of capital (rU).
- **Step 2:** Calculate the net value of the debt financing (PVF), which is the sum of various effects, including:
  - PV(Interest tax shields) – our main focus
  - PV(Issuance costs)
  - PV(Financial distress costs)
  - PV(Other market imperfections)
- **Step 3:** Sum up the value of the unlevered project and the net value of debt financing to find the adjusted present value of the project. That is, VL = VU + PVF.

6.3.5. Applications of Adjusted Present Value

Since the APV method can readily account for the side effects of financing, such as interest tax shields, it is most helpful when evaluating businesses or projects with a fixed debt schedule. By dissecting a project's value into its essential elements, APV offers insightful data that is necessary to improve the transaction and keep an eye on its progress (Fernandez, 2005).

One classic use case for APV is leveraged buyouts (LBOs), in which one company uses debt to finance the acquisition of another company. Because of the shifting capital structure, the APV approach is the most applicable in this case.

6.4. ASSET-BASED VALUATION

The asset-based business valuation is the most notable approach available for business valuation. This is due to the fact that it looks at the overall value of your company's assets. The company's assets include both tangible possessions like real estate and vehicles and intangible assets like intellectual property like trademarks and copyrights.

With the aid of the company books, it is easy to ascertain the market value of some of these items, the majority of which are tangible. However, figuring out the value of intangibles gets really tough.

You will be able to calculate an asset-based valuation for a company using the help of the following two approaches:

- **Going Concern**: The company must list each asset's net balance sheet value under this method. Next, the value of the company's liabilities are deducted from its asset value. Businesses who want to stay in business for a while and do not intend to liquidate or sell their assets are advised to use this valuation approach.
- **Liquidation Value**: You can guess this approach from its name. Compared to its counterpart, going concern, it needs a little more urgency. If the company is in the process of liquidating, it needs to figure out how much net cash it has right away. This is the money that is obtained as soon as the debts are paid off and the assets are sold. It usually has a lower value than market value because of the surrounding "everything has to go" situation.

6.4.1. Calculating Asset-Based Value

As previously stated, the asset-based approach determines the valuation of a business entity based on the value of its assets. To put it simply, the book value of the business or the equity held by the shareholders is the same as the asset-based value. And the value is calculated by deducting the obligations from the possessions (Brennan & Schwartz, 1978).

Due to timing and other variables, the value of the assets less the liabilities will typically differ from the values shown on the balance sheet. It may be possible to use market values rather than balance sheet values in an asset-based business valuation. Numerous intangible assets, which may or may not be listed on the balance sheet, can also be included by the analyst in the valuation.

6.4.2. Adjusting Net Assets

A significant obstacle in achieving an asset-based valuation is the adjustment of net assets. While balance sheet valuations use depreciation to gradually reduce the value of the assets, adjusted asset-based business valuations seek to determine the market value of the current environment. Therefore, an asset's book value and fair market value are not exactly equal. Numerous other factors, such as intangibles that are either entirely excluded from the balance sheet or have only a partial valuation, are taken into account when making asset adjustments. Additionally, many businesses might not think it's necessary to value a few trade secrets.

However, these intangibles would be significant to take into account because the adjusted asset-based business valuation examines what the company might possibly sell for in the market. Liabilities can also have adjustments made in the adjusted net asset calculation. In actuality, the market value adjustments may result in an increase or decrease in the liabilities' value, which has an immediate impact on the adjusted net asset computation.

6.4.3. Asset Business Valuation Methods

- **Asset Accumulation Valuation:** The first approach, known as the asset accumulation method, is remarkably similar to the commonly used balance sheet. This approach involves compiling a company's assets and liabilities and assigning a value to each one. Here, the company's value is determined by subtracting its liabilities from its asset value. Though it may seem straightforward, the details are what really matter. Each and every asset and liability needs to be precisely identified. In addition, the asset accumulation approach needs a reliable system for valuing each asset and liability. Furthermore, as was previously mentioned, not all of the items utilized in the business valuation are always present on the typical balance sheet. They consist of intangible assets produced internally, like trade secrets, trademarks, and patents. Provisional liabilities, which typically consist of unresolved legal cases or compliance costs, are also included in this list.
- **Excess Earning Valuation:** The excess earnings valuation approach is the second type of asset-based business valuation methodology. This method combines the asset-based valuation approach with the income method. With this approach, the company's goodwill is assessed in addition to its material assets and liabilities. The profits of the companies are considered as input for calculating the goodwill of the company, and a link to the income method is then made.

As a result, the excess earnings approach is strongly recommended for valuing sizable, well-run companies with significant goodwill. Professional service providers, including engineering firms, medical practices, law firms, accounting firms, and architectural firms, are among the most common examples. This approach works well for valuing the businesses of manufacturing and established technology companies as well. However, keep in mind that a business's value and its selling price are never the same. This will be clarified further in the following section.

- **Business value vs. Seling Price:** A business's selling price and its value are not the same thing. Many businesses use asset-based valuation to determine what an entity would theoretically be worth. However, in practice, the entity's value varies according to the individual performing the valuation. This implies that a greedy buyer looking to make up for lost revenue may decide to spend a large amount of money in order to purchase a business.

6.4.4. Pros and Cons of Asset-based Business Valuation

Now that everything is clear, let's examine the benefits and drawbacks of asset-based business valuation. Many businesses use the adjusted asset valuation approach when they are having difficulties with liquidation. Additionally, businesses in the investment sector are able to apply the asset-based business valuation method, in which the assets are determined using either the market approach or income.

Despite how excellent this approach is for valuing any kind of business, it is not without its problems. This approach, in contrast to the others, ignores the company's potential for future profit. As a matter of fact, when a company's current assets are sold off piece by piece, their business value can often be substantially higher.

Furthermore, when conducting a business valuation using this method, the process of measuring the intangible assets can be highly complex because internally generated products are not available on the balance sheet. Having said that, valuing a company requires much more than science. The asset-based business valuation specialist requires expertise, experience, precision, and close attention to detail.

6.5. VALUATION USING DISCOUNTED CASH FLOWS

A technique for determining a company's current value that takes into account time value of money adjustments and projected future cash flows is called discounted cash flow valuation, or DCF valuation. The cash flows consist of the cash flows that occur during the explicit forecast period plus a continuing or terminal value that denotes the cash flow stream that occurs beyond the forecast period. The income approach is another name for DCF valuation that is used in various contexts.

Discounted cash flow valuation was first applied in industry in the 1700s or 1800s. John Burr Williams explained it in his 1938 book The Theory of Investment Value, and it gained widespread use in the United States of America during the 1960s financial economics debate the 1980s and 1990s courts.

6.5.1. Basic Formula for firm Valuation using DCF Model

$$\text{Value of firm} = \sum_{t=1}^{n} \frac{FCFF_t}{(1+WACC_t)^t} + \frac{\left[\dfrac{FCFF_{n+1}}{(WACC_{n+1} - g_{n+1})}\right]}{(1+WACC_n)^n}$$

Where;

- FCFF is the free cash flow to the firm (essentially operating cash flow minus capital expenditures) as reduced for tax
- WACC is the weighted average cost of capital, combining the cost of equity and the after-tax cost of debt
- t is the time period
- n is the number of time periods to "maturity" or exit
- g is the sustainable growth rate at that point

"Value of firm" generally refers to the enterprise value of the company, which is its market value as opposed to its price; in the context of corporate finance valuations, this is the net present value, or NPV, of the project. Using a "perpetuity growth model," the second term indicates the continuing value of future cash flows after the forecasting term (Dittmann, Maug, & Kemper, 2004).

It should be noted that free cash flow to equity (FCFE) or dividends are valued at the cost of equity rather than WACC, which takes the cost of debt into account, when valuing equity as opposed to the firm. Free cash flows to equity are distributed to shareholders exclusively; to the firm, they are distributed among, or at least due to, all holders of securities in a corporate entity. In cases where the latter are dividends, the above formula can be modified by applying the dividend discount model.

6.5.2. Use

The diagram aside shows an overview of the process of company valuation. All steps are explained in detail below.

6.5.2.1. Determine Forecast Period

The first step is to choose the forecast period, or the duration for which the DCF formula's individual annual cash flows will be explicitly modeled. After the forecast period, cash flows are shown as a single figure.

A forecast period of five to 10 years is typical in practice, but it should be chosen in accordance with the company's strategy, market, and industry. Theoretically, this corresponds to the time it will take for the company's (excess) return to converge to that of its industry, with continuous, long-term growth applying to the continuing value thereafter.

The duration for venture capital and private equity investments will vary based on the exit strategy and investment timeframe.

6.5.2.2. Determine Cash flow for Each Forecast Period

As above, an explicit cash flow forecast is required for each year during the forecast period. These must be "Free cash flow" or dividends.

This forecast will usually be built using historical data from internal accounting and sales as well as external industry and economic indicators (the latter typically coming from published surveys and industry reports outside of large institutions).

Predicting revenue, which is dependent on the analyst's projections for market size, demand, inventory availability, the firm's market share, and market power, is perhaps the most important part of the forecast. Then, using a common-sized analysis, future fixed and variable costs as well as PPE investment and related capital requirements can be estimated as a function of sales.

The resulting line items must also be in communication with the business's operations: generally speaking, increases in revenue will necessitate matching increases in working capital, fixed assets, and related financing; additionally, profitability (as well as other financial ratios) should eventually trend toward the industry average.

The methods for determining which assumptions have the greatest influence on the value, and therefore require the greatest care, as well as for model calibration are covered below (the procedure is then somewhat iterative).

There are several context dependent modifications:

- Importantly, in the case of a startup, substantial costs are often incurred at the start of the first year – and with certainty – and these should then be modeled separately from other cash flows, and not discounted at all. Forecasted ongoing costs, and capital requirements, can be proxied on a similar company, or industry averages; analogous to the "common-sized" approach mentioned; often these are based on management's assumptions re COGS, payroll, and other expenses.

- For corporate finance projects, cash flows should be estimated incrementally, i.e., the analysis should only consider cash flows that could change if the proposed investment is implemented. (This principle is generally correct, and applies to all (equity) investments, not just to corporate finance; in fact, the above formulae do reflect this, since, from the perspective of a listed or private equity investor all expected cash flows are incremental, and the full FCFF or dividend stream is then discounted.)
- For an M&A valuation the free cash flow is the amount of cash available to be paid out to all investors in the company after the necessary investments under the business plan being valued. Synergies or strategic opportunities will often be dealt with either by probability weighting/haircutting these, or by separating these into their own DCF valuation where a higher discount rate reflects their uncertainty. Tax will receive very close attention. Often each business-line will be valued separately in a sum-of-the-parts analysis.
- When valuing financial services firms, FCFE or dividends are typically modeled, as opposed to FCFF. This is because, often, capital expenditures, working capital and debt are not clearly defined for these corporates, and cash flows to the firm, and hence enterprise value, cannot then be easily estimated. Discounting is correspondingly at the cost of equity. Further, as these firms operate within a highly regulated environment, forecast assumptions must incorporate this reality, and outputs must similarly be "bound" by regulatory limits.

Different definitions of cashflow, such as EVA, will apply to alternative approaches to DCF valuation, which will take a more direct look at economic profit. When the cost of capital is appropriately and appropriately adjusted, the valuation ought to produce the same outcome in typical scenarios. These strategies might be more suitable for businesses that have negative free cash flow for a few years but are anticipated to turn a profit later on. These might also be less susceptible to the final value.

6.5.2.3. Determine Discount Factor/Rate

Choosing the right required rate of return based on the company's and its market's level of risk is a crucial step in the valuation process.

Typically, for an established (listed) company:

- For the cost of equity, the analyst will apply a model such as the CAPM most commonly. An unlisted company's Beta can be based on that of a listed proxy as adjusted for gearing, ie debt, via Hamada's equation. (Other approaches, such as the "Build-Up method" or T-model are also applied.)
- The planned after-tax interest payment as a percentage of the total amount of outstanding debt can be used to compute the cost of debt for each period.
- The appropriate discount rate for each year of the forecast period

will then be returned by combining these in a value-weighted manner. Each period's discount factor will be compounded over the periods to that date because the weight (and cost) of debt may change over the forecast.

In contrast, the discount factor is typically determined by funding stage rather than modeled for venture capital and private equity valuations, especially in cases where the company is a startup, as in the example. A higher return is required in compensation during the early phases of the business, when there is a greater chance of failure; when the business matures, a strategy akin to the one above may be used.

Corporate finance analysts typically use the first strategy, which is for listed companies; however, in this case, the project's risk characteristics—rather than those of the parent company—must be taken into account when determining the cost of equity. M&A analysts also use the first method, with the target capital structure and risk influencing WACC as well as the cost of equity.

6.5.2.4. Determine Current Value

By multiplying the cash flow of each period by the applicable discount factor, the analyst can easily compute the current value of the future cash flows.

In cases where the forecast is annual, an adjustment may be made because, even though annual cash flows are discounted, cash will actually flow in over the course of the entire year rather than all at once. This is taken into account by applying a mid-year adjustment to the discount rate, which modifies the necessary averaging without changing the forecast itself.

6.5.2.5. Determine the Continuing Value

The continuing, or "terminal" value, is the estimated value of all cash flows after the forecast period.

- Usually, a perpetuity growth model is used to calculate this value, which is essentially a geometric series that returns the value of the future cash flows. The way the long-term growth rate is handled in this case, as well as the number of years that are anticipated to pass before the company reaches this mature stage, are crucial.
- Alternatively, the exit multiple approach (see Valuation using multiples) implicitly assumes that the business will be sold at some multiple of its final explicitly forecast cash flow at the end of the projection period. This method is frequently used for venture capital valuations in cases where an exit strategy is clearly laid out.

The terminal value is then discounted by the factor that corresponds to the final explicit date, regardless of the approach used.

It should be noted that this step is riskier than the previous one because it is farther off in time and effectively summarizes the company's future. Compared to the explicit forecast period, there is (much) greater uncertainty, but there is also a greater chance that the outcome will contribute a sizeable amount to the overall value. In this case, a very high proportion might point to a problem with the valuation (as mentioned in the example), but it might also represent how investors profit from equity investments, which is primarily from capital gains or price appreciation. The perpetuity derived number can then be checked, or triangulated, using its implied exit multiple.

Owing to this reliance on terminal value, analysts frequently create a valuation range, or sensitivity table (see graphic), that correlates to different exit multiples, perpetuity growth rates, and appropriate, internally consistent discount rates.

A continuing value is not included in the valuation of mining projects because the forecast period is the same as the mine's life (i.e., the DCF model will explicitly forecast all cashflows due to mining the reserve, including the expenses due to mine closure), as opposed to listed mining corporates.

6.5.2.6. Determine Equity Value

The continuing value and the present values of the cash flows that are explicitly predicted add up to the equity value. When free cash flow to the firm is forecasted, as in the above example, the value of equity is determined by deducting any outstanding debts from the total of all discounted cash flows. This last step is not necessary if free cash flow to equity (or dividends) has been modeled; in that case, the discount rate would have been the cost of equity rather than WACC. Some increase the FCFF value with easily accessible cash.

The accuracy of the many (many) inputs and assumptions will affect the DCF valuation's accuracy. Analysts that specialize in venture capital and private equity specifically use (some of) the following strategies to address this. With the first two, the model will be influenced by the pertinent variables and presumptions, and the output price will then be related to the market. The latter two are only applicable at this point.

- Using the share price or most recent transaction as a basis, the DCF value is always verified by comparing its corresponding P/E or EV/EBITDA to that of a pertinent company or sector. When the terminal value is estimated using the perpetuity approach, this assessment is particularly helpful and can also be used to calibrate the model. In the case of startups, where profit and cash flows are frequently negative, the use of traditional multiples may be limited; instead, ratios like price/sales are used.
- Analysts will frequently generate a valuation range, particularly when based on the various terminal value hypotheses that were previously discussed. To show how reliable the stated value is and to determine which model inputs are most important to the value, they might also perform a sensitivity analysis, which measures the impact on value for a tiny change in the input. This eliminates the need to estimate dozens of variables and allows attention to be focused on the inputs that actually drive value.
- Private equity and corporate finance analysts frequently produce scenario-based valuations as well, based on various assumptions about both company-specific and global economic factors. The probability-weighted average of the different scenarios—discounted using a WACC appropriate for each—is, in theory, an unbiased value.
- An extension of scenario-based valuations is to use Monte Carlo simulation, passing relevant model inputs through a spreadsheet risk-analysis add-in, such as @Risk or Crystal Ball. The output is a histogram of DCF values, which

allows the analyst to read the expected (i.e., average) value over the inputs, or the probability that the investment will have at least a particular value, or will generate a specific return.

Depending on the situation, the DCF value may be applied differently. Along with other stock selection criteria, an investor in listed equity will compare the value per share to the share's traded price. She will be more likely to invest if the price is lower than the DCF figure; for more information, see Undervalued stock, Value investing, and Financial Margin of Safety. In this case, reasonable and solid assumptions will be more relevant than the calibration mentioned above. A related approach is to "reverse engineer" the stock price; i.e., to "figure out how much cash flow the company would be expected to make to generate its current valuation. [then] depending on the plausibility of the cash flows, decide whether the stock is worth its going price."

6.6. PRICE–EARNINGS RATIO

The ratio of a company's share (stock) price to its earnings per share is called the price-earnings ratio, or P/E ratio, P/E, or PER. The ratio is used to assess a company's worth and determine if it is overvalued or undervalued.

$$P/E = \frac{\text{Share Price}}{\text{Earnings per Share}}$$

Depending on the type of earnings and whether they are realized or projected, there are several variations of the P/E ratio:

- Trailing P/E uses the weighted average share price of common shares in issue divided by the net income for the most recent 12-month period. This is the most common meaning of P/E if no other qualifier is specified. Monthly earnings data for individual companies are not available, and in any case usually fluctuate seasonally, so the previous four quarterly earnings reports are used and earnings per share are updated quarterly. Note, each company chooses its own financial year so the timing of updates varies from one to another.
- "Trailing P/E from continued operations" uses operating earnings, which exclude earnings from discontinued operations, extraordinary items (e.g., one-off windfalls and write-downs), and accounting changes
- "Forward P/E": Instead of net income, this uses estimated net earnings over next 12 months. Estimates are typically derived as the mean of those published by a select group of analysts (selection criteria are rarely cited).

There are frequently changes made to the conventional trailing and forward P/E ratios. Alternative P/E ratios typically replace other earnings measures, like rolling averages over longer time periods or corrected earnings figures that take out specific exceptional events or one-time gains or losses. There might be some variation in the definitions. A primary P/E, which is based on the earnings projections made for the upcoming years to which a discount calculation is applied, can be used in place of P/E for companies that are losing money or whose earnings are predicted to fluctuate significantly.

6.6.1. Interpretation

The P/E ratio has time units and is defined as the ratio of a stock (share price) to a flow (earnings per share). It can be understood as the period of time that the business would have to maintain its current earnings in order to generate sufficient revenue to cover the current share price. Although the P/E ratio can be expressed in terms of any time unit in theory, in actuality it is almost always reported implicitly in years, with the year as the unit of measurement being very rarely stated explicitly.

The most popular technique for assessing whether shares are fairly valued in relation to one another is the price/earnings ratio (PER). However, the PER by itself cannot tell us if the share is a good deal or not. The market's assessment of the risk and projected earnings growth determine the PER. In comparison to a company with a higher PER, one with a lower PER suggests that the market views it as having higher risk, lower growth, or both. The market's overall assessment of a company's risk and its prospects for earnings growth relative to other companies determines the PER of its shares, which is determined by the listing company. Investors use the price-earnings ratio (PER) to assess how well a company aligns with their own assessment of risk and growth versus the market's overall assessment, which is reflected in the current PER. Investors are free to choose to buy or sell based on their perception that it is superior to the market's.

6.6.2. In Business Culture

For many managers, a company's P/E ratio is a primary concern. Typically, they receive payment in the form of options on their company's stock or company stock; this payment arrangement is meant to balance the interests of other stockholders and management. Either higher earnings or a higher multiple that the market gives those earnings are the two paths that can lead to an increase in the stock price. Consequently, higher and longer-term rates of earnings growth are the main forces behind multiples like the P/E ratio.

Managers are therefore highly motivated to increase earnings per share, even temporarily, and/or enhance long-term growth rates. This may affect corporate choices in a number of ways:

- If a company wants to acquire companies with a higher P/E ratio than its own, it usually prefers paying in cash or debt rather than in stock. Though in theory the method of payment makes no difference to value, doing it this way offsets or avoids earnings dilution.
- Conversely, companies with higher P/E ratios than their targets are more tempted to use their stock to pay for acquisitions.
- Companies with high P/E ratios but volatile earnings may be tempted to find ways to smooth earnings and diversify risk—this is the theory behind building conglomerates.
- Conversely, companies with low P/E ratios may be tempted to acquire small high-growth businesses in an effort to "rebrand" their portfolio of activities and burnish their image as growth stocks and thus obtain a higher PE rating.
- Companies try to smooth earnings, for example by "slush fund accounting" (hiding excess earnings in good years to cover for losses in lean years). Such measures are designed to create the image that the company always slowly but steadily increases profits, with the goal to increase the P/E ratio.
- Companies with low P/E ratios are usually more open to leveraging their balance sheet. As seen above, this mechanically lowers the P/E ratio, which means the company looks cheaper than it did before leverage,

and also improves earnings growth rates. Both of these factors help drive up the share price.

- Strictly speaking, the ratio is measured in years, since the price is measured in dollars and earnings are measured in dollars per year. Therefore, the ratio demonstrates how many years it takes to cover the price, if earnings stay the same.

6.6.3. Investor Expectations

When a company's price to earnings ratio is higher than that of its competitors, it generally means that investors anticipate the company's earnings to grow at a faster rate in the future. A low price-earnings ratio can mean that a business is doing exceptionally well in comparison to its historical trends, or it can mean that the business is currently undervalued. One way to standardize the value of one dollar of earnings across the stock market is to use the price-to-earnings ratio. Theoretically, a standardized P/E ratio could be created by taking the median of P/E ratios over a range of years.

This ratio could then be used as a benchmark to determine whether or not a stock is worthwhile purchasing. Stale investments are the driving force behind the extrapolation of past performance in private equity. The extrapolative effects of past returns are not lessened by the assumption of higher inflation by state and local governments that are more financially burdened by higher unfunded pension liabilities.

6.6.3.1. Negative Earnings

P/E is shown as N/A when a company is either reporting losses or no earnings. Although a negative P/E can be calculated, this is not the standard practice.

CASE STUDY

ENTERPRISE VALUE ANALYSIS: THE CASE OF PEPSICO

In the stock exchange and investment market, a great number of investors want to receive a high expected return. A company which has a higher valuation and growth potential may create more profits for investors. Pepsi is a famous consumer products company which has over 1000 products. As a large, listed company, PepsiCo is probably one of the typical companies in the food industry that represents a consumer products company. Valuing PepsiCo could be helpful in understanding the market trend and investment direction in the comparable industry. In the listed company valuation, although the company information has high transparency, the growth potential and profitability cannot be reflected completely in the public information. The executive compensation change is internal information in a company, which is a relatively opaque factor in company valuation. In addition, evaluating a company with an appropriate valuing method could be helpful in making distressed companies solve financial problems. And can help the distressed company identify the internal management problem to maintain operations. In that case, valuing a company accurately with an appropriate valuation method could be helpful to earn higher returns at lower prices and avoid risks for investors. On the other hand, reasonable company valuation can also help managers understand asset situations and make decisions. Therefore, company valuation is a pivotal indicator for company decision analysis and financing. This study has selected Pepsi Corporation as the research object and used Discounted Free Cash Flow method (DCF) and Adjusted Present Value method (APV) to value the company.

- **Methods**

This study has used the two valuation methods mentioned above to value the corporate valuation of PepsiCo. The DCF method is based on the theory that the value of an asset is equal to the expected future yields discounted to today. The DCF method usually has two stage processes:

$$PV = \sum \frac{FCF_t}{(1+WACC)^t} + \frac{PV_t}{(1+WACC)^t} \tag{1}$$

In the DCF model, PV is the company value, PVt represents the terminal value of a company in a time period. FCFt is the free cash flow for different years, and WACC represents the weighted average cost of capital which is used as a discount rate. According to the calculation of free cash flow and terminal value in the future, the company value could be estimated. Free Cash Flow (FCF)is the remaining cash flow after the need for general operation and development in a company. Free cash flow is used to repay the debt or pay the dividends, which is a main indicator in enterprise value assessment. The free cash flow can be expressed as the difference between operating cashflow and the capital expenditures:

$$FCF=EBIT\ 1\text{-}T_c\ +Depreciation\text{-}Capital\ expenditures\text{-}\Delta Working\ capital \quad (2)$$

The EBIT is yields before interest and taxes, Tc represents the tax rate in local, capital expenditures represent the investment of fixed assets, and the Δ working capital is the net increase of working capital. In this model, the capital expenditures are represented by the change value of total fixed assets. The free cash flow for Pepsi on December 31, 2022, can be calculated as 5.86 billion dollars. The discount rate is WACC (Weighted Average Cost of Capital), which is used to calculate the weighted average of different capitals:

$$WACC=r_D*\frac{D}{V}*(1\text{-}T_c)+r_E*\frac{E}{V} \quad (3)$$

The D/V is represented as the percentage of debt to total financing, and E/Vis the percentage of equity in total financing. T_C is the corporate income tax rate which is about 18.14%. r_D is the cost of debt in a company, which represents the interest rate paid by a company for debt. In order to estimate r_D, it is necessary to find the type of bonds that a company has issued and determine the interest rates as the expected return of bonds. r_E is the cost of equity, which determines there turn investors expect to earn by investing in a company. The r_E can be estimated by the CAPM model (a method used to estimate the relationship between the yield of assets and risks), which is an effective way to estimate the cost of equity and evaluate the systematic risk.

$$r_E=r_f+\beta*(r_m-r_f) \quad (4)$$

In the CAPM model, rf represents the zero-risk rate, which is the minimum expected yield when risk is zero. In this study, rf is regarded as the treasury bond rate. β is the systematic risk factor that cannot be diversified. rm is the yield of market investment. To calculate the cost of equity (r_E), this paper has selected a risk-free rate from Federal Reserve, which is the long-term government bond yields. The risk-free rate is 3.75% on December 31st, 2022. And the β was estimated by using the data from Fin box in the last 5 years. In order to maintain the stability of r_E, the β has been calculated by using average values from the past 5 years. Thus, the systematic risk (β) of Pepsi is 0.58. This paper has selected rm = 13.66% as the market investment yield, which is from Stock Analysis Database. Finally, based on the CAPM model, the cost of equity r_E = 9.50%canbecalculated.

After calculating r_E, the next is to estimate the weighted average cost of capital to discount cashflows. According to the analysis of Pepsi's 2022 balance sheet, debt and equity can be estimated. In addition, according to the bonds issued by Pepsi in 2022, the cost of debt r_D can be estimatedas4.40%. Hence, the discount rate WACC can be estimated as 5.44%. Suppose that PepsiCo is continuously operating, valuing the company by sales revenue forecast could be effective. Inorderto obtain relatively reliable results, this paper has chosen 5 years as the forecast horizon, which can avoid long-term uncertainty and short-term underdevelopment. According to the analysis of the growth of sales revenue in the past decade, suppose that the average growth of revenue is 2.92%inthe next 1 to 3 years. And the growth rate of revenue is 4% in the next 4 to 5 years. In addition, assuming that the sales revenue is lasting growth, then the growth rate of sales is set to 3%after the fifth year. The terminal value can be represented as:

$$PV_t = \frac{FDF_{i+1}}{WACC_{-g}} \tag{5}$$

Based on the analysis of the US food industry growth rate, the annual growth rate of the food industry is about 3.40%. Thus, the perpetuity growth rate g=3% is in line with the development of the US food industry.

The Adjusted Present Value is a company's net present value (NPV) plus the other present value of financing side effect. The net present value of a company is represented as the base-case company value, and the formula is:

APV=PV(Base Case Company Value)+PV(Financing Side Effects) (6)

The APV method has used opportunity costs of capital as the discount rate, which can be viewed as an unleveled WACC

$$\text{Opportunity cost of capital} = r_D \frac{D}{V} + r_E \frac{E}{V} \tag{7}$$

The financing side effect means that when a company conducts financing activities, the tax shield, equity costs (rE), and debt costs (r_D) could be changed and further affect company valuation. Thus, the APV method should consider the effects of the debt interest tax shield, which is the interest that companies raise funds through liabilities. The debt interest tax shield could be useful for companies to reduce tax payments by paying for debt interests.

$$\textit{Debt Interest Tax Shield} = \textit{Debt} * r_D * T_c \tag{8}$$

The APV method considers the risks of different assets, which could be flexible to adjust company valuation and reduce errors.

- **Results**

According to the analysis of the research results, the company valuation of PepsiCo is about 428.31billion as shown in Table 6.1. In 2022, the outstanding shares of PepsiCo are about 1.38 bsillion. Thus, the value per share of PepsiCo is approximately 310.37 dollars per share. By contrast, the real stock value of Pepsi is 189.71 dollars per share. The company value in the results is more than the real value. It is because the revenue growth is not constant, and the sales growth rate varies continuously. On the other hand, in the process of free cash flow calculation, the capital expenditures could be larger than the real value. It is because in order to compute the investment infixed assets easily, the gross fixed assets have been replaced by company assets in the long term. All of the company's long-term assets include more extensive assets such as goodwill and apart of intangible assets. Thus, the real investment in total assets could be smaller than the calculation. Although using the total long-term assets may lead to smaller free cash flow, it could still be valid to decrease the unclear asset differentiation. For example, in some cases, the distinction between fixed assets and current assets may not be clear; companies may consider certain high-value as sets as current assets. In the process of sales revenue growth forecast for the next 5 years, this paper assumed that the sales revenue is continuously growing. However, based on the analysis of PepsiCo's sales revenue in the past 10 years, it could easily find that PepsiCo's sales revenue growth has shown significant volatility. In order to reduce the volatility and achieve as table forecast, this paper has decided the growth rate based on the US food industry growth rate and average sales growth rate for Pepsi. It could be helpful to obtain accurate results when choosing a sales growth rate that aligns with industry development. Furthermore, due to the unstable market environment and economic situation, the company value of Pepsi is different every year.

Table 6.1. DCF Vww

Setting: billion	0	1	2	3	4	5	6
Sales	43.00	44.26	45.55	46.88	48.76	50.71	52.23
EBITDA	13.80	14.20	14.62	15.04	15.65	16.27	16.76
Depreciation & Amortization	1.26	1.30	1.33	1.37	1.43	1.49	1.53
Profit before tax (EBIT)	12.54	12.91	13.28	13.67	14.22	14.79	15.23
Income Tax	2.12	2.09	2.16	2.22	2.31	2.40	2.47
Profit after tax	10.42	10.81	11.13	11.45	11.91	12.39	12.76
Investment in fixed assets	1.64	2.65	1.43	1.47	2.08	2.16	1.68
Investment in working capital	0.27	0.08	0.09	0.09	0.13	0.13	0.10
FCF	9.78	9.37	10.94	11.26	11.14	11.58	12.50
PV(FCF) (1-5)	46.16	8.88	9.83	9.59	8.99	8.86	500.06
PV Horizon value	382.61						
PV (company)	428.77						

Source: Shihao Guo, Enterprise ValueAnalysis: The Case of PepsiCo, DOI: 10.54254/2754-1169/34/20231686.

The adjusted present value (APV) for Pepsi is 420.2 billion dollars in Table 6.2, which is less than the DCF valuing results. According to the summary of the results, it could be found that in the process of APV method for valuation, the company value has been divided into base-case company value and the sum of net effect of debt. In addition, the APV method also considers the debt interest tax shield, which could be useful to decrease the tax burden. However, the DCF method is mainly focus on the free cash flow in the company operation, which neglects the effects of debts or tax. On the other hand, DCF used WACC as discount rate, which assumes the debt ratio and financial structure are constant. In that case, when the debt changes over time, different results may be obtained by using DCF method. In the APV calculation, assume that the debt is continuously changing, and the opportunity cost of capital is the discount rate. Then, the discounted value of debt interest tax shield is the financing side effect. In general, APV method has considered more about debt tax shield rather than single operation activity. Furthermore, APV method could be helpful to distinguish the value-adding factors and value-decreasing factors for managers.

Table 6.2. APV Valuation Results

Setting: billion	0	1	2	3	4	5	6
Free Cash Flow	9.78	9.37	10.94	11.26	11.14	11.58	12.50
Debt	39.07	37.51	36.01	34.57	33.18	31.86	
Interest		1.72	1.65	1.58	1.52	1.46	
Interest Tax shield		0.28	0.27	0.26	0.25	0.24	
PV (Interest Tax Shield)	1.04	0.26	0.24	0.16	0.20	0.18	
PV(FCF1-5)	45.51	8.84	9.74	9.46	8.82	8.65	500.06
PV Horizon Value	373.67						
PV(Company)Base	419.18						
APV	420.22						

Source: Shihao Guo, Enterprise ValueAnalysis: The Case of PepsiCo, DOI: 10.54254/2754–1169/34/20231686.

Conclusion

This study has researched the company value of Pepsi Corporate by using the discounted free cashflow (DCF) method and adjusted present value (APV) method. According to the summary of valuing results and compared with Pepsi's value from NASDAQ, this study yields a higher value for Pepsi than the market value. It could be concluded that Pepsi may have greater upside in the future operation. In addition, this study has forecasted the free cash flow in the next 5 years based on the sales growth rate, which can reflect the financial stability and development of Pepsi. However, in the calculation of discounted free cash flow, the EBITDA, capital expenditures, and the value of change in working capital are all estimated as a percentage of sales revenue. As sales revenues are assumed to be continuously growing, the free cash flow will also show continuous growth. In that case, the company value calculated by the DCF method may be higher than the real value. Similarly, the APV method has also used free cash flow from the result of the DCF method. The company value calculated by using APV method is also higher than market value. Although the higher company value of Pepsi may be subject to error, it can still help investors understand the financial situation of Pepsi corporate. In other words, sales revenue is a direct indicator reflecting the company's operation and market competition. Investors can understand the financial structure easily and make decisions quickly based on this indicator. Therefore, using the sales growth rate to estimate the free cash flow and company valuation could be useful for investors to analyze the company's market position. According to the analysis of Pepsi valuation, it could be concluded that the company value is related to financial situation, which is always reflected in the free cashflow. In addition, the industry development and environment can also affect company valuation. If a company is operating in a poor market environment, the demand of consumers and corporate competitiveness will be influenced, the company may suffer a decline in sales and an increase in debt. In that case, expand the market share and enhance talent management could be effective to improve the company valuation.

CLASS ACTIVITY

Let's assume Sky Limited intends to pay a $1 dividend per share next year and it is expected that this would increase by 5% per year thereafter. Let's further assume the required rate of return on Sky Limited's stock is 10%. Currently, XYZ Company stock is trading at $10 per share. Further, assume that during the next few years Sky Limited's dividends will increase rapidly and then grow at a stable rate. Next year's dividend is still expected to be $1 per share, but dividends will increase annually by 7%, then 10%, then 12%, and then steadily increase by 5% after that.

Compute the intrinsic value and fair value of Sky Limited's stock.

SUMMARY

- In finance, valuation is the process of determining the value of a (potential) investment, asset, or security.
- Comparable company analysis (CCA) is a method of valuing a company based on the market multiples of similar companies in the same industry or sector.
- CCA is based on the idea that companies with similar characteristics, such as size, growth, profitability, risk, and competitive advantage, should trade at similar multiples of their financial metrics, such as revenue, earnings, cash flow, or book value.
- One of the most important steps in comparable company analysis (CCA) is gathering financial data of the target company and its peers. This data is used to calculate various valuation multiples and ratios that can help compare the relative value of different companies in the same industry or sector.
- Interpreting the results of a comparable company analysis (CCA) is a crucial step in the valuation process. CCA is a method of valuing a company by comparing it to similar companies in the same industry or sector, based on various financial metrics and ratios.
- Precedent Transaction Analysis (PTA) is a valuation method used to determine the value of a company by comparing it to other similar companies that have been sold in the past.
- Adjusted Present Value (APV) is used for the valuation of projects and companies. It takes the net present value (NPV), plus the present value of debt financing costs, which include interest tax shields, costs of debt issuance, costs of financial distress, financial subsidies, etc.
- Valuation using discounted cash flows (DCF valuation) is a method of estimating the current value of a company based on projected future cash flows adjusted for the time value of money.

- The price–earnings ratio, also known as P/E ratio, P/E, or PER, is the ratio of a company's share (stock) price to the company's earnings per share. The ratio is used for valuing companies and to find out whether they are overvalued or undervalued.

REVIEW QUESTIONS

1. Discuss the process of selecting comparable companies.
2. How to adjust financial statements? Explain.
3. What are the steps to perform precedent transaction analysis.
4. How debt and equity affect the value of a project?
5. What do you understand by the adjusted present value for valuation?
6. Describe asset business valuation methods.
7. Discuss the pros and cons of asset-based business valuation.
8. Give a detailed overview about valuation using discounted cash flows.

REFERENCES

1. Booth, L. (2002). Finding value where none exists: Pitfalls in using adjusted present value. *Journal of Applied Corporate Finance, 15*(1), 9–17.
2. Bowman, R., & Graves, L. (2004). A test of the usefulness of comparable company analysis in Australia. *Accounting Research Journal, 17*(Special Issue), 121–135.
3. Brennan, M., & Schwartz, E. (1978). Finite difference methods and jump processes arising in the pricing of contingent claims: A synthesis. *Journal of Financial and Quantitative Analysis, 13*(3), 461–474.
4. Cheng, A., & McNamara, R. (2000). The valuation accuracy of the price-earnings and price-book benchmark valuation methods. *Review of Quantitative Finance and Accounting, 15*, 349–370.
5. Dittmann, I., Maug, E., & Kemper, J. (2004). How fundamental are fundamental values? Valuation methods and their impact on the performance of German venture capitalists. *European Financial Management, 10*, 609–638.
6. Fama, E., & French, K. (1996). Multifactor explanation of asset pricing anomalies. *Journal of Finance, 51*(1), 55–84.
7. Fernandez, P. (2005). Equivalence of ten different methods for valuing companies by cash flow discounting. *International Journal of Financial Education, 1*(1), 141–168.
8. Graham, J., & Harvey, C. (2001). The theory and practice of corporate finance: Evidence from the field. *Journal of Financial Economics, 60*, 187–243.
9. Laitinen, E. K. (2006). Financial statement data in assessing the potential of a technology firm: The case of Nokia. *International Review of Financial Analysis, 15*, 256–286.

10. Lakonishok, J., Shleifer, A., & Vishny, R. (1994). Contrarian investment, extrapolation, and risk. *Journal of Finance, 49*(5), 1541–1578.
11. Modigliani, F., & Miller, M. (1958). The cost of capital, corporate finance, and the investment decision. *American Economic Review, 48*(3), 261–297.
12. Rajan, R., & Zingales, L. (1995). What do we know about capital structure? Some evidence from international data. *Journal of Finance, 50*(5), 1421–1460.
13. Taggart, R. (1977). Capital budgeting and the financing decision: An exposition. *Financial Management, 6*(2), 59–64.
14. Willis, J., & Clark, D. (1989). An introduction to mezzanine finance and private equity. *Journal of Applied Corporate Finance, 2*(2), 77–86.
15. Yagil, J. (1982). On valuation, beta, and the cost of equity capital: A note. *Journal of Financial and Quantitative Analysis, 17*(3), 441–449.

CHAPTER

7 Corporate Finance and Capital Structure Modeling

LEARNING OBJECTIVES

After studying this chapter, you will be able to:

- Understand capital structure and cost of capital
- Explain debt and equity financing models
- Focus on dividend discount models (DDM)
- Describe capital budgeting and project valuation
- Discuss leveraged buyout (LBO) modeling.

KEY TERMS FROM THIS CHAPTER

Arbitrage	Asset	Capital market
Capital structure	Capital supply	Debt
Dividend discount model	Equity	Finance operations
Investments	Leverage	Modigliani–Miller theorem
Net present value	Trade-off theory	Pecking order theory
Shareholders	Time value of money (TVM)	Optimal Capital Structure

INTRODUCTION

Corporate finance is the study of a company's capital structure, including funding and management's efforts to raise the enterprise value. The instruments and analysis used to allocate and prioritize financial resources are also included in corporate finance. Corporate finance's overarching goal is to optimize a company's worth via resource allocation and implementation that strikes a balance between risk and profitability.

The amount of debt and/or equity a company uses to finance its assets and operations is referred to as its capital structure. Typically, a debt-to-equity or debt-to-capital ratio is used to describe a company's capital structure. A company's operations, capital expenditures, acquisitions, and other investments are financed by debt and equity capital. When deciding whether to finance operations with debt or equity, businesses must weigh trade-offs; managers will balance the two to determine the best capital structure.

7.1. CAPITAL STRUCTURE AND COST OF CAPITAL

A company's capital structure refers to the specific mix of debt and equity that it uses to fund its overall operations and expansion. Ownership of stock in a company and claims to its future earnings and cash flows are the sources of equity capital. Bonds and loans are examples of debt, whereas common stock, preferred stock, and retained earnings are examples of equity. Another debt that is regarded as a component of the capital structure is short-term debt (Groppelli & Nikbakht Ehsan, 2000).

7.1.1. Basic Concepts

In the US, capital structure plays a significant role in determining the rates that regulated utilities charge their consumers. Although regulators determine the appropriate capital structure and cost of capital for ratemaking purposes, the utility company is free to choose any capital structure it sees fit. Financial analysts monitor different leverage or gearing ratios closely in order to determine how much debt is present in a company's capital structure.

7.1.1.1. Leverage

The use of debt (bonds or bank loans) in a company's capital structure is advantageous up to a certain amount. A company that includes debt in its capital structure can achieve higher earnings per share than it could through the issuance of equity. This is due to the fact that the company's interest on the debt is tax deductible. A larger portion of the business's operating income can be distributed to investors thanks to the tax cut. In the UK and Australia, the corresponding rise in earnings per share is referred to as financial leverage, or gearing. When a business is growing and profitable, financial leverage can be helpful; however, when a business enters a contraction phase, it can be harmful. Regardless of the amount of operating income the business generates, the interest on the debt must be paid; otherwise, bankruptcy may ensue. If the company struggles and its earnings fall short of management's projections, excessive debt (i.e., excessive leverage) raises the possibility that the business won't be able to pay its debts. This eventually causes investors to become uneasy and raises the cost of borrowing money or issuing new stock for the company.

7.1.1.2. Optimal Capital Structure

It is imperative that the management of a company acknowledges the risks associated with debt and upholds an ideal capital structure that strikes a suitable balance between debt and equity. A capital structure that maximizes the firm's value while minimizing the cost of debt and equity financing is considered optimal. Understanding how outsiders perceive the strength of the company's financial position is important when making internal policy decisions about capital structure and debt ratios (Melicher Ronald & Welshans Merle, 1988). Maintaining a stable dividend policy, a strong track record of earnings, and a credit rating that allows the company to draw in new outside funding on fair terms are all important factors to take into account.

7.1.1.3. Term Structure of Debt in Capital Structure

Management must choose the right balance between short-term and long-term debt after determining how much debt should be included in the capital structure. A company's financial flexibility may be improved by raising the proportion of short-term debt since the borrower's obligation to pay interest is for a shorter time. However, short-term debt also increases the risk of refinancing for the company. According to a 2022 article in *The Journal of Finance*, equity holders will therefore expect higher returns on equity to offset the increased risk as the percentage of short-term debt in a firm's capital structure increases (Friewald Nils, Nagler Florian, & Wagner Christian, 2022).

7.1.1.4. Seniority

The seniority of the capital structure matters in the event of bankruptcy. A typical company has the following seniority structure listed from most senior to least:

- senior debt, including mortgage bonds secured by specifically pledged property;
- junior or subordinate debt, such as debenture bonds, whose security is based on the company's overall creditworthiness and financial stability;
- preferred stock, whose holders of this stock are entitled to have their claims fulfilled before those of common stockholders; and
- equity, which includes common stock and retained earnings.

In practice, the capital structure may be complex and include other sources of capital.

7.1.2. Leverage or Capital Gearing Ratios

To measure the amount of debt and equity in a company's capital structure and to compare companies, financial analysts employ leverage ratios of one kind or another. It is possible to compute the debt-to-capital ratio using the balance sheet figures, as indicated below.

Debt-to-capitalization ratio = Dollar amount of debt/ dollar amount of total capitalization

Both the capital gearing ratio and the debt-to-equity ratio are frequently used for the same objective.

Capital gearing ratio = Dollar amount of capital bearing risk/ dollar amount of capital not bearing risk Debentures (risk of paying interest) and preference capital (risk of paying dividends at a set rate) are examples of instruments carrying capital risk. Equity is categorized as non-risk bearing capital.

Therefore, one can also say, Capital gearing ratio = (Debentures + Preference share capital): (shareholders' funds).

7.1.3. In Public Utility Regulation

In the US, capital structure plays a significant role in determining the rates that regulated utilities charge their consumers. The usage of rates in the U.S. maintains that the rates that consumers pay for utilities should be set at a level that ensures the provider can offer dependable service at a fair price. Depending on the capital structure of the business, the cost of capital is one of the expenses that a utility must be permitted to recover from consumers. The utility company is free to select any capital structure that it thinks fit, but regulators set the cost of capital and suitable capital structure in order to set rates.

7.1.4. Modigliani–Miller Theorem

The foundation of contemporary academic theory on capital structure is the Modigliani–Miller theorem, which was put forth by Merton Miller and Franco Modigliani in 1958. Since it ignores a number of significant capital structure process factors, such as fluctuations and uncertain scenarios that may arise during a firm's financing, it is typically seen as a purely theoretical result. According to the theorem, a firm's value is unaffected by its financing structure in a perfect market. This finding serves as the foundation for examining the practical justifications for capital structure, namely the ways in which a company's capital structure influences its value. Taxes, agency fees, bankruptcy expenses, and information asymmetry are a few more causes. The question of whether there is, in fact, an ideal capital structure—that is, a structure that maximizes the firm's value—can then be further investigated using this analysis.

Imagine a perfect capital market where everyone can borrow money at the same interest rate, there are no taxes, no transaction or bankruptcy fees, and investment returns are unaffected by fluctuations in the financial system. It is unrealistic to expect perfection in the capital, as Modigliani and Miller suggest.

In these circumstances, Modigliani and Miller came to two conclusions. Their initial "proposition" held that a company's value is unaffected by its capital structure. According to their second "proposition," a leveraged company's cost of equity is the same as that of an unleveraged company plus an additional premium for financial risk. In other words, as leverage rises, risk is distributed among various investor classes, but overall firm risk remains unchanged, meaning that no additional value is produced.

The impact of taxes and high-risk debt were added to their analysis. In a traditional tax system, debt financing is advantageous because interest is tax deductible; as a result, the cost of capital falls as the share of debt in the capital structure rises. Having almost no equity at all would be the ideal structure, i.e., 99.99% of the capital structure is made up of debt.

7.1.5. Variations on the Miller-Modigliani Theorem

If capital structure is meaningless in a perfect market, then its significance must stem from flaws in the actual world. The theories that follow attempt to alleviate some of these flaws by easing some of the Modigliani–Miller theorem's stipulations.

- **Trade-off Theory:** The benefit of using debt as a tax shelter is offset by the existence of bankruptcy costs according to the trade-off theory of capital structure. It claims that there are costs associated with financing with debt, including the costs associated with bankruptcy and financial distress, as well as benefits associated with debt financing, including tax benefits. This theory also discusses the notion that a business weighs the costs and benefits of using different levels of debt and equity financing when making its decision. When deciding how much debt and equity to use for financing, a company maximizing its overall value will consider this trade-off because the marginal benefit of additional debt increases as debt increases while the marginal cost increases. In terms of empirical explanation, this theory might be able to explain variations in debt-to-equity ratios between industries, but not within them.

- **Pecking Order Theory:** The costs of asymmetric information are attempted to be captured by Pecking Order Theory. According to this, businesses prioritize their funding sources (from internal to equity) in accordance with the law of least resistance or effort, with equity raising being a "last resort" method of financing. Therefore, internal financing is used first; debt is issued when it runs out; and equity is issued when it makes no sense to issue debt at all. This theory says that companies follow a hierarchy of financing sources and that when available, internal financing is preferred. If external financing is needed, debt is preferred over equity because equity would require issuing shares, which would mean "bringing external ownership" into the company. As a result, a company's choice of debt may indicate that it needs outside funding.

The pecking order theory was made popular by Myers (1984), who contended that equity is a less preferred method of raising capital because investors assume that managers, who are presumed to be more knowledgeable about the true state of the company than investors, are taking advantage of the assumed overvaluation when they issue new equity. Investors might therefore give the new equity issuance a lower value.

- **Capital Structure Substitution Theory:** The capital structure substitution theory is predicated on the idea that management of the company may alter the capital structure to maximize earnings per share (EPS) (Timmer Jan, 2011). The model is not normative i.e., and does not state that management should maximize EPS, it simply hypothesizes they do.

Public companies were able to repurchase their own stock on the open market and manipulate capital structure more easily thanks to the 1982. SEC rule 10b–18. There are more testable predictions resulting from this hypothesis. First, the "Fed model" has been reformulated to show that the market average earnings yield will balance with the market average interest rate on corporate bonds following corporate taxes. Second, it has been predicted that businesses with low valuation ratios will be more leveraged, and businesses with high valuation ratios, or low earnings yield, will have little to no debt (Fama, & French, 2001). This explains why certain companies use dividends and others do not—they have a dynamic debt-equity target. The fourth prediction holds that the relative price volatilities of companies and their leverage have a negative relationship in the market. This runs counter to what Hamada found, who found a positive correlation between these two variables based on the research of Modigliani and Miller.

- **Agency Costs:** The relevance of capital structure can be explained by three different types of agency costs:
  - **Asset substitution effect**: Management is incentivized to take on riskier projects with potentially negative net present value (NPV) when the debt-to-equity ratio rises. This is because debtors bear the consequences of an unsuccessful project, while shareholders benefit from a successful endeavor.
  - **Underinvestment problem** or debt overhang problem: In the event that debt is hazardous e.g., the project's benefits will go to debt holders rather than shareholders in a growing company. Therefore, even though positive NPV projects have the potential to raise firm value, management is incentivized to reject them.
  - **Free cash flow**: Without returning free cash flow to investors, management is incentivized to erode the value of the company by constructing empires, offering lavish benefits, etc. Leverage forces management to exercise financial restraint.
- **Structural Corporate Finance:** The attempt to translate the aforementioned models, along with others, into a time-consistent, structured theoretical framework with a dynamic structure akin to what is observed in reality is a current area of research in finance. Investment returns, debt, equity, and management contracts all have long-term, multi-period effects. Because of this, it is challenging to consider how the aforementioned basic models might affect reality if they are not incorporated into a dynamic framework that closely resembles it. Under the guise of credit risk research, a comparable kind of study is carried out, in which the modeling of the probability of default and its pricing is done with respect to various assumptions about investors and the motivations of management, shareholders, and debt holders.
- **Capital Structure and Macroeconomic Conditions:** Researchers discover that the choice of capital structure is significantly influenced by macroeconomic conditions in addition to firm-specific traits. Korajczyk, Lucas, and McDonald (1990) offer proof that a cluster of equity issues arises after the equity market experiences a surge. Target leverage is found to be pro-cyclical for constrained firms but counter-cyclical for unconstrained firms by Korajczyk and Levy (2003). Additionally, macroeconomic conditions have an impact on issue choice for firms that can align their decision-making with periods of favorable macroeconomic conditions, but not for constrained firms. Levy and Hennessy (2007) point out that the observed patterns can be the outcome of trade-offs between agency problems and risk sharing, which vary throughout the business cycle. Some have connected these patterns to puzzles involving asset pricing (Chen Hui, 2010).
- **Capital Structure Persistence:**

First, corporate leverage ratios are calculated. Despite variations in time, low to high leverage ratios tend to remain stable. The main factors influencing variation in capital structures are those that hold steady over an extended length of time. These constants are not observable (Lemmon Michael, Roberts, Michael, & Jaime Zender, 2008).

- **Growth Type Compatibility:** Businesses logically make investments and look for funding in ways that fit their growth types. Low growth type firms are more eager to issue new debt than equity when market and economic conditions improve, while high growth type firms are less likely to issue debt and more eager to issue equity. Different growth patterns endure. Growth type compatibility, in line with a generalized Myers–Majluf framework, permits different growth types and, consequently, specifications of market imperfection or informational environments to endure, producing capital structure persistence (Wu Xueping, Au Yueng, & Chau Kin, 2012).
- **Other:**
  - Capital supply — capital structure also depends on the relative supply of equity vs. debt capital available to the firm (Adhikari Binay, Cicero, David, & Sulaeman Johan 2021).
  - The neutral mutation hypothesis — firms fall into various financing habits that do not impact value.
  - Market timing hypothesis: capital structure results from managers' cumulative historical market timing (Baker Malcolm, & Wurgler Jeffrey 2002).
  - Accelerated investment effect—even in the absence of agency costs, levered firms invest faster because of the existence of default risk.
  - Research has shown that capital structure, particularly short-term debt, has a major impact on a firm's performance in transition economies. One example of this is the case of the Vietnamese emerging market economy (Vuong Quan Hoang, 2014).

7.1.6. Arbitrage

A capital structure arbitrageur aims to make money by taking advantage of differences in the prices of different securities that a single company issues. Take conventional bonds and convertible bonds, for instance. The latter are bonds that can be converted into equity shares under certain contractual terms. A convertible bond's stock-option component has a monetary value all by itself. The combined value of the option feature and the conventional bonds should equal the instrument's total value. The capital-structure arbitrageur will wager that the spread—the difference between convertible and non-convertible bonds—will converge if it increases unnecessarily.

7.2. DEBT AND EQUITY FINANCING MODELS

When starting or growing a startup, one of the most important choices you'll have to make is how to raise money for your business. Instead of slowly bootstrapping, most founders opt for debt or equity financing; however, each has unique benefits and drawbacks. With debt financing, you borrow money that has to be repaid over time, usually with interest. The lender, however, has no say over how your business is run. Conversely, equity financing entails raising money through the sale of your company's shares. This implies that investors give money in return for a stake in the company and maybe even a vote in how the business is run.

Beyond just the financial consequences, deciding between debt and equity financing is a strategic move that can impact every facet of your company, including:

- Control
- Ownership
- Financial health
- Company culture
- Growth trajectory
- Investor relations
- Exit strategy
- Risk profile
- Tax implications

7.2.1. Debt Financing

Debt financing is the process by which a business sells debt instruments to individual and/or institutional investors in order to raise money for working capital or capital expenditures. The people or organizations that lend the money become creditors in exchange for a guarantee that the principal and interest will be paid back.

7.2.1.1. How Debt Financing Works

A company can raise funds in one of three ways: by selling equity, taking on debt, or by utilizing a combination of the two. An ownership position in the business is represented by equity. It does not have to be repaid; instead, it grants the shareholder an entitlement to future profits. Equity holders are the last to get paid in the event that the company files for bankruptcy. Equity financing refers to the alternative method of raising capital in the debt markets through the issuance of stock shares through a public offering.

A business can choose debt financing to raise the money it needs to develop and expand by selling investors fixed income products like bonds, bills, or notes. Bond buyers are lenders, who can be either institutional or retail investors who provide the business with debt financing when it issues bonds. At a future date that has been set, the principal amount of the investment loan must be repaid. Lenders have a greater claim than shareholders on any liquidated assets in the event that the company files for bankruptcy.

7.2.1.2. Cost of Debt

The capital structure of a company consists of debt and equity. Dividend payments to shareholders represent the cost of equity, and interest payments to bondholders represent the cost of debt. A company that issues debt makes two promises to its bondholders: it will repay the principal amount and ensure that the bondholders receive annual interest payments, also referred to as coupon payments. The cost of borrowing for the issuer is reflected in the interest rate paid on these debt instruments.

A company's cost of capital is the total of its debt and equity financing costs. The least amount of return on capital that a business needs to generate in order to appease its creditors, shareholders, and other capital providers is known as the cost of capital. Investment choices made by a business for new initiatives and operations should always result in profits higher than the cost of capital. A business is not making a profit for its investors if the returns on its capital expenditures are less than its cost of capital. In this situation, the corporation might have to review and adjust its capital structure.

The formula for the cost of debt financing is:

KD = Interest Expense x (1 – Tax Rate)

Where; KD = cost of debt

The interest expense is calculated on an after-tax basis to make it more comparable to the cost of equity because stock earnings are taxed, even though the interest on the debt is typically tax deductible.

7.2.1.3. Measuring Debt Financing

The debt-to-equity ratio (D/E) is one statistic used to compare and assess how much of a company's capital is being financed by debt. For instance, the D/E ratio is $2 billion/$10 billion = 1/5, or 20%, if the total debt is $2 billion and the total equity held by investors is $10 billion. This indicates that there is $5 in equity for every $1 in debt financing. While some industries are more tolerant of debt than others, in general, a low D/E ratio is better than a high one. The balance sheet statement shows both debt and equity.

7.2.1.4. Other Types of Debt Financing

Apart from merely issuing bonds, the following is a summary of the most popular forms of debt financing. Keep in mind that small businesses might find it more difficult to obtain some options, particularly if they are newer to the market or have weaker finances than larger companies.

- **Term Loans**: Term loans are when you borrow money from a bank or other financial institution in one lump sum that you have to pay back over a set amount of time. The interest rates on it could be variable or fixed. Principal and interest are typically paid on a monthly basis under the terms of these loans.

- **Lines of Credit**: A line of credit is a type of flexible loan that gives companies access to a fixed amount of funds that they can use as needed. Similar to how a credit card functions, only the money that businesses really use is subject to interest payments. Credit lines are especially helpful for handling unforeseen expenses, controlling cash flow, and paying for temporary operating costs.
- **Revolving Credit Facilities**: Similar in function to lines of credit, revolving credit facilities are usually larger and utilized by larger companies. These facilities offer a capital pool that the company can use and repay over time (up to a predetermined credit limit, of course).
- **Equipment Financing**: Equipment financing is taking out a loan specifically to buy equipment that is necessary for a business, using the equipment as collateral. With this kind of loan or lease, companies can purchase the equipment, cars, technology, and other assets they need to run their operations without having to make an upfront cash payment.
- **Merchant Cash Advances**: Businesses can receive a one-time payment in exchange for a portion of future credit card sales from merchant cash advances. When a business needs cash right away and has a high volume of credit card transactions, this kind of financing is popular. However, when compared to conventional loans, merchant cash advances may have higher fees.
- **Trade Credit**: Suppliers can provide short-term financing in the form of trade credit. It's when a business purchases an item and makes a payment 30 or 60 days later. In order to have the cash flow to pay that invoice, this kind of financing helps businesses make the goods they need and manage inventory.
- **Convertible Debt**: Convertible debt is a hybrid type of financing in which loans have the potential to be converted at a later time into company equity shares. An issuer may decide to issue bonds with the caveat that holders may later convert from debt-to-equity financing.

7.2.1.5. Pros of Debt Financing

One benefit of debt financing is that it makes it possible for a company to grow faster than it otherwise might by leveraging a small amount of capital into a much larger sum. The ability to deduct debt payments from taxes is an additional benefit. Businesses can also maintain ownership and control through debt financing. In contrast to equity financing, which involves selling ownership stakes to investors, business owners retain all control and decision-making authority over their company. As we previously discussed, debt financing may be less expensive than equity financing. Furthermore, there are no more responsibilities after the debt is paid off and the lender-borrower relationship ends. Equity investors, on the other hand, usually anticipate continuing dividend payments and a portion of the profits, which can end up costing more over time. This can only be put out of the way through share reacquisition.

7.2.1.6. Cons of Debt Financing

The primary drawback of debt financing is that interest payments to lenders must be made, resulting in a payment amount that is greater than the amount borrowed. Regardless of the company's revenue, debt payments are mandatory, and this can be especially dangerous for startups or smaller companies that don't yet have a stable cash flow. The balance sheet and financial ratios of a company can be adversely affected by high levels of debt. This may give the impression that the company is riskier to lenders and investors, which could eventually result in higher borrowing costs. A company's flexibility may also be restricted by high debt levels since a large portion of its earnings will go toward debt servicing. Restrictive covenants are another common feature of debt financing. Lenders have the power to impose restrictions on further borrowing, mandate the maintenance of specific financial ratios, or restrict the kinds of investments or expenses that a business can make. This is a risk-reduction tactic meant to reassure the lender about the business's operations.

- **Examples of Debt Financing:** Bank loans, loans from friends and family, government-backed loans like SBA loans, credit card loans, mortgages, lines of credit, and equipment loans are all examples of debt financing.

7.2.2. Equity Financing

The process of raising money through the sale of shares is known as equity financing. Businesses may need to raise money for a long-term project that fosters growth or for the immediate need to pay bills. A business can effectively sell ownership of its company for cash by selling shares. Diverse sources provide equity financing. Sources of needed capital for an entrepreneur could include professional investors, the entrepreneur's friends and family, or an initial public offering (IPO). Private companies go through an initial public offering (IPO) process to sell shares of their company to the general public in a new stock issuance. A business can raise funds from the general public by issuing public shares. Through IPOs, major players in the market like Google and Meta (formerly Facebook) raised billions of dollars. Equity financing encompasses both private and public company financing, although it is most commonly used to describe the financing of publicly traded companies.

7.2.2.1. How Equity Financing Works

Common stock as well as other equity or quasi-equity instruments like convertible preferred stock, preferred stock, and equity units that comprise common shares and warrants are sold as part of equity financing. Both current shareholders and the capacity to attract new shareholders may be impacted by this action. A successful startup will go through multiple rounds of equity financing as it develops. A startup may employ different equity instruments to meet its financing needs because, at different phases of its development, it usually draws in a variety of investors. For instance, convertible preferred shares are preferred over common stock by angel and venture capitalists, who are typically the initial investors in a startup, as the former offer greater upside potential and some protection against downside.

A company may think about selling common stock to institutional and retail investors once it has grown big enough to contemplate going public. In the future, if the business requires more funding, secondary equity financing options like a rights offering or an equity unit offering with warrants included as a sweetener may be selected. Note that debt financing and equity financing are not the same. When a business uses debt financing, it takes on debt and gradually repays it with interest. Seling ownership shares in exchange for cash is known as equity financing.

7.2.2.2. Types of Equity Financing

- **Individual Investors**: These are frequently business owners' friends, family, and coworkers. More money is needed to meet financing objectives because individual investors typically have smaller investment portfolios. These investors might not have the necessary business acumen, industry experience, or advice to benefit a company.
- **Angel Investors**: These are frequently affluent people or organizations looking to invest in ventures they think will yield profitable returns. Because they have experience in the industry, angel investors are able to make significant investments and offer valuable guidance, contacts, and insight. Angel investors typically make investments in the initial phases of a company's growth.
- **Venture Capitalists**: Those with the ability to invest large sums of money in companies they believe have strong growth potential, a competitive edge, and excellent chances of success are known as venture capitalists. They typically expect a sizeable ownership stake in a company in exchange for their monetary contribution, connections, and resources. To safeguard their investment, they might even demand a large degree of control over the day-to-day operations, planning, and activities of the business. Usually, venture capitalists enter the business early and leave when the company goes public, at which point they can make huge profits.
- **Initial Public Offerings:** An established company can raise capital by going public with initial public offerings (IPOs) of its stock. Owing to the cost, duration, and labor involved in initial public offerings (IPOs), this kind of equity funding takes place later in the business's growth. Less control is expected by IPO investors compared to venture capitalists and angel investors.
- **Crowdfunding:** Through online platforms like Kickstarter, Indiegogo, and Crowdfundr, individual investors can contribute small amounts to support a company's financial objectives. These investors frequently have a similar view on the objectives and mission of the business.

7.2.2.3. Reasons to Choose Equity Financing

- **You're a Startup:** Angel and venture capitalists may be especially interested in early-stage businesses. This is because their experience and skills could yield a high return on investment.
- **Established Lending Sources Ignore You:** When traditional financing options are unavailable because of the nature of the business, equity financing can be a viable alternative. For instance, because of an owner's lack of prior business experience or an unproven business concept, traditional lenders like

banks frequently won't extend loans to businesses they deem to be too significant a risk.

- **You Don't Want to Incur Debt:** You incur no new debt and no repayment obligations when you use equity financing. Investors take on the risk of losing their money.
- **You Get Guidance from Experts:** More than just money is delivered by equity financing. You might also get and profit from the important tools, advice, abilities, and experience of investors who wish you well, depending on where the money came from.
- **Your Goal Is the Sale of Your Company:** By providing the sizeable capital you might require to encourage faster and more significant growth, equity financing can increase your company's appeal to potential buyers and pave the way for a sale.

7.2.2.4. Pros and Cons of Equity Financing

While equity financing has benefits, there are some disadvantages to being funded this way.

- **Pros:** With equity financing, there is no debt to be paid back. If your company is unable to secure a loan, this is an additional choice. Because investors want a return on their investment rather than a loan repayment, it's viewed as a lower risk financing option. Plus, because the rewards can be substantial, investors are usually more interested in seeing you succeed than lenders are. Access to exceptional business expertise, insight, and advice can be obtained through equity financing provided by angel investors and venture capitalists. Additionally, it can introduce you to new and important networks and business contacts that could result in funding.
- **Cons:** The risks assumed by investors offering equity financing can be high, which lowers the profits that go to the company owners. Profits are divided among all stockholders, even the smallest ones. Furthermore, whenever you intend to make decisions that will have an effect on the business, investors might want to be consulted. Business owners have to cede some ownership in exchange for the substantial sums that venture capitalists and angel investors may invest. This may result in you having less authority over your own business. Large investors' generally higher rate of return demands can easily surpass what lenders charge. Dividends to shareholders are also not tax deductible. Loan interest payments are, with a few exceptions.

7.2.2.5. Example of Equity Financing

Let's say you have invested $1.5 million of your own funds in starting a small tech company. You are in complete control and ownership at this point. Angel investors and venture capitalists are drawn to your company because of its unique social media concept and the industry you operate in. You decide to look into hiring an outside investor because you know you'll need more money to maintain your fast growth. You meet with several potential investors and go over your company's plans, objectives, and financial requirements with them. Eventually, you accept a $500,000 offer from an angel investor who you believe has sufficient experience in addition to the funding. This funding round will not require the entire amount. Furthermore, you don't want to take a bigger amount and give up a bigger portion of your company's ownership. As a result, $2 million has been invested in your business overall ($1.5 million plus $500,000. You retain a 75% stake, while the angel investor owns a 25% stake ($500,000/$2 million).

7.2.3. Equity Financing vs. Debt Financing

When a company wants to raise money for financing, it usually has two options: debt financing and equity financing. Financing debt entails borrowing money. Seling a portion of the company's equity is required for equity financing. Even though each form of funding has certain benefits, the majority of businesses combine debt and equity financing.

- **No Ownership Issues with Debt:** A loan is the most typical method of financing debt. Debt financing necessitates that a business repay the money it receives plus interest, in contrast to equity financing, which has no repayment obligations. A loan's (and debt financing's, generally) benefit is that it spares a business from having to cede a portion of its ownership to shareholders. When a company uses debt financing, the lender has no say over how the company runs. Your relationship with the lender terminates when the loan is repaid. When a company chooses to raise capital through the sale of stock to investors, it is required to divide profits and confer with these investors on decisions that have a broad company impact.
- **Operational and Expense Differences:** Additionally, a company's operations may be restricted by debt financing, making it more difficult for it to seize opportunities outside of its primary business. Generally speaking, businesses prefer a low debt-to-equity ratio. If a critical need arises in the future, creditors are more likely to approve further debt financing because they will view this metric more favorably. Lastly, interest paid on loans is deductible from taxes in the form of business expenses. Due to the fixed amount of loan payments, budgeting for future needs is simple.
- **Factors to Consider:** When deciding whether to seek debt or equity financing, companies usually consider these three factors:
  - What source of funding is most easily accessible for the company?
  - What is the company's cash flow?
  - How important is it for principal owners to maintain complete control of the company?

The only method to get rid of investors—and their stake in the business—when a company offers them a portion of the company through the sale of equity is to buy back their shares, a move known as a buy-out. Repurchasing the shares, however, is probably going to be more expensive than what you were paid for issuing them.

7.3. DIVIDEND DISCOUNT MODELS (DDM)

The dividend discount model, or DDM for short, is a quantitative technique that projects a company's stock price based on the idea that the current price of the stock is equal to the total of all of the future dividend payments, discounted back to their present value. It makes an effort to determine a stock's fair value regardless of the state of the market and accounts for market expected returns and dividend payout parameters. The stock is cheap and should be purchased if the value determined by the DDM exceeds the share price as of right now, and vice versa.

7.3.1. Understanding the DDM

A business makes products or provides services in order to make money. The profits derived from these kinds of business operations are what drive the company's stock prices. Additionally, businesses pay dividends to their investors; these payments are typically derived from corporate profits. The foundation of the DDM model is the idea that a company's value is equal to the present value of all of its anticipated future dividend payments [Gordon Myron, 1959).

7.3.2. Time Value of Money

Let's say you lent your friend $100 with no interest. You visit them to pick up the money you were loaned after a while. Your pal offers you the following two options:

1. Take your $100 now
2. Take your $100 after a year

The majority of people will select the first option. You can deposit the money in a bank if you take it now. After a year, your money will increase to $105, assuming the bank pays a meager interest rate of, say, 5%. It will be preferable to the second option, in which your friend gives you $100 after a year. Mathematically;

Future Value=Present Value ⊠(1+interest rate%)(for one year)

The time value of money is demonstrated by the example above, which can be summed up as follows: "The value of money depends on time." Put another way, you can use the same interest rate model to determine the present value of an asset or receivable if you know its future value.

Rearranging the equation;

Present Value=Future Value/(1+interest rate%)

In essence, given any two factors, the third one can be computed. This principle is applied in the dividend discount model. Using the time value of money (TVM) concept, it determines a company's net present value (NPV) based on the estimated future cash flows it will produce. The foundation of the DDM is essentially the total of all anticipated future dividend payments made by the company, which is then valued at present using a net interest rate factor, also known as a discount rate.

7.3.3. Expected Dividends

It can be difficult to predict a company's future dividend payments. In order to project future dividend payments, analysts and investors may make specific assumptions or look for patterns based on historical dividend payment data. It is possible to assume that the company will continue to grow its dividends at a fixed rate indefinitely, or in perpetuity, which is a term used to describe an endless stream of identical cash flows with no end in sight. For instance, if a business paid a $1 dividend per share this year and is projected to continue paying dividends at a growth rate of 5%, the dividend is anticipated to be $1.05 the following year. Alternatively, an assumption about this year's dividend payment being $4.00 can be made if a particular trend is noticed, such as a company paying dividends of $2.00, $2.50, $3.00, and $3.50 over the previous four years. In mathematics, this kind of expected dividend is represented by (D).

7.3.4. Discounting Factor

Investing in stocks entails risk for shareholders because the value of their purchases could decrease. They anticipate receiving a payout or return in exchange for this risk. Like a landlord who rents out their property, the stock investors provide funding to the company in exchange for a predetermined rate of return. The amount that investors and the market are willing to pay a company to own an asset and assume ownership risk is known as the cost of equity capital. You can use the Dividend Growth Model or the Capital Asset Pricing Model (CAPM) to estimate this rate of return, which is denoted by (r). But an investor can only realize this rate of return if they sell their shares. Investor discretion may cause the necessary rate of return to change.

Businesses that distribute dividends do so at a specific yearly rate, denoted by (g). The effective discounting factor for a company's dividend is equal to the rate of return minus the dividend growth rate (r – g). The shareholders receive and realize the dividend. The return on equity (ROE), which is the opposite of the dividend payout ratio, can be multiplied by the retention ratio to estimate the dividend growth rate. Since the dividend is derived from the company's earnings, it should ideally not be greater than the earnings. In order for the model to work and produce results with negative stock prices, which are not achievable in reality, the rate of return on the entire stock must be higher than the rate at which dividends grow in subsequent years.

7.3.5. DDM Formula

Based on the expected dividend per share and the net discounting factor, the formula for valuing a stock using the dividend discount model is mathematically represented as:

Value of Stock=EDPS/(CCE–DGR)

Where; *EDPS* is the expected dividend per share; *CCE* is the cost of capital equity; and *DGR*=dividend growth rate

The value is subject to certain assumptions because the formula takes into account variables like the dividend per share and the net discount rate, which are represented by the required rate of return or cost of equity and the expected rate of dividend growth, respectively. The DDM is thought to only apply to companies that regularly pay dividends because dividends and their growth rate are important formulaic inputs. Nevertheless, it can still be applied to stocks that do not pay dividends by assuming what dividend the company would have paid in the absence of dividends.

7.3.6. DDM Variations

There are numerous, varying degrees of complexity in the DDM. The simplest iteration of the dividend discount model assumes zero dividend growth, which is inaccurate for the majority of companies but results in a value for the stock equal to the dividend value divided by the expected rate of return. The Gordon growth model (GGM), which was named in honor of American economist Myron J. Gordon in the 1960s, is the most widely used and simple method for calculating a DDM. It is based on the assumption of a steady dividend growth rate. Gordon. This model makes the assumption that dividends will grow steadily each year. Three factors are considered by the GGM when determining the price of a dividend-paying stock:

D=the estimated value of next year's dividend

r=the company's cost of capital equity

g=the constant growth rate for dividends, in perpetuity

Using these variables, the equation for the GGM is:

Price per Share=$D/r-g$

The supernormal dividend growth model is a third variation that accounts for a phase of rapid expansion followed by a period of slower, steady growth. Each dividend amount can be taken from the high growth period and discounted back to the current period. The GGM model is used in the computations for the constant growth period. The total of these computed factors is used to determine the stock price.

7.3.7. Examples of the DDM

Assume that this year, Company X distributed a $1.80 dividend per share. The company's cost of equity capital is 7%, and it anticipates dividend growth of 5% annually for all of eternity. In order to determine D_1, the projected dividend for the following year, the $1.80 dividend for this year must be modified by the growth rate. This calculation is: $D_1 = D_0 \times (1 + g) = \$1.80 \times (1 + 5\%) = \$1.89$. The price per share of Company X is then determined by applying the GGM, and it is D(1)/(r – g) = $1.89/(7% – 5%) = $94.50.

An examination of the dividend payment record of top US retailer Walmart Inc. (WMT) reports that, in chronological order, it distributed annual dividends of $2.08, $2.12, $2.16, $2.20, and $2.24 between 2019 and 2024. It is evident that Walmart's dividend has been steadily rising each year by 4 cents, or roughly 2 percent on average. Let's say an investor needs a 5% rate of return. Using an estimated dividend of $2.28 at the beginning of 2024, the investor would use the dividend discount model to calculate a per-share value of $2.28/ (.05 –.02) = $76.

7.3.8. Shortcomings of the DDM

Despite being widely used, the DDM's GGM method has two well-known drawbacks. The model makes the assumption that dividend growth will always be constant. This presumption is usually safe for extremely well-established businesses with a track record of consistent dividend payments. DDM, however, might not be the ideal model to value more recent companies with erratic dividend growth rates or none at all. The DDM can still be applied to these businesses, although its accuracy declines as more assumptions are made. The output of the DDM is highly sensitive to the inputs, which is its second problem. For instance, in the above example of Company X, if the dividend growth rate is reduced by 10% to 4.5%, the stock price that results is $75.24, which is less than 20% of the $94.50 price that was previously calculated. When a company's rate of return (r) is lower than the dividend growth rate (g), the model also breaks down. This could occur if a business keeps paying dividends despite losing money or having substantially lower earnings.

7.3.9. Using the DDM for Investments

Every DDM version, but notably the GGM, permits valuing a share independently of the state of the market. It also helps with direct comparisons between businesses, regardless of which industry they are in. Investors can use it to identify overbought or oversold stocks if they subscribe to the underlying theory that a stock's current intrinsic value represents the discounted value of its future dividend payments. If the computed value is greater than the share's current market price, this suggests a good time to buy because the stock is currently trading below the DDM's estimate of its fair value. It is important to remember that the DDM is just one of many quantitative tools for stock valuation that are available. The DDM is one of several widely used stock valuation techniques that can be used in addition to one another to ascertain a stock's intrinsic value. It might not be the only best approach to base investment decisions because it necessitates a lot of assumptions and forecasts.

7.4. CAPITAL BUDGETING AND PROJECT VALUATION

The planning process used to assess whether an organization's long-term capital investments, such as new machinery, machinery replacement, new plants, new products, and research development projects, are worth the funding of cash through the firm's capitalization structures (debt, equity, or retained earnings), is known as capital budgeting in corporate finance, corporate planning, and accounting. It is the process of distributing funds for significant investments or capital costs. Increasing the firm's value for the shareholders is a fundamental objective that aligns with the corporate finance methodology.

Since capital budgeting is not included in the revenue model, the models of most types of businesses, or even the day-to-day operations, it is generally regarded as a non-core business activity. It serves a business's strategic financial purpose. Investment banks are one company type where capital budgeting makes sense as part of the core business operations because their revenue model or models heavily rely on financial strategy. [O'Sullivan Arthur & Sheffrin Steven, 2003).

7.4.1. Nature of Capital Budgeting

Capital expenditure plans involving a sizable investment in fixed assets are the essence of capital budgeting. Once authorized, capital expenditures are long-term investments that cannot be withheld or withdrawn without incurring a loss. Forecasting profits for multiple years ahead of time and evaluating project profitability are key components of creating capital budget plans. Here, it could be argued that decisions about capital investments should be carefully considered to ensure they do not conflict with the company's future goals.

7.4.2. Importance of Capital Budgeting

Capital budgeting lowers the risk of funding unprofitable projects and maximizes returns by assisting businesses in prioritizing investments and more efficiently allocating financial resources. All things considered, capital budgeting is a crucial tool for companies looking to grow and succeed over the long run.

- Informs long-term investment decisions

- Reduces risk of unprofitable investments
- Maximizes profits by aligning with business goals
- Prioritizes investments and allocates resources efficiently
- Provides a framework for evaluating opportunities
- Promotes long-term growth and success
- Enables planning and budgeting for future investments

7.4.3. How Capital Budgeting Works

When a business is making capital budgeting decisions, figuring out whether or not a project will be profitable is crucial. While we will cover every capital budgeting technique, the following are the most widely used techniques for project selection.

1. Payback Period (PB);
2. Internal Rate of Return (IRR); and
3. Net Present Value (NPV).

Although it would seem that a capital budgeting strategy that yields positive results for each of the three metrics would be ideal, these strategies frequently lead to inconsistent outcomes. Depending on the needs of the company and the management's selection criteria, some strategies will be chosen over others. Nevertheless, there are advantages and disadvantages to these popular methods of valuation. Capital budgeting is meant to do just that—it determines capital asset investments based on how they will impact cash flow down the road. While increasing the amount of cash that enters the business later is preferred, the capital investment uses less cash in the future.

Paying attention to the timing is just as crucial. If you take the time value of money into account, it is always preferable to generate cash sooner rather than later. Considerations should also be made for scale. It might be necessary for a large company to concentrate its resources on assets that can generate large amounts of cash in order to have a noticeable effect on the overall performance of the company. Smaller businesses may have to turn down a project that could generate significant and quick cash flow because the necessary investment exceeds their capacity. The risk of making a poor choice and its possible rewards will determine how much effort and time will go into capital budgeting. If the company is afraid of going bankrupt in the event that decisions don't work out, then making a smaller investment might be a better course of action. Under capital budgeting, sunk costs are not taken into account. Rather than past expenses, the process concentrates on future cash flows.

7.4.4. Techniques

Many formal methods are used in capital budgeting, including the techniques such as:

- Accounting rate of return
- Average accounting return
- Payback period
- Net present value
- Profitability index
- Internal rate of return
- Modified internal rate of return
- Equivalent annual cost
- Real options valuation

The incremental cash flows from each possible project or investment are used in these methods. Though economists believe this to be improper, techniques like the accounting rate of return and "return on investment" are occasionally employed. These are based on accounting earnings and accounting rules. Payback period and discounted payback period are two examples of simplified and hybrid approaches that are employed.

7.4.4.1. Net Present Value

The cash present value (NPV) added to the company is calculated by discounting cash flows at the cost of capital. In order to maximize value added to the firm, the firm would accept all projects with positive net present value (NPV) unless capital was restricted or there were dependencies between projects. The time value of money is taken into account in this method. Projects that are mutually exclusive are those that accomplish the same goal together, for example, of which only one will be accepted out of the group. As a result, when selecting between projects that are mutually exclusive, more than one project may meet the capital budgeting requirement, but only one project may be approved.

7.4.4.2. Internal Rate of Return

The discount rate that results in a net present value (NPV) of zero is known as the internal rate of return, or IRR. It is a frequently employed indicator of investment performance. Projects should be arranged according to IRR to maximize return. A common cash flow structure for projects is a negative cash flow at first, followed by positive cash flows. Applying this criterion to non-mutually exclusive projects in an unconstrained environment will yield the same decision as the NPV method because in such a scenario, if the IRR is greater than the cost of capital, the NPV is positive.

One project whose cash flows don't follow this pattern is a loan, which has positive cash flows initially and then negative cash flows later on. Obviously, a lower IRR is preferable in this situation because the borrower must pay a higher rate the greater the loan's internal rate of return (IRR). An NPV is positive for any loan of this type whose IRR is less than the cost of capital. With the exception of these situations, the decision rule that chooses the project with the highest IRR will maximize return on investment for projects that are mutually exclusive and where the cash flow pattern dictates that the higher the IRR, the higher the NPV. However, it may also choose a project with a lower NPV.

There may be more than one IRR in a situation where there are multiple solutions to the equation NPV = 0. If there are one or more years of net investment (negative cash flow) followed by years of net revenues, then the IRR is real and distinct. However, multiple IRRs could exist if the cash flow signs fluctuate. Usually, the IRR equation can only be iterated rather than analytically solved. The return on capital invested (IRR) over the invested sub-period is calculated. Reinvesting intermediate cash flows at the IRR's rate might not be feasible. In order to address this problem, a metric known as the Modified Internal Rate of Return (MIRR) simulates the reinvestment of cash flows at a second rate of return. Executives seem to favor maximizing returns over maximizing the firm's value as measured by net present value (NPV), despite a strong academic preference for the latter.

7.4.4.3. Equivalent Annuity Method

By dividing the NPV by the present value of the annuity factor, the equivalent annuity method expresses the NPV as an annualized cash flow. It is frequently applied when evaluating just the expenses of particular projects with comparable cash inflows. This method, referred to as the equivalent annual cost (EAC) method, calculates the annual cost of owning and operating an asset for the duration of its life.

When comparing investment projects with different lifespans, it is frequently used. It would not be appropriate to compare the net present values (NPVs) of two projects, for instance, if project A has a 7-year expected lifetime and project B has an 11-year expected lifetime, unless the projects could not be repeated. The project will be replaced with an identical project if the EAC method is used.

As an alternative, the chain method and the NPV method can be applied together, provided that the projects will always be replaced with identical cash flows. To compare projects of unequal length, say, 3 years and 4 years, the projects are *chained together*, i.e., four repetitions of the 3-year project are compare to three repetitions of the 4-year project. The results obtained from the chain method and the EAC method are equivalent mathematically. Real interest rates, as opposed to nominal interest rates, are typically used in the computations because the assumption of identical cash flows for every link in the chain is effectively an assumption of zero inflation.

7.4.4.4. Real Options

Since the 1970s, real options analysis has gained significance due to the advancement of option pricing models. Projects are essentially valued using the discounted cash flow methods, which treat them like risky bonds with known promised cash flows. However, managers will have a wide range of options for raising or decreasing future cash outflows. To put it another way, managers oversee the projects rather than just approve or disapprove them. In real options analysis, the option values that the managers will have in the future are valued and added to the net present value (NPV).

7.4.5. Process of Capital Budgeting

The process of Capital Budgeting involves the following points:

- **Identifying and Generating Projects:** Proposals for investments are the initial stage of capital budgeting. There exist several incentives for making investments in a business. One possibility is the growth or addition of a new product line. It could also be suggested to increase production or decrease production costs.
- **Evaluating the Project:** It mostly entails choosing every criterion required to determine whether a proposal is necessary. It needs to align with the company's mission in order to maximize market value. Here, it is imperative to take the time value of money into account. You ought to assess the process's advantages and disadvantages in addition to the costs and benefits. The overall inflows and outflows of cash could carry a number of risks. Before continuing, this must be carefully examined.
- **Selecting a Project:** There is no set method for choosing a project because there is no "one-size-fits-all" factor. Because every business has different needs, a project's approval is contingent upon the goals of the company. The other elements must be completed after

the project has been concluded. These include raising money, which the company's finance department may investigate. Before coming to a decision and approving the project, the companies must consider all of their options. In addition, the selection of the project is heavily influenced by variables such as market conditions, profitability, and viability.

- **Implementation:** After the project is put into action, other crucial components like finishing it within the allotted budget or time frame come into play. After that, it is the management's responsibility to keep an eye on the project's implementation's effects.
- **Performance Review:** Analyzing and comparing the actual results to the projected outcomes is part of this process. This stage assists management in locating the shortcomings and removing them from subsequent proposals.

7.4.6. Ranked Projects

Ranking projects is where capital budgeting really adds value. Many of the projects that most organizations are working on have the potential to be financially lucrative. When a project has proven to have overcome a challenge, it ought to be evaluated in relation to other similar projects (e.g., – from the highest to the lowest profitability index. Prioritizing projects should be carried out until all allocated funds have been used.

7.4.7. Funding Sources

Retained earnings, debt capital, or equity capital must be raised in order to provide the excess cash needed for capital budgeting investments and projects. Debt capital is money that has been borrowed; it typically takes the form of bonds issued to creditors or bank loans. Investments made by shareholders who buy stock in the company are known as equity capital. Exceeding cash surplus from the company's previous and current earnings is known as retained earnings. Each of these sources has unique qualities regarding (i) the required rate of return that capital providers expect, which has an effect on the total cost of capital, and (ii) cash flow implications. The choice of "financing mix" will consequently impact the firm's valuation: Corporate finance and capitalization structure addresses these two interconnected factors.

7.4.8. Limitations of Capital Budgeting

Even though capital budgeting offers a great deal of insight into a company's future prospects, it is not a perfect approach. We study about some of the restrictions on capital budgeting in this section.

- **Cash Flow:** Determining whether the increased value of a project justifies the necessary investment is a straightforward process. The main goal of capital budgeting is to estimate the potential revenue that a project could produce. The estimate itself might be the issue. As of right now, neither the up-front expenses nor the projected revenue are more than estimates. Either an overestimation or an underestimate could eventually hurt the company's performance.
- **Time Horizon:** The process of capital budgeting often takes many years to complete. Forecasts with shorter durations might be estimated, but those with longer durations will almost certainly be off. Thus, when

calculating figures with capital budgeting, an extended time horizon may present a challenge. In addition, there might be other variables that present challenges, like competition, new laws, or technological advancements.

- **Time Value:** The capital budgeting technique known as the payback period method is very important, particularly for small businesses. It's an easy method that just needs the company to pay back within the agreed upon period. Its failure to account for the time value of money, however, is a concern. In other words, the same amounts of money have different values depending on when they are spent.
- **Discount Rates:** One of three ways to account for the time value of money is to use one's own funds, pay interest, or borrow money. Understanding discount rates is crucial. Its accurate calculation and estimation may prove to be a difficult undertaking. Even in the event that this is accomplished, additional variations such as fluctuating interest rates may negatively impact future cash flows. As such, this contributes to the list of drawbacks associated with capital budgeting.

7.5. LEVERAGED BUYOUT (LBO) MODELING

Using borrowed money to acquire a company is known as a leveraged buyout. Usually, private equity (PE) firms carry out these transactions by borrowing a significant amount of the acquisition's total cost from multiple lenders while making the least amount of their own money available. Then, the loan is secured by the assets of both the acquiring and the acquiring companies. Because employing debt (leverage) to finance acquisition deals can raise return on equity (ROE) and internal rate of return (IRR), allowing businesses to maximize profit back from their investments, leveraged buyouts are popular among PE firms. Businesses can consistently generate higher profits and better total returns because the cost of debt is often lower than the expected return on those assets. Leveraged buyouts are frequently pursued by businesses or private equity firms for the following reasons: to acquire a competitor, to take a publicly traded company private, or to restructure and swiftly resell a business.

7.5.1. Definition of Leveraged Buyout Model

An Excel-based financial model called a leveraged buyout model is used to assess possible LBO transactions. An LBO model's purpose is to assist investment banking or private equity analysts in evaluating risk and potential return in order to make informed decisions about which businesses to target for acquisition.

7.5.2. Components of Leveraged Buyout Model

LBO models typically consist of a few key components:

- **Financial Statements for the Target Company:** This comprises cash flow statements, balance sheets, and historical income statements. These financial statements serve as a foundation for understanding the company's historical performance and financial projections for the future.
- **Assumptions and Projections:** It is important to base assumptions and projections on the anticipated future performance of the target company. These presumptions may concern capital expenditures, expense levels, and rates of revenue growth. The resulting cash flows are then computed using the LBO model, which accounts for interest costs and any debt repayments.
- **Acquisition Structure:** The purchase price, the amount of debt that needs to be raised, and the equity contribution from the acquiring company or investor group are all included in the acquisition structure. Based on the capital structure and

transaction risk profile, the LBO model determines the necessary internal rate of return (IRR) for the investors.

- **Key Financial Metrics:** The LBO model can be used to compute a number of financial metrics that are helpful in determining the deal's attractiveness in addition to IRR. These measures include the debt service coverage ratio (a measure of how much cash flow is available to pay debt obligations) and the cash-on-cash multiple (the total cash earned on the total cash invested). These metrics aid in assessing the transaction's financial viability and the degree to which the projected returns satisfy the needs of the investors.
- **Sensitivity Analysis:** In order to evaluate the potential future effects of both internal and external factors on the target company's financial performance, LBO models usually incorporate some kind of scenario planning. Sensitivity analysis is another tool that analysts frequently use to evaluate how particular variables or presumptions might affect an LBO's result. This step assists in determining the main factors influencing the transaction's success as well as any possible investment risks.
- **Exit Strategy:** The LBO model also takes into account the acquiring company's ultimate exit strategy, which may entail recapitalizing, selling the acquired business to a different buyer, or selling it through an IPO. The potential proceeds from the exit and the potential return on investment from each can be estimated by the model.

7.5.3. Steps to Building a Leveraged Buyout Model

It's crucial for businesses thinking about pursuing a leveraged buyout to understand what steps to take in order to build a leveraged buyout model and begin the exploration process. These actions comprise:

1. **Have a Process for Targeting Companies:** You might base your leveraged buyout strategy on a specific profile that describes the kinds of businesses you hope to acquire through LBOs. Establish a clear definition of your ideal target company so that you can analyze your LBO model with clarity.
2. **Determine Your Capital Structure:** The target company's purchase price (as established by a company valuation) and the transaction's capital structure, which specifies the precise debt-to-equity ratio that will be utilized to finance the acquisition, must then be ascertained. In this step, you will also have to decide which kinds of debt you will use (i.e., bank debt, debt with a high yield, etc.).
3. **Assess Risk:** The next crucial stage in creating your LBO model is scenario planning, which is also how you'll primarily determine how risky your LBO transaction is. Through the use of predictive analytics, scenario planning examines a range of possible future scenarios, allowing you to assess the potential effects of various outcomes or economic factors on the success of your deal.
4. **Build Financial Projections and Plan Cash Flows:** After you've thoroughly described the deal's

structure in terms of risk and return potential, it's time to base your financial projections on the upcoming financial statements of your target company. Next, forecast future cash flows and figure out how much money is available to pay off debt. Lastly, use financial projections to establish the timetable and structure of your intended repayment.

5. **Plan Your Exit Strategy:** The optimal possible exit strategy for selling the target company should be determined by your LBO model based on the details of your deal, expected returns, and possible risk factors. You can work toward a specific goal and adjust your strategies throughout the course of your deal by planning your exit strategy at the outset of your leveraged buyout (LBO).

CASE STUDY

ASSET ALLOCATION AND INVESTMENT MANAGEMENT STRATEGIES

The Client is one of the prominent investment companies in Kuwait which operates a wide range of investment and financial activities, including direct investments, asset management, and corporate finance services. The Client had a strong foothold in the Kuwaiti market with an asset base of KD 289.38. Million as of Sep 30, 2009. The asset base was skewed heavily towards Kuwait and other G.C.C countries, with minimal investments spread across U.S, Asia, North Africa and European Market. Additionally, significant amount of the Company's assets were in privately held companies.

The Challenge

Economic downturn impacted the asset prices, and the liquidity of the company. Over a period of time, the Company's portfolio had significantly drifted to suboptimal levels. The management of the company felt the need for an optimal allocation of its portfolio which would reduce the risk levels, meet target returns, and provide sufficient liquidity. The Client was also looking for developing effective and suitable portfolio management strategies and in developing performance measurement standards.

Approach

The existing portfolio of Client has been analyzed, the strengths and weaknesses of the Company, and the current investment environment regionally, and globally. Further, AB sat with individual departmental heads and asset managers, circulated questionnaires and assessed the feedback in terms of suitability of the asset allocation to the Company.

After assessment the investment environment, returns expectations, risk capacity, liquidity requirements, expertise, and other advantages and constraints, AB developed a framework for strategic and tactical optimal asset allocation of its portfolio, and periodical rebalancing. In the strategic asset allocation, recommendations were made to increase its investment in Fixed Income Assets in order to meet the liquidity of the company and also recommendations were made for the inclusion of additional asset classes like commodities which would enhance the risk return tradeoff, and diversification of the portfolio. The tactical asset allocation aimed at an optimal allocation amongst sectors across different regions.

Conclusion

The client has been assisted by developing portfolio management strategies and guidelines spanning from investment screening, monitoring to exiting its investments. They also advised on adopting a synthetic credit scoring mechanism for arriving at the appropriate fixed income asset pricing since a majority of its fixed income assets were priced arbitrarily. Further, AB suggested appropriate benchmark against which the investment performance should be analyzed, and developed a mechanism for measurement and attribution analysis of its Investments and portfolios' performance.

CLASS ACTIVITY

GROUP ACTIVITY – WOULD YOU GIVE YOURSELF A LOAN?

Typically, people think they are great candidates for a loan, whether it's a car loan, a personal loan, or mortgage loan. This activity forces students to flip the conversation and discuss what it would take for them to give a loan to someone else or even themselves, especially if their own money or livelihood were on the line. Break your students into small groups of 3–4 members. Assign one group member to act as a bank while the remaining group members act as loan applicants. Once roles have been assigned, tell your students that are acting as bank employees to conduct interviews of loan applicants to determine who they would and would not give a loan to (Students should have the option of using authentic answers or creating a different financial "persona"). Some key components to consider while bankers are interviewing their applicants include:

- Does the applicant have verifiable income? Applicants should be prepared to provide ways to verify income.
- What other proof would you need of the borrower's ability to repay? Ask bankers to decide if income is enough to determine this as well as list what other factors (debts, for example) play a role and why.
- What is the loan for and who does the applicant owe? Bankers should ask questions to determine the reason for a loan. This will constitute good and bad reasons for a loan.

SUMMARY

- Capital structure is the particular combination of debt and equity used by a company to finance its overall operations and growth. Equity capital arises from ownership shares in a company and claims to its future cash flows and profits.
- Financial analysts use some form of leverage ratio to quantify the proportion of debt and equity in a company's capital structure, and to make comparisons between companies.
- A capital structure arbitrageur seeks to profit from differential pricing of various instruments issued by one corporation.
- Debt financing involves borrowing funds that must be paid back over time, typically with interest—however, the lender has no control over your business operations. Equity financing, on the other hand, involves raising capital by selling shares of your company. This means investors provide funds in exchange for ownership interest, potentially having a say in business decisions.
- A firm's capital structure is made up of equity and debt. The cost of equity is the dividend payments to shareholders, and the cost of debt is the interest payment to bondholders.
- The dividend discount model (DDM) is a quantitative method used for predicting the price of a company's stock based on the theory that its present-day price is worth the sum of all of its future dividend payments when discounted back to their present value.
- Shareholders who invest their money in stocks take a risk as their purchased stocks may decline in value. Against this risk, they expect a return/compensation. Similar to a landlord renting out their property for rent, the stock investors act as money lenders to the firm and expect a certain rate of return.
- Capital budgeting in corporate finance, corporate planning and accounting is an area of capital management that concerns the planning process used to determine whether an organization's long term capital investments such as new machinery, replacement of machinery, new plants, new products, and research development projects are worth the funding of cash through the firm's capitalization structures (debt, equity or retained earnings).
- Capital budgeting helps businesses prioritize investments and allocate financial resources more effectively, reducing the risk of investing in unprofitable projects and maximizing returns.
- Capital budgeting investments and projects must be funded through excess cash provided through the raising of debt capital, equity capital, or the use of retained earnings. Debt capital is borrowed cash, usually in the form of bank loans, or bonds issued to creditors. Equity capital are investments made by shareholders, who purchase shares in the company's stock.
- A leveraged buyout is the acquisition of a company using borrowed funds. They're typically done by private equity (PE) firms that borrow a large portion of the total cost of acquisition from a variety of lenders, putting as little of their own money down as they can.

REVIEW QUESTIONS

1. What is capital structure?
2. Why do different companies have different capital structure?
3. What are the different types of financing debt and equity?
4. What is the debt financing method?
5. What is the dividend discount model of cost of equity?
6. What is capital budgeting valuation?
7. Why do businesses need capital budgeting?
8. What are the steps to an LBO model?

REFERENCES

1. Adhikari, B. K., Cicero, D. C., & Sulaeman, J. (2021). Does local capital supply matter for public firms' capital structures? *Journal of Financial and Quantitative Analysis, 56*(5), 1809–1843. https://doi.org/10.1017/S0022109020000423.
2. Baker, M. P., & Wurgler, J. (2002). Market timing and capital structure. *Journal of Finance, 57*(1), 1–32. https://doi.org/10.1111/1540-6261.00414.
3. Chen, H. (2010). Macroeconomic conditions and the puzzles of credit spreads and capital structure. *Journal of Finance, 65*(6), 2171–2212. https://doi.org/10.1111/j.1540-6261.2010.01613.x.
4. Fama, E., & French, K. (2001). Disappearing dividends: Changing firm characteristics or lower propensity to pay. *Journal of Financial Economics, 60*(1), 3–43. https://doi.org/10.1016/S0304-405X(01)00038-1.
5. Friewald, N., Nagler, F., & Wagner, C. (2022). Debt refinancing and equity returns. *Journal of Finance, 77*(4), 2287–2289. https://doi.org/10.1111/jofi.13162.
6. Gordon, M. J. (1959). Dividends, earnings, and stock prices. *Review of Economics and Statistics, 41*(2), 99–105. https://doi.org/10.2307/1927792.
7. Groppelli, A. A., & Nikbakht, E. (2000). *Finance* (4th ed.). Hauppauge, NY: Barron's Educational Services, Inc. ISBN 0-7641-1275-9.
8. Korajczyk, R. A., Lucas, D., & McDonald, R. L. (1990). Understanding stock price behavior around the time of equity issues. In *Asymmetric Information, Corporate Finance, and Investment* (pp. 257–278). National Bureau of Economic Research. ISBN 0-226-35585-3.
9. Lemmon, M., Roberts, M., & Zender, J. (2008). Back to the beginning: Persistence and the cross-section of corporate capital structure. *Journal of Finance, 63*(4), 1575–1608. https://doi.org/10.1111/j.1540-6261.2008.01369.x.
10. Melicher, R. W., & Welshans, M. T. (1988). *Finance: Introduction to Markets, Institutions, and Management* (7th ed.). Cincinnati, OH: South-Western Publishing Co. ISBN 0-538-06160-X.

11. O'Sullivan, A., & Sheffrin, S. M. (2003). *Economics: Principles in Action*. Upper Saddle River, NJ: Pearson Prentice Hall. ISBN 0-13-063085-3.

12. Timmer, J. (2011). Understanding the Fed model, capital structure, and then some. *SSRN Electronic Journal*. https://doi.org/10.2139/ssrn.1322703.

13. Vuong, Q. H. (2014). Operational scales, sources of finance, and firms' performance: Evidence from Vietnamese longitudinal data. *CEB Working Paper Series* (N° 14/017). Retrieved from: https://doi.org/10.2139/ssrn.2470425.

14. Wu, X., & Au Yueng, C. K. (2012). Firm growth type and capital structure persistence. *Journal of Banking and Finance, 36*(12), 3427–3443. https://doi.org/10.1016/j.jbankfin.2012.08.008.

CHAPTER 8

Asset Pricing Models

LEARNING OBJECTIVES

After studying this chapter, you will be able to:

- Discus the concept of asset pricing
- Focus on pricing strategy
- Explain the different types of pricing strategy
- Learn about value pricing.

KEY TERMS FROM THIS CHAPTER

Equilibrium theory
Financial performance
Premium pricing
Value
Finance
Investors
Price

INTRODUCTION

The term "asset pricing" describes the formal treatment and development of the two main principles of pricing that are described below, along with the models that are produced. Numerous models have been created for various scenarios, but they all originate from either rational asset pricing—which is equivalent to risk-neutral pricing—or general equilibrium asset pricing. The body of knowledge used to support the process of choosing investments is referred to as investment theory, which is almost synonymous with asset pricing models. These models are then used to determine the asset-specific required rate of return on the investment in question or to price derivatives on these for trading or hedging.

The Capital Asset Pricing Model (CAPM) is one tool used by investors to determine the risks and return on their investment. Throughout the study, the CAPM will be referred to as the standard model. In 1960, William Sharpe presented the model. The standard model looks at how the investment portfolio is affected by systematic risk (beta coefficient). Regression analysis is used to determine the beta coefficient between the return of a managed portfolio and a benchmark portfolio. Applying this model piqued the interest of numerous investors and financial analysts. Researchers found that data distributions aren't always normal in their follow-up studies, and they adjusted the CAPM accordingly. The researchers developed the Downside Capital Asset Pricing Model (D-CAPM), a brand-new model.

8.1. BASIC CONCEPT OF ASSET PRICING

The foundation of capital market theory is asset pricing, a topic that has been extensively studied in the literature on finance. The way market participants price securities is depicted by asset-pricing theories. A positive correlation between the expected risk premiums and the systematic risk of each individual security is the main result of the CAPM. The CAPM has been used for a long time in corporate finance and performance evaluation of securities and portfolios by academics and investment managers due to its enticing and simple outcome. Similar to most theories, the CAPM has faced criticism from a number of researchers who have shown that market beta cannot account for the cross-sectional variation in average security returns. the correlations between market capitalization, book-to-market, price-earnings, and cash flow to price ratios, in that order, and average stock returns. These results opened the door for the development of a different asset-pricing model that expanded on the CAPM by incorporating the book-to-market ratio and size.

8.1.1. General Equilibrium Asset Pricing

According to the general equilibrium theory, supply and demand drive market pricing, which sets prices. The requirement that the quantities of each asset supplied and the quantities demanded at that price be equal is here jointly satisfied by asset prices, a process known as "market clearing." The capital asset pricing model (CAPM), which is the archetypal outcome of modern portfolio theory, is the source of these models. Here, prices are set in relation to macroeconomic variables, which take individual preferences into account. For the CAPM, these variables are the overall market; for the CCAPM, they are overall wealth. These large-dimension models are intended to represent the statistically derived probability distribution of all securities' market prices at a specific future investment horizon. Then, in assessing heterogeneous portfolios, general equilibrium pricing is applied, resulting in a single asset price for numerous assets. In order to calculate an investment or share value, one must first: (i) create a financial forecast for the company or project in question; and (ii) discount the output cash flows at the rate that the chosen model returns, which reflects the project's level of risk. e. the unique risk associated with these cash flows, also known as the undiversifiable risk; (iii) these present values are then combined. A different, albeit less popular, strategy is to use a fundamental valuation method, like the T-model, which instead makes use of accounting data in an effort to model return based on the anticipated financial performance of the company.

8.1.1.1. Rational Pricing

For a summary of the reasoning behind rational pricing derivatives, consider the following: under rational pricing, derivative prices are typically computed so as to be arbitrage-free with regard to more fundamental (equilibrium determined) securities prices. This method typically produces a unique risk price for each asset rather than grouping assets together; as a result, the models are low dimensional. Combining the following methods yields the option prices (or Greeks): (i) a model of the underlying price behavior, or process – i.e., the chosen asset pricing model; and (ii) a formula that determines the premium—also known as sensitivity—based on this behavior.

The Black-Scholes model, which is the traditional model in this case, describes the dynamics of a market that includes derivatives (and its formula for option pricing); it also generally leads to Martingale pricing and aside models. The Black-Scholes model presupposes a log-normal process, whereas the other models might include characteristics like mean reversion or be aware of the volatility surface, utilizing either local volatility or stochastic volatility.

8.1.2. Capital Asset Pricing Model (CAPM)

Adding assets to a well-diversified portfolio requires deciding on an asset's theoretically appropriate required rate of return, which can be done using the capital asset pricing model (CAPM). The model considers the asset's sensitivity to non-diversifiable risk (also called systematic risk or market risk), which is commonly represented in the financial industry by the quantity beta (β). It also accounts for the market's expected return and the expected return of an asset that is theoretically risk-free. CAPM assumes a specific form of utility functions (i.e., asset returns whose probability distributions are entirely described by the first two moments (e.g., the normal distribution) and zero transaction costs (necessary for diversification to get rid of all idiosyncratic risk). In other words, risk is measured by variance, for example, a quadratic utility. In these circumstances, the CAPM demonstrates that beta alone determines the cost of equity capital. The CAPM is still widely used because of its adaptability and simplicity in a range of scenarios, even though it has failed multiple empirical tests and more contemporary methods of asset pricing and portfolio selection (like arbitrage pricing theory and Merton's portfolio problem) have been developed.

8.1.3. What Is CAPM?

The foundation of modern financial theory is the belief that: (1) securities markets are highly competitive and efficient, meaning that pertinent company information is swiftly and widely disseminated and absorbed; and (2) rational, risk-averse investors, who aim to maximize their satisfaction from investment returns, dominate these markets. The first presupposes a highly developed, knowledgeable buyer and seller populating the financial market. The second assumption characterizes wealth-conscious investors who would rather have more than less. Furthermore, the modern financial theory's hypothetical investors demand a premium in the form of higher expected returns for the risks they take on.

Even though these two presumptions form the basis of contemporary financial theory, additional, more specific limiting assumptions are made during the formal development of CAPM. These consist of perfect markets devoid of imperfections such as transaction fees, levies, and limitations on borrowing and short sales. Limiting assumptions about the statistical nature of securities returns and investor preferences are also necessary for the model to work. Lastly, based on a shared time horizon, investors are presumed to concur on the expected performance and risk of securities. Even though the CAPM's underlying assumptions are obviously false, it is frequently necessary to simplify reality in order to create models that are useful. The validity and usefulness of a model's prescription serve as its true tests, in addition to the plausibility of its underlying assumptions. An idealized but concrete model of how financial markets measure risk and convert it into expected return can be derived by tolerating the somewhat unrealistic assumptions of the CAPM.

8.1.4. Portfolio Diversification

When it comes to financial securities, CAPM handles risks and returns and defines them precisely, if arbitrarily. The cash dividends received plus the capital gain (or loss) during the holding period divided by the purchase price of the security is the rate of return an investor receives from purchasing common stock and holding it for a specific amount of time. Investors may be pleasantly surprised or disappointed by the fluctuating returns they receive from a particular stock, even though they may have anticipated a specific return when purchasing the stock.

Common stocks are therefore regarded as risky investments. (In contrast, certain securities, like Treasury bills, are regarded as riskless since their returns are consistent with their expected returns. According to financial theory, risk is the likelihood that actual returns will differ from expected returns; risk is measured by the degree of potential fluctuation.

The idea that hazardous stocks can be bundled so that the resulting portfolio (or combination) is less risky than any of its parts forms the basis of the capital asset pricing model (CAPM). Even though this kind of diversification is widely known, it could be beneficial to revisit how diversification lowers risk. Assume that two businesses with a focus on tourism are situated on a remote island. One business produces lotion for suntans. Rainy years see its stock perform poorly, and sunny years see it perform well. The other business makes throwaway umbrellas. Its stock does well in rainy years and equally poorly in sunny ones. An average return of 12% is earned by each company.

Investors take a significant risk when buying either stock because weather-related variations in the stock price can cause volatility. Regardless of the weather, investing half of the money in the stock of suntan lotion and half in the stock of the umbrella manufacturer yields a 12% return. Through portfolio diversification, two risky stocks with a 12% average return each become a risk-free portfolio that is guaranteed to generate the anticipated 12% return. Regretfully, in real life, it is extremely uncommon for there to be a perfect negative relationship between the returns on these two stocks. Corporate securities move in tandem to some extent, making it impossible to completely eliminate risk through straightforward portfolio diversification. However, diversification will always lower risk as long as there is a lack of parallelism in the securities' returns.

8.1.5. Employment of CAPM

The ideas behind these concepts are easily applied. For instance, the cost of equity component should represent the risk inherent in the division's operations rather than the risk of the parent company when a manager is computing divisional costs of capital or hurdle rates. It is recommended to use an equity cost that is proportionate to the risk involved, even if it is significantly greater than the parent company's equity cost. Calculating the CAPM estimates of the cost of equity for comparable, independent businesses that are involved in the same industry is one method for estimating the cost of equity for a division.

The industry's level of risk is reflected in these companies' betas. Of course, adjustments could be required to account for variations in financial leverage and other elements. A second illustration relates to purchases. The appropriate cost of equity in discounted cash flow evaluations of acquisitions should take into account the risks associated with the discounted cash flows. Once more, disregarding adjustments needed for modifications to capital structures and similar matters, the cost of equity ought to represent the target company's risk profile rather than the acquirer's.

8.1.6. Does CAPM Work?

The model is obviously an idealized theory of financial markets with unrealistic assumptions. Naturally, the effectiveness of CAPM is the real litmus test. Numerous empirical tests of CAPM have been conducted. The majority of these have looked at historical data to assess how closely stock returns and betas have tracked the direction indicated by the security market line (Figure 8.1).

With few exceptions the major empirical studies in this field have concluded that:

- As a measure of risk, beta appears to be related to past returns. Because of the close relationship between total and systematic risk, it is difficult to distinguish their effects empirically. Nonetheless, inclusion of a factor representing unsystematic risk appears to add little explanatory power to the risk/return relationship.
- The relationship between past returns and beta is linear—that is, reality conforms to what the model predicts. The relationship is also positively sloped—that is, there is a positive trade-off between the two (high risk equals high return, low risk equals low return).
- The empirical SML appears less steeply sloped than the theoretical SML. As illustrated in Exhibit VI, low-beta securities earn a return somewhat higher than CAPM would predict, and high-beta stocks earn less than predicted. A variety of deficiencies in CAPM and/or in the statistical methodologies employed have been advanced to explain this phenomenon.

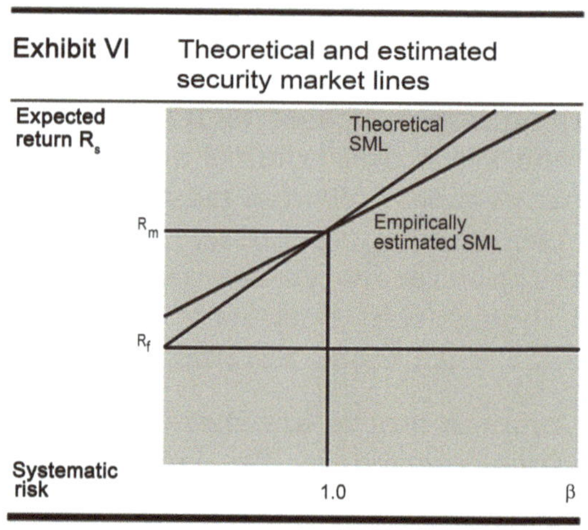

Figure 8.1. Theoretical and estimated security market lines.

Source: https://hbr.org/resources/images/article_assets/hbr/8201/82106_F.gif.

These empirical tests support the main implications of CAPM, even though they do not definitively validate it. There is a positive risk/return trade-off, and the relationship between risk and return appears to be linear. The systematic risk measure, beta, does appear to be correlated with historical returns. Research on the conflicting results regarding the SML's slope is still ongoing. Based on these results, some researchers recommend utilizing a more gradually sloped "empirical market line" in place of the theoretical SML.

Recent research in the field of investment management has cast doubt on the idea that systematic risk alone is significant. It would be improbable to find just one pertinent kind of risk in a complex world—market risk. The development of richer asset-pricing models has advanced significantly. But none of these more advanced models have yet demonstrated a definite advantage over CAPM. Research in this field is still very active, with a primary focus on applications related to investment management.

8.1.7. The CAPM and the Efficient Frontier

The Capital Asset Pricing Model (CAPM) makes the assumption that a portfolio's risk-return profile can be optimized, with an optimal portfolio showing the least amount of risk relative to its return.

Furthermore, since every new asset added to a portfolio increases its diversification, the ideal portfolio should include every asset and be value-weighted to achieve the aforementioned results (assuming that no asset is infinitely divisible, assuming no trading costs). Each of these ideal portfolios, i.e., one for every return level, make up the efficient frontier.

The goal of using the CAPM to construct a portfolio is to assist investors in risk management. The following graph illustrates the efficient frontier, which is where a portfolio would lie if an investor could precisely optimize a portfolio's return in relation to risk using the CAPM (Figure 8.2).

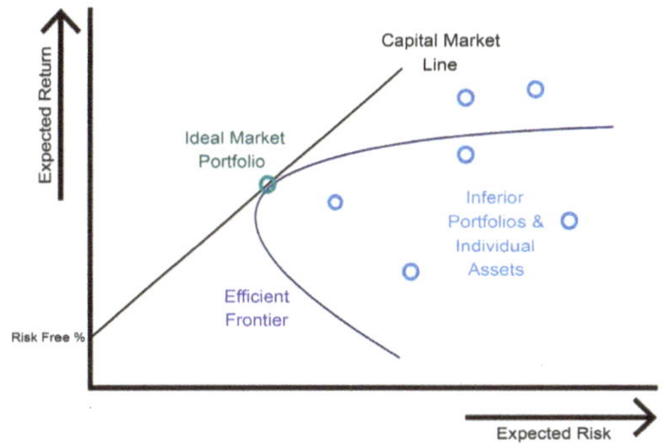

Figure 8.2. *The CAPM and the efficient frontier.*

Source: https://www.investopedia.com/thmb/nM4YLmelnnoslrkTjVByogAuGqU=/750x0/filters:no_upscale():max_bytes(150000):strip_icc():format(webp)/CapitalAssetPricingModelCAPM1_2-e6be6eb7968d4719872fe0bcdc9b8685.png.

The graph illustrates how higher expected risk (x-axis) necessitates higher expected returns (y-axis). According to modern portfolio theory, a portfolio's expected return rises with increasing risk, starting at the risk-free rate. There comes a point at which a theoretical portfolio can be constructed on the Capital Market Line (CML) with the best return for the amount of risk being taken, but any portfolio that fits on the CML is better than any possible portfolio to the right of that line. Although it can be challenging to define, the efficient frontier and CML highlight a crucial idea for investors: there is a trade-off between higher return and higher risk.

Due to the fact that it is impossible to construct a portfolio that precisely fits on the CML, investors frequently take on excessive risk in an attempt to increase returns. Two portfolios that have been built to fit along the efficient frontier are displayed in the following chart. Portfolio A has a 10% standard deviation, or risk level, and an expected annual return of 8%.

The expected annual return for Portfolio B is 10%, with a standard deviation of 16%. Portfolio B's risk increased more quickly than its anticipated returns (Figure 8.3).

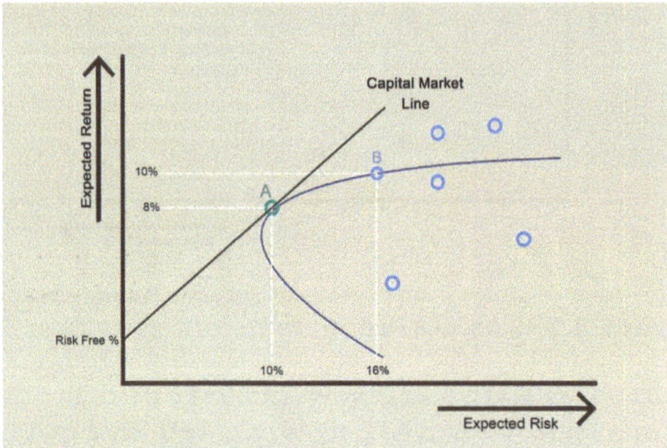

Figure 8.3. *That have been constructed to fit along the efficient frontier.*

Source: https://www.investopedia.com/thmb/hFGVxgltwekXVbd8ufHz8MPtdWo=/750x0/filters:no_upscale():max_bytes(150000):strip_icc():format(webp)/CapitalAssetPricingModelCAPM2_2-b5f6378f74164191a5e589e307d88c51.png.

The efficient frontier is only calculable in theory and is predicated on the same assumptions as the CAPM. A portfolio would be offering the maximum return for its degree of risk if it were located on the efficient frontier. But since future returns are unpredictable, it is hard to determine whether a portfolio is on the efficient frontier or not.

The efficient frontier graph can be rearranged to show the trade-off for specific assets. This risk-return trade-off is applicable to the CAPM. As you can see, the CML is now known as the Security Market Line (SML) in the following chart. The stock's beta is used on the x-axis in place of expected risk. The illustration shows that the expected return rises as beta increases from one to two (Figure 8.4).

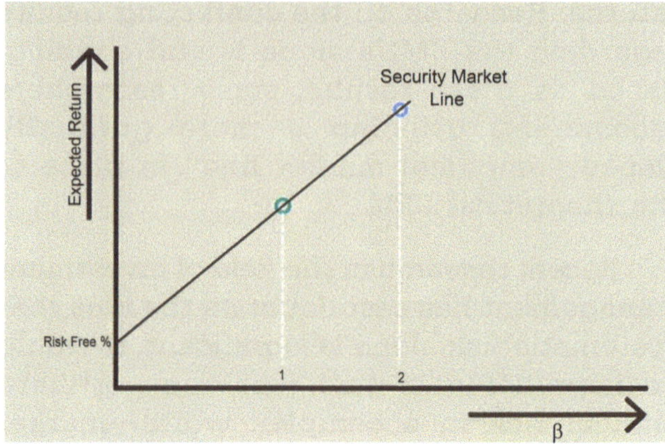

Figure 8.4. *The value of these two models.*

Source: https://www.investopedia.com/thmb/I063VGT1GkUOPG1_pKGMOxeXLfs=/750x0/filters:no_upscale():max_bytes(150000):strip_icc():format(webp)/CapitalAssetPricingModelCAPM3_2-0caa4bc4faf6446c86d857b2253a15eb.png.

The relationship between a stock's beta and expected risk is established by the CAPM and SML. Greater beta translates into greater risk, but there may be high beta stock portfolios on the CML where the trade-off is tolerable, if not optimal. Assumptions about beta and market participants that are not true in real markets reduce the usefulness of these two models.

For instance, when comparing a stock with an equally high beta to another that does not see the same type of downward price movements, beta does not take into consideration the relative riskiness of the stock that is more volatile than the market and experiences a high frequency of downside shocks.

8.1.8. Practical Value of the CAPM

It could be challenging to see the CAPM's potential value in light of the criticisms leveled at it and the presumptions underlying its application in portfolio construction.

Nonetheless, there may still be some benefit to using the CAPM as a tool for comparisons or to assess whether future expectations are reasonable. Consider an advisor who suggests putting a $100 share price stock into a portfolio.

The advisor justifies the price with a 13% discount rate by using the CAPM. With this data, the advisor's investment manager can assess whether a 13% return is realistic by comparing it to the company's historical performance and that of its competitors.

In this case, let's say that over the past few years, the peer group's performance has been slightly above 10%, while this stock has consistently underperformed, returning 9 percent. The investment manager ought to provide a rationale for the higher expected return before following the advisor's advice. The efficient frontier and CAPM concepts can also be used by investors to assess how well their individual stocks or portfolios are performing in comparison to the market as a whole.

Assume, for illustration purposes, that an investor's portfolio has returned 10% annually over the previous three years, with a 10% standard deviation of returns (risk). On the other hand, with an 8 percent risk, market averages have returned 10% over the past three years.

This observation may be used by the investor to reconsider the composition of their portfolio and identify holdings that might not be on the SML.

The reason the investor's portfolio is to the right of the CML may be explained by this. An investor can enhance returns by making adjustments to holdings that are either negatively impacting returns or disproportionately raising the risk of the portfolio.

8.1.9. Application Problems

There are multiple possible sources of error in CAPM applications used in corporate finance. First off, the behavior of financial markets might not be well described by the straightforward model. Numerous model extensions have been created by researchers in an effort to increase the model's realism. The fact that betas are unstable over time is a second issue.

This fact makes things complicated when equity costs are calculated using betas derived from historical data to assess future cash flows. Betas ought to alter in tandem with shifts in capital structures and business fundamentals. Furthermore, statistical estimation error can affect betas that are estimated based on historical data. There are numerous methods for addressing these sources of instability.

Errors can also be found in the projections of the market return and the future risk-free rate. A last set of issues is specific to CAPM applications in corporate finance. Using the CAPM, or any other financial market model, in capital budgeting decisions involving real assets is not without its theoretical and practical challenges. Research on these challenges is still very active.

The failure of the CAPM in empirical tests implies that most applications of the model are invalid:

- The traditional CAPM using historical data as the inputs to solve for a future return of asset i. However, the history may not be sufficient to use for predicting the future and modern CAPM approaches have used betas that rely on future risk estimates.
- Most practitioners and academics agree that risk is of a varying

nature (non-constant). A critique of the traditional CAPM is that the risk measure used remains constant (non-varying beta). Recent research has empirically tested time-varying betas to improve the forecast accuracy of the CAPM.

- The model assumes that the variance of returns is an adequate measurement of risk. This would be implied by the assumption that returns are normally distributed, or indeed are distributed in any two-parameter way, but for general return distributions other risk measures (like coherent risk measures) will reflect the active and potential shareholders' preferences more adequately. Indeed, risk in financial investments is not variance in itself, rather it is the probability of losing: it is asymmetric in nature as in the alternative safety-first asset pricing model. Barclays Wealth have published some research on asset allocation with non-normal returns which shows that investors with very low risk tolerances should hold more cash than CAPM suggests.
- Some investors prefer positive skewness, all things equal, which means that these investors accept lower returns when returns are positively skewed. For example, Casino gamblers pay to take on more risk. The CAPM can be extended to include co-skewness as a priced factor, besides beta.
- The model assumes that all active and potential shareholders have access to the same information and agree about the risk and expected return of all assets (homogeneous expectations assumption).
- The model assumes that the probability beliefs of active and potential shareholders match the true distribution of returns. A different possibility is that active and potential shareholders' expectations are biased, causing market prices to be informationally inefficient. This possibility is studied in the field of behavioral finance, which uses psychological assumptions to provide alternatives to the CAPM.
- The model does not appear to adequately explain the variation in stock returns. Empirical studies show that low beta stocks offer higher returns than the model would predict. Either that fact is itself rational (which saves the efficient-market hypothesis but makes CAPM wrong), or it is irrational (which saves CAPM, but makes the EMH wrong – indeed, this possibility makes volatility arbitrage a strategy for reliably beating the market). The puzzling empirical relationship between risk and return is also referred to as the low-volatility anomaly.
- The model assumes that there are no taxes or transaction costs, although this assumption may be relaxed with more complicated versions of the model.
- The market portfolio consists of all assets in all markets, where each asset is weighted by its market capitalization. This assumes no preference between markets and assets for individual active and potential shareholders, and that active and potential shareholders choose assets solely as a function of their risk-return profile. It also assumes that all assets are infinitely

divisible as to the amount which may be held or transacted.

- The market portfolio should in theory include all types of assets that are held by anyone as an investment (including works of art, real estate, human capital.). In practice, such a market portfolio is unobservable and people usually substitute a stock index as a proxy for the true market portfolio. Unfortunately, it has been shown that this substitution is not innocuous and can lead to false inferences as to the validity of the CAPM, and it has been said that due to the in observability of the true market portfolio, the CAPM might not be empirically testable. However, others find that the choice of market portfolio may not be that important for empirical tests. Other authors have attempted to document what the world wealth or world market portfolio consists of and what its returns have been.
- The model assumes economic agents optimize over a short-term horizon, and in fact investors with longer-term outlooks would optimally choose long-term inflation-linked bonds instead of short-term rates as this would be more risk-free asset to such an agent.
- The model assumes just two dates, so that there is no opportunity to consume and rebalance portfolios repeatedly over time.
- CAPM assumes that all active and potential shareholders will consider all of their assets and optimize one portfolio. This is in sharp contradiction with portfolios that are held by individual shareholders: humans tend to have fragmented portfolios or, rather, multiple portfolios: for each goal one portfolio.
- Empirical tests show market anomalies like the size and value effect that cannot be explained by the CAPM.

Even with its own limited set of assumptions, the CAPM is essentially faulty, showing that it is either circular or irrational. The term "circularity" describes how the price of covariance risk alone determines the price of total risk, and vice versa. This "revision of prices," as declared by the CAPM, results in the same discount rates for the (lower) amount of covariance risk alone as for the (higher) amount of total risk (i.e., irrationality the same discount rates for varying levels of risk).

8.2. PRICING STRATEGY

All of the techniques a business owner employs to decide on the appropriate price for a good or service are collectively referred to as a pricing strategy. You will usually have to do some research, gather consumer insights, or conduct market analysis in order to implement a great strategy. Naturally, not all pricing strategies are exhaustive.

Certain business owners would rather keep things straightforward and use manufacturer suggested retail prices (MSRPs) or set markups, which are also referred to as cost-plus pricing. You already have a pricing strategy in place if you set your prices using any kind of regular procedure. You will, however, be able to gain the competitive edge in your sector if you develop a strategy that more fully takes into consideration the state of the market and other elements that affect consumer behavior.

8.2.1. Pricing Objectives

When determining the price of its goods or services, a company sets pricing objectives that it hopes to meet. The pricing process needs to be integrated with the rest of the marketing mix in order to be effective. The four Ps of a marketing mix are product, price, place/distribution, and promotion. Every choice made regarding the price points, or costs of goods or services to consumers, must align with the marketing strategy or plan that takes into account the product's value as well as the costs associated with distribution and promotion. To stay in business, the company needs to turn a profit, or a profitable return on investment (ROI), but it also needs to meet competitive pricing goals in order to draw in clients.

Getting media attention for a company is one kind of pricing goal. For instance, a brand-new bread company might center its marketing campaign on the idea of offering reasonably priced, high-quality grain products to assist consumers in hard times. Because the pricing and marketing strategies would differ from those of competitors, a positioning that can draw in the target market with a distinctive selling proposition (USP) is the outcome. Unique selling propositions (USPs) are powerful, convincing marketing messages that attract a lot of new consumers by providing an enticing reason for them to choose that specific brand over those of rivals.

Matching techniques are used in other, more popular pricing objectives. For example, a business might say to prospective clients in its marketing communications that it will match the prices of all of its competitors. When using this kind of price point strategy, many companies include a tagline like "You get true value with Smith's Flooring.." When a business is struggling, survival pricing is a goal. In this case, the primary objective of pricing is to ensure the survival of the business rather than taking ROI into account. Survival pricing is only ever appropriate as a short-term business strategy; it should never be used as part of a permanent marketing mix.

One pricing strategy that a business may employ to attract clients who aren't particularly motivated by a product's or service's price is skimming. This is how luxury goods are usually priced; if the product is the best, its demand indicates that it is worth it at nearly any cost. This kind of pricing goal offers high-end, in-demand products to a select target market, thereby skimming the cream, or highest value, from the marketplace. Pricing goals (i.e., what the business hopes to achieve with its pricing strategy) should be connected to its goals and should come after the choice of how to position its goods and services. Depending on factors such as business size, internal capabilities, and whether profit, sales, or government action is the primary focus, different small businesses within the same industry might have distinct pricing objectives.

- **Sales-Based Objectives:** Increasing sales volume and market share relative to the competition may involve penetration pricing, where a business prices a new product below that of the competition to quickly penetrate the market at the competitor's expense, acquire a large market share, and then gradually raise the price. This objective might be appropriate for a small business that is introducing a new product or service to a very competitive marketplace.
- **Profit-Maximization Objectives:** Quickly recovering the costs of product development while providing customer value may involve price skimming, where a new product is priced higher than that of the competition to maximize profit. This objective would work for a small business with customers who are more concerned with quality, uniqueness, and status rather than price. However, a product's image and quality must warrant the high price.
- **Status-Quo-Based Objectives:** Used to minimize the impact of competitors, government, or channel members and to avoid a sales decline, these objectives are reactive rather than proactive, so they should be adopted for the short term only. Small businesses must be able to meet the needs of their target market.

8.2.1.1. Competitive Pricing

The practice of basing a product or service's price on that of a rival is known as competitive pricing. Pricing strategy includes determining whether to charge the same as the competition, less than the competition, or more than the competition. Competitive pricing is typically examined in terms of undercutting rivals or imposing a price that is less than the going rate. However, there is a thin line separating lawful anti-competitive behavior from healthy competition. Owners of businesses need to be careful that their competitive pricing does not cross the line into illegal predatory pricing.

The owner of the business has three options in theory. He can find other businesses in his region that offer comparable or identical goods, and he can set his prices to reflect going rates. As an alternative, he might attempt to differentiate his goods from those that are already available and charge more. Lastly, he can undercut the competition by pricing his goods less than the market.

Competitive pricing is built on these pricing tactics. Entrepreneurs base critical pricing decisions on the kind of relationship they hope to build with their rivals. A business owner's relationships with other owners are rarely strained by setting prices at or above the market. Following the market puts the company on a path to keep things as they are. Establishing a premium price opens up a new market and calls for a marketing plan that emphasizes persuading customers of a product's special qualities in order to support a higher price. On the other hand, undercutting the competition can have a number of consequences.

Competitive pricing of this kind primarily takes clients away from rivals' wallets. A new company that plans to use lower prices to draw clients is more likely to create a hostile work environment. A strategy like this could start a pricing war in which companies alternately lower and lower their prices. While price wars benefit consumers, the participating businesses cannot sustain them.

Governments keep a careful eye out for price undercutting. Setting prices low to force a competitor out of business can be seen as anti-competitive predatory pricing that increases the market's susceptibility to a monopoly, even though regular competitive pricing is encouraged. Simple competitive pricing is typically applied when a business owner can set prices lower due to operational efficiency. However, the tactic will probably be viewed as predatory if a business owner uses cash reserves to maintain lower prices and then raises them after forcing a rival out of business.

8.2.2. Benefits of a Pricing Strategy

In order to account for the pricing model of the goods, a pricing strategy takes into account variables such as market conditions, consumer trends, competitor actions, and other variable costs. The second most significant advantage of online shopping for consumers is the capacity to compare prices. Customers will increasingly look for the best deal they can find as e-commerce grows and makes price comparison easier every day.

By providing a rationale for your price changes, a solid pricing strategy can assist you in exceeding customer expectations. Your plan will establish a recurring procedure that motivates you to think about the reactions of your target market and possibly even your rivals to the prices you choose. With continued practice, you'll be able to win over even the pickiest consumers in terms of price. In the long term, your pricing strategy may even help you change the perception of the value of your goods or services when combined with an effective marketing plan.

8.2.2.1. Price Target

When it comes to trading, a price target is the amount that a trader hopes to obtain in order to maximize the return on their investment. Since the desired rate is the price the seller hopes to receive for the securities that are currently being offered for sale, this usually has to do with the sale of an investment. Traders employ a diverse array of approaches to ascertain the optimal price target for a particular asset. These methods span from basic intuition to intricate formulas that forecast the market price at the moment the investor desires to commence the sale.

Some investors base their price target determination on evaluating the investment's historical performance and tying it to the expected movement of the asset's price over a given time frame. This can help the investor estimate the potential profit on their investment should they decide to hold onto the asset for a month, six months, or a year. The investor may set the target price at the rate the security is anticipated to reach at the end of the year if they believe the price of the security will be at a desirable level in a year.

The investor has two options if the security performs better than expected and hits the price target before then: they can sell the asset when the target is reached, or they can keep holding it for the duration of the projection. This investment carries some risk because there's always a chance that it will peak early, start to decline, and ultimately drop back below the price target.

Because of this, investors who employ this strategy should keep a close eye on market conditions and take prompt action if the asset's value starts to decline. Setting a price target also involves other factors, like calculating a moving average or using Fibonacci extensions. Price levels known as Fibonacci extensions allow one to project market support and resistance for the duration of the study period. From this angle, the extensions can help determine the best time to sell the asset and maximize the proceeds from the transaction.

Using the advice of financial experts when determining a price target is an alternative strategy. For instance, some investors would accept a Wall Street analyst's six-month price target of $100 in US dollars (USD) for a stock that is currently trading at $60 USD, without taking the time to conduct their own independent analysis of the data. Although this strategy has the benefit of drawing on the experience of reputable experts, there's always a chance that the analyst missed something important that the investor would have taken into account before establishing the goal.

As determining a price target is highly individualized, no single optimal approach will be adopted by all investors to determine the price. It is possible for two different investors to set different price targets for the same investment, even when they are taking into account the same set of factors. This is because their interpretation of the data and the expected rate of return on the trade will differ. Setting a target, like with most projections, establishes a target to strive toward but does not ensure that the intended result will materialize.

8.2.3. High Price Strategy

A high price strategy is a marketing tactic in which producers, retailers, or manufacturers set a high price for a good or service. There are many different pricing strategies and tactics that can be used to sell goods or services; this is just one of them. A high price strategy can be applied to the sale of these kinds of products for a number of reasons, such as the item's quality, rarity, or uniqueness, or just as a way to fleece gullible buyers.

When a product stands out from a large number of similar products, its sellers may take advantage of this and use a high price strategy. A product's uniqueness may stem from a variety of factors, such as color, rarity, ingredients, presentation, or packaging. The sale of various kinds of jewelry serves as an excellent illustration of this. Jewelers will use the distinctive qualities of a precious stone—such as a color or size that deviates from the norm—to pursue a high price strategy.

Customers may have responded to the jewelers' high price strategy in this instance if they were offered a price for that specific precious stone that was significantly higher than what they would typically pay for such a stone. When an item's quality surpasses that of similar items, a high price strategy may also be employed in this situation. For example, a beauty salon that employs the best stylists in the industry, offers a ton of extra services, and is situated in a posh neighborhood may use a high price strategy with success because customers will value the service highly. This value may stem from the sense of exclusivity that visiting that specific beauty salon offers, even if its prices are more than three times higher than those of its closest competitors.

This tactic may also be used by marketers who want to trick consumers into parting with their money in order to make quick cash. Under such circumstances, a subpar good will have its value marked up and be offered or sold for a hefty price. Though some individuals may be able to spot the scam for what it is, others may still be duped by this kind of tactic.

8.2.3.1. Issue Price

The initial asking price for bonds and stocks is known as the issue price. Trades made by participants on secondary markets, whether above or below the issue price, can reveal information about how customers perceive the company. Prices that are rising indicate investor confidence in the business, while those that are falling reflect waning confidence and concerns about the company's sustainability. Finding out the original asking price requires researching information about the original issue, as it is a matter of public record.

When it comes to stocks, the process of figuring out an issue price takes place in the lead-up to the IPO. In order to find out how much prospective investors and underwriters believe shares will be worth based on the quantity of shares and the overall health of the company, the company will meet with them. In order to quickly sell out, it will set an issue price that must balance high and low pricing. If the price is too high, the business won't be able to sell the first issue. If it is too low, the company may not receive the full amount of capital from the sale. Usually, an underwriter handles the sales process on behalf of the company. The issues are purchased by the underwriter at a reduced cost and subsequently offered for sale at the issue price. Institutional investors may be eligible for special incentives, and regular investors frequently cannot purchase shares when they are first offered; instead, they must wait until the stock hits the secondary market to make their purchases.

Determining the amount of debt the company wishes to issue and dividing it by the total number of bonds is the process of setting the issue price for bonds. Together with their purchase, buyers lend money to the business, expecting to be paid back eventually with interest. In order to immediately recover their investment, they can sell bonds on the secondary market, where buyers can offer prices that are marginally higher or lower than the issue price, depending on the terms they agree upon with sellers.

8.2.3.2. Share Price

The value of a company's stock is expressed as its share price. Shares of stock will be sold by publicly traded companies in order to raise capital reserves through equity investments. Companies will first go through an initial public offering procedure. An initial share price for stock will be set by a financial services underwriter taking into account the state of the market and the company's financial standing. The demand for the company's stock will determine how much it costs after the initial offering.

8.2.3.3. Price Stability

One indicator of economic stability is price stability. When prices are stable, year-over-year changes in the cost of goods and services are negligible and the impact of inflation and deflation is minimal. Price stability is generally regarded as a desirable, if not entirely attainable, objective for an economy. Some critics contend that this measurement's significance may be exaggerated and that basing a financial system's health on it can lead to risky oversimplifications.

8.2.3.4. What does a Pricing Analyst Do?

A business expert with a focus on pricing analysis, a pricing analyst seeks to ascertain the optimal prices for the organization they represent. Since pricing is a very delicate art and a skilled pricing analyst can make or break a company's future, these professionals frequently have degrees from business schools and have received highly specialized training. In addition to employing pricing analysts as consultants for specific projects or issues, many businesses also keep full-time pricing analysts on staff. Pricing analysts keep a close eye on their competitors' pricing tactics while examining industry norms. In addition to studying consumer behavior to find patterns in consumer spending and the amount of money people are willing to pay for different products, they use mathematical analysis to track pricing trends. When deciding on prices and the best time to launch new products, it can be important to know whether consumers are willing to pay more for particular kinds of goods at particular times of the year.

A pricing analyst must also consider internal concerns. Pricing analysts are interested in a company's intended profit margin, marketing expenses, and the cost of producing different goods. They may offer guidance during the research and development stage to maximize revenue for the business. They are also concerned with the presentation and packaging of products, which can affect consumers' willingness to pay. Since pricing is highly psychological, a pricing analyst must possess both a thorough understanding of business and an understanding of human psychology.

Pricing analysts must consider how customers interact with pricing, how other products in the same line are priced, and how prices may change in-store when setting prices for their products. Even in cases where there is little difference between the prices being considered, selecting the appropriate price can have a significant impact on sales. The pay for pricing analysts can differ based on their position, degree of training, and experience. Because many employers seek out candidates with real-world experience in addition to business school degrees, it can be difficult for recent graduates to break into this field. Those who are interested in this line of work might begin their careers in different divisions and sections of an organization before advancing into the pricing analysis division.

8.2.4. The Best Pricing Strategy and Tactics

The proper pricing strategy and tactics are essential to the marketing process for any individual or business that has goods or services to offer. The types of products or services, the reason for applying the pricing strategy, and the environment in which the products or services will be sold are some of the criteria that determine which pricing strategy and tactics to apply in a given situation, given the variety of pricing strategies available. A combination of these elements, such as identifying the target consumer group that the pricing strategy is intended for, may also result in the appropriate pricing strategy and tactics (Figure 8.5).

Figure 8.5. *Stores without a large amount of competition can also adjust their price optimization upwards.*

Source: https://www.healthgrades.com/right-care/hepatitis-c/6-ways-to-prepare-for-hepatitis-c-treatment.

Because it enables the marketer to customize the pricing of the goods or services to the target customer base, a target consumer demographic analysis is crucial when attempting to determine the best pricing strategy and tactics. An example of a company that makes jeans for adult men and teenage boys can be used to demonstrate this. A business of this kind might choose to set the price of its jeans for teenage boys based on how much money they think their target market can afford. The business will weigh the total cost of manufacturing the jeans or the cost of production overall in relation to the lowest price it can charge for the jeans and still turn a profit.

However, if the business determines that the children of wealthy parents will be the teenage jeans' target market, it will have no qualms about employing the exclusivity pricing strategy when choosing which kind of pricing plan to implement. The marketer's objective for the goods or services can be used to inform another use of pricing strategy and tactics. A grocery store owner, for example, may choose to employ the pricing strategy of marking down products in order to get rid of inventory that is close to expiring. Since the products are going to expire, this kind of pricing strategy can be used in this situation. The best course of action in this situation for the owner of the grocery store would be to salvage as much as possible from the products before they go bad.

8.2.5. Types of Marketing Tactics

Three essential elements are needed for a business to succeed in order to implement effective marketing tactics: attraction, conversion, and retention. Typically, the objectives are to draw in new business, win over clients from rivals, and hold onto existing clientele. A company that combines all three typically has an advantage over rivals that provide comparable goods or services. An idea, or marketing strategy, that prompts action in each of the three areas is the starting point for marketing tactics.

Name recognition, also referred to as branding, is one of the most crucial components of attraction marketing strategies since it helps prospective buyers become familiar with a brand or service. According to business executives, it typically takes 10 interactions with a customer for them to make a purchase. The first step for any business is to determine who its target audience is and then use marketing strategies to reach them.

The most costly and time-consuming area of marketing is usually attraction. Guerrilla marketing is a non-conventional way for some businesses to invest more time and energy than cash. Guerrilla marketing uses techniques like bumper stickers, open houses, and t-shirts with an advertising slogan and logo to expose a company to a large number of potential customers. Another well-liked method for producing an advertising campaign that could be seen by a large audience is through social media.

Websites can target users who are already interested in a product that is being sold. They can also inform present customers about sales and promotions and entice the clients of rival businesses. Internet newsletters are low-cost marketing strategies that can help a business achieve its objectives for attraction, conversion, and retention.

Conversion marketing strategies are designed to persuade potential customers to make a quick phone call or purchase a product. These tactics typically try to persuade a person that they need a product by offering it for a limited time at a discounted price. Promotions may link to another website when utilizing the Internet for conversion efforts in order to target consumers who regularly purchase the product. Although retention marketing strategies are frequently the least expensive, they are occasionally disregarded in favor of attraction and conversion strategies.

Holding onto previous or present clients may result in recommendations and new business. Experts in market research advise maintaining contact with clients through email lists or newsletters. A strategy that could work is rewarding consumers with a gift or discount for each referral. Organizing an event for current clients and inviting them to bring guests is another concept for rewarding loyalty.

8.3. DIFFERENT TYPES OF PRICING STRATEGY

The practice of charging different amounts to sell the same type of product to different customer groups is known as differential pricing. It is also referred to as multiple pricing and discriminatory pricing. Differential pricing is frequently employed in conjunction with marketing initiatives. For instance, a good or service might be promoted as being more affordable for students. A prevalent reason for charging a lower price to a particular group is their perceived lack of resources or financial strain. Typically, senior citizens, kids, families, students, and active military personnel receive discounted prices. Businesses in the entertainment and restaurant industries commonly provide this kind of differential pricing. This type of pricing may also be used for other reasons, such as the terms of payment, the quantity of goods bought, and the deadline for delivery. The item's price could be much higher with a longer payment term than it would be for someone who finished paying off their debt faster. Purchasing a product in large quantities can often result in a lower unit cost. Even so, the cost may change based on the quantity of the item ordered. There might be an additional fee for a customer's requested expedited delivery of an item or service.

As a marketing tactic, differential pricing can also be employed. A business may conduct an analysis of its clientele to ascertain the type of person most likely to purchase its goods at full price. Once this has been established, the company can schedule sales, promotions, and other related campaigns to avoid launching them during the peak buying season for that particular customer base. The objective is to sell as much merchandise as possible at full price and then pursue clients who are interested in the company's offerings but do not view them as necessities. At that point, the business will move its inventory at a reasonable rate and optimize its profits.

Differential pricing also takes the form of negotiation. This is a particularly widespread procedure in the automotive sector. The customer will haggle for a lower price while the dealer will try to sell the car at that amount. The ultimate cost is contingent on how each side of the dispute is resolved. Differential pricing may result in a loss of sales if the parties are unable to come to an agreement. Businesses that want to turn a profit in a cutthroat market must sell their goods at a price that makes sense. Business managers must take into account a variety of factors, including rivals' prices, production and distribution costs, how customers perceive a product, and identifying the demographics of possible customers.

8.3.1. Premium Pricing Strategy

Premium pricing refers to the practice of setting prices artificially higher in order to convey an air of exclusivity, luxury, or superior quality. When a business sells an uncommon or unique product, it may also employ the premium pricing strategy because consumers could be prepared to pay more for such an item. It is crucial to consider product quality when implementing premium pricing because consumers will only be prepared to pay extra for a product if they feel that its value justifies its price.

Premium pricing can be a very profitable tactic for a number of reasons. First off, market research has consistently demonstrated that a large number of people believe that an expensive item must necessarily be more valuable. This means that, regardless of the actual truth, charging a high price for a product can automatically give the impression that it is of higher quality. When someone thinks they must have the highest quality possible, they might select the priciest product on the basis of this belief. Second, because they can afford it, higher-income consumers are more likely to purchase luxury goods, which enhances their status and financial worth and may deter them from looking for deals.

Even though any product can benefit from premium pricing, companies with a specialized market niche tend to use it most successfully. A manufacturer may raise the price of a product if it is rare or there is a significant gap between supply and demand. This is because more customers are willing to pay for the item. Businesses that directly compete with one another for a nearly identical product frequently attempt to undercut one another's prices in an effort to win over a larger proportion of the market. A business has no incentive to maintain low prices when customers are willing to pay more if it is not facing direct competition.

It is crucial to comprehend the current pricing range for comparable products in order to appropriately set a premium price. The premium price should be close to or slightly above the top of the range if the bath towel's price range is $5–$20 USD. The product's quality determines how much the premium price should be, but some speculation is also necessary. Depending on how much they think a towel is worth, the average consumer might or might not be willing to pay $25 USD, but it's unlikely that many would be willing to pay $75 USD for one. Premium pricing may be determined through trial and error.

There are those who argue that premium pricing is an unfair technique of manipulating the market, and there are laws in certain places that restrict the amount of markup that can be applied to particular products. Generally speaking, though, premium pricing only works if customers are prepared to shell out extra money for a product they believe to be better. It is up to the customer to determine the fair value of a product, regardless of whether that air of superiority is produced by a well-known designer name, a reputation for quality, or just the price itself. There wouldn't be a market for such a tactic if consumers weren't prepared to spend a premium product.

When businesses launch a new product that offers clear advantages over comparable products, they employ a premium pricing strategy. A product that is considered premium is more expensive than its rivals.

The best time to use premium pricing in a product's life cycle is at launch. Small companies that offer products with distinctive qualities are better equipped to implement premium pricing. Companies attempt to project an image where customers believe the products are valuable and worthy of the higher prices in order to make premium pricing acceptable to them. In addition to presenting the product as being of superior quality, the business must coordinate its marketing initiatives, and the product packaging and store design should all reinforce the idea that the product is worthy of the premium price.

8.3.2. Penetration Pricing Strategy

As part of a marketing strategy known as penetration pricing, a new product or an established one is introduced to a new market by using extremely competitive pricing. The purpose of this kind of pricing strategy is to get customers to try the product, see if they like it, and then become more inclined to use it going forward. After a product gains a certain amount of traction in the market and establishes itself, the manufacturer switches from a penetration pricing strategy to one that maintains competitiveness while offering a larger profit margin.

The concept of price skimming is distinct from that of penetration pricing. A product is introduced at a higher price rather than a lower one when using the skimming approach. In order to increase consumer awareness of the product and pique their interest, aggressive advertising campaigns are typically employed. Even though initial sales are typically rather low, the manufacturer makes more money on each unit sold. The unit price is then reduced to appeal to a wider consumer base after the advertising has drawn in customers. This also increases the likelihood that previous customers will refer the product and its new, lower price to others.

The goal of penetration pricing is to attract bargain-hunting customers and increase sales. It is anticipated that after using the product, customers will place more emphasis on quality and less emphasis on price. Following a suitable period of time, the price is raised gradually while the effects of each increase on total sales are carefully considered. The manufacturer typically designates that price as the standard retail price and uses it as the base figure for any special promotions or sales that may occur during the course of the business year, or whenever the price has increased as much as possible without losing customers.

The penetration price strategy may be the most effective way for new businesses looking to gain market share from more established rivals in terms of generating interest and starting to acquire clients.

This tactic may also be employed by well-established companies to deter potential competitors from joining the market and luring away customers. For instance, a sizable communications company with high sales volume may find out that a rival company is getting ready to introduce a new line of related services.

Equipped with greater resources, the established company employs penetration pricing proactively to attract new customers ahead of the competition and fortify its relationships with existing ones. Because there is now less chance of drawing away customers, the competitor may decide to postpone or scrap plans to launch the product line entirely.

By offering their products and services at a lower cost than their rivals, marketers employ penetration pricing to increase their market share. Marketers aim to introduce their products into the market with the intention of increasing consumer awareness and encouraging potential buyers to give them a try. Although the company may initially lose money using this lower price strategy, marketers anticipate raising prices to a more profitable level once they have a greater market penetration.

8.3.3. Economy Pricing Strategy

Economy pricing is a volume-based pricing strategy in which you set a low price for your goods and make money from the quantity of customers who buy them. It is usually applied to commodity goods that do not have the same marketing and advertising expenses as their name-brand equivalents, such as generic-brand groceries or pharmaceuticals.

In order to turn a tiny profit, an economy pricing strategy sets prices as low as possible. Businesses cut back on the expenses of marketing and promotion. The secret to a successful economy pricing strategy is to offer a large number of goods and services at discounted costs. Small businesses will find it difficult to sell enough products at low prices to stay in business, but large companies like Walmart can benefit from this low-price strategy.

- **How Do You Execute Economy Pricing?:** At its core, an economy pricing strategy is similar to a cost-plus pricing strategy. You take a product with relatively low production costs and set a price for it that provides you with a small profit.

Production Cost + Profit Margin = Price

With such a low price, economy pricing is very much a volume play. The only way you will make a profit is if you bring in a large amount of customers on a consistent basis. That makes acquisition incredibly important because you would not be able to rely on existing customers to drive revenue over time.

- **Common Products That Use Economy Pricing:** Economy pricing is used a lot in the commodity goods market. It's a great strategy for companies that have low overhead costs and the ability to sell a larger number of products to new customers on a regular basis.
- **Supermarket Store Brands:** Every grocery store you go into has their own version of popular brands. Companies like Trader Joe's and ALDI are two examples that capitalize on economy pricing to drive their growth.
- **Generic Drugs and Medications:** Much like supermarket store brands, there are lots of different types of generic over-the-counter medications available through companies like CVS and Rite-Aid.
- **Big Box Stores:** Companies like Costco and BJ's take the economy pricing model to the next level by selling primarily their own brands. While name brands are still available, the major draw of these types of stores is the quality-to-price ratio of their generic brands.
- **Budget Airlines:** In order to fill seats on their aircraft, many airlines will offer economy pricing, which includes premium pricing as well. Economy pricing starts much lower for the first seats that are purchased and increases in price as availability drops. Although economy pricing is less common in the SaaS and subscription sectors, there are examples of successful subscription e-commerce companies using economy pricing.

Dollar Shave Club is a prime example of economy pricing in action; it employed this tactic to lure consumers away from well-known brands like Gillette. In order to achieve this, it had to account for the higher marketing and advertising expenses, which are uncommon for the majority of economy pricing businesses.

- **Pros and Cons of Economy Pricing:** Economy pricing is a useful method of acquisition for subscription and SaaS companies. However, the unit economics of selling at such a low price makes it difficult to gradually develop a revenue base because subscriptions are based on recurring customer relationships.
- **Pros of Economy Pricing:** There are some intriguing advantages to economy pricing for bigger, more established businesses. It is low-cost, simple to implement, and appealing to buyer personas who are specifically interested in "getting a deal" for your product or service. In addition to allowing you to acquire customers more quickly, these pricing strategies typically have lower customer acquisition costs (CAC) than alternative approaches.

Quicker and less expensive market entry can also aid newcomers in establishing themselves, but the price is lost in terms of pricing power. Economy pricing is less of a pricing strategy and more of an acquisition one.

- **Cons of Economy Pricing:** It's crucial to realize that economy pricing is only effective in a limited range of market circumstances. Businesses without any market share or recognition would find it impossible to maintain low enough operating costs for this pricing strategy to be successful. Furthermore, economy pricing can have a detrimental effect on how much customers think your brand is worth if you're just getting started.

The model needs a steady stream of new clients to sustain revenue and depends on slim profit margins to keep prices low. Setting a low price for your good or service makes it difficult for prospective buyers to understand the value for the money and makes it more difficult to raise prices or generate additional revenue down the road.

- **Does Profit-Well Recommend Economy Pricing?:** If market conditions are not exactly right, economy pricing can cause issues for SaaS and subscription businesses. In order to develop your product or service, you must not only be aware of the true costs of operations, but also maintain low operating costs as your business and clientele expand. There isn't much leeway for error with these narrower profit margins.

Nevertheless, it can be effective as an acquisition strategy if you are in a market where consumers are price conscious, marketing and advertising costs are low, and the population size is sufficient to support the economy pricing model. Profit-Well advises against employing economy pricing unless you have a well-defined strategy in place for making money off of these new clients once they are brought on board.

- **What Is Economic Stability?:** An economy that grows steadily and has low inflation is said to be stable. Low unemployment, higher productivity, and enhanced efficiency are benefits of a stable economy. Prolonged periods of recession or crisis, increasing rates of inflation, and fluctuations in currency exchange rates are indicative of instability. Consumer confidence declines, economic growth is slowed, and foreign investments are decreased in an unstable economy.

The expansion of global trade and commerce has made it possible for the stability of one nation's economy to impact that of other nations. International spending and investments may significantly decline in a nation when its economy becomes unstable. If an investor is located in an unstable nation, they may also suffer large financial losses. For instance, if a French investor bought property in the U.S. S. Prior to the 2008 financial crisis, the investment's value might have fallen to unrecoverable levels even after the U.S. S. recuperation.

Business cycles are frequently employed in the analysis of economic stability. A business cycle consists of four stages: peak, recession, recovery, and depression. An economy may be deemed unstable if there are significant differences between its peak and depression phases. The economy is deemed unstable if it remains in a state of depression or recession for a prolonged duration. When a nation enters a financial crisis or the depression or recession stages of the business cycle, it typically experiences periods of instability.

Typically, policymakers try to lessen the effects of an unstable economy and steer it in the direction of recovery. Policymakers employ a variety of strategies, such as boosting the economy, reducing inflation, and maintaining the value of the nation's currency. As a means of reviving the economy, funding for company expansion and startup initiatives should continue. Controlling inflation is necessary because high inflation deters foreign investors from buying goods and securities because they are now more expensive than they were in the past. Establishing investor confidence, promoting investment, and accelerating business expansion should be the overarching objectives. The International Monetary Fund (IMF) was established to provide member nations with financial and economic policy advice aimed at bolstering economic stability. Additionally, it offers data and statistics regarding the state of the economies of all nations. The gross domestic product (GDP), inflation, unemployment, payment balances, exports, imports, external debt, capital flows, and commodity prices are just a few of the variables that the IMF tracks in order to determine stability. It is the primary source of information on the current conditions in the majority of nations.

8.3.4. Price Skimming Strategy

Setting prices high by launching new products in a market with few competitors is known as price skimming. By using this strategy, companies can increase profits before rivals join the market, which causes prices to decline.

8.3.4.1. Benefits of Price Skimming

One of the most crucial ways a business competes in a market is through pricing strategies, which are mainly used to entice customers to make purchases. Price skimming, in which products have high initial prices that decrease over a predetermined period of time, is one tactic used when selling goods in a market. Businesses may reduce the price of a good for a variety of reasons, such as when new competitors enter the market or when customers start to pay more for particular products. Price skimming has several advantages, such as large profits, the development of exclusivity, and market dominance. Price skimming should be flexible, just like many other business strategies, in response to changes in the market brought about by factors such as customer demand.

Price skimming is a tactic to increase profits with a new or unique product in certain market situations. For instance, a new piece of software or hardware may provide a business the ability to charge a premium because there is little rivalry. This just indicates that a business can charge a high initial price because of the product itself, not because the new product was expensive to develop. Sometimes a business sets these exorbitant prices to cover certain, sometimes very high, production-related expenses. In any case, there are situations when this is a well-liked tactic to employ.

A price skimming strategy also helps to create exclusivity for a particular good or service. For certain consumers, a high price only indicates that the good or service has to be exceptionally valuable to warrant such a high cost. The product might be unique in the market, of excellent quality, or designed for a specific purpose. Now, this does not always imply that the product offers customers better service than any other product. Even though the item might not be all that valuable, the price strategy's main goal is to persuade a customer to buy it by instilling a sense of value in their mind. Companies may use price skimming as a means of attempting to control a market. A rival may occasionally attribute a high product price to high production costs. Alternatively, a business that sets high prices for a particular category of goods is aiming for a niche market that cannot support a large number of rivals. In either case, price skimming allows a business to control a particular market segment while extracting profits.

8.3.5. Psychological Pricing Strategy

The theory behind psychological pricing in business is that consumers are more receptive to certain price points and are therefore more inclined to purchase products at those prices. These prices typically end in 9, 99, or 95, which is thought to reassure customers that they are saving money on their purchases. When a product is priced at $19.99 instead of $20 US dollars (USD), some businesses hope that customers will think they are saving money and feel more comfortable making a purchase, even if that savings is just one penny.

Numerous historical instances of psychological pricing exist, going all the way back to the late 1800s, when newspaper salesmen would occasionally use this strategy. It started to be used more frequently in the 20th century, and some stores now seem to use it constantly. Those who think psychological pricing works contend that there are several ways in which this decreased quantity could affect customers.

They might only consider dollar value, and in the rush of that particular purchase, they might overlook the possibility that the cents portion may only be a penny or two less than a dollar. A price of $9.99 might be interpreted as $9.00 rather than nearly $10.00. This is known as the left-digit effect at times. Even when this is not the case, the absence of a round, solid price indicates that the item is discounted or on sale.

The purpose of the purposeful and somewhat obvious attempt at price fixing is to ensure that customers are drawn in by the prices and buy the associated goods. It's interesting to note that some businesses charge differently in order to cater to what they perceive to be additional customer needs. Some businesses set their prices at whole numbers to represent their unwavering, trustworthy attitude toward their clients. This may appeal to some customers who aren't really searching for a deal. There are some effective ways to avoid psychological pricing for the person who feels influenced by it. To begin with, shoppers ought to bring a calculator with them so they can total their purchases and determine the true cost of items before making a purchase. This is particularly crucial in areas where sales tax is in effect. Just raising the sales tax can serve as a wake-up call.

Reading prices backwards is the next useful trick that might be applied. The cents portion is usually printed smaller, so always pay attention to it first and round it up to the nearest dollar. To see a more accurate estimate of the price, add it to the listed dollar price. Customers can reduce the impact of psychological pricing with a few simple techniques, especially if they are aware that the merchant is attempting to influence them rather than typically saving them money.

Marketers use psychological pricing that encourages consumer to buy products based on emotions rather than on common-sense logic. The best example is when a company prices its product at $199 instead of $200. Even though the difference is small, consumers perceive $199 as being substantially cheaper. This is known as the "left-digit effect."

8.3.5.1. Bundle Pricing Strategy

Companies sell a number of products at a discounted price when they are bundled together, as opposed to when they are bought separately. This is a good way to get rid of unsold merchandise that is just taking up room. Additionally, bundling gives the impression to the customer that he is receiving a very good value for his money. Packaged pricing is a good fit for businesses that offer a range of related products.

For instance, on a specific day of the week, a restaurant might provide a complimentary dessert with an entrée. A Blu-ray is frequently included in the price of older video games that are nearing the end of their useful lives. Businesses must research and create pricing plans that fit their products and services. While some pricing strategies are effective for launching new products, others are used for more established products with a larger number of competitors in the market.

8.3.5.2. Nail the Right Price

You can be sure that you're setting prices that your clients will be willing to pay when you employ a pricing strategy that is specifically designed for your company. You can simultaneously maximize your profits and sales volume by setting a product or service's price logically. Keep in mind that customer opinions are subject to change as you evaluate the prices they are willing to pay for your brand.

8.3.6. Pricing Schedule

A pricing schedule is typically a document that lists the costs associated with a business's products or services. This sheet is usually referred to as a pricing schedule, for instance, if a business charges a slightly lower rate for larger volume purchases.

A company typically doesn't share its pricing or schedule with just anybody; instead, the sheet is typically made available to businesses or customers who make purchases from the company. Furthermore, a business may have different schedules for various clientele or companies operating in particular industries. This enables a business to customize its offerings to particular customers and their business processes.

Pricing schedules are typically used by suppliers and vendors on behalf of their customers. Here, the vendors provide a schedule of goods or services with prices for various items to each customer. To encourage new business, a small discount may be offered to prospective customers; this strategy typically works for larger purchases. In other cases, a larger discount might be given to loyal customers to keep them coming back. In either case, the pricing schedule is an adaptable method of collaborating with customers.

A pricing schedule can help a business maintain control over the market or fend off competition from other companies. For instance, if a business is aware of the going rate for a certain good or service, it can develop a competitive pricing schedule that accommodates this price. For this reason, when it comes to the cost of goods or services, a lot of these schedules have a tendency to be regressive. Businesses are more inclined to reduce their profits on high-volume transactions to keep a rival from gaining the clientele.

This technique might occasionally resemble a different variation of price skimming, a popular pricing tactic. The inclusion of this item in a bid or contract for goods and services is an alternative format for a pricing schedule. Several businesses compete for a set amount of business with a single client during a bid process. A pricing schedule with lower prices can help win the business of this new client in order to gain future business or more contracts. Alternatively, the supplier or vendor offering the largest volume discounts in the contract or bid may be able to win over the new client and receive additional business. The pricing schedule functions the same in either case.

8.3.6.1. Pricing Power

In the business sector, the term "pricing power" is frequently used to describe how a shift in produce prices will affect consumer demand for that particular good. Although the phrase can be used to describe both rising and falling current prices, most businesses will concentrate on the consequences of raising prices. A good or service's pricing power is determined by a variety of factors, such as its uniqueness in the market, competition from similar products, customer perception of the product's quality, and the success of the company's advertising campaign.

8.3.6.2. Variable Pricing

A marketing strategy known as variable pricing allows different prices to be charged to different clients for the same products or services. This strategy is frequently used in societies where haggling over prices is accepted as normal or where prospective purchasers are permitted to take part in auctions or other bidding processes. Variable pricing may apply even in nations where fixed pricing is the norm if the customer commits to buying a significant quantity of goods or services. In these situations, the client is typically required to meet certain requirements in order to receive pricing that is different from the going rate.

The fixed price policy that is typically in place differs from the variable pricing strategy. With fixed pricing, the seller assesses all pertinent variables, decides whether to grant a buyer a discount from the going rate, and then applies that discount to all purchases made during a predetermined window of time. Typically, a contract is utilized to guarantee those reduced prices for a predetermined amount of time that is agreed upon by the seller and the buyer. Variable pricing, on the other hand, is typically offered only once. If the buyer decides to place another order later, the seller will evaluate the situation again and, if justified, offer different pricing.

8.3.6.3. Dynamic Pricing

Dynamic pricing, which is also referred to as time-based pricing, is a type of price discrimination where a business modifies a product or service's price in response to a range of variables. It is typical of sectors like tourism and transportation, whose businesses frequently see significant fluctuations in response to foreseeable events. Because dynamic pricing makes it easier to set prices that account for fluctuating levels of demand and willingness to pay, it enables businesses to maximize their profits.

Dynamic pricing is frequently used in the tourism sector. At different times of the year, different places see higher numbers of visitors. For example, a beach resort will see far higher demand in the summer than it will in the winter; alternatively, if the beach resort is always warm, business may increase in the winter in other places. However, during the winter, there will be a higher demand for a ski lodge. A hotel that uses dynamic pricing will increase its rates in the busiest times of the year and decrease them in the slowest times.

8.4. VALUE PRICING

Value pricing is arguably the most significant pricing tactic available. This considers how valuable, important, and high-quality your customers think your goods and services are. Value pricing is the reason why a high-end salon haircut is more valuable than quick Great Clips services, and why a wedding dress is worth thousands more than a prom dress. Setting value-based prices requires a thorough understanding of both your brand's reputation and the needs, pain points, and motivations of your target audience. It is imperative to consider the impact of market conditions on individuals' perceptions of value.

For instance, during a recession, the value of a non-necessity, such as a Netflix subscription, may decline. Even though value pricing is being highlighted as a distinct strategy, we always advise considering value even if it's not your main tactic. By making sure you don't undersell yourself with competitive pricing or start price skimming at an excessively high price, this can help you lower risk.

8.4.1. Value-Pricing Strategy

The term "value-pricing strategy" refers to the tactical approaches that companies take when promoting their goods. Value pricing is just one of many pricing strategies that companies can employ to promote their goods in an efficient manner. This pricing strategy determines the value of a product targeted at a market based on the outcome of evaluating the worth of the good or service the business is providing to the target market or customers. It does this by evaluating a potential or existing market. That is, the product's price is not determined by factoring in the typical production costs and profit margins that are used to determine a product's price. Under the value-pricing strategy, the product price may be entirely disproportionate to the cost of production or service; however, the product's value will be determined by the target consumer's perception of the product, which they are persuaded of by the company's marketing campaigns.

As a result, depending on how different markets are evaluated under the value-pricing strategy, the same product may have different prices for different markets. The target consumer's belief that the product or service adds something new or fills a gap in the category of goods or services that other products don't could be the deciding factor in determining the product's value under the value-pricing strategy. It might be the result of a calculated attempt by the business to give customers the impression that the good or service is more valuable than it actually is.

Value pricing is frequently used in the fashion industry, where items of clothing are sold for outrageous prices that exceed the cost of production or the quality of the workmanship involved in making them. The emotional attachment to the brand behind the label and the value that such a brand attracts are the primary causes of some products in this industry having a tendency to be more expensive than other products of comparable, or even better quality. Because of the value that consumers have attached to the brand, the company could therefore produce a plain piece of paper and sell it for far more than an entire box of books.

8.4.2. Value-Based Pricing

Value-based pricing is a method of setting prices that takes into account the consumer's perception of value rather than any other variables. Using this tactic, a company tries to set the price of its goods based on what the market determines to be a fair price. This strategy does not make use of any of the metrics that other strategies do, such as the cost of the goods or particular profit margins. This strategy has the benefits of greater profitability, ease of use, and improved customer understanding.

A popular pricing strategy used by many companies in the market today is value-based pricing. The company tries to figure out how much a specific customer would pay for the product rather than basing pricing on a predetermined profit margin on top of the product's cost. As a result, businesses now need to have a keen understanding of their clientele. The business must conduct some research to find out how much consumers are willing to pay for a product. This research will frequently take the shape of customer panels or surveys.

Through this research, the company hopes to learn what consumers perceive to be the product's inherent value. Businesses who don't employ this pricing strategy may be losing out on revenue. Consumers typically have a preconceived notion of what a product should cost. The company can maximize sales and profit margins by setting its product prices at this level. Businesses that don't employ value-based pricing occasionally choose a price that differs from the product's perceived value. When this occurs, sales volume may decline or profit margin may be less than it could have been with appropriate pricing.

This pricing strategy has the benefit of being easy to implement. The customer research is the most challenging aspect of it. After that is finished, the business can just set the price for its goods. It can determine the price of each product without the need for complex formulas. Overall, this saves time and eases the burden on the business.

A further benefit of value-based pricing is that it will help the business better understand its clientele. The business must invest significant resources in researching its clientele, which frequently yields ideas with high potential for profit. Value-based pricing can improve a business's relationship with its clients and result in higher future sales.

8.4.3. Connection between Pricing Strategy and Channel Distribution

Effective control or monitoring of the distribution channels helps guarantee that the prices of products stay within the price limits set by an organization, and a proper pricing strategy is one of the business strategies employed by an organization. This is where the relationship between pricing strategy and channel distribution comes from. Pricing strategy and channel distribution are related in that careful observation of the channels of distribution helps prevent price conflicts because different distributors may be inclined to tack on extra costs of their own, resulting in disparate prices and the appearance of price inconsistency. Another connection is that a company with insufficient resources for internal product distribution can benefit from having a well-balanced external distribution channel. This can help the company lower the price of its products because it eliminates the need to pay for the establishment and upkeep of a sales team for direct sales, among other costs.

Pricing strategy and channel distribution are linked in part because of the impact that price instability has on the product's importer or manufacturer. Pricing is one of the most common ways that businesses use effective strategy. Therefore, any departure from the established price range will jeopardize the company's efforts to execute the predetermined price. A candle manufacturer might, for instance, establish a maximum price for a box containing 50 individual candles at a price that accounts for a distributor and retailer's profit margin. The company's goal is defeated when distributors and retailers tack on extra costs above the maximum price set by the candle manufacturer. For this reason, the company must implement measures to limit these practices.

The availability of effective distribution channels spares a company the financial burden of establishing its own internal distribution channel, which is another way in which pricing strategy and channel distribution are related. Establishing a private distribution channel entails recruiting, preparing, and compensating a sales force, offering the sales force the logistics they need to perform their jobs well, and establishing channels for the product's additional distribution. If the business does not need to take this action, the money it would have saved will enable it to lower the product's price even further.

CASE STUDY

CAPITAL STRUCTURE MODELING

One of the most important aspects of capital structure modeling is to understand how different scenarios and assumptions affect the credit rating and risk profile of a company. Capital structure modeling involves building and testing various models that simulate the impact of changes in debt, equity, cash flow, interest rates, and other factors on the company's financial performance and creditworthiness.

By using capital structure modeling, analysts and managers can evaluate the trade-offs between different financing options, optimize the *capital structure* for a given objective, and assess the sensitivity and robustness of the model results. You will look at some case studies and examples of capital structure modeling from different perspectives and contexts.

We will see how different models can be used to address different questions and challenges related to capital structure decisions. We will also discuss some of the best practices and limitations of capital structure modeling, and how to improve the quality and reliability of the model outputs.

The following are some of the topics that we will cover:

1. **How to Build a Capital Structure Model Using Excel:** We will start with a simple example of how to create a basic *capital structure* model using Excel. We will use the data and assumptions from a hypothetical company, ABC Inc., to illustrate the steps and formulas involved in building the model. We will also show how to use *Excel functions* and features, such as data tables, *scenario manager*, and solver, to perform various analyzes and optimizations on the model.
2. **How to Test a Capital Structure Model Using Monte Carlo Simulation:** We will then introduce a more advanced technique of testing a capital structure model using monte Carlo simulation, monte Carlo simulation is a method of generating random samples from a probability distribution and using them to estimate the possible outcomes and risks of a model. We will use a software tool, to perform monte Carlo simulation on the capital structure model that we built in Excel. We will see how to define the input variables, output variables, and *distribution functions*, and how to interpret the simulation results and statistics.
3. **How to Compare Different Capital Structure Models Using Rating Agencies' Methodologies:** We will then explore how to compare different capital structure models using the rating agencies' methodologies. Rating agencies, such as Moody's, S&P, and Fitch, have developed their own criteria and models to assess the credit quality and rating of a company based on its capital structure and other factors. We will use the rating agencies' models as a benchmark to evaluate

the performance and implications of our own capital structure models. We will see how to apply the rating agencies' models to our hypothetical company, ABC Inc., and how to compare the results with *our own model outputs*.

4. **How to Apply Capital Structure Modeling to Real-World Cases and examples:** Finally, we will look at some real-world cases and examples of *capital structure* modeling from different industries and sectors. We will see how *capital structure* modeling can be used to address various issues and challenges, such as mergers and acquisitions, refinancing, restructuring, dividend policy, and capital budgeting. We will also see how *capital structure* modeling can be influenced by external factors, such as market conditions, regulations, and stakeholders' expectations. We will use some publicly available data and information to illustrate the application and limitations of *capital structu*re modeling in practice.

CLASS ACTIVITY

In today's class activity on asset pricing, we delved into the core principles governing the valuation of financial assets. We explored the concepts of risk and return, emphasizing how investors assess these factors to determine the appropriate price for assets. The discussion covered various models such as the Capital Asset Pricing Model (CAPM) and the Arbitrage Pricing Theory (APT), highlighting their assumptions and practical applications. Through interactive examples and simulations, students gained insights into how market conditions, investor behavior, and economic factors collectively influence asset pricing dynamics in real-world scenarios. This session aimed to deepen our understanding of financial markets and investment decision-making processes.

SUMMARY

- Asset pricing refers to a formal treatment and development of two main pricing principles, outlined below, together with the resultant models.
- Although investors may expect a particular return when they buy a particular stock, they may be disappointed or pleasantly surprised, because fluctuations in stock prices result in fluctuating returns.
- The term "pricing strategy" encompasses all the methods that a business owner uses to determine how much to charge for a product or service.
- Pricing objectives are goals that a business hopes to achieve when deciding on the cost of its products or services. In order to be effective, the pricing process must be connected to the overall marketing mix.
- Critics of stability-based fiscal policy tend to cite the high costs of keeping inflation to minimum. By setting a price stability goal to be maintained regardless of outside circumstances, governments may increase taxes and tariffs on citizens to artificially reduce inflation in the name of price stability.
- The importance of using an analysis of a target consumer demographic when trying to arrive at the right pricing strategy and tactics is due to the fact that it allows the marketer to tailor the pricing of the products or services to suit the target consumer base.
- Premium pricing is a business practice in which prices are artificially elevated to create an aura of luxury, exclusivity, or higher quality.
- Penetration pricing is a marketing strategy that involves the use of highly competitive pricing to introduce a new product to consumers, or to introduce an older product into a new market.

REVIEW QUESTIONS

1. Discus the general equilibrium asset pricing.
2. What is CAPM?
3. Explain the practical value of the CAPM
4. What does a pricing analyst do?
5. Discuss the premium and economy pricing strategy.
6. Focus on value-pricing strategy.

REFERENCES

1. Acharya, V., & Pedersen, L. (2005). Asset pricing with liquidity risk. *Journal of Financial Economics, 77*(2), 375–410.
2. Adams, M., Mullins, T., & Thornton, B. (2007). Pedagogical strategies for incorporating behavioral finance concepts in investment courses. *Journal of College Teaching & Learning, 4*(3), 21–32.

3. Adrian, T., & Franzoni, F. A. (2009). Learning about beta: Time-varying factor loadings, expected returns, and the conditional CAPM. *Journal of Empirical Finance, 16*(4), 537–556.
4. Arora, D., & Gakhar, D. V. (2019). Asset pricing models: A study of CNX Nifty 500 index companies. *Indian Journal of Finance, 13*(4), 20–35.
5. Belimam, D., Tan, Y., & Lakhnati, G. (2018). An empirical comparison of asset-pricing models in the Shanghai A-share exchange market. *Asia-Pacific Financial Markets, 25*(3), 249–265.
6. Cochrane, J. H. (2005). *Asset Pricing*. Princeton University Press.
7. Dash, S. R., & Mahakud, J. (2013). Conditional multifactor asset pricing model and market anomalies. *Journal of Indian Business Research, 5*(4), 271–294.
8. Fama, E. F., & French, K. R. (2015). A five-factor asset pricing model. *Journal of Financial Economics, 116*(1), 1–22.
9. Fama, E. F., & French, K. R. (2017). International tests of a five-factor asset pricing model. *Journal of Financial Economics, 123*(3), 441–463.
10. Guo, B., Zhang, W., Zhang, Y., & Zhang, H. (2017). The five-factor asset pricing model tests for the Chinese stock market. *Pacific-Basin Finance Journal, 43*, 84–106.
11. Harshita, S., & Yadav, S. S. (2015). Indian stock market and the asset pricing models. *Procedia Economics and Finance, 30*, 294–304.
12. Krause, A. (n.d.). An overview of asset pricing models. Retrieved from: https://people.bath.ac.uk (accessed on 4 July 2024).
13. Kubota, K., & Takehara, H. (2017). Does the Fama and French five-factor model work well in Japan? *International Review of Finance, 18*(1), 137–146.
14. Lin, Q. (2017). Noisy prices and the Fama-French five-factor asset pricing model in China. *Emerging Markets Review, 31*, 141–163.
15. Nichol, E., & Dowling, M. (2014). Profitability and investment factors for U.K. asset pricing models. *Economics Letters, 125*(3), 364–366.
16. Qian, J. (n.d.). An introduction to asset pricing theory. Retrieved from: https://jhqian.org (accessed on 4 July 2024).

CHAPTER

9 Portfolio Model

LEARNING OBJECTIVES

After studying this chapter, you will be able to:

- Understand the capital asset pricing model (CAPM)
- Discus arbitrage pricing theory (APT)
- Explain the modern portfolio theory
- Understand the dynamic asset allocation (DAA)
- Define black-litterman model and multi-index models
- Explain the robust portfolio optimization (RPO).

KEY TERMS FROM THIS CHAPTER

Alpha	Beta	Capital Asset Pricing Model
Capital budgeting	Capital markets	Dividend growth model (DGM)
Efficient Frontier	Market Timing	Modern Portfolio Theory (MPT)
Sharpe Ratio	Stock	Strategic Asset Allocation
Tactical Asset Allocation	Unsystematic risk	

INTRODUCTION

The Portfolio Model in financial modeling is a fundamental concept used to optimize the allocation of assets within an investment portfolio. The Portfolio Model aims to achieve the best possible balance between risk and return, guided by the principles of diversification and modern portfolio theory. Diversification involves spreading investments across various assets to reduce risk, while modern portfolio theory, introduced by Harry Markowitz, emphasizes the importance of constructing portfolios that maximize returns for a given level of risk. By quantifying the relationship between different assets, the Portfolio Model helps investors identify the optimal mix that minimizes risk and maximizes returns.

In practical terms, the Portfolio Model involves several key steps. First, it requires the identification of potential assets for inclusion in the portfolio, which can range from stocks and bonds to real estate and alternative investments. Each asset is evaluated based on its expected return, risk (typically measured by standard deviation or variance), and correlation with other assets. The next step involves the use of optimization techniques, such as mean-variance optimization, to determine the ideal asset allocation that meets the investor's risk tolerance and return objectives. This process often involves creating an efficient frontier, a graphical representation of optimal portfolios that offer the highest expected return for a given level of risk.

The Portfolio Model also incorporates ongoing monitoring and rebalancing to ensure that the portfolio remains aligned with the investor's goals and market conditions. This dynamic aspect of the model recognizes that market conditions and asset performance can change over time, necessitating adjustments to maintain the desired risk-return profile. Additionally, the Portfolio Model can be tailored to incorporate specific investor preferences, such as ethical considerations or sectoral biases, further enhancing its applicability and relevance. By providing a structured framework for decision-making, the Portfolio Model empowers investors to make informed choices, manage risk effectively, and achieve their financial objectives in a disciplined and systematic manner.

9.1. CAPITAL ASSET PRICING MODEL (CAPM)

The Capital Asset Pricing Model (CAPM) is one of the foundational models in finance for understanding the relationship between risk and return in the context of capital markets. Developed independently by Jack Treynor, William Sharpe, John Lintner, and Jan Mossin in the early 1960s, CAPM provides a framework for evaluating the expected return of an asset given its systematic risk as measured by beta. (Fama Eugene, & French Kenneth, Summer 2004).

9.1.1. Theoretical Foundations of CAPM

CAPM builds on the principles of modern portfolio theory introduced by Harry Markowitz in 1952. It extends Markowitz's mean-variance optimization framework by introducing a model that prices risk.

- **Assumptions:** CAPM relies on several key assumptions:
  - Investors are rational and risk-averse.
  - Markets are frictionless, with no transaction costs or taxes.
  - All investors have homogeneous expectations regarding asset returns.
  - Investors can lend and borrow at a risk-free rate.
  - There is a single-period investment horizon.
  - All assets are infinitely divisible.
- **The Security Market Line (SML):** The core of CAPM is the Security Market Line, which represents the relationship between the expected return of an asset and its beta:

$$ER_i = R_f + \beta_i(ER_m - R_f)$$

Where; ER_i is the expected return of investment; R_f is the risk-free rate; β_i is the beta of the investment; and $(ER_m - R_f)$=market risk premium

- **Beta: Measure of Systematic Risk:** Beta (β) measures the responsiveness of an asset's return to the return of the market portfolio. A beta greater than 1 indicates higher sensitivity to market movements, while a beta less than 1 indicates lower sensitivity.

9.1.2. Empirical Testing of CAPM

The empirical validity of CAPM has been a subject of extensive research. While CAPM is elegant and theoretically appealing, empirical evidence presents a mixed picture.

- **Early Tests:** Initial tests by Black, Jensen, and Scholes (1972) and Fama and MacBeth (1973) found support for the CAPM. However, these tests also identified potential anomalies and limitations.

- **Anomalies and Challenges:** Empirical challenges to CAPM include:
  - **Size Effect:** Small-cap stocks tend to outperform large-cap stocks on a risk-adjusted basis.
  - **Value Effect:** Value stocks (with high book-to-market ratios) tend to outperform growth stocks.
  - **Momentum Effect:** Stocks that have performed well in the past continue to perform well in the short term.
- **Fama-French Three-Factor Model:** In response to CAPM's limitations, Fama and French (1993) introduced the three-factor model, which includes market risk, size, and value factors to better explain asset returns.

9.1.3. Practical Applications of CAPM

Despite its empirical limitations, CAPM remains a cornerstone of financial practice due to its simplicity and intuitive appeal.

- **Cost of Equity Capital:** CAPM is widely used to estimate the cost of equity capital for firms. The cost of equity is a critical input in various financial decisions, including capital budgeting, valuation, and performance measurement.
- **Portfolio Management:** CAPM helps portfolio managers understand the trade-off between risk and return. By identifying assets with high expected returns for their level of risk, managers can construct optimal portfolios.
- **Performance Evaluation:** CAPM provides a benchmark for evaluating the performance of investment managers. By comparing actual returns to expected returns based on beta, investors can assess whether managers are generating alpha (excess returns).
- **Valuation:** Assists in determining the required rate of return for discounted cash flow models. Financial analysts often rely on CAPM to establish the appropriate discount rate when valuing companies.
- **Capital Budgeting:** In corporate finance, CAPM is used to determine the appropriate discount rate for evaluating investment projects. The risk-adjusted discount rate reflects the systematic risk of the project's cash flows.

9.1.4. Criticisms and Alternatives

CAPM has faced various criticisms over the years, leading to the development of alternative models.

- **Assumption Criticisms:** Critics argue that CAPM's assumptions are unrealistic. Markets are not frictionless, investors do not have homogeneous expectations, and borrowing and lending rates are not always equal.
- **Behavioral Finance:** Behavioral finance challenges the rationality assumption of CAPM, suggesting that investor behavior is influenced by psychological biases and heuristics, leading to market inefficiencies.

- **Arbitrage Pricing Theory (APT):** APT, developed by Stephen Ross (1976), provides an alternative to CAPM by considering multiple sources of systematic risk. APT does not rely on a single market portfolio but instead uses multiple factors to explain asset returns.
- **Multi-Factor Models:** Building on CAPM and APT, multi-factor models incorporate additional risk factors such as momentum, profitability, and investment patterns. These models aim to provide a more comprehensive explanation of asset returns.

9.1.5. Examples of CAPM (Capital Asset Pricing Model)

- **Example 1.** Suppose a stock has the following information. It is listed on the London stock exchange and operates throughout Europe. The yield on a UK 10-year treasury is 2.8%. The stock in question will earn 8.6% as per historical data. The Beta for the stock is 1.4, i.e., it is 140% volatile to the changes in the general stock market.

The expected rate of return of the stock will be calculated as below.

B4 | Ra = Rrf + βa * (Rm – Rrf) | =B1+B2*(B3-B1)

		B
1	Risk Free Return (Rrf)	2.8
2	Beta of the Particular Stock (βa)	1.4
3	Return of Stock (Rm)	8.6
4	**Expected Rate of Return (Ra)**	**10.92**
5		

CAPM Formula (Expected return) = Risk free return (2.8%) + Beta (1.4) * Market risk premium (8.6%–2.8%)

- = 2.8 + 1.4*(5.8)
- = 2.8 + 8.12

Expected Rate of Return = 10.92

- **Example 2.** Thomas has to decide to invest in either Stock Marvel or Stock DC using the CAPM model illustrated by the following screenshot from work. Thomas has to decide to invest in Stock Marvel or Stock DC with the given information available to him. Marvel – Return 9.6%, Beta 0.95. DC – Return 8.7%, Beta 1.2. As measured by the return on government stock, a risk-free return in the market is 5.6%.

The expected rate of return of the stock marvel will be calculated below.

B5 | Ra = Rrf + βa * (Rm – Rrf) | =B2+B4*(B3-B2)

		B	C
1	**Stock Marvel**		
2	Risk Free Security Return (Rrf)	5.60%	
3	Return of the Stock (Rm)	9.60%	
4	Beta of Particular Stock (βa)	95.00%	
5	**Expected Rate of Return (Ra)**	**9.40%**	
6			

Formula – Expected return = Risk free return (5.60%) + Beta (95.00) * Market risk premium (9.60%–5.60%)

Expected Rate of Return = 9.40%

The expected rate of return of the stock DC will be calculated as below.

B11 | Ra = Rrf + βa * (Rm – Rrf) | =B8+B10*(B9-B8)

		B	C
7	**Stock DC**		
8	Risk Free Security Return (Rrf)	5.6%	
9	Return of the Stock (Rm)	8.7%	
10	Beta of Particular Stock (βa)	1.2	
11	**Expected Rate of Return (Ra)**	**9.32%**	
12			

Formula – Expected return = Risk free return (5.6%) + Beta (1.2) * Market risk premium (8.7%–5.6%).

9.1.6. Advantages of CAPM

- CAPM considers only the systematic or market risk or not the security's only inherent or systemic risk. This factor eliminates the vagueness associated with an individual security's risk, and only the general market risk, which has a degree of certainty, becomes the primary factor. The model assumes that the investor holds a diversified portfolio, and hence the unsystematic risk is eliminated between the stock holdings.
- It is widely used in the finance industry to calculate the cost of equity and ultimately the weighted average cost of capital, which is used extensively to check the cost of financing from various sources. It is seen as a much better model to calculate the cost of equity than the other present models like the
- It is a universal and easy-to-use model. Dividend growth model (DGM)Given the extensive presence of this model, this can easily be utilized for comparisons between stocks of various countries.

9.1.7. Disadvantages of CAPM

- The capital asset pricing model is hinged on various assumptions. One of the assumptions is that a riskier asset will yield a higher return. Next, the historical data is used to calculate Beta. The model also assumes that past performance is a good measure of the future results of a stock's functioning. However, that is far from the truth.
- The model also assumes that the risk-free return will remain constant throughout the stock investment. If the return on the government treasury securities rises or falls, it will change the risk-free return and potentially the calculation of the model. It is not taken into account while calculating the CAPM.
- The model assumes that the investors have access to the same information and have the same decision-making process concerning the risks and returns associated with the securities. It assumes that the investors will prefer low-risk securities to high-risk securities for a given return. Investors will prefer higher returns to lower returns for a given risk. Although this is a general guideline, some of the more extravagant investors might not be in agreement with this theory.

9.2. ARBITRAGE PRICING THEORY (APT)

The Arbitrage Pricing Theory (APT) is a theory of asset pricing that holds that an asset's returns can be forecasted with the linear relationship of an asset's expected returns and the macroeconomic factors that affect the asset's risk. The theory was created in 1976 by American economist, Stephen Ross. The APT offers analysts and investors a multi-factor pricing model for securities, based on the relationship between a financial asset's expected return and its risks (Burmeister Edwin, & Wall Kent, 1986).

The APT aims to pinpoint the fair market price of a security that may be temporarily incorrectly priced. It assumes that market action is less than always perfectly efficient, and therefore occasionally results in assets being mispriced – either overvalued or undervalued – for a brief period of time.

However, market action should eventually correct the situation, moving price back to its fair market value. To an arbitrageur, temporarily mispriced securities represent a short-term opportunity to profit virtually risk-free. The APT is a more flexible and complex alternative to the Capital Asset Pricing Model (CAPM). The theory provides investors and analysts with the opportunity to customize their research. However, it is more difficult to apply, as it takes a considerable amount of time to determine all the various factors that may influence the price of an asset.

9.2.1. Assumptions in the Arbitrage Pricing Theory

The Arbitrage Pricing Theory operates with a pricing model that factors in many sources of risk and uncertainty. Unlike the Capital Asset Pricing Model (CAPM), which only takes into account the single factor of the risk level of the overall market, the APT model looks at several macroeconomic factors that, according to the theory, determine the risk and return of the specific asset. These factors provide risk premiums for investors to consider because the factors carry systematic risk that cannot be eliminated by diversifying. The APT suggests that investors will diversify their portfolios, but that they will also choose their own individual profile of risk and returns based on the premiums and sensitivity of the macroeconomic risk factors. Risk-taking investors will exploit the differences in expected and real returns on the asset by using arbitrage.

9.2.2. Arbitrage in the APT

The APT suggests that the returns on assets follow a linear pattern. An investor can leverage deviations in returns from the linear pattern using the arbitrage strategy.

Arbitrage is the practice of the simultaneous purchase and sale of an asset on different exchanges, taking advantage of slight pricing discrepancies to lock in a risk-free profit for the trade. However, the APT's concept of arbitrage is different from the classic meaning of the term. In the APT, arbitrage is not a risk-free operation – but it does offer a high probability of success. What the arbitrage pricing theory offers traders is a model for determining the theoretical fair market value of an asset. Having determined that value, traders then look for slight deviations from the fair market price, and trade accordingly.

For example, if the fair market value of stock A is determined, using the APT pricing model, to be $13, but the market price briefly drops to $11, then a trader would buy the stock, based on the belief that further market price action will quickly "correct" the market price back to the $13 a share level.

9.2.3. Mathematical Model of the APT

The Arbitrage Pricing Theory can be expressed as a mathematical model:

$$ER(x) = Rf + \beta_1 RP_1 + \beta_2 RP_2 + \ldots + \beta_n RP_n$$

Where;

- *ER(x)* – Expected return on asset
- *Rf* – Riskless rate of return
- β_n *(Beta)* – The asset's price sensitivity to factor
- RP_n – The risk premium associated with factor

Historical returns on securities are analyzed with linear regression analysis against the macroeconomic factor to estimate beta coefficients for the arbitrage pricing theory formula.

9.2.4. Empirical Testing of APT

The empirical validity of APT has been extensively studied. Researchers have focused on identifying the relevant factors and testing the model's ability to explain asset returns.

- **Identification of Factors:** The selection of factors is critical in APT. Researchers have used various macroeconomic variables such as inflation, interest rates, industrial production, and market indices. Statistical techniques like factor analysis and principal component analysis are often employed to identify these factors.
- **Empirical Evidence:** Empirical tests of APT have shown mixed results. Some studies have found that APT performs well in explaining asset returns, while others have pointed out limitations and inconsistencies. Factors such as data limitations, model specification, and estimation techniques can affect the results.
- **Comparison with CAPM:** Compared to CAPM, APT offers a more flexible approach by considering multiple sources of risk. Empirical studies have shown that APT can sometimes provide a better fit for asset returns than CAPM, particularly in capturing the effects of macroeconomic factors.

9.2.5. Criticisms and Limitations

While APT is a robust model, it is not without its criticisms and limitations.

- **Identification of Factors:** One of the main challenges of APT is the identification of relevant factors. The choice of factors can significantly impact the model's accuracy and explanatory power. Different studies have used different sets of factors, leading to varying results.

- **Estimation Issues:** Estimating the sensitivities (β coefficients) to multiple factors can be complex and data-intensive. The accuracy of these estimates depends on the quality and availability of data, as well as the statistical techniques used.
- **Model Specification:** The specification of the APT model, including the number and type of factors, can influence its performance. There is no universally accepted method for determining the optimal set of factors, and this can lead to model uncertainty.
- **Empirical Challenges:** Empirical tests of APT have faced challenges such as data limitations, model specification errors, and estimation biases. These challenges can affect the reliability of the results and the model's practical applicability.

9.3. MODERN PORTFOLIO THEORY

Modern Portfolio Theory (MPT), introduced by Harry Markowitz in his seminal 1952 paper "Portfolio Selection," revolutionized the field of finance by providing a systematic framework for constructing investment portfolios that maximize expected return for a given level of risk. This theory laid the groundwork for much of the subsequent development in finance, including the Capital Asset Pricing Model (CAPM) and Arbitrage Pricing Theory (APT). MPT emphasizes diversification, efficient portfolios, and the trade-off between risk and return.

According to modern portfolio theory, all the investments that are selected are combined together in a way that reduces the risk in the market through the means of diversification and, at the same time, also generates a good return in the long term to the investors.

In case two different portfolios are given to the investor having the same level of expected return, then the rational decision would be to choose the portfolio having lower total risk.

Even though it is accepted widely all over the world and also applied by different investment institutions, but at the same time, there are also some modern portfolio theory criticism by different persons. However, regardless of the different criticisms, Modern portfolio theory is a working strategy having a diversified investment that is implemented by different risk managers, investment institutions, and related persons (Figure 9.1).

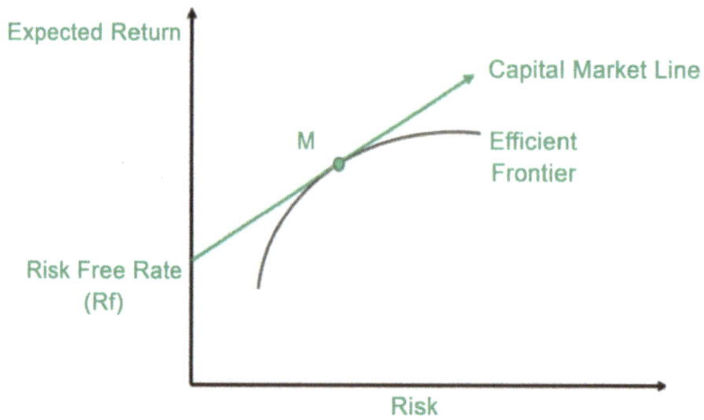

Figure 9.1. *Modern-portfolio-theory.*

Source: https://www.wallstreetmojo.com/modern-portfolio-theory/.

- **Example**

There is an individual who wants to invest in a portfolio. He got an option of two portfolios, which are as follows:

1. The first portfolio consists of a mix of the bonds and different stocks that gave the return of 10% annually on an average, but at the same time differed by the range of as much as 15% annually (returns, in this case, usually differed between –5% and + 25%).
2. On the other hand, the second portfolio consists of a mix of the bonds and different stocks that gave the return of 10% annually on an average, but at the same time differed by a range of only 3% annually (returns, in this case, usually differed between 7% and 13%).

According to the modern portfolio theory graph, which investment portfolio should a person consider?

Analysis

- In both scenarios, the average expected return on the investment is 10%. However, in the first portfolio, one could get the return of as much as 25%, which sounds attractive, but at the same time, there prevails a huge risk where one might lose 5% as well because the range usually differs between –5% and + 25%.
- On the other hand, in the case of the second portfolio, a less return range of between 7% and 13% may be less attractive to the investor, but in that case, it is expected that one will not lose his money, which makes the investment less risky than the first portfolio.
- According to the modern portfolio theory graph, an investor invests with the motive of taking the minimum level of risk and earning the maximum amount of return with that minimum risk taken, so in the present case, one should choose the second portfolio as he is getting the same average expected return with the less level of risk.

9.3.1. Assumptions

Modern Portfolio theory has a certain assumption that is to be considered while making any decisions in order to arrive at the conclusion that risk, return, and diversification relationships hold true. The different assumptions of the modern portfolio theory are as follows:

- Returns from the assets are distributed normally. Due to this assumption, various statistical measures like standard deviation or correlation in analysis or portfolio can be used.
- The theory assumes that the investor making the investment is rational and will avoid all the unnecessary risk associated. This implies that any decision maker who acts in a rational manner will have the aim of maximizing the utility and will evaluate their investments based on the return and risk associated with it. It also leads to the fact that all information collected is relevant to the process.
- Investors will give their best in order to maximize returns for all the unique situations provided.
- All investors have access to the same information. Even though this is assumed, such a situation is not always realistic.

- The cost pertaining to taxes and trading is not considered while making decisions. The theory assumes that there is no tax or any kind or transaction cost while holding the asset of transacting with it.
- All the investors are having the same views on the rate of return expected. Thus, all investors have same expectations about the return that they will get in future, the volatility of the asset value or correlation within assets. Therefore, it offers a consistent framework.
- The single investors alone are not sizable and capable enough to influence the prices prevailing in the market. There are a number of investors and all of them are equally important in the process.
- Unlimited capital at the risk-free rate of return can be borrowed.
- It does not account for the market fluctuations or changes in the economic conditions. It assumes that the characteristics of return from the market remains unchanged.

9.3.2. Criticisms and Alternatives

- **Behavioral Finance:** Behavioral finance challenges the rationality assumption of MPT. It suggests that investors are influenced by psychological biases, such as overconfidence and loss aversion, leading to market inefficiencies and suboptimal investment decisions.
- **Market Inefficiencies:** Critics argue that MPT's assumption of efficient markets is unrealistic. Factors such as transaction costs, taxes, and information asymmetries can lead to deviations from the predicted risk-return trade-offs.
- **Black-Litterman Model:** The Black-Litterman model is an extension of MPT that incorporates investor views and market equilibrium. It provides a more robust framework for portfolio optimization by blending subjective views with objective market data.
- **Post-Modern Portfolio Theory (PMPT):** PMPT addresses some of the limitations of MPT by considering downside risk measures, such as semi-variance and Value at Risk (VaR). PMPT provides a more comprehensive view of risk by focusing on the potential for losses rather than overall volatility.

9.3.3. Advantages

There are several different importance of modern portfolio theory providing the opportunity for the investors investing their money in the market. Some of the advantages are of the Modern portfolio theory as follows:

- It helps in evaluating and managing risks and returns associated with the investments. With the help of analysis, the assets which are underperforming assets and the assets having an excessive risk with respect to returns can be scrutinized and then replaced with the new one.
- The importance of modern portfolio theory lies in the fact that it is an important tool for avoiding financial ruin because by following these theories, traders don't rely on only one investment for their financial stability; rather, they diversify their portfolio in order to get the maximum return with minimum risk.

9.3.4. Disadvantages

Along with the different advantages, there modern portfolio theory criticism, which includes the following:

- In the case of the modern portfolio theory, the past performance of the company under consideration is taken. The performance of the past never provides a guarantee for the result that could arise in the future. Considering only the past performances sometimes leads to overpassing the newer circumstances, which might not be there when historical data were considered but could play an important role in making the decision.
- Another limitations of modern portfolio theory is that this theory assumes that there is a normal distribution of the return on an asset within a class of assets, which is proved to be wrong for individual equities as the correlations of asset class may change over the period of time.
- In this theory, there is an assumption that securities of any of the sizes can be bought and sold, which doesn't hold true as some of the securities have minimum order sizes, which cannot be dealt with in the fraction.
- Modern Portfolio Theory even though is accepted widely all over the world and also applied by different investment institution, but at the same time it has also been criticized by different persons particularly by representatives of the behavioral economics who challenges the assumptions of the Modern portfolio theory on the parameters of investor rationality and the expectations for the return.

9.4. DYNAMIC ASSET ALLOCATION (DAA)

Dynamic Asset Allocation (DAA) models are investment strategies that adjust the portfolio composition in response to changing market conditions and economic environments. Unlike static allocation, which maintains a fixed asset mix, DAA models are designed to optimize the risk-return trade-off over time by adapting to new information and trends. This approach aims to enhance portfolio performance, manage risks more effectively, and capitalize on emerging opportunities.

9.4.1. Background and Rationale

The traditional approach to asset allocation involves setting a strategic asset mix based on an investor's risk tolerance, investment horizon, and financial goals. While this method provides a stable and straightforward framework, it may not be responsive enough to capture short-term market fluctuations or shifts in economic conditions. DAA models address this limitation by incorporating flexibility and adaptability, allowing for adjustments that reflect the evolving investment landscape. The rationale behind DAA models is grounded in the belief that markets are not always efficient and that asset returns are influenced by a variety of factors, including economic cycles, interest rates, inflation, and geopolitical events. By continuously monitoring these factors and adjusting the asset allocation accordingly, investors can potentially improve their risk-adjusted returns.

9.4.2. Theoretical Foundations

DAA models are rooted in several key financial theories and principles:

1. **Modern Portfolio Theory (MPT):** Proposed by Harry Markowitz in 1952, MPT emphasizes the benefits of diversification and the trade-off between risk and return. DAA extends this concept by dynamically adjusting the portfolio to maintain an optimal risk-return profile over time.
2. **Efficient Market Hypothesis (EMH):** While EMH suggests that markets are efficient and it is difficult to consistently outperform the market, DAA models operate on the premise that inefficiencies and anomalies exist, which can be exploited through active management.
3. **Intertemporal Capital Asset Pricing Model (ICAPM):** Developed by Robert Merton, ICAPM extends the traditional CAPM by incorporating multiple time periods and considering the investor's changing investment opportunities over time.
4. **Behavioral Finance:** DAA models also draw on insights from behavioral finance, which acknowledges that investors are not always rational and that

psychological biases can influence market behavior. By accounting for these biases, DAA models aim to mitigate their impact on investment decisions.

9.4.3. Types of Dynamic Asset Allocation Models

There are several types of DAA models, each with its unique approach and methodology:

1. **Tactical Asset Allocation (TAA):** TAA involves making short-term adjustments to the portfolio based on market conditions and economic indicators. The goal is to take advantage of perceived mispricings or trends by temporarily deviating from the strategic asset allocation.
2. **Constant Proportion Portfolio Insurance (CPPI):** CPPI is a risk management strategy that dynamically adjusts the allocation between a risky asset and a risk-free asset to ensure a minimum portfolio value. The allocation is based on a cushion value, which is the difference between the current portfolio value and the floor value.
3. **Dynamic Strategic Asset Allocation (DSAA):** DSAA combines elements of both strategic and tactical asset allocation. It involves setting a long-term strategic asset mix while making periodic adjustments based on changing economic conditions and market outlook.
4. **Risk Parity:** Risk parity strategies aim to allocate risk equally across various asset classes, rather than focusing on capital allocation. This approach often involves leveraging low-risk assets to achieve a balanced risk exposure.
5. **Trend Following:** Trend following strategies adjust the asset allocation based on observed trends and momentum in asset prices. The goal is to capitalize on the persistence of trends by increasing exposure to assets that are performing well and reducing exposure to those that are underperforming.
6. **Volatility Targeting:** Volatility targeting involves adjusting the asset allocation to maintain a consistent level of portfolio volatility. By increasing or decreasing exposure to risky assets based on their volatility, investors aim to achieve more stable returns.

9.4.4. Key Components and Implementation

Implementing DAA models involves several key components and steps:

1. **Market and Economic Analysis:** The foundation of DAA models is a thorough analysis of market conditions and economic indicators. This can include evaluating macroeconomic data, interest rates, inflation, corporate earnings, and geopolitical events.
2. **Factor Identification:** Identifying the key factors that influence asset returns is critical for developing DAA models. These factors can include economic growth, interest rates, inflation, market volatility, and investor sentiment.
3. **Model Development:** Developing a DAA model involves selecting the appropriate methodology and algorithms for adjusting the asset allocation. This can range from simple rules-based approaches to complex quantitative models that

incorporate machine learning and artificial intelligence.

4. **Backtesting and Validation:** Before implementing a DAA model, it is essential to backtest the strategy using historical data to evaluate its performance and robustness. This involves simulating the model's performance over various market conditions and time periods.
5. **Implementation and Monitoring:** Once the model is validated, it can be implemented in the portfolio. Continuous monitoring is necessary to ensure that the model is performing as expected and to make adjustments based on new information and changing conditions.
6. **Risk Management:** Effective risk management is a critical component of DAA models. This involves setting appropriate risk limits, diversifying the portfolio, and using hedging strategies to mitigate potential losses.

9.4.5. Advantages of Dynamic Asset Allocation Models

DAA models offer several advantages over static allocation strategies:

1. **Flexibility:** DAA models provide the flexibility to adjust the portfolio in response to changing market conditions, potentially improving returns and reducing risk.
2. **Improved Risk Management:** By continuously monitoring and adjusting the asset allocation, DAA models can better manage risk and protect against downside losses.
3. **Enhanced Return Potential:** DAA models aim to exploit market inefficiencies and trends, potentially enhancing the portfolio's return potential.
4. **Adaptability:** DAA models can be tailored to different market environments and investment objectives, making them suitable for a wide range of investors.
5. **Diversification:** By dynamically adjusting the asset allocation, DAA models can achieve better diversification and reduce the impact of individual asset class performance on the overall portfolio.

9.4.6. Challenges and Limitations

Despite their advantages, DAA models also face several challenges and limitations:

1. **Complexity:** Developing and implementing DAA models can be complex and require sophisticated analytical tools and expertise.
2. **Data and Model Risk:** The accuracy of DAA models depends on the quality and reliability of the data used. Additionally, models can be sensitive to assumptions and parameter settings.
3. **Transaction Costs:** Frequent adjustments to the portfolio can result in higher transaction costs, which can erode returns.
4. **Behavioral Biases:** DAA models are not immune to behavioral biases and may be influenced by investor sentiment and market noise.
5. **Regulatory Constraints:** Regulatory constraints and restrictions on certain investment strategies can limit the implementation of DAA models.

9.5. BLACK-LITTERMAN MODEL

The Black-Litterman Model, developed by Fischer Black and Robert Litterman at Goldman Sachs in 1990, is a sophisticated asset allocation model that addresses some of the limitations of Modern Portfolio Theory (MPT). It combines the equilibrium market returns implied by the Capital Asset Pricing Model (CAPM) with the investor's unique views on expected returns. This model has become a vital tool for portfolio managers seeking to create more robust and diversified investment portfolios.

9.5.1. Theoretical Foundations of the Black-Litterman Model

Assumptions

The Black-Litterman Model builds on several key assumptions:

- **Market Equilibrium**: Markets are assumed to be in equilibrium, meaning that asset prices fully reflect all available information.
- **Investor Views**: Investors have unique views on the expected returns of certain assets, which may differ from the market equilibrium returns.
- **Combining Views with Market Equilibrium**: The model combines investor views with market equilibrium returns to generate a new set of expected returns, leading to a more diversified and balanced portfolio.

9.5.2. The CAPM and Market Equilibrium

The CAPM provides the foundation for the Black-Litterman Model by suggesting that the expected return on an asset is proportional to its systematic risk (beta) relative to the market. The market equilibrium returns (π) can be derived from CAPM as follows:

$$\pi=\lambda\Sigma w_m$$

Where;

- π is the vector of equilibrium returns.
- ⊠ is the market risk premium.
- Σ is the covariance matrix of asset returns.
- w_m is the market capitalization-weighted vector of assets.

9.5.2.1. Incorporating Investor Views

The Black-Litterman Model allows investors to incorporate their unique views into the expected return estimates. These views can be expressed as absolute or relative:

- **Absolute Views:** Direct opinions on the expected returns of specific assets.
- **Relative Views:** Opinions on the expected returns of one asset relative to another.

9.5.2.2. The Black-Litterman Formula

The core of the Black-Litterman Model is the formula that combines the equilibrium returns with the investor's views to generate a new set of expected returns:

$$E(R) = [(\tau\Sigma - 1 + PT\Omega P] - 1\,[(\tau\Sigma) - 1\Pi + PT\Omega Q]$$

Where; E(R) is the expected return; τ is the A scalar number indicating the uncertainty of the CAPM distribution; P is a matrix with investors views; each row a specific view of the market and each entry of the row represents the weights of each asset; Q is the expected returns of the portfolios from the views described in matrix P; Ω is the diagonal covariance matrix with entries of the uncertainty within each view; Σ is the Covariance matrix of returns; and Π = Vector of implied equilibrium expected returns.

- **Example of Black-Litterman Model:** An equity portfolio manager believes that the tech sector will outperform the market by 3%. She also has a bearish view on the consumer discretionary sector and expects it to underperform by 2%. The expected market return (market equilibrium) is 10%. After applying the Black-Litterman adjustments, the expected return for the tech sector can be revised to 13% (market consensus of 10% + 3% the subjective view of the investor), while consumer discretionary is revised to 8% (market consensus of 10% – 2% subjective forecast). The manager can then use these revised expected returns in a mean-variance optimization to determine an optimal portfolio allocation that aligns with both market equilibrium and her unique insights.

Overall, the model is expected to tilt the portfolio towards the outperforming security/asset if the view exceeds the difference between the two implied equilibrium returns.

- **Black-Litterman Model Excel Example**

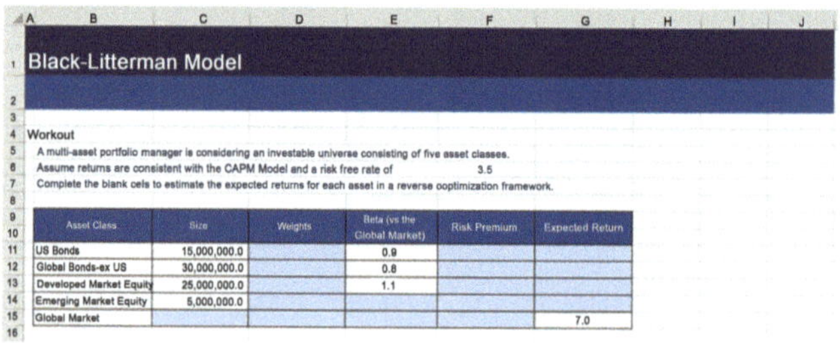

Black-Litterman Model

Workout

A multi-asset portfolio manager is considering an investable universe consisting of five asset classes.

Assume returns are consistent with the CAPM Model and a risk free rate of 3.5

Complete the blank cels to estimate the expected returns for each asset in a reverse ooptimization framework.

Asset Class	Size	Weights	Beta (vs the Global Market)	Risk Premium	Expected Return
US Bonds	15,000,000.0		0.9		
Global Bonds-ex US	30,000,000.0		0.8		
Developed Market Equity	25,000,000.0		1.1		
Emerging Market Equity	5,000,000.0				
Global Market					7.0

We need to find the estimated return for each asset class in a reverse optimization framework, which then could be used to be applied as own views in a Black-Litterman model.

1. First, we calculate the total size of the market by adding up all asset classes.
2. Then we find the size of each asset class by dividing its size by the total market size (all should add up to 1, i.e., 100%).
3. Then we need to find the beta for Emerging Market equities. The beta for the Global Market should

equal 1 so in that cell we use the SUMPRODUCT function and multiply together the individual weights by their relevant beta. Then we need to use the Goal Seek function to find the Emerging Markets beta (Data-What if Analysis-Goal Seek). As noted, cell E15 should equal 1 by changing cell E14.

4. Next, to calculate the risk premium, we need to use the expected return for the Global Market of 7% and deduct the risk-free rate of 3.5%. This is consistent across each asset class in the portfolio.
5. Finally, to calculate the expected return we take the risk-free rate and add the individual beta for each asset class multiplied by the risk premium. Download the full model to check your answer.

9.5.3. Empirical Testing of the Black-Litterman Model

- **Early Applications:** Early applications of the Black-Litterman Model focused on its ability to generate more stable and intuitive portfolio weights compared to the traditional mean-variance optimization. Studies found that the model improved portfolio performance by incorporating investor views and reducing estimation errors.
- **Empirical Evidence:** Empirical studies have shown that the Black-Litterman Model can effectively balance the equilibrium market returns with investor views, leading to more diversified and less concentrated portfolios. The model has been tested across various asset classes, including equities, fixed income, and alternative investments, with generally positive results.
- **Comparison with MPT:** Compared to MPT, the Black-Litterman Model addresses several key limitations, such as:
  - **Estimation Risk:** By combining market equilibrium returns with investor views, the model reduces the sensitivity to estimation errors.
  - **Intuitive Weights:** The model generates more stable and intuitive portfolio weights, avoiding extreme allocations that can result from traditional mean-variance optimization.
  - **Flexibility:** The model allows for the incorporation of both absolute and relative views, providing greater flexibility in portfolio construction.

9.5.4. Criticisms and Limitations

- **Complexity:** One of the main criticisms of the Black-Litterman Model is its complexity. The model requires a deep understanding of both the theoretical framework and the practical implementation, which can be challenging for some investors.
- **Parameter Estimation:** Accurate estimation of the model's parameters, such as the market risk premium (λ), the covariance matrix (Σ), and the uncertainty scalar (τ), is crucial for the model's success. Estimation errors can lead to suboptimal portfolio allocations.
- **Incorporating Views:** Incorporating investor views into the model requires a clear and structured

approach. Inaccurate or biased views can negatively impact the portfolio's performance.

- **Market Assumptions:** The Black-Litterman Model relies on the assumption that markets are in equilibrium and that CAPM accurately reflects market returns. Deviations from these assumptions can limit the model's effectiveness.

9.5.5. Advantages

One advantage of the model is that it uses the mean-variation approach. This method allows investors to take their risk tolerance into account so they can maximize their expected returns.

Investors can also use their own views when using this tool, which gives them more control and confidence over how their portfolio is structured in terms of asset allocation and how it's rebalanced when it comes time to make any changes. Furthermore, it is more instinctive, which helps prevent heavy changes in portfolio weight over time.

9.5.6. Disadvantages

One of the main drawbacks of using the Black-Litterman model is that it doesn't promise or guarantee the best portfolio. Rather, it devises a portfolio (and rebalances it if/when needed) based on the investor's or portfolio manager's views about the market.

Another key disadvantage is that since it works on assumptions, it is sensitive to the investor's views. This means that the model is based on the fact that these views act independently of one another and, therefore, don't act together.

9.6. MULTI-INDEX MODELS

Multi-index models, also known as multi-factor models, play a crucial role in financial economics and investment analysis. These models extend the basic single-index model (such as the Capital Asset Pricing Model, or CAPM) by incorporating multiple risk factors that can influence asset returns. This approach provides a more comprehensive understanding of the dynamics that drive asset prices and allows for better risk management and portfolio optimization.

9.6.1. Background and Rationale

The single-index model, primarily exemplified by CAPM, posits that the return on an asset can be explained by its sensitivity to the overall market return. While this model provides a useful starting point, it oversimplifies the complex nature of financial markets by attributing all risk to a single market factor. Multi-index models address this limitation by recognizing that asset returns are influenced by a variety of factors, such as macroeconomic variables, industry-specific conditions, and firm-specific characteristics.

The development of multi-index models was largely driven by empirical observations that single-index models failed to capture all the systematic risk components that affect asset returns. For instance, studies showed that asset returns are often correlated with variables like interest rates, inflation, and industrial production, suggesting the need for a more nuanced approach.

9.6.2. The Structure of Multi-Index Models

Multi-index models can be generally expressed as:

$$R_i = \alpha_i + \quad {}_{j=1}^{k} \beta_{ij} F_j + \epsilon_i$$

Where; R_i is the return on asset I; ⊠$_i$ is the intercept term for asset i, representing its expected return independent of the factors; β_{ij} is the sensitivity of asset i's return to the jth factor; F_j is the jjjth factor; and ⊠$_i$ is the error term, representing the idiosyncratic risk of asset iii not explained by the factors.

The choice of factors F_j is critical and can include various macroeconomic variables, financial metrics, or statistical constructs derived from historical data. Commonly used factors in multi-index models include:

- **Market Factor:** The excess return of the market portfolio over the risk-free rate.
- **Size Factor (SMB – Small Minus Big):** The difference in returns between small-cap and large-cap stocks.
- **Value Factor (HML – High Minus Low):** The difference in returns between high book-to-market and low book-to-market stocks.
- **Momentum Factor:** The tendency of stocks to continue performing well or poorly based on past performance.
- **Interest Rate Factor:** The sensitivity of asset returns to changes in interest rates.
- **Inflation Factor:** The impact of inflation on asset returns.

9.6.3. Theoretical Foundations

- **Arbitrage Pricing Theory (APT):** One of the foundational theories underlying multi-index models is the Arbitrage Pricing Theory (APT), proposed by Stephen Ross in 1976. APT posits that the return on any asset can be modeled as a linear function of various macroeconomic factors, and that arbitrage opportunities will force the expected return on an asset to align with its factor exposures.

The APT model can be expressed as:

$$R_i = E(R_i) + \sum_{j=1}^{k} \beta_{ij}(F_j - E(F_j)) + \epsilon_i$$

Where; $E(R_i)$ is the expected return on asset I; $E(F_j)$ is the expected value of the jth factor; and Other terms are as previously defined. APT is less restrictive than CAPM as it does not require the assumption of a market portfolio and allows for multiple factors to explain asset returns. It provides a more flexible framework for understanding the impact of various economic forces on asset prices.

- **Fama-French Three-Factor Model:** Eugene Fama and Kenneth French expanded on the CAPM by introducing the Fama-French Three-Factor Model in 1992. This model adds two additional factors to the CAPM: size and value. The model is expressed as:

$$R_i - R_f = \alpha_i + \beta_i(R_m - R_f) + s_i SMB + h_i HML + \epsilon_i$$

Where; R_{fR} is the risk-free rate; R_m is the market return; SMB is the size factor; HML is the value factor; and s_i and h_i are the factor loadings for SMB and HML, respectively. The Fama-French model provided empirical evidence that small-cap stocks and high book-to-market stocks tend to outperform the market, thus offering a better explanation of asset returns compared to the single-factor CAPM.

- **Carhart Four-Factor Model:** Mark Carhart extended the Fama-French model by adding a momentum factor, leading to the Carhart Four-Factor Model. The inclusion of momentum acknowledges the empirical observation that stocks with strong past performance tend to continue performing well in the short term. The model is expressed as:

$$R_i - R_f = \alpha_i + \beta_i(R_m - R_f) + s_i SMB + h_i HML + m_i MOM + \epsilon_i$$

Where; MOM is the momentum factor; and m_i is the factor loading for MOM.

9.6.4. Empirical Implementation

The empirical implementation of multi-index models involves several steps:

1. Factor Selection: Identifying and selecting appropriate factors that are believed to influence asset returns. This can involve economic intuition, statistical analysis, and empirical validation.
2. Data Collection: Gathering historical data on asset returns and the chosen factors. This data is typically sourced from financial databases and macroeconomic reports.
3. Estimation of Factor Loadings: Using regression analysis to estimate the factor loadings (β_{ij} for each asset. This involves regressing the asset returns on the selected factors.
4. Model Validation: Testing the model's explanatory power and predictive accuracy using out-of-sample data. This step often involves statistical tests and robustness checks.

9.6.5. Advantages of Multi-Index Models

Multi-index models offer several advantages over single-index models:

1. Enhanced Explanatory Power: By incorporating multiple factors, these models provide a more comprehensive explanation of asset returns.
2. Improved Risk Management: Multi-index models allow for better identification and management of various sources of risk, leading to more effective portfolio diversification.
3. Flexibility: These models can be tailored to specific investment strategies and market conditions by selecting relevant factors.
4. Empirical Validation: Multi-index models have been empirically validated and widely adopted in both academic research and practical investment management.

9.6.6. Challenges and Limitations

Despite their advantages, multi-index models also face several challenges and limitations:

1. Factor Selection: Choosing the appropriate factors is a critical and often subjective process that can significantly impact the model's performance.
2. Data Availability: Accurate and comprehensive data on both asset returns and factors is essential for reliable model estimation.
3. Overfitting: The inclusion of too many factors can lead to overfitting, where the model captures noise rather than true relationships.
4. Dynamic Nature of Markets: Financial markets are dynamic, and the relevance of certain factors can change over time, necessitating continuous model updates.

9.7. ROBUST PORTFOLIO OPTIMIZATION (RPO)

Robust Portfolio Optimization (RPO) is a sophisticated approach to investment management that seeks to construct portfolios resilient to uncertainty and model inaccuracies. Traditional portfolio optimization methods, such as Mean-Variance Optimization (MVO), rely on precise estimates of asset returns, variances, and covariances, which can be highly sensitive to estimation errors. RPO addresses these limitations by incorporating uncertainty directly into the optimization process, aiming to create portfolios that perform well across a range of plausible scenarios.

9.7.1. Background and Rationale

The foundation of portfolio optimization lies in Modern Portfolio Theory (MPT), introduced by Harry Markowitz in 1952. MPT emphasizes the benefits of diversification and the trade-off between risk and return. The core idea is to construct an "efficient frontier" of portfolios that offer the highest expected return for a given level of risk. However, MPT's reliance on precise input parameters makes it vulnerable to estimation errors, which can lead to suboptimal or highly concentrated portfolios. RPO emerges from the recognition that financial markets are inherently uncertain and that traditional models often fail to capture this uncertainty adequately. By explicitly considering uncertainty in the optimization process, RPO aims to create portfolios that are more robust to estimation errors and unexpected market events, leading to more stable and reliable investment outcomes.

9.7.2. Theoretical Foundations

RPO builds on several key theoretical concepts:

1. **Uncertainty Sets:** These are predefined ranges or distributions within which the true values of input parameters (e.g., asset returns, covariances) are expected to lie. By considering these uncertainty sets, RPO can construct portfolios that are less sensitive to estimation errors.
2. **Worst-Case Optimization:** RPO often involves optimizing the portfolio for the worst-case scenario within the defined uncertainty sets. This approach ensures that the portfolio remains robust even in adverse conditions.
3. **Stochastic Programming:** This technique models uncertainty by incorporating random variables and their distributions into the optimization problem. RPO can use stochastic programming to generate solutions that account for a wide range of possible outcomes.

4. **Distributionally Robust Optimization (DRO):** DRO extends robust optimization by considering uncertainty in the probability distributions of input parameters. This approach seeks to optimize the portfolio based on the worst-case distribution within a given ambiguity set.

9.7.3. Types of Robust Portfolio Optimization Models

Several RPO models have been developed, each with its unique approach to handling uncertainty:

1. **Box Uncertainty Model:** This model assumes that the true values of input parameters lie within a specified range (box). The optimization process aims to minimize the worst-case scenario within this box.
2. **Ellipsoidal Uncertainty Model:** This model defines uncertainty sets as ellipsoids, capturing correlations between input parameters. The optimization process minimizes the worst-case scenario within the ellipsoid.
3. **Polyhedral Uncertainty Model:** This model uses polyhedra to define uncertainty sets, offering more flexibility in representing complex uncertainty structures. The optimization seeks the worst-case scenario within the polyhedral set.
4. **Norm-Constrained Models:** These models constrain the norm (e.g., L1, L2) of deviations from estimated parameters. By minimizing the worst-case deviation, the portfolio becomes more robust to estimation errors.
5. **Scenario-Based Models:** These models generate multiple scenarios representing different possible future states of the world. The optimization process seeks to construct a portfolio that performs well across these scenarios.

9.7.4. Key Components and Implementation

Implementing RPO involves several key components and steps:

1. **Defining Uncertainty Sets:** The first step is to define the uncertainty sets for input parameters. This can involve statistical analysis, historical data, expert judgment, or a combination of these methods.
2. **Model Formulation:** The next step is to formulate the optimization problem, incorporating the defined uncertainty sets. This involves selecting the appropriate RPO model and mathematical formulation.
3. **Optimization Algorithms:** Solving RPO problems requires specialized algorithms capable of handling uncertainty and complexity. Common algorithms include interior-point methods, cutting-plane methods, and scenario decomposition techniques.
4. **Backtesting and Validation:** Before implementing the RPO model in practice, it is essential to backtest the strategy using historical data. This step evaluates the model's performance, robustness, and stability.
5. **Implementation and Monitoring:** Once validated, the RPO model can be implemented in the portfolio. Continuous monitoring and periodic

adjustments are necessary to ensure the portfolio remains robust to changing market conditions.

9.7.5. Advantages of Robust Portfolio Optimization

RPO offers several advantages over traditional optimization methods:

1. **Enhanced Stability:** By considering uncertainty, RPO constructs portfolios that are more stable and less sensitive to estimation errors.
2. **Improved Risk Management:** RPO explicitly accounts for worst-case scenarios, leading to better risk management and protection against adverse market events.
3. **Flexibility:** RPO models can accommodate a wide range of uncertainty structures and investor preferences, making them adaptable to different investment contexts.
4. **Resilience to Model Errors:** RPO mitigates the impact of model inaccuracies, leading to more reliable and consistent investment outcomes.
5. **Better Performance:** Empirical studies have shown that RPO can lead to improved risk-adjusted returns compared to traditional optimization methods.

9.7.6. Challenges and Limitations

Despite its advantages, RPO also faces several challenges and limitations:

1. **Complexity:** RPO models can be complex to formulate and solve, requiring specialized mathematical and computational expertise.
2. **Data Requirements:** Defining accurate uncertainty sets requires extensive and reliable data, which may not always be available.
3. **Computational Intensity:** Solving RPO problems can be computationally intensive, especially for large portfolios with many assets.
4. **Subjectivity:** Defining uncertainty sets and worst-case scenarios can involve subjective judgment, leading to potential biases.
5. **Regulatory Constraints:** Regulatory constraints and restrictions on certain investment strategies can limit the implementation of RPO models.

ROLE MODEL

HARRY MARKOWITZ

Harry Markowitz is an American economist and creator of the influential Modern Portfolio Theory (MPT) still widely used today.

Harry Markowitz was born in Chicago, Illinois, on August 24, 1927. After completing his bachelor's in philosophy at the University of Chicago, Markowitz returned to the university for a master's in economics, studying under influential economists such as Milton Friedman.

While writing his dissertation on the application of mathematics to stock market analysis, Markowitz took great interest in John Burr Williams' "Theory of Investment Value." Williams emphasized investors' consideration of the expected value of assets within the portfolio, but Markowitz realized the argument lacked considerations of risk.

Markowitz identified the risk as variance – the measurement of volatility from the mean. Furthermore, he determined that investors could benefit from diversifying their portfolio due to idiosyncratic risk. Idiosyncratic risk is the risk inherent in specific assets. By incorporating different assets into a portfolio, diversification removes such a risk if the assets show low covariance (correlation of movement between assets).

Using risk and return as the primary considerations of investors, Markowitz pioneered the modern portfolio theory (MPT), published in 1952 by the Journal of Finance. He continued his work with colleague George Dantzig, where he refined his research on optimal portfolio allocation. His resulting work on graphing the Modern Portfolio Theory (MPT) would later be named the efficient frontier. He went on to receive a Ph.D. in economics and published his new findings on portfolio allocation.

His work earned him the John von Neumann Theory Prize in 1989 and the Nobel Memorial Prize in Economic Sciences in 1990. Almost a decade after Markowitz's initial publication on MPT, the famous capital asset pricing model (CAPM) was introduced, based on Markowitz's theory of risk and diversification.

Currently, Harry Markowitz spends his time teaching at the University of California San Diego and consulting at Harry Markowitz Company.

SUMMARY

- The Capital Asset Pricing Model (CAPM) is an equation that describes the relationship between the expected return of an investment and its risk. The model posits that the expected return on an investment is equal to the risk-free rate plus a risk premium, which is based on the beta of that investment. Beta measures an investment's volatility relative to the market as a whole.
- Arbitrage Pricing Theory (APT) is a financial model that investors use to determine the expected return of an asset based on various risk factors. It suggests that the future performance of an asset can be modeled by its sensitivity to multiple sources of risk.
- The Modern Portfolio Theory (MPT) refers to an investment theory that allows investors to assemble an asset portfolio that maximizes expected return for a given level of risk. The theory assumes that investors are risk-averse; for a given level of expected return, investors will always prefer the less risky portfolio.
- The Black-Litterman model is an asset allocation tool that portfolio managers use to optimize investor portfolios according to their risk tolerance and market outlook. The model uses market equilibrium as a starting point and considers the investors' subjective market views to calculate how the optimal asset weights should differ from the initial portfolio allocation. The model attempts to create more stable and efficient portfolios based on investors' unique insight, which overcomes the issues of input sensitivity.

REVIEW QUESTIONS

1. What is the basic premise of the CAPM, and how does it define the relationship between expected return and risk?
2. How does the APT account for multiple risk factors in determining asset prices?
3. What is the efficient frontier in Modern Portfolio Theory, and how is it determined?
4. How does Dynamic Asset Allocation differ from static asset allocation?
5. How does the Black-Litterman Model incorporate investor views into the asset allocation process?
6. What are Multi-Index Models, and how do they extend the single-index model in asset pricing?
7. What is Robust Portfolio Optimization, and why is it important in portfolio management?

REFERENCES

1. Benson, E. D., Bortner, B. D., & Kong, S. (2011). Stock return expectations and P/E10. *The Journal of Portfolio Management, 38*, 91–99.

2. Bodie, Z., Kane, A., & Marcus, A. J. (2008). *Investments* (7th International ed.). Boston: McGraw-Hill. p. 303. ISBN 978-0-07-125916-3.

3. Burmeister, E., & Wall, K. D. (1986). The arbitrage pricing theory and macroeconomic factor measures. *Financial Review, 21*(1), 1–20.

4. Campbell, J., & Shiller, R. (2001). Valuation ratios and the long-run stock market outlook: An update. *The Journal of Portfolio Management Winter 1998, 24*(2), 11–26.

5. Chen, N.-F., Roll, R., & Ross, S. A. (1986). Economic forces and the stock market. *The Journal of Business, 59*(3), 383–403. doi:10.1086/296344.

6. Fama, E. F., & French, K. R. (1992). The cross-section of expected stock returns. *Journal of Finance, 47*, 427–465.

7. Fama, E. F., & French, K. R. (2004). The Capital Asset Pricing Model: Theory and evidence. *Journal of Economic Perspectives, 18*(3), 25–46.

8. French, J. (2016). Estimating time-varying beta coefficients: An empirical study of US & ASEAN portfolios. *Research in Finance, 32*, 19–34. ISBN 978-1-78635-156-2.

9. Jansen, D. W., Koedijk, K. G., & de Vries, C. G. (2000). Portfolio selection with limited downside risk. *Journal of Empirical Finance, 7*, 247-269.

10. Kritzman, M., Page, S., & Turkington, D. (2012). Regime shifts: Implications for dynamic strategies. *Financial Analysts Journal, 68*(3), 22–39.

11. Rosenberg, B., Reid, K., & Lanstein, R. (1984). Persuasive evidence of market inefficiency. *The Journal of Portfolio Management, 11*, 9–17.

CHAPTER

10 Risk Analysis and Management

LEARNING OBJECTIVES

After studying this chapter, you will be able to:

- Define financial risk
- Identify the sources, drivers, and potential impacts of financial risks
- List the assessing financial risks in corporate venturing
- Describe financial risk analysis
- Explain financial risk management.

KEY TERMS FROM THIS CHAPTER

Business Risk	Credit risk	Debt
Financial assets	Investment decision	Liquidity risk
Market risk	Operational risk	Risk analysis
Risk management	Strategic risk	Volatility risk
Working capital		

INTRODUCTION

Risk analysis and management are critical components of financial modeling, providing a structured approach to identifying, assessing, and mitigating potential risks that can affect financial performance and decision-making. Financial models are designed to forecast future financial performance, but they inherently involve uncertainty and risk due to variables such as market fluctuations, economic changes, and operational challenges. Effective risk analysis helps modelers understand the range of possible outcomes and the impact of different risk factors on the financial metrics.

In financial modeling, risk analysis typically involves the use of quantitative techniques to evaluate the potential variability of outcomes. This includes sensitivity analysis, which examines how changes in key assumptions affect model outputs, and scenario analysis, which explores the effects of different hypothetical situations on financial projections. More sophisticated methods, such as Monte Carlo simulations, generate a range of possible outcomes by running thousands of simulations based on random variations in input variables. This helps to quantify the probability of various outcomes and understand the risk profile of a financial model.

Risk management, on the other hand, focuses on developing strategies to minimize the adverse effects of identified risks. This can include diversification, hedging, and the use of financial instruments like options and futures to protect against price volatility. It also involves setting risk tolerance levels and developing contingency plans to mitigate the impact of adverse events. In financial modeling, risk management practices are essential to ensure that models remain robust under different conditions and provide reliable information for decision-making.

Overall, integrating risk analysis and management into financial modeling enhances the accuracy and reliability of financial forecasts. It equips businesses and investors with the tools to make informed decisions and to prepare for uncertainties, ultimately supporting better financial planning and risk mitigation strategies.

10.1. FINANCIAL RISK

One of the main worries of any business, regardless of industry or location, is financial risk. This explains why financial professionals all over the world are beginning to highly regard the Financial Risk Manager FRM Exam. The highest credential available to risk management professionals globally is the FRM. Once more, the fundamental idea of the FRM Level 1 exam is financial risk. Prior to comprehending the methods for managing and controlling risk, it is crucial to grasp the definition and categories of risk. Let's talk about various kinds of risk in this article.The possibility of losing money on a business or investment decision is referred to as financial risk. Financial risks have the potential to cause capital losses for both individuals and companies. Financial risks include credit, liquidity, and operational risks, among others.

Stated differently, financial risk is an inherent danger that has the potential to result in capital loss. The probability of losing money is relevant. When a business faces a financial risk, there's a chance that its cash flow won't be enough to cover its responsibilities. Credit, operational, foreign investment, legal, equity, and liquidity risks are a few typical financial hazards. Financial risk in the public sector refers to the incapacity to manage debt and/or monetary policy. Find out more about the relationship between financial risk and various entities, including markets, governments, businesses, and individuals.

10.1.1. Types of Risks

Risk is synonymous with the possibility of an unanticipated or unfavorable result. Risk is any action or activity that has the potential to result in a loss of any kind. A company has to overcome a variety of risks that it may encounter. In general, risks can be divided into three categories: financial, non-financial, and business risk.

- **Business Risk:** Businesses themselves take these kinds of risks in an effort to increase profits and value for shareholders. For instance, businesses take on expensive marketing risks when launching a new product in an effort to increase sales.
- **Non- Business Risk:** Firms have no control over these kinds of risks. We refer to risks resulting from political and economic imbalances as non-business risks.
- **Financial Risk:** Financial risk is, as the name implies, the risk of financial loss to businesses. Financial risk is typically brought on by market volatility and losses brought on by changes in interest rates, stock prices, and other variables.

10.1.2. Types of Financial Risks

The various risk categories are divided into multiple groups. Market risk, credit risk, operational risk, strategic risk, liquidity risk, and event risk are some of the categories into which risks are divided.

For any business, one of the most important categories of risk is financial risk.

Market fluctuations are what lead to financial risk, and these fluctuations can be caused by a variety of factors. This allows for the classification of financial risk into a number of different categories, including legal, operational, market, credit, and liquidity risk (Figure 10.1).

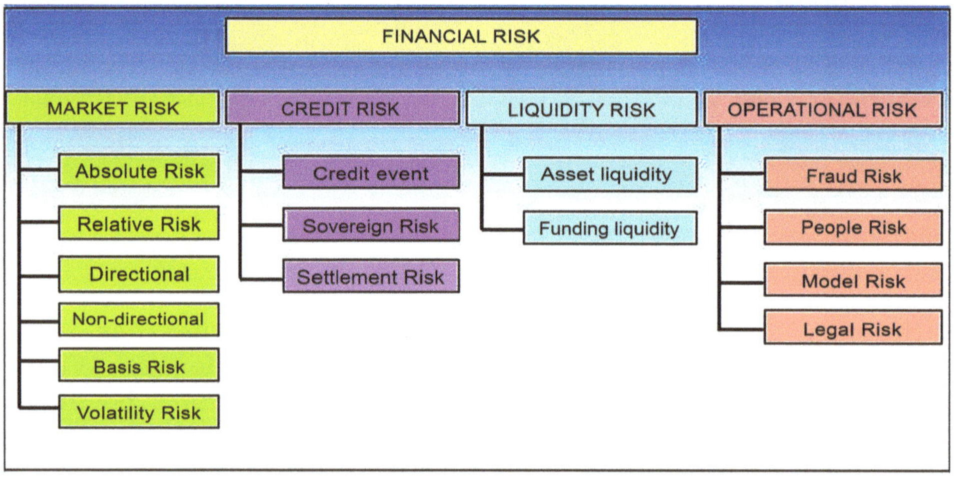

Figure 10.1. *Types of financial risks.*

Source. https://www.simplilearn.com/ice9/article_detailed_content_img/types-of-financial-risks.jpg.

- **Market Risk:** This kind of risk results from fluctuations in financial instrument prices. There are two categories of market risk: directional risk and non-directional risk. Variations in interest rates, stock prices, and other factors can lead to directional risk. However, there can be volatility risks associated with non-directional risk.
- **Credit Risk:** This kind of risk appears when someone doesn't carry out their responsibilities to their counterparties. Sovereign risk and settlement risk are two categories into which credit risk falls.

  The main cause of sovereign risk is often complex foreign exchange regulations. Conversely, settlement risk appears when one party pays while the other does not carry out their end of the bargain.
- **Liquidity Risk:** This kind of risk results from a failure to complete transactions. There are two types of liquidity risk: funding liquidity risk and asset liquidity risk. Insufficient sellers or buyers in relation to buy and sell orders, respectively, can result in asset liquidity risk.
- **Operational Risk:** Technical malfunctions or poor management are examples of operational failures that give rise to this kind of risk. Fraud risk and model risk are two categories under which operational risk falls. Inadequate controls lead to fraud risk, while improper model application results in model risk.
- **Legal Risk:** Lawsuits and other legal restrictions give rise to this kind of risky financial situation. Legal risk arises whenever an organization must deal with monetary losses as a result of legal proceedings.

10.1.3. Financial Risks for Businesses

Financial risk can arise from various macroeconomic factors, such as shifting market interest rates and the potential for major corporations or industries to fail. Individuals who manage businesses take financial risks when they make choices that could affect their capacity to make ends meet or pay off debts. Starting a business from scratch is costly. Companies frequently require outside funding in order to maintain consistent growth. The company seeking the money and the stakeholder investing in the business are both exposed to financial risk by this funding requirement.

We refer to the risk that comes with taking out a loan as credit risk or default risk. Investors experience a decrease in income from loan repayments, principal, and interest if the borrower defaults on the loan. Costs associated with collecting debts frequently increase for creditors.

A different phrase, "specific risk," is applied when only a few or a single company experiences financial difficulties. This kind of risk pertaining to an organization or collection of organizations involves financial transactions, default risk, and capital structure. As a result, specific risk represents investors' apprehension about receiving returns and possible financial loss.

Moreover, operational risk is something that businesses deal with. This kind of risk arises when companies use poor management practices or flawed financial reasoning, i.e., they experience internal factors that prevent them from succeeding in their endeavors.

Financial risks can impact companies of all sizes and shapes. Understanding financial risk is essential. Although it lessens the likelihood of bad things happening, being aware of the risks and protective measures does not completely eliminate the risk.

10.1.4. Financial Risks for the Market

Financial markets are frequently a center for financial risks because a variety of factors can affect them. The financial situation of the entire market is impacted when a crucial market sector faces difficulties in the financial system. Market risk is demonstrated by the global financial crisis of 2007–2008. As companies shut down, investors suffered huge losses, and the government was compelled to reevaluate its monetary policies.

In addition, other factors like volatility have an impact on the market. Regarding the fair value of market assets, it creates uncertainty. Implied volatility is a measure of volatility. The statistical value is expressed as a percentage, signifying the stakeholders' level of confidence that the market returns align with the overall market valuation. It provides information about growing and declining markets. Therefore, stock market shares may experience sharp price swings as a result of volatility risk. Financial risks can arise from changes in market interest rates and defaults. Defaults mostly happen in the bond or debt market when businesses or issuers don't make their payments on time. Defaults cause serious harm to investors. Simultaneously, fluctuations in the market interest rate often force investors to abandon individual securities. They are compelled to invest in debt securities with lower payoffs or riskier returns. Risks associated with asset-backed securities emerge when their value fluctuates along with that of the underlying securities. The following example clarifies an asset-backed category that is commonly used. A borrower who takes out a loan for a predetermined amount of time settles it early. The income stream from repayments is terminated by this early payment. Additionally, it eliminates the potential revenue from notable fluctuations in interest rates.

10.1.5. Financial Risks for Governments

Financial risk for a government arises in the following situations:

- Government losing control of its monetary policy
- Its inability or unwillingness to control inflation
- Government defaulting on its bonds
- Other debt issues

A government issues debt in the following form:

- Bonds
- Funding wars
- Building bridges
- Building infrastructure
- Paying for general day-to-day operations

Treasury bonds are one type of debt that the US government issues. Numerous governments, such as those in Venezuela, Russia, Argentina, and Greece, have fallen behind on their debt. Certain governments only postpone paying their debts; others make smaller than agreed-upon payments. Investors and stakeholders face financial risk in both situations.

10.1.6. Financial Risks for Individuals

If you make bad decisions, you could also become a victim of financial risks. Taking an extra day off work can be a common source of financial risk. Highly speculative investments are one of the other causes. People have to understand that there is always a chance of risk involved in any endeavor. There are risks that are out of one's control. Thus, it is imperative to fully comprehend the ramifications.

Liquidity risk has the following two situations for investors:

- **Market Liquidity Risk:** Involves assets and securities that cannot be sold or purchased at a rate that compensates for the losses in a volatile market. It arises when there are many sellers but few buyers.
- **Funding/ Cash Flow Liquidity Risk:** The possibility that a company might not have the necessary capital to pay its debt. Thereby it gets forced to default and harms stakeholders.

People are also exposed to speculative risks, which are those in which the success of a profit or gain is uncertain. Speculative risks are possible when an investor makes poor research decisions prior to making an investment. It occurs when they aim too high for profits or devote an excessive amount of their net worth to a single venture.

Do you have an inflow of foreign currencies? You can also be exposed to currency financial risks as the following factors affect your calculated finances:

- Interest rate changes
- Monetary policy changes
- Changes in prices due to market differences
- Political changes
- Natural calamities

- Diplomatic changes
- Economic conflicts

10.1.7. Pros and Cons of Financial Risk

The flip side of reward is risk. An uncertain situation is a financial risk. It is present in varying degrees. Financial risk is particularly serious because it can spread from one business to another or to an entire sector, market, or even the world.

The word "risk" carries a negative connotation. Therefore, making better and more informed business decisions can result from knowing and evaluating the level of financial risk associated with an asset.

The pros and cons of knowledge of financial risks are as follows:

Pros of Financial Risks	Cons of Financial Risks
• Facilitates more informed decisions • Assists in assessing value, i.e., the risk-reward ratio • It can be recognized via analysis tools	• Often arises from unpredictable outside forces • It can be uncontrollable or difficult to overcome • Can spread to different sectors or markets

10.2. IDENTIFY THE SOURCES, DRIVERS, AND POTENTIAL IMPACTS OF FINANCIAL RISKS

The process of determining the origins, causes, and possible effects of financial risks that could have an impact on a project, an organization, or a person is known as financial risk identification. The uncertainties and losses resulting from financial transactions, markets, instruments, or events are referred to as financial risks. Effective financial risk management, which attempts to lessen the possibility and severity of unfavorable outcomes, depends on the ability to identify financial risks. This section will cover the various methods of identifying financial risks, including internal, external, qualitative, and quantitative approaches. We'll also give some illustrations of typical financial risks and how they affect things.

To identify financial risks, we can use the following steps:

1. **Define the Scope and Objectives of the Risk Identification Process:** THE goal, parameters, and scope of the risk identification process must be established. These include the project, organization, or person that is exposed to financial risks, the time horizon, the risk appetite, and the risk criteria. The entity's overarching goals and strategies should be in line with the scope and goals of the risk identification process.
2. **Identify the Sources and Drivers of Financial Risks:** This entails identifying the variables, such as financial transactions, markets, instruments, or events, that contribute to or affect financial risks. Financial risks have two main sources and drivers: internal and external factors. Internal factors are those that come from within the organization and include things like processes, policies, strategies, systems, and culture. Factors classified as external come from outside the entity and can include legal, social, political, economic, and environmental aspects. Some examples of sources and drivers of financial risks are:

i. **Credit Risk:** The risk of loss due to the failure of a borrower, counterparty, or issuer to meet its financial obligations, such as loans, bonds, or derivatives. The sources and drivers of credit risk include the creditworthiness, default probability, and *recovery rate* of the borrower, counterparty, or issuer, as well as the terms and conditions of *the financial contract*, such as the maturity, interest rate, collateral, or covenants.

ii. **Market Risk:** The risk of loss due to changes in the market prices or rates of financial assets, liabilities, or instruments, such as stocks, bonds, currencies, commodities, or derivatives. The sources and drivers of *market risk* include the supply and demand, volatility, liquidity, and correlation of the *market prices* or rates, as well as the exposure, sensitivity, and hedging of *the financial position*.

iii. **Liquidity Risk:** The risk of loss due to the inability to meet cash flow needs or to sell or buy financial assets, liabilities, or instruments at a reasonable price or in a timely manner. The sources and drivers of liquidity risk include the cash flow mismatch, funding availability, *market liquidity*, *asset liquidity*, and contagion effects of *the financial position*, as well as the liquidity preferences, expectations, and behaviors of *the market participants*.

iv. **Operational Risk:** The risk of loss due to the failure of people, processes, systems, or external events to perform adequately or as expected, such as fraud, human error, cyberattack, natural disaster, or legal dispute. The sources and drivers of *operational risk* include the complexity, efficiency, reliability, security, and compliance of the people, processes, systems, or *external events*, as well as the controls, mitigation, and *contingency plans* of the entity.

3. **Identify the Potential Impacts of Financial Risks:** This entails determining the potential ramifications or results of financial risks, including gains, losses, or modifications to the entity's value, performance, or financial status. There are two categories of possible financial risk effects: qualitative and quantitative. Qualitative impacts include things like staff morale, stakeholder confidence, and customer loyalty that have an effect on the entity's quality, reputation, or level of satisfaction. The term "quantitative impacts" refers to effects that have an effect on an entity's measurement, quantity, or valuation. Examples of these include costs, profits, assets, liabilities, equity, and cash flows. Some examples of *potential impacts* of financial risks are:

i. **Credit risk:** The potential impacts of credit risk include the loss of principal, interest, or fees due to default, the impairment or write-off of financial assets, the increase in provisions or allowances for credit losses, the decrease in credit ratings or credit quality, the increase in *borrowing costs* or *capital requirements*, or the reduction in profitability or solvency of the entity.

ii. **Market Risk:** The potential impacts of market risk include the loss or gain of market value or fair value due to changes in market prices or rates, the change in cash flows or income due to changes in market prices or rates, the change in hedging effectiveness or hedge accounting due to changes in market prices or rates, the change in risk exposure or risk profile due to changes in *market prices* or rates, or the change in performance or value indicators, such as return on investment, net present value, or economic value added, due to changes in *market prices* or rates.

iii. **Liquidity Risk:** The potential impacts of liquidity risk include the loss of liquidity or solvency due to cash flow shortages or funding difficulties, the increase in liquidity costs or premiums due to cash flow imbalances or market illiquidity, the loss of market value or fair value due to forced sales or purchases of financial assets, liabilities, or instruments, the loss of business opportunities or competitive advantages due to liquidity constraints or market illiquidity, or the change in liquidity or solvency indicators, such as liquidity ratios, cash flow coverage, or net working capital, due to *liquidity risks*.

iv. **Operational Risk:** The potential impacts of *operational risk* include the loss of assets, income, or reputation due to operational failures or incidents, the increase in operational costs or expenses due to operational inefficiencies or errors, the increase in *operational risks* or exposures due to operational vulnerabilities or threats, the decrease in operational performance or quality due to operational disruptions or delays, or the change in operational indicators, such as *operational risk* capital, *operational risk* appetite, or key risk indicators, due to *operational risks*.

We can determine the causes, trends, and possible effects of financial risks that could have an impact on our organization by taking the actions listed below. This will support us in efficiently and effectively measuring, managing, and reducing financial risks.

10.3. ASSESSING FINANCIAL RISKS IN CORPORATE VENTURING

A critical component of corporate venturing is evaluating the monetary risks associated with exploring new avenues. The potential losses or unfavorable effects of investing in a new business venture, such as market volatility, intense competition, ineffective operations, changes in regulations, or legal disputes, are known as financial risks. Corporate venturers can reduce potential risks, allocate resources wisely, and make well-informed decisions by evaluating financial risks. This section will cover some of the most important procedures and techniques for evaluating the financial risks associated with corporate venturing, along with some best practices and difficulties that venturers encounter.

Some of the steps and methods for assessing financial risks in *corporate venturing* are:

10.3.1. Identify the Sources and Types of Financial Risks

Finding potential sources and categories of financial risks—such as those related to market volatility, customer demand, competitor behavior, technological disruption, operational costs, regulatory compliance, or legal liability—that could have an impact on the new business is the first step. These risks can be divided into three categories: idiosyncratic risks, which are specific to a given situation or context, unsystematic risks, which affect a particular venture or company, and systematic risks, which affect the entire market or industry. Corporate venturers can prioritize and concentrate on the most pertinent and significant financial risks for their venture by understanding the sources and types of risks.

10.3.2. Estimate the Probability and Impact of Financial Risks

The next stage is to use quantitative or qualitative methods to estimate the likelihood and magnitude of financial risks that could arise in the new venture. When calculating the likelihood and impact of financial risks, such as expected value, standard deviation, variance, beta, or value at risk, quantitative methods make use of numerical data and statistical models. Qualitative methods, like the Delphi method, SWOT analysis, or Monte Carlo simulation, entail utilizing expert opinions, scenarios, or simulations to evaluate the likelihood and consequences of financial risks. Corporate venturers can assess and weigh the possible returns and trade-offs of their venture by estimating the likelihood and impact of financial risks.

10.3.3. Evaluate the Risk-Return Profile of the New Venture

Assessing the new venture's risk-return profile—that is, the correlation between the amount of risk involved and the anticipated return—is the last stage. A risk-return curve, which displays the various combinations of risk and return that are feasible for the venture, can be used to illustrate the risk-return profile. The corporate venturer's risk appetite, or the amount of risk they are ready and able to take on in order to achieve their goals, determines the ideal risk-return profile for a new venture. Corporate venturers can decide whether a new venture is worth pursuing and how best to allocate their capital and resources by assessing the risk-return profile of the project.

Some of the best practices and challenges for assessing financial risks in *corporate venturing* are:

1. **Use a Multidisciplinary and Collaborative Approach:** Assessing financial risks in corporate venturing requires a multidisciplinary and collaborative approach, involving different stakeholders and perspectives from within and outside the organization. This can help to ensure that the assessment is comprehensive, objective, and realistic, and that it considers the various aspects and implications of the new venture, such as strategic, operational, financial, legal, or ethical. A multidisciplinary and collaborative approach can also help to foster a culture of risk awareness and learning, and to facilitate communication and alignment among the *corporate venturers* and their partners.
2. **Adapt to the Changing and Uncertain Environment:** Assessing financial risks in corporate venturing also requires adapting to the changing and uncertain environment, which may pose *new or unexpected challenges* or opportunities for the new venture. This can involve updating and revising the assessment as new information or feedback becomes available, or as the market or industry conditions evolve. Adapting to the changing and uncertain environment can also involve being flexible and agile, and being able to adjust or pivot *the venture strategy* or execution as needed, based on the assessment results and the risk-return profile.
3. **Balance the Risks and Rewards of Innovation:** Assessing financial risks in corporate venturing ultimately requires balancing the risks and rewards of innovation, which is the core objective and value proposition of corporate venturing.

   This can involve finding the optimal balance between taking calculated risks and pursuing attractive returns, between being proactive and being prudent, and between being creative and being disciplined.

   Balancing the risks and rewards of innovation can also involve recognizing and embracing the inherent uncertainty and ambiguity of *corporate venturing*, and being prepared to face and overcome *the potential failures* or setbacks that may occur along the way.

10.3.4. Evaluating Non-Financial Factors

Quantifying the possible gains or losses from different sources of uncertainty, such as market swings, credit defaults, operational lapses, or legal disputes, is only one aspect of financial risk analysis. It also involves being aware of the qualitative elements of the industry, competitors, clients, suppliers, regulators, and stakeholders that can have an impact on an organization's stability and financial performance. The process of assessing these non-financial factors through a variety of techniques, including SWOT, PESTEL, scenario, stakeholder, and Porter's five forces analysis, is known as qualitative analysis. The opportunities, threats, weaknesses, and strengths that can affect an organization's financial risk profile can all be found through qualitative analysis, along with the tactics and plans of action that can be used to either take advantage of or lessen those risks. The advantages and difficulties of performing a qualitative analysis for financial risk management will be covered in this section. Additionally, we will give some instances of qualitative variables that may impact the financial risks associated with various kinds of organizations. We will cover the following topics:

1. **What Is Qualitative Analysis and Why Is It Important for Financial Risk Management?:** The assessment of non-financial elements that may have an impact on an organization's stability and financial performance is known as qualitative analysis. A few examples of these factors are the industry structure and dynamics, the competitive advantages and disadvantages, customer preferences and behaviors, supplier relationships and dependencies, regulatory requirements and compliance, stakeholder expectations and interests, and the political, economic, social, technological, environmental, and legal aspects of the business environment. Qualitative analysis is a useful tool for determining the causes and origins of financial risks as well as their possible effects and outcomes. The development and assessment of plans and courses of action that can improve, diversify, hedge, or take advantage of financial opportunities as well as minimize, transfer, avoid, or accept financial risks can also be assisted by qualitative analysis.

2 **How to Conduct a Qualitative Analysis for Financial Risk Management?:** Conducting a qualitative analysis for financial risk management cannot be done in a way that is universally applicable because different organizations may have different goals, environments, and resources. However, some general steps that can be followed are:

i. Define the scope and purpose of the analysis. What are the *financial risks* that need to be assessed and managed? What are the *qualitative factors* that can affect these risks? What are the goals and criteria for the analysis?

ii. Collect and review *the relevant data* and information. What are the sources and methods of obtaining the data and information? What are the reliability and validity of the data and information? What are the gaps and limitations of the data and information?

iii. analyze and interpret the data and information. What are the tools and techniques that can be used to analyze and interpret the data and information? What are the assumptions and biases that can affect the analysis and interpretation? What are the findings and insights that can be derived from the analysis and interpretation?

iv. Communicate and report the results and recommendations. What are the formats and channels that can be used to communicate and report the results and recommendations? What are the audiences and stakeholders that need to be informed and involved? What are the feedback and *follow-up mechanisms* that need to be established and implemented?

3. **What Are the Benefits and Challenges of Qualitative Analysis for Financial Risk Management?**: Qualitative analysis can provide several benefits for *financial risk management*, such as:

i. It can complement and enrich the quantitative analysis by providing a broader and deeper perspective on the financial risks and opportunities.

ii. It can help identify and understand the root causes and interrelationships of the *financial risks* and opportunities, as well as *the potential scenarios* and outcomes of these risks and opportunities.

iii. It can help evaluate and prioritize the financial risks and opportunities, as well as the strategies and actions that can address them, based on multiple criteria and dimensions, such as feasibility, desirability, sustainability, and impact.

iv. It can help foster a culture of risk awareness and risk management within the organization, by engaging and involving the relevant stakeholders and decision-makers in the qualitative analysis process and outcomes.

However, qualitative analysis can also pose some challenges for financial risk management, such as:

i. It can be subjective and biased, depending on the data and information sources, *the analysis and interpretation methods*, and the perspectives and preferences of the analysts and stakeholders.

ii. It can be complex and ambiguous, as there may be multiple and conflicting *qualitative factors*, as well as uncertainties and unpredictabilities in *the financial risk environment*.

iii. It can be time-consuming and resource-intensive, as it may require a large amount of data and information collection, analysis, interpretation, communication, and reporting.

iv. It can be difficult to measure and monitor, as there may be no clear and consistent indicators and metrics to evaluate the effectiveness and efficiency of the qualitative analysis and its outcomes.

4. **What Are Some Examples of Qualitative Factors That Can Affect the Financial Risks of Different Types of Organizations?**: The qualitative factors that can affect the *financial risks* of different types of organizations may vary depending on the nature, size, scope, and sector of the organizations. However, some common examples

of qualitative factors that can affect the *financial risks* of different types of organizations are:

i. For a manufacturing company, some qualitative factors that can affect the financial risks are the quality and safety standards of the products, the innovation and differentiation capabilities of the products, the customer satisfaction and loyalty levels, the supplier reliability and availability, the environmental and social impacts of *the production processes*, and the regulatory and legal compliance of the operations.

ii. For a service company, some qualitative factors that can affect the financial risks are the reputation and brand image of the company, the service quality and customer experience, the employee engagement and retention, the intellectual property and data protection, the technological adoption and adaptation, and the ethical and social responsibility of the company.

iii. For a financial institution, some qualitative factors that can affect the financial risks are the trust and confidence of the customers and investors, the governance and risk management practices of the institution, the diversification and liquidity of the assets and liabilities, the capital adequacy and solvency of the institution, the market and *competitive position* of the institution, and *the regulatory and supervisory oversight* of the institution.

These are just some examples of qualitative factors that can affect the *financial risks* of different types of organizations. There may be other qualitative factors that are specific or relevant to a particular organization or industry. Therefore, it is important to conduct a comprehensive and customized qualitative analysis for *financial risk management*, based on the objectives, context, and resources of each organization.

10.3.5. Importance of Mitigating Financial Risks

Financial risk mitigation is essential to the success of any business. A business's ability to manage its finances may suffer if financial risks are not managed. This can lead to large losses. One such financial risk that companies must reduce to maintain their financial stability is lease balance default. Businesses can employ a number of techniques to reduce the financial risks related to lease balance default.

1. **Develop a Clear Understanding of Lease Terms:** It is essential to have a clear understanding of the lease terms to mitigate *financial risks*. Businesses need to ensure that they have a clear understanding of the lease terms, including payment schedules, interest rates, and default clauses. A clear understanding of the lease terms can help businesses avoid *financial risks* associated with lease balance default.
2. **maintain a Positive Cash Flow:** Maintaining a positive cash flow is crucial for mitigating financial risks associated with lease balance default. Businesses need to ensure that they have sufficient cash flow to meet their lease payment obligations. Maintaining a positive cash flow can help businesses avoid the *financial risks* associated with lease balance default.

3. **negotiate Lease Terms:** Negotiating lease terms can help mitigate financial risks associated with lease balance default. Businesses need to negotiate favorable lease terms that can help them avoid financial risks associated with lease balance default. For example, businesses can negotiate for lower interest rates and flexible payment schedules to mitigate *financial risks*.
4. **Diversify the Portfolio:** Diversifying the portfolio is another strategy that businesses can use to mitigate financial risks associated with lease balance default. Businesses need to ensure that they have a diversified portfolio that can help them avoid financial risks associated with lease balance default. For example, businesses can invest in different asset classes to mitigate *financial risks*.

To protect their finances, businesses must reduce the financial risks connected to lease balance default. Some of the tactics that businesses can employ to reduce the financial risks associated with lease balance default include developing a clear understanding of the terms of the lease, keeping a positive cash flow, negotiating the terms of the lease, and diversifying the portfolio. Businesses can safeguard their long-term financial stability and prevent financial losses related to lease balance default by putting these strategies into practice.

10.3.6. The Importance of Identifying Financial Risks

In risk management, one of the most important steps is identifying financial risks. It enables businesses to recognize, evaluate, and control the risks they encounter. A multitude of factors can give rise to financial risks, such as fluctuations in the market, credit risk, liquidity risk, operational risk, and legal and regulatory risks. Companies can make educated decisions about risk mitigation strategies that can reduce the impact of these risks by having a clear understanding of the potential effects of these risks on the financial health of their organization.

Identifying financial risks can provide many benefits for organizations. Some of these benefits include:

1. **improved Decision-Making:** Identifying financial risks can help organizations make better decisions by providing accurate information about *potential risks*. This information can help organizations to make informed decisions about investments, financing, and *other important financial decisions*.
2. **Enhanced Transparency:** Identifying financial risks can provide transparency to stakeholders by allowing them to understand the *potential risks* that an organization faces. This can help improve trust between stakeholders and the organization.
3. **improved Risk Management:** Identifying financial risks can help organizations to develop appropriate risk management strategies that can help to minimize the impact of these risks. This can help to protect the organization's financial health and improve its overall performance.
4. **Compliance with Regulations:** Identifying financial risks can help organizations to comply with regulatory requirements. For example, International Financial

Reporting Standards (IFRS) require organizations to identify and disclose financial risks in their financial statements.

5. **improved Financial performance:** Identifying financial risks can help organizations to improve their financial performance by minimizing the impact of these risks. This can help to improve profitability and increase shareholder value.

For instance, a business involved in the energy industry might be exposed to monetary risks as a result of fluctuations in oil prices.

By identifying these risks, the business can reduce the impact of those risks on its financial performance by implementing suitable risk management strategies, like hedging.

One of the most important aspects of risk management is identifying financial risks.

It can support businesses in making wiser decisions, increasing transparency, adhering to rules, and safeguarding their financial stability. Comprehension of the possible consequences of financial risks on the financial well-being of an organization aids in decision-making regarding risk mitigation tactics that reduce these risks' effects.

10.4. FINANCIAL RISK ANALYSIS

Financial risk analysis is an essential procedure for any company hoping to maximize profits, prevent losses, and accomplish its objectives. The identification, measurement, and management of various financial risks, including market, credit, liquidity, operational, and legal risks, have been covered. We will review the key ideas and offer some suggestions or best practices for financial risk analysis in this concluding section.

Some of the key takeaways are:

- Financial risk analysis is the process of assessing the potential impact of various factors that can affect the financial performance of a business, such as changes in market conditions, *customer behavior*, *competitor actions*, regulatory requirements, *operational failures*, and *legal disputes*.
- Financial risk analysis can help a business to anticipate and mitigate the negative effects of *financial risk*s, as well as to exploit the opportunities that arise from them.
- *Financial risk analysis* involves three steps: identification, measurement, and management of *financial risk*s.
- Identification of financial risks requires a thorough understanding of the business environment, the sources and drivers of *financial risk*s, and the exposure and vulnerability of the business to those risks.
- Measurement of financial risks requires the use of appropriate tools and techniques, such as sensitivity analysis, scenario analysis, value at risk, stress testing, and Monte Carlo simulation, to quantify the probability and magnitude of potential losses or gains from *financial risk*s.
- Management of financial risks requires the implementation of effective strategies and policies, such as diversification, hedging, insurance, contingency planning, and risk transfer, to reduce, transfer, or accept the *financial risk*s.

Some of the recommendations or best practices for *financial risk* analysis are:

1. Adopt a holistic and integrated approach to *financial risk* analysis. Consider the interrelationships and dependencies among different types of *financial risk*s, as well as the impact of *financial risk*s on the overall objectives and performance of the business.
2. Align the financial risk analysis with the business strategy and risk appetite. Define the acceptable level and tolerance of financial risk for the business, and ensure that the financial risk analysis supports the strategic goals and priorities of the business.
3. Involve the relevant stakeholders in the financial risk analysis. Engage the management, employees, customers, suppliers, investors, regulators, and other

parties that have an interest or influence on the financial performance of the business, and solicit their input and feedback on the identification, measurement, and management of *financial risks*.

4. update the financial risk analysis regularly and frequently. Monitor the changes in the internal and external environment that can affect the *financial risks*, and review and revise the *financial risk* analysis accordingly. Use the *financial risk* analysis as *a dynamic and continuous process*, rather than *a static and one-time exercise*.
5. Communicate and report the financial risk analysis effectively. Use clear and concise language, charts, graphs, tables, and other visual aids to present the results and findings of the *financial risk* analysis. Highlight *the key risks*, opportunities, and actions that need to be taken. Provide recommendations and suggestions for improvement and follow-up.

10.4.1. Analyzing Financial Risks

There are always financial risks associated with running a business. To minimize potential losses and make educated decisions, it is imperative to recognize and examine them. A number of factors, including market volatility, credit risk, liquidity risk, operational risk, and more, can give rise to financial risks. Financial risks must be identified, measured, and managed to reduce any potential impact on the company.

1. **Identify Financial Risks:** The first step in analyzing financial risks is to identify them. Financial risks can be identified by analyzing the company's financial statements, market trends, and economic indicators. The company's balance sheet, income statement, and cash flow statement can provide valuable insights into the financial risks the company faces. For example, if a company has a high debt-to-equity ratio, it may face a higher risk of default.
2. **Quantify Financial Risks:** Once you have identified the financial risks, the next step is to quantify them. This involves assessing the potential impact of the risks on the company's financial performance. For instance, if a company's revenue is highly dependent on a single product or customer, it faces a significant revenue risk if that product or customer is lost. Quantifying financial risks can help the company prioritize its risk management strategies.
3. **manage Financial Risks:** Once you have identified and quantified the *financial risks*, the next step is to manage them. There are several ways to manage *financial risks*, including risk transfer, risk avoidance, risk reduction, and risk acceptance. Risk transfer involves transferring the risk to another party, such as an insurance company. Risk avoidance involves avoiding activities that pose a significant *financial risk*. *Risk reduction* involves taking steps to reduce the likelihood or impact of the risk. *Risk acceptance* involves accepting the risk and *its potential impact*.
4. **Monitor Financial Risks:** The final step in analyzing financial risks is to monitor them continuously. Financial risks can change over time, and it is essential to monitor them to ensure that the risk management strategies are effective.

Monitoring financial risks involves analyzing the company's financial statements regularly, staying abreast of market trends and economic indicators, and assessing the effectiveness of the risk management strategies.

For any business to operate, financial risk analysis is essential. Businesses can reduce potential losses and make well-informed decisions by recognizing, measuring, managing, and keeping an eye on financial risks. A comprehensive approach that considers all potential sources of financial risk is imperative when conducting financial risk analysis.

10.4.2. Monitoring and Reviewing Financial Risks for Continuous Improvement

One of the most important aspects of managing a business's financial stability and success is keeping an eye on and reviewing financial risks for ongoing improvement. Through vigilant observation and assessment of financial risks, enterprises can detect possible hazards and adopt preemptive actions to offset them. The purpose of this section is to offer insights from various angles on how to efficiently track and evaluate financial risks, guaranteeing ongoing advancements in risk management procedures.

1. **Establishing Key Performance Indicators (KPIs):** One way to monitor financial risks is by defining and tracking relevant KPIs. These indicators can include metrics such as liquidity ratios, debt-to-equity ratios, and *profitability margins*. By regularly reviewing these KPIs, businesses can identify any deviations from *the desired benchmarks* and take appropriate actions.
2. **Conducting Regular Financial Audits:** Regular financial audits help in assessing the accuracy and reliability of financial information. Audits provide an opportunity to identify any potential errors, fraudulent activities, or internal control weaknesses that may pose financial risks. By conducting thorough audits, businesses can ensure the integrity of their financial data and make informed decisions based on reliable information.
3. **implementing Risk management Frameworks:** Developing and implementing robust risk management frameworks is essential for effectively monitoring and reviewing financial risks. These frameworks should include processes for identifying, assessing, and mitigating various types of financial risks, such as credit risk, market risk, operational risk, and liquidity risk. By following a structured approach, businesses can systematically address potential risks and minimize their impact on financial performance.
4. **Utilizing Technology Solutions:** Leveraging technology solutions, such as financial management software and data analytics tools, can significantly enhance the monitoring and review of financial risks. These tools can automate data collection, analysis, and reporting processes, enabling businesses to gain real-time insights into their financial risks. By harnessing the power of technology, businesses can make more informed decisions and respond promptly to *emerging risks*.
5. **Conducting Scenario Analysis:** Scenario analysis involves simulating various hypothetical scenarios to assess the potential impact of different risk events on

financial performance. By conducting scenario analysis, businesses can identify vulnerabilities, evaluate the effectiveness of existing risk mitigation strategies, and develop contingency plans. This approach helps in proactively managing financial risks and preparing for unexpected events.

6. **learning from Past Mistakes:** Reviewing past financial risks and their outcomes is crucial for continuous improvement. By analyzing previous risk incidents, businesses can identify patterns, root causes, and lessons learned. This knowledge can be used to refine risk management strategies, update policies and procedures, and enhance the overall risk culture within the organization.

10.5. FINANCIAL RISK MANAGEMENT

Any business must have financial risk management, which entails identifying, assessing, and prioritizing risks that could jeopardize the organization's financial stability. It is a procedure that aids companies in reducing monetary risks and guaranteeing their long-term viability.

The process of locating, assessing, and ranking risks that could jeopardize an organization's financial stability is known as financial risk management. It entails creating plans to control these risks and guarantee the company's long-term viability. A number of factors, including market volatility, credit risk, operational risk, liquidity risk, and regulatory risk, can result in financial risks.

Because it enables companies to recognize possible risks and create effective risk management plans, financial risk management is crucial. Businesses can safeguard their financial stability, guarantee business continuity, and enhance overall performance by effectively managing financial risks. Financial risk management also aids companies in staying in compliance with legal requirements and upholding stakeholder confidence.

Businesses may be exposed to a variety of financial risks, such as credit risk, operational risk, market risk, liquidity risk, and regulatory risk. Market risk is the possibility of suffering financial losses as a result of shifts in variables that affect the market, such as interest rates, currency rates, and commodity prices. Credit risk is the possibility of suffering financial losses if a borrower defaults on a loan or doesn't fulfill its financial commitments. Operational risk is the possibility of suffering financial losses as a result of fraud, natural disasters, or other internal or external calamities. The risk of suffering financial losses as a result of not being able to pay short-term debts is known as liquidity risk. The risk of financial losses as a result of modifications to regulatory requirements or non-compliance with regulatory standards is known as regulatory risk.

Businesses can manage financial risks in a number of ways, such as through risk acceptance, transfer, avoidance, and reduction. Avoiding actions that could expose the company to financial risks is part of risk avoidance. Implementing strategies to lessen the possibility or impact of financial risks is known as risk reduction. Transferring financial risks to another party, like an insurance company, is known as risk transfer. Accepting risk entails acknowledging the financial risks and creating plans to successfully manage them. The application of best practices, including frequent risk assessments, the creation of risk management policies and procedures, the formation of risk management committees, and the utilization of risk management tools and techniques, is necessary for effective financial risk management. In order to guarantee the efficacy of their risk management strategies, businesses should also make sure they have enough resources to handle financial risks and that they routinely review and assess these strategies.

Any business that wants to survive in the long run needs to manage its financial risk. Businesses can create efficient plans to manage financial risks and guarantee their financial stability by recognizing, assessing, and prioritizing them.

Businesses can safeguard their financial stability, adhere to legal requirements, and uphold stakeholder trust by putting best practices in financial risk management into practice.

10.5.1. Mitigating Financial Risks in Business Consolidation

Financial risks associated with business consolidation can have a big influence on an organization's success and profitability. These risks can affect the consolidated company's financial stability in a number of ways, including changes in market demand, currency fluctuations, and regulatory requirements. Therefore, reducing financial risks is a crucial part of any consolidation plan and calls for a thorough and well-planned strategy. There are several ways that organizations can mitigate financial risks during consolidation:

1. **Develop a Robust Financial Risk Management Plan:** A financial risk management plan can help an organization in identifying, assessing, and mitigating potential financial risks. This plan should be an integral part of the consolidation strategy and should be developed by experienced financial experts who can provide insights into the *potential risks* and how to mitigate them.
2. **Conduct a Thorough Due Diligence:** A thorough due diligence process can help identify *potential financial risks* associated with the consolidation. This process should be comprehensive and should take into account all aspects of the business, including *financial statements*, contracts, tax obligations, and *regulatory requirements*.
3. **Establish a Robust Financial Reporting System:** Consolidated companies need to have a robust financial reporting system that can provide timely and accurate financial information. Such a system can help in identifying potential financial risks and in taking appropriate measures to mitigate them.
4. **Consider the Use of Financial Instruments:** Financial instruments such as forward contracts, options, and swaps can help in mitigating financial risks associated with currency fluctuations and interest rate changes. Companies can use these instruments to hedge against *potential risks* and to protect *their financial position*.
5. **Monitor and Review Financial Risks Regularly:** Financial risks are dynamic, and they can change rapidly. Therefore, it is essential to monitor and review financial risks regularly to identify any changes and take appropriate actions to mitigate them. Regular reviews can also help in identifying potential new risks and in taking *proactive measures* to mitigate them.

One of the most important aspects of any consolidation strategy is risk mitigation. A complete financial risk management plan, a rigorous due diligence procedure, a strong financial reporting system, the use of financial instruments, and routine monitoring and assessment of financial risks are all essential components of an organization's comprehensive financial risk management strategy. Organizations can reduce financial risks and guarantee the success of their consolidation strategy by using such an approach.

10.5.2. Importance of Monitoring and Reporting Financial Risks

An organization's stability and success can be significantly impacted by the financial risks it faces. As a result, in order to make sure that these risks are adequately managed, it is essential to track and report on them. The Asset Liability Committee, or ALCO, steps in at this point. The ALCO is in charge of overseeing and reporting on an organization's financial risks as part of its risk management process. We will talk about the significance of keeping an eye on and disclosing financial risks in this section.

1. **Identifying Risks:** The first step in managing financial risks is to identify them. Monitoring and reporting financial risks can help organizations identify potential risks before they become significant issues. For example, monitoring market trends and economic indicators can help an organization identify potential risks to its investments and financial stability.
2. **Mitigating Risks:** Once risks have been identified, they must be mitigated. Monitoring and reporting financial risks can help organizations develop strategies to mitigate these risks. For example, if an organization is exposed to interest rate risk, it can use interest rate swaps or other hedging strategies to mitigate the risk.
3. **Compliance:** Monitoring and reporting financial risks is essential for compliance purposes. Many regulatory bodies require organizations to report on their financial risks, and failure to do so can result in significant penalties. Therefore, it is critical to have a robust monitoring and reporting system in place to ensure compliance.
4. **Decision-Making:** Monitoring and reporting financial risks can help organizations make informed decisions. For example, if an organization is considering investing in a new market, it can use its risk reporting to assess the potential risks and benefits of such an investment.
5. **Stakeholder Communication:** Monitoring and reporting financial risks can help organizations communicate with stakeholders effectively. This includes investors, lenders, and other stakeholders who may be interested in an organization's financial stability. Providing regular updates on financial risks can help build trust and confidence with stakeholders.

To effectively manage their financial stability, organizations must monitor and report financial risks. It supports the identification of possible risks, the creation of mitigation plans, the maintenance of compliance, the making of well-informed decisions, and the efficient interaction with stakeholders. Thus, in order to protect an organization's financial stability, the ALCO must have a strong monitoring and reporting system in place.

10.5.3. Mitigating Financial Risks

Financial risks should be recognized and then minimized, in addition to being identified. By taking steps to lessen the possibility or impact of future financial losses, one can mitigate financial risks. Numerous strategies, such as risk acceptance, transfer, avoidance, and reduction, can be used to accomplish this. We will go over each of these approaches in detail and offer perspectives from various angles in this section.

1. **Risk Transfer:** Transferring the risk to a different party is one way to mitigate financial risks. This can be accomplished by outsourcing, hedging, or insurance. For instance, a business can buy credit insurance to transfer its credit risk. In this manner, in the event that a client misses payments, the insurance provider will pay the loss. Similarly, a business can use a forward contract with a bank to mitigate its currency risk. In this way, the bank will absorb the loss in the event of an unfavorable change in the currency exchange rate. Another method of transferring risk is outsourcing. A business can shift the risks involved in specific operations to the outsourcing partner by outsourcing those operations.
2. **Risk Reduction:** Reducing the possibility or magnitude of possible losses is one way to mitigate financial risks. Internal controls, asset allocation, and diversification can all help achieve this. One way for a business to lower its market risk is to diversify its holdings across several asset classes. In this manner, the overall performance of the portfolio will not be greatly impacted if one asset class underperforms. Similar to this, internal controls like duty segregation and frequent audits can help a business lower operational risk. In this manner, the consequences of an employee engaging in fraudulent activity will be reduced.
3. **Risk Avoidance:** One way to reduce financial risks is to steer clear of activities that carry a high risk. This technique is known as risk avoidance. This can be accomplished by passing up on some business prospects or by not making certain investments in particular assets. One way for a business to reduce credit risk is to avoid giving credit to clients who have a bad credit history. Comparably, a business can steer clear of market risk by avoiding investments in erratic assets like cryptocurrencies.
4. **Risk Acceptance:** A technique for reducing financial risks is risk acceptance, which involves acknowledging possible losses and doing nothing to lessen them. When the expense of risk mitigation exceeds the possible loss, this is typically done. For instance, if settling a lawsuit will save money compared to going to court, a business might decide to take on the risk of being sued.

A crucial component of any financial risk assessment is risk mitigation. It's critical to recognize the risks and take the necessary steps to lessen their impact or likelihood. Effective strategies for reducing financial risks include risk acceptance, transfer, avoidance, and reduction. But it's crucial to weigh the advantages and disadvantages of each approach and select the one that works best in the given circumstance.

10.5.4. Strategies for Mitigating Financial Risks in Affiliate Relationships

Affiliate relationships are becoming more and more common in the world of business partnerships as a way to reach a wider audience, boost sales, and generate income.

These connections do, however, carry some inherent risks that should be properly managed, just like any other business venture.

If this isn't done, there may be monetary losses, relationship problems, and reputational damage. We will examine practical methods for reducing financial risks in affiliate partnerships in this section. We will also examine insights from different angles and offer comprehensive information to assist you in navigating this difficult terrain.

1. **Establish Clear Expectations:** One of the most critical aspects of managing financial risks in affiliate relationships is setting clear expectations from the outset. This involves defining the scope of the partnership, the responsibilities of each party, and *the financial arrangements* involved. By clearly outlining expectations, both parties can have a shared understanding of their roles and obligations, minimizing the potential for misunderstandings and disputes later on. For example, if an affiliate expects *a certain commission rate* for each sale generated, it should be clearly communicated and agreed upon by all parties involved.
2. **Conduct Thorough Due Diligence:** Before entering into an affiliate relationship, it is crucial to conduct thorough due diligence on potential partners. This includes researching their reputation, financial stability, and track record. By delving into these aspects, you can gain insights into their past performance, assess their ability to meet financial obligations, and identify any red flags that may indicate *potential risks*. For instance, if a potential affiliate has a history of *financial instability* or a poor track record of fulfilling *payment obligations*, it may be wise to reconsider entering into a partnership with them.
3. **Implement Robust Contractual Agreements:** A well-drafted and comprehensive contract is a vital tool for mitigating financial risks in affiliate relationships. The contract should clearly outline the terms and conditions of the partnership, including payment schedules, dispute resolution mechanisms, termination clauses, and confidentiality provisions. It should also include provisions for addressing potential financial risks, such as non-payment or fraud. By having a solid contractual agreement in place, both parties can have legal recourse in case of any breaches or disputes. For example, a contract may include provisions for regular financial audits to ensure transparency and identify any *potential financial risks*.
4. **Monitor Performance and Track Metrics:** Regular monitoring of performance and tracking of key metrics is essential to identify and address any financial risks in

affiliate relationships. By closely monitoring the performance of affiliates, businesses can identify any discrepancies, such as underperformance or fraudulent activities, and take corrective actions promptly. Establishing clear metrics and regularly analyzing performance data can help uncover any *potential financial risks* early on. For instance, if a certain affiliate consistently underperforms or generates suspiciously high refund rates, it may be an indication of *financial risks* that need to be addressed.

5. **Foster Open Communication and Collaboration:** Effective communication and collaboration between the business and its affiliates are crucial for managing financial risks. Maintaining open lines of communication allows both parties to address any concerns, clarify expectations, and resolve any potential issues promptly. By fostering a collaborative environment, businesses can work closely with their affiliates to identify and mitigate financial risks together. For example, if an affiliate identifies a potential fraud or *financial irregularity*, they should feel comfortable reporting it to the business promptly, enabling *timely action* to be taken.

In order to reduce financial risks in affiliate partnerships, one must be proactive and strategic. Through the implementation of robust contractual agreements, clear expectations, thorough due diligence, performance monitoring, and open communication, businesses can effectively navigate the challenges associated with affiliate relationships. Never forget that handling financial risks in affiliate relationships is a continuous process that needs to be evaluated, adjusted, and improved on a regular basis to guarantee the partnership's success and longevity.

10.5.5. Establishing Effective Risk Oversight

The monitoring and reporting of risks that have an impact on an organization's financial strength is one of the most important components of financial risk analysis. Effective risk oversight is the process of making sure that the organization's risk appetite and strategic goals are met by the risk management practices and policies. Monitoring and reporting are key components of this process. Communicating the risk information to the appropriate parties, including the board of directors, senior management, regulators, and investors, is another aspect of risk oversight. The best practices for risk oversight and how to track and report financial risks are covered in this section. We will also give some instances of how various businesses have put in place systems for tracking and reporting financial risks.

Some of the points that we will cover in this section are:

1. **The Importance of Monitoring and Reporting the Financial Risks:** For the purpose of detecting, quantifying, and controlling risks that may have an impact on the organization's financial stability and performance, it is imperative to track and report financial risks. The organization can identify any changes or deviations in the risk profile and take prompt, appropriate action to control or mitigate the risks by keeping an eye on and

reporting the financial risks. The organization can demonstrate its ability to manage risk to external stakeholders and comply with regulatory requirements by keeping an eye on and disclosing financial risks.

2. **The Types of Financial Risks That Need to be Monitored and Reported:** The kind and extent of the company's operations, goods, and services determine the financial risks that must be tracked and disclosed. Credit risk, market risk, liquidity risk, operational risk, legal risk, reputational risk, strategic risk, and emerging risk are a few examples of common financial risk types that must be tracked and reported. Every kind of financial risk is different, with unique characteristics, sources, and effects. To monitor and report on it, particular techniques and resources are needed.
3. **The Methods and Tools for Monitoring and Reporting the Financial Risks:** The kind and degree of the risks, as well as the accessibility and caliber of the data, determine the different approaches and instruments for tracking and disclosing the financial risks. Risk indicators, risk dashboards, risk reports, risk registers, risk matrices, risk maps, risk models, stress tests, scenario analysis, and sensitivity analysis are a few of the frequently used techniques and instruments for tracking and reporting financial risks. These techniques and resources support the organization in clearly and consistently quantifying, visualizing, and communicating the financial risks.
4. **The Best Practices for Risk Oversight:** The board of directors and senior management are in charge of risk oversight since they establish the guidelines and expectations for the organization's risk culture and risk governance. Defining and communicating the organization's risk appetite and risk tolerance, creating and reviewing a risk management framework and policies, designating and empowering the risk management function and committees, guaranteeing the function's independence and accountability, allocating sufficient resources and training to the function and committees, and interacting with internal and external auditors and regulators regarding the risks and findings are some of the best practices for risk oversight.
5. **The Examples of Monitoring and Reporting Systems for Financial Risks:** Depending on their size, complexity, and industry, different organizations use different methods and systems for tracking and reporting their financial risks. The Basel III framework for banks, which establishes minimum capital, liquidity, and leverage requirements, as well as requiring banks to disclose their risk-weighted assets, capital ratios, liquidity ratios, and leverage ratios; the Solvency II framework for insurance companies, which establishes minimum solvency and capital requirements, as well as requiring them to disclose their minimum capital requirement, risk margin, and risk assessment; and the COSO framework for enterprises, which offers a comprehensive and integrated model for enterprise risk

management, are a few examples of monitoring and reporting systems for financial risks.

10.5.6. Developing a Risk Management Strategy

Creating a risk management strategy is one of the most crucial elements of financial risk management. A plan that describes how to recognize, evaluate, reduce, and keep an eye on the financial risks that could have an impact on your project is known as a risk management strategy. You can lessen the negative effects of financial volatilities and uncertainties, such as market volatility, interest rate fluctuations, currency exchange rates, inflation, credit risk, liquidity risk, operational risk, and legal risk, by implementing a risk management strategy. Moreover, a risk management plan can assist you in seizing opportunities like leverage, arbitrage, hedging, and diversification that come with financial risks. In this section, we'll go over how to create a risk management plan for your project and offer some perspectives from various angles. Additionally, some examples will be used to highlight the important ideas and procedures.

To develop a risk management strategy, you need to follow these steps:

1. **Identify the Financial Risks**: Finding possible sources and categories of financial risks that could have an impact on your project is the first step. To do this, you can use a variety of tools and methods, including risk registers, SWOT analysis, PESTLE analysis, scenario analysis, and sensitivity analysis. Along with these, you should think about other external and internal factors like your project's goals, scope, budget, schedule, resources, stakeholders, contracts, laws, and market conditions that could affect the financial risks. To get their opinion and guidance, you should also speak with professionals like risk managers, accountants, auditors, auditors, attorneys, and financial analysts. The risks that have been identified should be documented along with their attributes, including probability, impact, timing, and interdependencies.
2. **Assess the Financial Risks**: Evaluating the size and probability of the financial risks you have identified is the second step. This can be accomplished using a variety of techniques and models, including decision trees, Monte Carlo simulation, expected value, standard deviation, variance, coefficient of variation, and value at risk. The project's and your organization's risk appetite and tolerance—that is, the amounts of risk you can and will tolerate—should also be taken into account. The hazards should be ranked in order of importance and seriousness, and you should give each one a risk rating—high, medium, or low.
3. **Mitigate the Financial Risks**: In order to lessen or completely eradicate the financial risks that you have evaluated, the third step is to decide on and put into practice the suitable risk response techniques. Avoidance, reduction, transfer, sharing, acceptance, retention, insurance, futures, options, swaps, forwards, and contracts are just a few of the tools and options available to you for doing this. Each risk response strategy's advantages

and disadvantages, as well as any trade-offs and potential effects on your project and organization, should be taken into account. It is advisable to record the selected risk response tactics along with the anticipated results, including risk exposure, residual risk, and backup plans.

4. **Monitor the Financial Risks**: Monitoring and reviewing the financial risks and the risk-response tactics you have put in place is the fourth and last step. To do this, you can use a variety of tools and methods, including risk audits, reviews, dashboards, reports, indicators, triggers, and logs. Additionally, as the project develops and the financial environment shifts, you should update and modify the processes for risk identification, assessment, and mitigation. The appropriate stakeholders, including project sponsors, managers, team members, clients, suppliers, and regulators, should be informed about the risk status and performance. Along with documenting the best practices and lessons discovered during the risk management process, you should also distribute these documents to other projects and your organization.

A key component of financial risk management is creating a risk management plan. It can assist you in reaching your project's goals and objectives as well as in managing the project's financial volatility and uncertainties. By following the above-mentioned steps, you can improve your knowledge and abilities in financial risk management while developing a thorough and successful risk management strategy for your project.

10.5.7. Key Factors to Consider Financial Risk Management

Finding the possible sources of financial risks that could have an impact on your personal or business finances is one of the most crucial parts of financial risk analysis. The uncertainties and losses resulting from changes in market conditions, the conduct of financial agents, and regulatory actions are collectively referred to as financial risks. You can evaluate the financial risks' impact and likelihood by identifying them, and you can then come up with effective management or mitigation plans. We'll go over some important things to think about when identifying financial risks in this section, along with some illustrations of how they might impact your financial stability.

Some of the key factors to consider when identifying financial risks are:

1. **The type and nature of the financial risk:** Financial risks come in a variety of forms, including credit, market, liquidity, operational, legal, and reputational risks. Every kind of risk has unique traits, origins, and effects. The risk of losing money as a result of shifts in the market prices of derivatives, assets, or liabilities, for instance, is known as market risk. The possibility of a borrower or counterparty defaulting or not making payments is known as credit risk. The risk of not having enough cash on hand to pay bills or selling assets for a fair price is known as liquidity risk. Operational risk is the possibility of suffering losses as a result of personnel, systems, or internal processes going wrong. Legal risk is the possibility of suffering losses as a result of breaking rules, laws, or contracts. Reputational risk is the possibility

of losing stakeholders' faith and confidence as a result of bad press or scandals. You should be aware of the kind and extent of the financial risk to which you are exposed, as well as the potential effects on your performance and financial situation.

2. **The Source and Origin of the Financial Risk:** There are many different sources of financial risks, including the external environment, internal operations, and relationships with other parties. The external environment, for instance, can present financial risks because of shifts in the political and economic landscape, societal trends, technological advancements, and natural disasters. Financial risks may arise from internal operations as a result of inefficiencies, mistakes, frauds, or poor management. Financial risks may arise from dealings with other parties if there are disagreements, conflicts, or defaults. It is important to determine the origin and source of the financial risk you are experiencing, as well as its cause and mode of transmission.
3. **The Magnitude and Frequency of the Financial Risk:** The extent and frequency of financial risks are contingent upon the nature, duration, and volatility of the exposure. Certain financial risks, like a significant market crash or a catastrophic event, can, for instance, have a high magnitude but a low frequency. Certain financial risks, like slight price swings or operational mistakes, can be small in size but occur frequently. Certain financial risks, like credit defaults or liquidity shortages, can occur occasionally and in moderate amounts. In addition to estimating the expected value and probability distribution of the financial risk you are handling, you should measure its frequency and magnitude.
4. **The Impact and Consequence of the Financial Risk:** Depending on the sensitivity, resilience, and contingency of the affected entity, financial risks can have a variety of effects and outcomes. Certain financial risks, for instance, may directly affect the entity's cash flows, revenues, expenses, assets, liabilities, or equity. Certain financial risks may indirectly affect the company's standing, clientele, morale among staff members, or relationships with stakeholders. Certain financial risks may cascade into other risks, into other entities, or into the system as a whole. You should consider the implications and effects of the financial risk you are taking on, as well as the possibility of harm and recovery.

Some examples of how financial risks can affect *your financial strength* are:

i. Market risk can affect your financial strength by eroding the value of your investments, increasing the cost of your borrowings, or reducing the income from your operations. For instance, if you have invested in stocks, bonds, or currencies, you may lose money if the market prices go down. If you have borrowed money at a variable interest rate, you may pay more if the market interest rate goes up. If you have a business that depends on *the market demand*, you may earn less if *the market demand* goes down.

ii. Credit risk can affect your financial strength by impairing the quality of your assets, increasing the provision for bad debts, or reducing the availability of credit. For example, if you have lent money to customers, suppliers, or partners, you may not receive the full amount or on time if they default or delay. If you have a high level of credit risk, you may need to set aside more money to cover the potential losses. If you have a low credit rating, you may have difficulty accessing credit or pay a higher interest rate.

iii. Liquidity risk can affect your financial strength by limiting your ability to meet your obligations, forcing you to sell your assets at a discount, or increasing your reliance on external funding. For instance, if you have a mismatch between your inflows and outflows of cash, you may not be able to pay your bills, salaries, or taxes on time. If you have illiquid assets that are hard to sell, you may have to accept a lower price or incur a loss. If you have insufficient liquidity, you may have to borrow more money or raise more capital, which can be costly or dilutive.

10.5.8. Monitoring and Reviewing Financial Risks

Financial risks should be regularly monitored and reviewed after they have been identified and evaluated. This makes it easier to guarantee that risks are adequately managed and that adjustments to the business environment are considered. Financial risk monitoring and review is a continuous process that necessitates the participation of numerous organization stakeholders.

1. **Establish a Monitoring Framework:** Establishing a monitoring framework is crucial for efficiently reviewing and monitoring financial risks. Every stakeholder participating in the process should have defined roles and responsibilities within this framework. It should also specify how often monitoring and reporting will occur, as well as the methods and instruments for determining and evaluating risks.
2. **Regular Reporting:** An essential part of tracking and evaluating financial risks is regular reporting. Regularly generated reports should contain details on the current state of risks, newly identified risks, and modifications to already identified risks. Senior management and the board of directors should be among the important parties in the organization with whom these reports are shared.
3. **Use of Key Performance Indicators (KPIs):** KPIs are a useful instrument for keeping an eye on and assessing financial risks. They offer a means of gauging the success of risk management techniques and pinpointing areas in need of development. To make sure that risks are being effectively managed, KPIs should be set for each identified risk and monitored over time.
4. **Scenario Analysis:** Using hypothetical scenarios, scenario analysis evaluates the possible effects of various risks on the company. This enables stakeholders to evaluate the possible impact of various risks and create mitigation strategies, making it a useful tool for monitoring and reviewing financial risks.
5. **Reviewing Risk Management Strategies:** It's critical to continuously assess risk management techniques to make sure they remain current and effective. The effectiveness of

current strategies should be evaluated, and any new strategies that might be needed to handle emerging risks should also be considered.

6. **Best option:** Establishing a thorough monitoring framework with frequent reporting, scenario analysis, KPI use, and reviews of risk management techniques is the best way to keep an eye on and evaluate financial risks. This strategy makes sure that risks are adequately managed and that any modifications to the business environment are considered.

Financial risk monitoring and review is a continuous process that necessitates the participation of many organization stakeholders.

Organizations can effectively manage financial risks and ensure their long-term success by putting in place a thorough monitoring framework that includes regular reporting, the use of KPIs, scenario analysis, and regular reviews of risk management strategies.

CASE STUDY

FINANCIAL RISK MANAGEMENT AT TOYOTA

Toyota Motor Corporation (Toyota), Japan's largest and the world's fourth-largest automobile manufacturer offered well-known car models like Camry, Corona, Corolla, and Lexus.

Though a late entrant, compared to General Motors and Ford, Toyota had become one of the strongest players in the automobile industry.

In an industry, generally considered to be mature in terms of technology, Toyota had continued to set new benchmarks for providing value to customers more effectively than competitors. Toyota had also redefined the rules of the game in various areas – product development, manufacturing, vendor management and human resources management.

Background Note

Sakichi Toyoda, born in 1868, founded Toyota. He showed little interest in the family's carpentry business. Instead, Toyoda concentrated on improving the handloom machinery used in textile factories. These efforts led to the Toyoda Automatic Loom.

In 1926, Sakichi founded Toyoda Automatic Loom Works (TALW) to make looms. He entrusted his son Kiichiro with the task of using the profits from the textile machinery business to develop a motor car. In 1933, Kiichiro opened an auto department within the loom works and began copying US engine designs. After Sakichi died in 1930, Kiichiro faced stiff competition from Ford and General Motors, who had set up their manufacturing units in Japan. Family members including brother Risaburo showed little interest in Kiichiro's plans. In spite of these difficulties, the articles of association of the company were amended in 1933 to permit automobile manufacturing.

Excerpts

- **Credit Risk**

Toyota used various financial instruments, in the normal course of business. These instruments were in general executed only with creditworthy financial institutions. Virtually all foreign currency contracts were denominated in U.S. dollars, euros and other currencies of major industrialized countries.

- **Market Risk**

Toyota was exposed to market risk due to changes in currency rates, interest rates and certain commodity and equity prices. In order to manage these risks, Toyota used various derivative financial instruments.

- **Derivative financial instruments: Accounting & Valuation**

Toyota employed derivative financial instruments, including foreign exchange forward contracts, foreign currency options, interest rate swaps, currency swap agreements and interest rate options to manage its exposure to fluctuations in interest rates and foreign exchange rates.

CLASS ACTIVITY

Assign a follow-up task where students individually analyze a different company's financial risks and propose a risk management plan. Students will work in teams to analyze a hypothetical company's financial data, identify potential risks, and develop risk management strategies.

SUMMARY

- Risk analysis and management are critical components of financial modeling, providing a structured approach to identifying, assessing, and mitigating potential risks that can affect financial performance and decision-making.
- Financial risk refers to the likelihood of losing money on a business or investment decision.
- Financial risk can be classified into various types such as Market Risk, Credit Risk, Liquidity Risk, Operational Risk, and Legal Risk.
- Financial risks are the potential losses or negative impacts that may arise from investing in a new venture, such as market uncertainty, competitive pressure, operational inefficiency, regulatory changes, or legal disputes.
- Mitigating financial risks is crucial for business success. The failure to mitigate financial risks can result in significant financial losses, which can be detrimental to the financial health of a business.
- Financial risks are an integral part of any business operation. It is essential to identify and analyze them to make informed decisions and mitigate potential losses.
- Monitoring and reviewing financial risks for continuous improvement is a crucial aspect of managing the financial stability and success of a business.
- Financial Risk Management is an integral part of any business, and it involves the identification, evaluation, and prioritization of risks that may affect the financial stability of an organization.

REVIEW QUESTIONS

1. What do you understand by financial risk?
2. What are the types of financial risks?
3. Elaborate the financial risks in corporate venturing.
4. How to analyzing financial risks?
5. How to developing a risk management strategy?

REFERENCES

1. Allen, S. L. (2012). Financial Risk Management: A Practitioner's Guide to Managing Market and Credit Risk (2nd ed.). John Wiley. ISBN 978-1118175453.
2. Baranoff, E., Brockett, P., & Kahane, Y. (2009). Risk Management for Enterprises and Individuals. Saylor. ISBN 9780982361801.
3. Blunden, T., & Thirlwell, J. (2021). Mastering Risk Management. FT Publishing International. ISBN 978-1292331317.

4. Christoffersen, P. (2011). Elements of Financial Risk Management (2nd ed.). Academic Press. ISBN 978-0-12-374448-7.
5. Coleman, T. (2011). A Practical Guide to Risk Management (PDF). CFA Institute. ISBN 978-1-934667-41-5.
6. Crockford, N. (1986). An Introduction to Risk Management (2nd ed.). Woodhead-Faulkner. ISBN 0-85941-332-2.
7. Crouhy, M., Galai, D., & Mark, R. (2013). The Essentials of Risk Management (2nd ed.). McGraw-Hill Professional. ISBN 9780071818513.
8. Damodaran, A. (2007). Strategic Risk Taking: A Framework sfor Risk Management. FT Press. ISBN 978-0137043774.
9. Farid, J. A. (2013). Models at Work: A Practitioner's Guide to Risk Management. Palgrave Macmillan. ISBN 978-1137371638.
10. Hampton, J. (2011). The AMA Handbook of Financial Risk Management. American Management Association. ISBN 978-0814417447.
11. Hull, J. (2023). Risk Management and Financial Institutions (6th ed.). John Wiley. ISBN 978-1-119-93248-2.
12. Jarrow, R. A., & Turnbull, S. M. (2000). The intersection of market and credit risk. Journal of Banking & Finance, 24(1–2), 271–299.
13. Kaplan, R. S., & Mikes, A. (2012). Managing risks: A new framework. Harvard Business Review, 90(6), 48–60.
14. Lam, J. (2003). Enterprise Risk Management: From Incentives to Controls. John Wiley. ISBN 978-0-471-43000-1.
15. McNeil, A. J., Frey, R., & Embrechts, P. (2015). Quantitative Risk Management: Concepts, Techniques and Tools (Revised ed.). Princeton University Press. ISBN 9780691166278.
16. Miller, M. B. (2019). Quantitative Financial Risk Management. John Wiley. ISBN 9781119522201.
17. Rockafellar, R. T., & Uryasev, S. (2002). Conditional value-at-risk for general loss distributions. Journal of Banking & Finance, 26(7), 1443–1471.
18. Roncalli, T. (2020). Handbook of Financial Risk Management. Chapman & Hall. ISBN 9781138501874.
19. Tapiero, C. (2004). Risk and Financial Management: Mathematical and Computational Methods. John Wiley & Sons. ISBN 0-470-84908-8.
20. Van Deventer, D. R., Imai, K., & Mesler, M. (2004). Advanced Financial Risk Management: Tools and Techniques for Integrated Credit Risk and Interest Rate Risk Management. John Wiley. ISBN 978-0-470-82126-8.
21. Wernz, J. (2021). Bank Management and Control: Strategy, Pricing, Capital and Risk Management (2nd ed.). Springer. ISBN 978-3030428686.

Index

V

W

FSC
www.fsc.org
MIX
Papier | Fördert gute Waldnutzung
FSC® C083411

Kolibri 360 GmbH
Ferdinand-Jühlke-Straße 7
99095 Erfurt, Deutschland
produktsicherheit@kolibri360.de